A FIRST BOOK OF C
Fundamentals of C Programming
Second Edition

A FIRST BOOK OF C
Fundamentals of C Programming
Second Edition

Gary J. Bronson
Fairleigh Dickinson University
Stephen J. Menconi
AT&T

West Publishing Company
Saint Paul New York Los Angeles San Francisco

PRODUCTION CREDITS

Text design: *David Farr, Imagesmythe, Inc.*
Copyeditor: *Natalie Zett*
Composition: *Alexander Teshin Associates, Mountain View, CA*

Copyright ©1988 By WEST PUBLISHING COMPANY
Copyright ©1991 By WEST PUBLISHING COMPANY
610 Opperman Drive
P.O. Box 64526
St. Paul, MN 55164-0526

Printed in the United States of America

98 97 96 95   8 7 6 5 4

Library of Congress Cataloging-in-Publication Data

Bronson, Gary J.
   A first book of C / Gary Bronson, Stephen Menconi. — 2nd ed.
   p.   cm.
   Includes index.
   ISBN 0-314-81348-9 (soft)
   1. C (Computer program language)   I. Menconi, Stephen J.
II. Title.
QA76.73.C15B75 1991
005.13'3—dc20   90-21085
                                                  CIP

dedicated to

Rochelle,
Matthew,
Jeremy,
David Bronson

Maryann,
Annamaria Menconi

Contents

CHAPTER TWO   Data Types, Declarations, and Displays   35

CHAPTER THREE   Assignments, Addresses, and Interactive Input   75

Preface

The C programing language is rapidly becoming the preeminent applications language of the 1990s. From its initial beginning as the development language for the UNIX operating system in the 1970s, C has evolved into the underlying development language for major spreadsheet, database, and word processing programs, the primary language for scientific and engineering applications, and a teaching language for introducing structured programming concepts in first and second level programming courses.

In recognition of C's growing importance in the applications and teaching areas, the first edition of this text was written. The primary purpose of the first edition was to make C more accessible as an applications programming language than was possible with texts that focused on C as an advanced operating systems language. The success of the first edition and the many comments we received from both students and faculty expressing how well the book helped them to learn and teach C, has been extremely gratifying.

The introduction of both Borland's Turbo C and Microsoft's Quick C have accelerated the acceptance of C as an applications language. As C has become more firmly entrenched as an introductory programming language, the requirements of introductory C texts have also increased. The most significant of these newer requirements is the necessity to include expanded software engineering concepts and material relating to Borland's Turbo-C and Microsoft's Quick C within an introductory C book. This permits the book to be used as an introduction to programming in addition to being an introduction to C.

The basic requirement, however, still remains that all topics be presented in a clear, unambiguous, and accessible manner to beginning students. As we stated previously, this was the purpose of the first edition and remains the purpose of the second edition. Thus, all of the topics, examples, explanations, and figures in the first edition remain in the second edition with one exception. The exception is that the material on program design in Chapter 6 of the first edition has been expanded, introduced earlier in the text, and integrated more fully throughout the text. Thus, except for Chapter 6, material has not been altered or deleted from that of the first edition; the second edition simply adds many new topics that were not in the first edition. These include:

- An early and expanded introduction to algorithms and software engineering, including top-down design and structure diagrams in Chapter 1. This expanded introduction includes the material on algorithms that was in Chapter 6 of the first edition.
- A new section on Errors, Testing, and Debugging in Chapter 4.
- A new section on Sorting Methods in Chapter 8.
- A new chapter on the current ANSI C standard.
- Four new appendixes on Program Life Cycle; Using the DOS, UNIX, VAX, and PRIME operating systems; Using Borland's Turbo-C Compiler; and Using Microsoft's C Compiler.

Distinctive Features of This Book

Writing Style. We firmly believe that introductory texts do not teach students—teachers teach students. An introductory textbook, if it is to be useful, must be the primary "supporting actor" to the "leading role" of the professor. Once the professor sets the stage, however, the textbook must encourage, nurture, and assist the student in acquiring and "owning" the material presented in class. To do this the text must be written in a manner that makes sense to the student. Our primary concern, and one of the distinctive features of this book is that it has been written for the student. As one of our reviewer's has said "This book addresses the student and not the professional." Thus, first and foremost, we feel the writing style used to convey the concepts presented, is the most important aspect of the text.

Modularity. C, by its nature, is a modular language. Thus, the connection between C functions and modules is made early in the text, in Section 1.2, and continues throughout the book. To stress the modular nature of C, the first complete `main()` function illustrates calling four other functions. The first program that can be compiled is then presented, which calls the `printf()` function.

The idea of argument passing into modules is also made early, in Section 1.3, with the use of the `printf()` function. In this manner, students are introduced to functions and argument passing as a natural technique of programming.

Software Engineering. This is the major addition to the second edition. Rather than simply introduce students to C, as was done in the first edition, the second edition introduces students to the fundamentals of software engineering. This introduction begins with a new Section 1.1, which introduces algorithms and the various ways that an algorithm can be described. The example illustrating three algorithms for summing the numbers from 1 to 100 (Figure 1-4) has been retained from the first edition, but moved from the middle of the text to the opening section.

The increased emphasis on software engineering is supported by a new section (Section 1.5) on top-down program development. Here the importance of understanding the problem and selecting an appropriate algorithm is highlighted and the relationship between analysis, design, coding, and testing introduced. Problem solving within this context is stressed throughout the text.

Introduction to Pointers. One of the unique features of the first edition was the early introduction of pointer concepts. This was done by first using the printf() function to display the addresses of variables and then using other variables to store these addresses. This approach always seemed a more logical and intuitive method of understanding pointers than the indirection description in vogue at the time the first edition was released.

Since the first edition we have been pleased to see that the use of the printf() function to display addresses has become a standard way of introducing pointers. Although this approach, therefore, is no longer a unique feature of our book, we are very proud of its presentation, and continue to use it in the second edition.

Program Testing. Every single C program in this text has been successfully compiled and run under Borland's Turbo C Compiler. The programs have been written following the Kernighan and Ritchie definition (standard C) using features fully supported under ANSI C. A source diskette of all programs is available to adopters.

Pedagogical Features

To facilitate our goal of making C accessible as a first level course, we have continued to use the following pedagogical features:

End of Section Exercises. Almost every section in the book contains numerous and diverse skill builder and programming exercises. Additionally, solutions to selected exercises are provided in Appendix H.

Pseudocode and Flowchart Descriptions. As in the first edition, pseudocode is stressed throughout the text. Although flowcharts were used in the first edition, no explicit definition or introduction to flowchart symbols was presented. In this edition we have added additional material on flowchart symbols and the use of flowcharts in visually presenting flow-of-control constructs.

Common Programming Errors and Chapter Review. Each chapter ends with a section on common programming errors and a review of the main topics covered in the chapter.

Appendices and Supplements

An expanded set of appendices has been provided in the second edition. In addition to the three appendices provided in the first edition on Operator Precedence, ASCII codes, and I/O-Standard Error Redirection, the new appendices contain material on Program Life Cycle; Using the DOS, UNIX, VAX, and PRIME operating systems; Using Borland's Turbo-C Compiler; and Using Microsoft's C Compiler.

As for the first edition, a solutions manual to selected exercises is available. Additionally, an IBM-PC compatible source code diskette for all example programs in the text is available to adopters.

Acknowledgments

The writing of the first edition of this book was a direct result of articles on pointers and command line arguments published in *UNIX World*, respectively, in June and August of 1985. The writing of the second edition of this book is a direct result of the success of the first edition. In this regard, our most heartfelt acknowledgment and appreciation is to the instructors and students who found the first edition to be of service to them in their respective quests to teach and learn C.

Once a second edition was planned, its completion depended on many people other than ourselves. For this we especially want to thank the staff of West Publishing Company for their many contributions. These included the continuous faith and encouragement of our editor, Richard Mixter, and the many suggestions and enthusiastic work of Lynette D'Amico and Sean Berres.

The direct encouragement and support of Dr. Paul Lerman, my Dean at Fairleigh Dickinson University must also be acknowledged. Without his support and the support of Dr. Naadimuthu and Dr. Yoon, this text could not have been written. Also, for their invaluable help in checking the details of the various operating systems presented in this text, we wish to express our appreciation to Neal Sturm, director of University Computing at Fairleigh Dickinson University, and Ralph Knapp, director of the computer facility at the Fairleigh Dickinson University Madison campus.

Finally, we both deeply appreciate and acknowledge the patience, understanding, and love provided by our wives and partners, Rochelle and Maryann.

Gary Bronson
Stephen Menconi

The authors thank these reviewers for their knowledgeable help in the completion of this book.

Jeff Slomka
Southwest Texas State University

Cary Laxer
Rose-Hulman Institute of Technology

Richard Walker
Moorhead State University

Howard K. Wolff
California State University—Chico

Gertrudis Weyzen
Ohlone College

Robert Burkhardt
Massachusetts Institute of Technology

Dwight Kirkpatrick
Southern Junior College of Business

Sunny Singh
Montana State University

Tom Tresser
Contra Costa College

Robert Shurtleff
Colorado Technical College

David A. Wellman
Wilson College

Fundamentals

Part One

Getting Started

Chapter One

1.1 Introduction to Programming

A computer is a machine. Like other machines, such as an automobile or lawn mower, it must be turned on and then driven, or controlled, to do the task it was meant to do. In an automobile, for example, the driver provides control by sitting inside of and directing the car. In a computer, the driver is a set of instructions, called a program. More formally, a *computer program* is a sequence of instructions used to operate a computer to produce a specific result. *Programming* is the process of writing these instructions in a language that the computer can respond to and that other programmers can understand. The set of instructions that can be used to construct a program is called a *programming language*.

Essentially, all computer programs do the same thing (Figure 1-1). They direct a computer to accept data (input), to manipulate the data (process), and to produce reports (output). This means that all programming languages must provide similar capabilities for performing these operations. These capabilities are provided either as specific instruction types, or prepackaged groups of instructions that can be used to do specific tasks. In C, the prepackaged groups of instructions are called *library functions*. Table 1-1 lists the fundamental set of instructions and library functions provided by FORTRAN, BASIC, COBOL, Pascal, and C for performing input, processing, and output tasks.

TABLE 1-1 Programming Language Instruction Summary

Operation	FORTRAN	BASIC	COBOL	Pascal	C
INPUT (Get the data)	READ	INPUT READ/DATA	READ ACCEPT	READ READLN	getchar() gets() scanf() sscanf() fscanf()
PROCESSING (Use the data)	= IF/ELSE DO	LET IF/ELSE FOR	COMPUTE IF/ELSE PERFORM	:= IF/ELSE FOR WHILE REPEAT	= if for while do
OUTPUT (Display the data)	WRITE PRINT	PRINT PRINT/ USING	WRITE DISPLAY	WRITE WRITELN	putchar() puts() printf() sprintf() fprintf()

If all programming languages provide essentially the same features, why are there so many? The answer is that there are vast differences in the types of input data, calculations needed, and output reports required by applications.

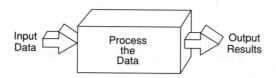

FIGURE 1-1 All Programs Perform the Same Operations

For example, scientific and engineering applications require precise numerical outputs, accurate to many decimal places. In addition, these applications typically use many algebraic or trigonometric formulae to produce their results. For example, determining a rocket's reentry point, as illustrated in Figure 1-2, requires a trigonometric formula and a high degree of numerical accuracy. For such applications, the FORTRAN programming language, with its algebra-like instructions, is ideal. FORTRAN, an acronym for FORmula TRANslation, was introduced in 1957 and specifically developed for translating formulas into a computer-readable form.

Business applications usually deal in whole numbers, representing inventory quantities, or dollar and cents data accurate to only two decimal places. These applications require simpler mathematical calculations than are needed for scientific applications. The outputs required from business programs frequently consist of reports containing extensive columns of formatted dollar and cents numbers and totals (see Figure 1-3). For these applications, the COBOL programming language, with its picture output formats, is ideal. COBOL, which was commercially introduced in the 1960s, is an acronym for COmmon Business Oriented Language.

FIGURE 1-2 FORTRAN Was Developed for Scientific and Engineering Applications

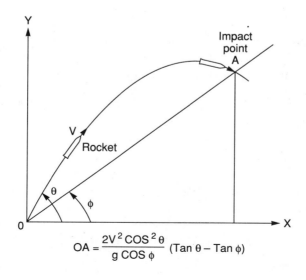

$$OA = \frac{2V^2 COS^2 \theta}{g\ COS\ \phi} (Tan\ \theta - Tan\ \phi)$$

```
┌─────────────────────────────────────────────────────┐
│                  INVENTORY REPORT                    │
│   Item                       In     On    Unit       │
│   No.        Description    Stock  Order   Cost       │
│                                                       │
│   10365   360KB - Diskette    20     0    5.95        │
│   10382   720KB - Diskette    10    50   10.70        │
│   10420   1.2MB - Diskette     2    60    8.40        │
│   10436  1.44MB - Diskette     6                      │
│   10449    20MB - Cartridge                           │
│   10486    40MB - Cartrid╌                            │
└─────────────────────────────────╮                    ╯
```

FIGURE 1–3   COBOL Is Ideal for Many Business Applications

Teaching introductory programming to students has its own set of requirements. Here, a straightforward, easy-to-understand computer language is
needed that does not require detailed knowledge of a specific application. Both
BASIC and Pascal programming languages were developed for this purpose.
BASIC stands for Beginners All-purpose Symbolic Instruction Code, and was
developed in the 1960s at Dartmouth College. BASIC is ideal for creating small,
easily developed, interactive programs.

Pascal was developed in the late 1970s to provide students with a firmer
foundation in modular and structured programming than could be provided
by BASIC. Modular programs consist of many small subprograms, each of which
performs a clearly defined and specific task that can be tested and modified
without disturbing other program sections. Pascal is not an acronym, like FOR-
TRAN, COBOL, and BASIC, but is named after the seventeenth-century math-
ematician, Blaise Pascal. The Pascal language is so rigidly structured, however,
that there are no escapes from the structured modules when such escapes would
be useful. This is unacceptable for real-world projects, and is one reason that
Pascal has not been widely accepted in the scientific, engineering, and business
fields. The design philosophy, called structured programming, that led to the
development of Pascal is relevant to C programmers. Using a structured programming approach results in readable, reliable, and maintainable programs.
We will introduce the elements of this program design philosophy in the next
section, and continue expanding upon it and using it throughout the text.

C language was initially developed in the 1970s at AT&T Bell Laboratories.
C evolved from a language called B, which was developed from the BCPL
language. C has an extensive set of capabilities and is a true general-purpose
programming language. As such, it can be used for creating simple, interactive
programs; for producing sophisticated applications, such as designing operating
systems; and for both business and scientific programming applications. An
indication of C's richness of library and instruction capabilities is clearly evident
from Table 1-1. Besides providing many existing tools to build programs with,
C also allows the programmer to easily create new tools to add to the existing
library routines. For this reason, C is known as the "professional programmer's
language."

Algorithms

Before writing a program, the programmer must clearly understand the desired result and how the proposed program will produce it. In this regard, it is useful to realize that a computer program describes a computational procedure called an algorithm. An *algorithm* is a step-by-step sequence of instructions that describes how to perform a computation.

An algorithm answers the question, "What method will you use to solve this computational problem?" Only after we clearly understand the algorithm, and know the specific steps required to produce the desired result, can we write the program. Seen in this light, programming is the translation of the selected algorithm into a language that the computer can use.

To illustrate an algorithm, we will consider a simple requirement. Assume that a program must calculate the sum of all whole numbers from 1 through 100. Figure 1-4 illustrates three methods we could use to find the required sum. Each method constitutes an algorithm.

Clearly, most people would not bother listing the possible alternatives in a detailed step-by-step manner, as is done in Figure 1-4, and then select one of the algorithms to solve the problem. But then, most people do not think algorithmically; they tend to think intuitively. For example, if you had to change a flat tire on your car, you would not think of all the steps required—you would simply change the tire or call someone else to do the job. This is an example of intuitive thinking.

Unfortunately, computers do not respond to intuitive commands. A general statement such as "add the numbers from 1 to 100" means nothing to a computer, because the computer can only respond to algorithmic commands written in an acceptable language such as C. To program a computer success-fully, you must clearly understand this difference between algorithmic and intuitive commands. A computer is an "algorithm-responding" machine; it is not an "intuitive-responding" machine. You cannot tell a computer to change a tire or to add the numbers from 1 through 100. Instead, you must give the computer a detailed, step-by-step set of instructions that, collectively, forms an algorithm. For example, the set of instructions

> Set n equal to 100
> Set $a = 1$
> Set b equal to 100
> Calculate sum = $n/2 * (a + b)$
> Print the sum

forms a detailed method, or algorithm, for determining the sum of the numbers from 1 through 100. Notice that these instructions are not a computer program. Unlike a program, which must be written in a language the computer can understand, an algorithm can be written or described in various ways. When English phrases are used to describe the algorithm (the processing steps), as in

Method 1. *Columns:* Arrange the numbers from 1 to 100 in a column and add them:

$$
\begin{array}{r}
1 \\
2 \\
3 \\
4 \\
\cdot \\
\cdot \\
98 \\
99 \\
+100 \\
\hline
5050
\end{array}
$$

Method 2. *Groups:* Arrange the numbers in convenient groups that sum to 100. Multiply the number of groups by 100 and add in any unused numbers:

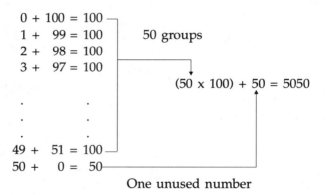

Method 3. *Formula:* Use the formula

$$\text{Sum} = n/2 * (a + 1)$$

where

n = number of terms to be added (100)
a = first number to be added (1)
1 = last number to be added (100)

$$\text{Sum} = 100/2 * (1 + 100) = 5050$$

FIGURE 1–4 Summing the Numbers 1 through 100

this example, the description is called *pseudocode*. When mathematical equations are used, the description is called a *formula*. When pictures that employ specifically defined shapes are used, the description is called a *flowchart*. A flowchart provides a pictorial representation of the algorithm using the symbols shown in Figure 1-5. Figure 1-6 illustrates the use of these symbols in depicting an algorithm for determining the average of three numbers.

FIGURE 1–5 Flowchart Symbols

SYMBOL	NAME	DESCRIPTION
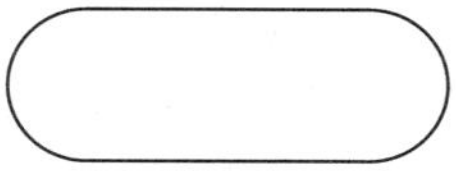	Terminal	Indicates the beginning or end of an algorithm
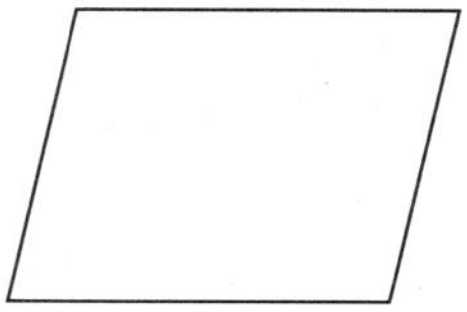	Input/Output	Indicates an Input or Output operation
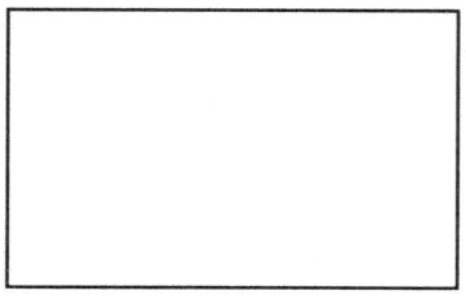	Process	Indicates computation or data manipulation
	Flow Lines	Used to connect the flowchart symbols and indicates the logic flow
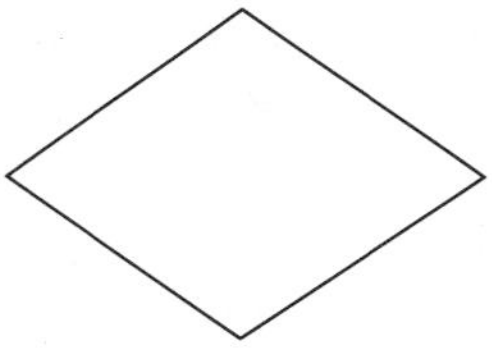	Decision	Indicates a decision point in the algorithm
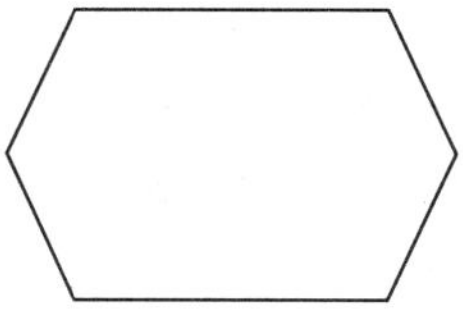	Loop	Indicates the initial, final, and increment values of a loop
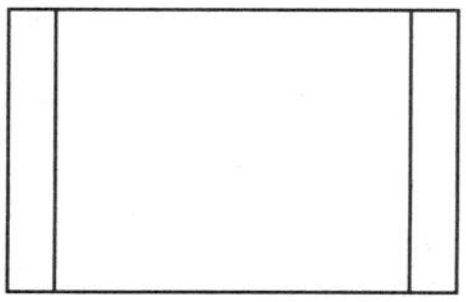	Predefined Process	Indicates a predefined process, as in calling a sorting process
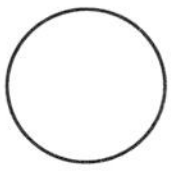	Connector	Indicates an entry to, or exit from, another part of the flowchart

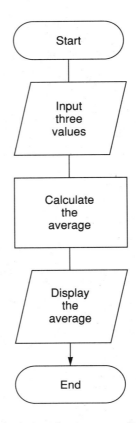

FIGURE 1-6 Flowchart for Calculating the Average of Three Numbers

Because flowcharts are cumbersome to revise, using pseudocode to express an algorithm's logic has gained increased acceptance among programmers. Unlike flowcharts, where standard symbols are defined, there are no standard rules for constructing pseudocode. Any short English phrase may be used to describe an algorithm using pseudocode. For example, acceptable pseudocode to describe the steps needed to compute the average of three numbers is

> *Input the three numbers into the computer*
> *Calculate the average by adding the numbers and*
>   *dividing the sum by three*
> *Display the average*

Only after the programmer selects an algorithm and understands the required steps can he or she write the algorithm using computer-language statements. When computer-language statements are used to describe the algorithm, the description is called a *computer program.*

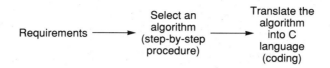

FIGURE 1–7   Coding an Algorithm

From Algorithms to Programs

After selecting an algorithm, it must be converted into a form that can be used by a computer. Converting an algorithm into a computer program, using a language such as C, is called *coding* the algorithm (see Figure 1-7). The remainder of this text is mostly devoted to showing you how to code algorithms into C.

Program Translation

Once a program is written in C, it cannot be executed without further translation on the computer. This is because the internal language of all computers consists of a series of 1s and 0s, called the computer's *machine language*. To generate a machine-language program that can be executed by the computer requires that the C program, which is referred to as a *source program*, be translated into the computer's machine language (see Figure 1-8).

A program can be translated into machine language in two ways. When each statement in the source program is translated individually and executed immediately, the programming language is called an *interpreted language*, and the program doing the translation is called an *interpreter*.

When all the statements in a source program are translated before any one statement is executed, the programming language used is called a *compiled language*. In this case, the program doing the translation is called a *compiler*. C is a compiled language. Here, the source program is translated as a unit into machine language. The machine-language version of the original source program is a separate entity called the *object program*. (See Appendix D for a complete description of entering, compiling, and running a C program.)

FIGURE 1–8   Source Programs Must Be Translated

Exercises 1.1

1. Define the terms:

a. computer program
b. programming
c. programming language
d. algorithm
e. pseudocode

f. flowchart
g. source program
h. object program
i. compiler
j. interpreter

2. Determine and list a step-by-step procedure to complete the following tasks:

Note: There is no single correct answer for each of these tasks. The exercise is designed to give you practice in converting intuitive commands into equivalent algorithms and making the shift between the thought processes involved in the two types of thinking.

a. Fix a flat tire.
b. Make a telephone call.
c. Go to the store and purchase a loaf of bread.
d. Roast a turkey.

3. Determine and write an algorithm (list the steps) to interchange the contents of two cups of liquid. Assume that a third cup is available to temporarily hold the contents of either cup. Each cup should be rinsed before any new liquid is poured into it.

4. Write a detailed set of step-by-step instructions, in English, to calculate the dollar amount of money in a piggybank that contains h half-dollars, q quarters, n nickels, d dimes, and p pennies.

5. Write a detailed set of step-by-step instructions, in English, to find the smallest number in a group of three integer numbers.

6. a. Write a detailed set of step-by-step instructions, in English, to calculate the change remaining from a dollar after making a purchase. Assume that the cost of the goods purchased is less than a dollar. The change received should consist of the smallest number of coins possible.

b. Repeat Exercise 6a, but assume the change is to be given only in pennies.

7. a. Write an algorithm to locate the first occurrence of the name JONES in a list of names arranged in random order.

b. Discuss how to improve your algorithm for Exercise 7a if the list of names was arranged in alphabetical order.

8. Write an algorithm to determine the total occurrences of the letter e in any sentence.

9. Determine and write an algorithm to sort four numbers into ascending (from lowest to highest) order.

1.2   Introduction to Modularity

A well-designed program is constructed using a design philosophy similar to that in constructing a well-designed building; it doesn't just happen, but depends on careful planning and execution for the final design to accomplish its intended purpose. Just as an integral part of a building design is its structure, the same is true for a program.

In programming, the term, structure, has two interrelated meanings. The first refers to the program's overall construction, which is discussed in this section. The second refers to the form used to carry out individual tasks within the program, which is discussed in Chapters 4 and 5. In relation to its first meaning, programs whose structure consists of interrelated segments, arranged in a logical and easily understandable order to form an integrated and complete unit, are referred to as *modular programs* (Figure 1-9). Modular programs are easier to develop, correct, and modify than programs constructed otherwise. In general programming terminology, the smaller segments used to construct a modular program are called *modules*.

Each module is designed and developed to perform a specific task, and is really a small subprogram all by itself. A complete C program is constructed by combining as many modules as necessary to produce the desired result. The advantage to modular construction is that the overall program design can be developed before any single module is written. Once each module's requirements are finalized, it can be programmed and integrated within the overall program as the module is completed.

Since a module is really a small subprogram, each module must do what is required of all programs: receive and process data and produce a result (see Figure 1-10). Unlike a larger program, however, a module performs limited operations. Modules are meant to handle, at most, one or two functions required by the complete program. Since each module is designed to perform a specific function, the modules themselves are called *functions* in C.

Functions

It helps to think of a function as a small machine that transforms the data it receives into a finished product. For example, Figure 1-11 illustrates a function

FIGURE 1–9   A Well-Designed Program Is Built Using Modules

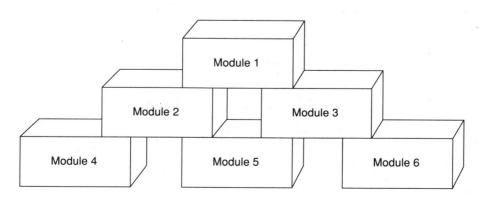

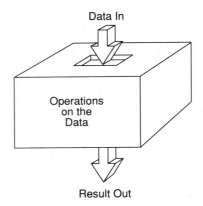

Data In

Operations
on the
Data

Result Out

FIGURE 1–10 A Module Must Accept Data, Process the Data, and Produce a Result

that accepts two numbers as inputs and multiplies the two numbers to produce one output.

One important requirement for designing a good function is to give it a name that conveys what the function does. Function names can be made up of any combination of letters, digits, or underscores (_) selected according to the following rules.

1. The function name must begin with a letter.
2. Only letters, digits, or underscores may follow the initial letter. Blank spaces are not allowed; use the underscore in place of a blank space.
3. A function name cannot be one of the reserved words listed in Table 1-2. (A *reserved word* is a word that is set aside by the language for a special purpose and can only be used in a specified manner.)
4. Only the first eight characters of a function name are actually used and recorded by the computer. (However, some systems recognize and use more than the first eight characters.)
5. All function names must be followed by parentheses.

FIGURE 1–11 A Multiplying Function

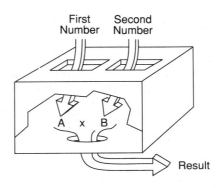

First
Number

Second
Number

A x B

Result

Examples of valid C function names, including the required parentheses, are:

```
grosspay()     tax_calc()     add_nums()     deg2rad()
mult_two()     salestax()     netpay()       bessel1()
```

Examples of invalid function names are:

```
1AB3()  (begins with a number, which violates Rule 1)
E*6()   (contains a special character, which violates Rule 2)
while() (this is a reserved word, which violates Rule 3)
```

Besides conforming to the rules for naming functions, a good function name should also be a mnemonic. A *mnemonic* is a word or name designed as a memory aid. For example, the function name `deg2rad()` is a mnemonic if it is the name of a function that converts degrees to radians. Here, the name, itself, helps identify what the function does.

Examples of valid function names that are not mnemonics are:

```
easy()      c3po()      r2d2()      theforce()      mike()
```

Nonmnemonic function names should not be used because they convey no information about the function.

Notice that all function names have been typed in lowercase letters. This is traditional in C, although it is not absolutely necessary. Uppercase letters are usually reserved for named constants, a topic covered in Chapter 3. It should be noted that C is a *case-sensitive* language. This means that the compiler distinguishes between uppercase and lowercase letters. Thus, in C, the names `TOTAL`, `total`, and `TotaL` represent three distinct names.

TABLE 1-2   Reserved Words

auto	do	for	return	typedef
break	double	goto	short	union
case	else	if	sizeof	unsigned
char	enum	int	static	void
continue	extern	long	struct	while
default	float	register	switch	

The `main()` Function

Once functions have been named, we need a way to combine them into a complete program (see Figure 1-12). Notice that we have not yet described the

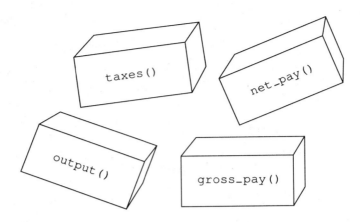

FIGURE 1–12 We Need Some Order Here!

actual writing of the functions. One of the nice features of C is that we can plan a program by first deciding what functions are needed and how they are to be linked together. Then we can write each function to perform the task it is required to do.

To provide for the orderly placement and execution of functions, each C program must have one function called main(). The main() function is sometimes referred to as a driver function, because it tells the other functions the sequence in which they are to operate (see Figure 1-13).

FIGURE 1–13 The main() Function Controls All Other Functions

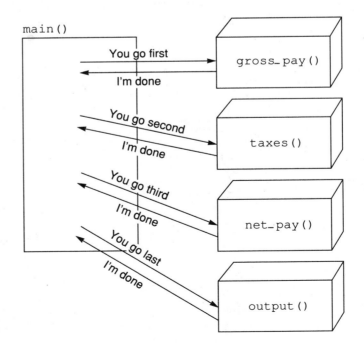

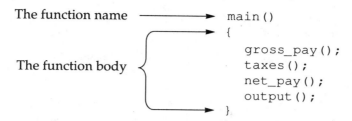

The function name ⟶ main()

The function body { gross_pay();
taxes();
net_pay();
output();
}

FIGURE 1–14 A Sample main() Function

Figure 1-14 illustrates a completed main() function. The word *main* identifies the start of each C program. The braces, { and }, determine the beginning
and end of the function body and enclose the statements making up the
function. The statements inside the braces determine what the function does.
Each statement inside the function must end with a semicolon (;).

The main() function illustrated in Figure 1-14 consists of four statements.
In this case, each statement is a command to execute another function. First the
gross_pay() function is called for execution. When gross_pay() is finished,
the taxes() function is called. After the taxes() function is completed, the
net_pay() function is called. Finally, the output() function is executed.
Although the functions gross_pay(), taxes(), net_pay(), and output()
must still be written, the main() function is completed. After the four other
functions are written, the program, consisting of main(), gross_pay(),
taxes(), net_pay(), and output(), is complete.

You will be naming and writing many of your own C functions. In fact, the
rest of this book is mostly about the statements required to construct useful
functions and about how to combine the functions to form useful programs.
Fortunately, however, many useful functions have already been written for us.
In the next section, we will use one of these functions to create our first working
C program.

Exercises 1.2

1. State whether the following are valid function names. If they are valid, state whether
they are mnemonic names. A mnemonic function name conveys some idea about what
the function might do. If they are invalid names, state why.

m1234()	new_bal()	abcd()	A12345()	1A2345()
power()	abs_val()	invoices()	do()	while()
add_5()	taxes()	net_pay()	12345()	int()
new_balance()	a2b3c4d5()	salestax()	amount()	$taxes()

2. Assume that the following functions have been written:

old_bal(),   sold(),   new_bal(),   report()

17

    a. Write a C program that calls these functions in the order that they are listed.
    b. From the functions' names, what do you think each function might do?

3. Assume that the following functions have been written:

```
input(),    salestax(),    balance(),    calcbill()
```

    a. Write a C program that calls these functions in the order that they are listed.
    b. From the functions' names, what do you think each function might do?

4. Determine names for functions that do the following:
    a. Find the maximum value in a set of numbers.
    b. Find the minimum value in a set of numbers.
    c. Convert a lowercase letter to an uppercase letter.
    d. Convert an uppercase letter to a lowercase letter.
    e. Sort a set of numbers from lowest to highest.
    f. Alphabetize a set of names.

Note for Exercises 5 through 10:

Most programming and nonprogramming projects can be structured into smaller subtasks or units of activity. These smaller subtasks can often be delegated to different people so that when all the tasks are finished and integrated, the project or program is completed. For exercises 5 through 10, determine a set of subtasks that, taken together, complete the required task.

    Note: The purpose of these exercises is to have you consider different ways that complex tasks can be structured. Although there is no single correct solution to these exercises, there are incorrect solutions and solutions that are better than others. An incorrect solution does not complete the task correctly. One solution is better than another if it more clearly or easily identifies what must be done.

5. You are given the job of planning a surprise birthday party. Determine a set of subtasks to accomplish this. (*Hint:* One such subtask would be to create a guest list.)

6. You are given the job of preparing a meal for five people next weekend. Determine the major tasks that must be handled to accomplish this. (*Hint:* One task, not necessarily the first one, is "Buy the food.")

7. You are a sophomore in college and plan to go to law school after graduation. List the major objectives that you must fulfill to meet this goal. (*Hint:* One objective is "Take the right courses.")

8. You wish to plant a vegetable garden. Determine the major tasks that must be handled to accomplish this. (*Hint:* One task is "Plan the garden.")

9. You are responsible for planning and arranging the family camping trip this summer. List the major tasks that must be accomplished to meet this objective successfully. (*Hint:* One task is "Select the camp site.")

10. *a.* A Wall Street investment firm desires a computer system to track all stock trades made during the year. The system must, of course, be capable of accepting and storing all the trades. Additionally, the company wants to retrieve and output a printed report listing all trades that meet certain criteria. For example, all trades made in a particular month with a net value of more than a given dollar amount, all trades made in a year with a particular client, or all trades made with firms in a particular

state. For this system, determine three or four major modules into which the system could be separated. (*Hint:* One module is "Input trades" to accept each day's trades.)

b. Suppose someone enters incorrect data about a trade, which is discovered after the trade has been entered and stored by the system. What module is needed to correct this problem? Discuss why such a module might or might not be required by most business systems.

c. Assume a module exists that allows a user to alter or change data that has been incorrectly entered and stored. Discuss the need for including an "audit trail" that would allow for a later reconstruction of the changes made, when they were made, and who made them.

1.3 The `printf()` Function

One of the most popular and useful prewritten functions in C is named `printf()`. This function, as its name suggests, is a print function that sends data given to it to the standard system display device. For most systems, this display device is a video screen. This function prints out whatever is given to it. For example, if the message `Hello there world!` is given to `printf()`, this message is printed (or displayed) on your terminal by the `printf()` function. Inputting data or messages to a function is called passing data to the function. The message `Hello there world!` is passed to the `printf()` function by simply putting the message inside the parentheses in the function's name (see Figure 1-15).

The purpose of the parentheses in all function names is to provide a funnel through which information can be passed to the function (see Figure 1-16). The items that are passed to the function through the parentheses are called arguments of the function.

FIGURE 1–15 Passing a Message to `printf()`

```
printf("Hello there world!");
```

FIGURE 1–16 Passing a Message to `printf()`

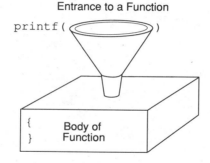

Entrance to a Function

printf( )

{ Body of
} Function

Now let's put all this together into a working C program that can be run on your computer. Consider Program 1-1.

Program 1-1

```
main()
{
    printf("Hello there world!");
}
```

As required, Program 1-1 has one `main()` function. The `main()` function itself has only one statement. Remember that statements end with a semicolon (;). The statement in `main()` calls the function `printf()` and passes one argument to it. The argument is the message `Hello there world!`

Since `printf()` is a prewritten function, we do not have to write it; it is available for use just by calling it correctly. Like all C functions, `printf()` was written to do a specific task, which is to print results. It is versatile and can print results in many different forms. When a message is passed to `printf()`, the function sees to it that the message is correctly printed on your terminal, as shown in Figure 1-17.

FIGURE 1–17 The Output from Program 1-1

```
Hello there world!
```

Messages are called strings in C, because they consist of a string of characters made up of letters, numbers, and special characters. The beginning and end of a string of characters is marked by using double quotes ("message in here") around the string. Thus, to pass a message to `printf()`, the string of characters making up the message must be enclosed in double quotes, as we have done in Program 1-1.

Let's write another program to illustrate `printf()`'s versatility. Read Program 1-2 to determine what it does.

Program 1-2

```
main()
{
    printf("Computers, computers everywhere");
    printf("\n    as far as I can C");

}
```

When Program 1-2 is run, the following is displayed:

```
Computers, computers everywhere
      as far as I can C
```

You might be wondering why the \n did not appear in the output. The two characters \ and n, when used together, are called a newline escape sequence. They tell `printf()` to start on a new line. In C, the backslash (\) character provides an "escape" from the normal interpretation of the character following it by altering the meaning of the next character. If the backslash was omitted from the second `printf()` call in Program 1-2, the n would be printed as the letter *n* and the program would print out:

```
Computers, computers everywheren    as far as I can C
```

Newline escape sequences can be placed anywhere within the message passed to `printf()`. See if you can determine what the following program prints:

```
main()
{
   printf("Computers everywhere\n as far as\n\nI can see");
}
```

The output for this program is:

```
Computers everywhere
 as far as

I can see
```

Exercises 1.3

1. a. Use the `printf()` function to write a C program that prints your name on one line, your street address on a second line, and your city, state, and zip code on the third line.
   b. Run the program you have written for Exercise 1a on a computer. (*Note:* You must understand the procedures for entering and running a C program on the particular computer installation you are using.)

2. a. Write a C program to print out the following verse:

```
Computers, computers everywhere
    as far as I can see
I really, really like these things,
    Oh joy, Oh joy for me!
```

b. Run the program you have written for Exercise 2a on a computer.

3. *a.* How many `printf()` statements would you use to print out the following:

PART NO.	PRICE
T1267	$6.34
T1300	$8.92
T2401	$65.40
T4482	$36.99

b. What is the minimum number of `printf()` statements that could be used to print the table in Exercise 3a? Why would you not write a program using the minimum number of `printf()` function calls?

c. Write a complete C program to produce the output illustrated in Exercise 3a.

d. Run the program you have written for Exercise 3c on a computer.

4. In response to a newline escape sequence, `printf()` positions the next displayed character at the beginning of a new line. This positioning of the next character actually represents two distinct operations. What are they?

5. *a.* Most computer operating systems provide the capability for redirecting the output produced by `printf()` either to a printer or directly to a floppy or hard disk file. Read the first part of Appendix C for a description of this redirection capability.

b. If your computer supports output redirection, run the program written for Exercise 2a using this feature. Have your program's display redirected to a file named poem.

c. If your computer supports output redirection to a printer, run the program written for Exercise 2a using this feature.

1.4 Programming Style

The word `main` in a C program tells the computer where the program starts. Since a program can have only one starting point, every C language program must contain one and only one `main()` function. As we have seen, all statements that make up the `main()` function are included within the braces { } following the function name. Although the `main()` function must be present in every C program, C does not require that the word `main`, the parentheses `()`, or the braces { } be placed in any particular form. The form used in the last section

```
main()
{
    program statements in here;
}
```

was chosen strictly for clarity and ease in reading the program. For example, the following general form of a `main()` function would also work:

```
main
(
){ first statement;second statement;
third statement;fourth
statement;}
```

Notice that more than one statement can be put on a line, or one statement can be written across lines. Except for messages contained within double quotes, function names, and reserved words, C ignores all white space (white space refers to any combination of one or more blank spaces, tabs, or new lines). For example, changing the white space in Program 1-1 and making sure not to split the message `Hello there world!` or the function names `printf` and `main` across two lines results in the following valid program:

```
main
(
){printf
("Hello there world!"
);}
```

Although this version of `main()` does work, it is an example of extremely poor programming style. It is difficult to read and understand. For readability, the `main()` function should always be written in standard form as:

```
main()
{
   program statements in here;
}
```

In this standard form, the function name starts in column 1 and is placed with the required parentheses on a line by itself. The opening brace of the function body follows on the next line and is placed under the first letter of the function name. Similarly, the closing function brace is placed by itself in column 1 as the last line of the function. This structure serves to highlight the function as a single unit.

Within the function itself, all program statements are indented two spaces. Indentation is another sign of good programming practice, especially if the same indentation is used for similar groups of statements. Review Program 1-2 to see that the same indentation was used for both `printf()` function calls.

As you progress in your understanding and mastery of C, you will develop your own indentation standards. Just keep in mind that the final form of your programs should be consistent and should always serve as an aid to the reading and understanding of your programs.

Comments

Comments are explanatory remarks made within a program. When used carefully, comments help clarify what the complete program is about, what a specific group of statements is meant to accomplish, or what one line is intended to do.

Any line of text bounded by asterisks and enclosed within slashes (/) is a comment. For example,

```
/* this is a comment */
/* this program prints out a message */
/* this program calculates a square root */
```

are all comment lines. The symbols /*, with no white space between them, designate the start of a comment. Similarly, the symbols */, as a single unit with no intervening white space, designate the end of a comment.

Comments can be placed anywhere within a program and have no effect on program execution. The computer ignores all comments—they are there strictly for the convenience of anyone reading the program.

A comment can be written either on a line by itself or on the same line containing a program statement. Program 1-3 illustrates the use of comments within a program.

 Program 1-3

```
main()     /* this program prints a message */
{
    printf("Hello there world!"); /* a call to printf() */
}
```

The first comment appears on the same line as the function name and describes what the program does. This is generally a good location to include a short comment describing the program's purpose. If more comments are required, they can be placed, one per line, between the function name and the opening brace that encloses the function's statements. If a comment is too long to be contained on one line, it can be separated into two or more comments, with each separate comment enclosed within the comment symbol set /* */.

The comment

```
/* this comment may be invalid because it
                extends over two lines */
```

may result in a C error message on your computer (however, some computers do accept comments written across lines). This comment is always correct when written as:

```
/* this comment is used to illustrate a */
/* comment that extends across two lines */
```

Typically, many comments are required when using nonstructured programming languages. These comments are necessary to clarify either the purpose of the program or of individual sections and lines of code within the program. In C, the program's structure is intended to make the program readable, making the use of extensive comments unnecessary. This is reinforced if both function names and variable names, described in the next chapter, are carefully selected to convey their meaning to anyone reading the program. However, if the purpose of a function or any of its statements is still unclear from its structure, name, or context, include comments where clarification is needed.

Exercises 1.4

1. a. Will the following program work?

```
main(){printf("Hello there world!");}
```

b. Why is the program given in Exercise 1a not a good program?

2. Rewrite the following programs to conform to good programming practice.

a.
```
main(
){
printf
(
"The time has come"
);}
```

b.
```
main
(){printf("Newark is a city\n");printf(
"In New Jersey\n"); printf
("It is also a city\n"
); printf("In Delaware\n"
);}
```

c.
```
main(){printf("Reading a program\n");printf(
"is much easier\n"
);printf("if a standard form for main is used\n")
;printf        ("and each statement is written\n");printf(
"on a line by itself\n")
;}
```

d.
```
main
(){printf("Every C program"
);printf
("\nmust have one and only one"
);
printf("main function"
);
printf(
"\n the escape sequence of characters")
;printf(
"\nfor a new line can be placed anywhere"
);printf
("\n within the message passed to printf()"
);}
```

3. *a.* When used in a message, the backslash character alters the meaning of the character immediately following it. If we wanted to print the backslash character, we would have to tell `printf()` to escape from the way it normally interprets the backslash. What character do you think is used to alter the way a single backslash character is interpreted?

b. Using your answer to Exercise 3a, write the escape sequence for printing a backslash.

4. *a.* A *token* of a computer language is any sequence of characters that, as a unit, with no intervening characters or white space, has a unique meaning. Using this definition of a token, determine whether escape sequences, function names, and the reserved words listed in Table 1-2 are tokens of the C language.

b. Discuss whether adding white space to a message alters the message. Discuss whether messages can be considered tokens of C.

c. Using the definition of a token given in Exercise 4a, determine whether the statement "Except for tokens of the language, C ignores all white space" is true.

1.5   Top-Down Program Development

Recall from Section 1.1 that writing a C program is essentially the last step in the programming process. The first step in the process is determining what is required and selecting the algorithm to be coded into C. In this section, we present a five-step program development procedure, called top-down development, for converting programming problems into working C programs. To make this development procedure more meaningful, we first apply it to a simple programming problem. As we will see, designing a program using a top-down approach results in a modular program design.

The five steps in the top-down development procedure are:

1. Determine the desired output items that the program must produce
2. Determine the input items
3. Design the program as follows:
   a. Select an algorithm for transforming the input items into the desired outputs
   b. Check the chosen algorithm, by hand, using specific input values
4. Code the algorithm into C
5. Test the program using selected test data

Steps 1 and 2 in the development procedure are referred to as the program *Analysis Phase,* Step 3 is called the *Design Phase,* Step 4 the *Coding Phase,* and Step 5 the *Testing Phase.*

In the analysis phase of program development (Steps 1 and 2) we are concerned with extracting the complete input and output information supplied by the problem. Together, these two items are referred to as the problem's input/output, or I/O, for short. Only after a problem's I/O has been determined is it possible to select an algorithm for transforming the inputs into the desired outputs. For example, consider the following simple programming problem:

> The volume, V, of a sphere is given by the formula $V = 4/3\pi r^3$, where π is the constant 3.1416 (accurate to four decimal places), and r is the radius of the sphere. Using this information, write a C program to calculate the volume of a sphere that has a 2-inch radius.

Step 1: Determine the Desired Output

The first step in developing a program for this problem statement is to determine the required outputs (Step 1 of the development procedure). Frequently, the statement of the problem will use such words as *calculate, print, determine, find,* or *compare,* which can be used to determine the desired outputs.

For our sample problem statement, the key phrase is "to calculate the volume of a sphere." This identifies an output item. Since there are no other such phrases in the problem, only one output item is required.

Step 2: Determine the Input Items

Having clearly identified the desired output, Step 2 of the development process requires that the input items be identified. It is essential, at this stage, to distinguish between input items and input values. An input *item* is the name of an input quantity, while an input *value* is a specific number or quantity that the input item can be. For example, in our sample problem statement, the input item is the radius of the sphere (the known quantity). Although this input item has a specific numerical value in this problem (the value 2), actual input item values are generally not important in Step 2.

The reason that input values are not needed at this point is because the initial selection of an algorithm is typically independent of specific input values; the algorithm depends on knowing the output and input items and whether there are any special limits. Let's see why this is so, as we determine a suitable algorithm for our sample problem statement.

Step 3a: Determine an Algorithm

From the problem statement, it is clear that the algorithm for transforming the input items to the desired output is given by the formula $V = 4/3\pi r^3$. Notice that this formula can be used regardless of the specific value assigned to r. Although we cannot produce an actual numerical value for the output item (volume) unless we have an actual numerical value for the input item, the correct relationship between inputs and outputs is expressed by the formula. Recall that this is precisely what an algorithm provides: a description of how the inputs are to be transformed into outputs that works for all inputs. Thus, the complete algorithm, in pseudocode, for solving this problem is:

Assign a value to r
Calculate the volume using the formula $V = 4/3\pi r^3$
Display the result

Step 3b: Do a Hand Calculation

Having selected an algorithm, the next step in the design procedure, Step 3b, is to manually check the algorithm using specific data. Performing a manual calculation, either by hand or by using a calculator, helps ensure that you really do understand the problem. An added feature of doing a manual calculation is that the results can later be used to verify the operation of your program in the testing phase. Then, when the final program is used with other data, you will have established a degree of confidence that a correct result is being calculated.

Doing a manual calculation requires that we have specific input values that can be applied to the algorithm to produce the desired output. For this problem, one input value is given: a radius of 2 inches. Substituting this value into the formula, we obtain a volume = $4/3$ (3.1416) 2^3 = 33.5104 in^3 for the sphere.

Step 4: Write the Program

Having selected an algorithm for the problem, all that remains is to write the algorithm in C. Since all of the statements for converting this algorithm into C are not presented until the next chapter, there are parts of the program that will be unfamiliar to you. Nevertheless, we present the completed program for you to examine and see how it follows our previous pseudocode description.

 Program 1.4

```
#include <math.h>    /* make the math library accessible, which */
main()               /* is needed for the power function, pow() */
{
   float radius, volume;
   radius = 2.0;
   volume = (4.0/3.0) * 3.1416 * pow(radius,3);
   printf("The volume of the sphere is %f",volume);
}
```

When this program is executed, the following output is produced:

```
The volume of the sphere is   33.510400
```

Having a working program that produces a result, the final step in the development process, testing the program, can begin.

Step 5: Test the Output

The purpose of testing is to verify that a program works correctly and fulfills its requirements. Once testing is completed, the program can be used to calculate outputs for differing input data without needing to retest. This is, of course, the real value in writing a program: the same program can be used over and over with new input data.

In theory, testing would reveal all existing program errors (in computer terminology, a program error is called a *bug*). In practice, this would require checking all possible combinations of statement execution. Due to the time and effort required, this is usually an impossible goal except for extremely simple programs such as Program 1-4. (We illustrate why this is generally an impossible goal in Section 4.7.)

The inability to completely test most programs has led to various testing methodologies. The simplest of these methods is to verify the program's operation for carefully selected sets of input data. One set of input data that should always be used is the data that was selected for the hand calculation made previously in Step 3b of the development procedure. If testing reveals an error (bug), the process of debugging, which includes locating, correcting, and verifying the correction, can be initiated. It is important to realize that although this type of verification testing may reveal the presence of an error, it does not necessarily indicate the absence of one. Thus, the fact that a test does not reveal an error does not indicate that another bug is not lurking somewhere else in the program.

In the case of Program 1-4, only a single calculation is performed and the result of the test run agrees with our hand calculation. Thus, the program has been completely tested and can now be used to calculate the volume of other spheres with confidence that the results being produced are accurate.

Modularity and Top-Down Design

The design of Program 1-4 was relatively simple because the algorithm was a simple formula that was given in the statement of the problem. For more complex problems the selection of an algorithm can be considerably more involved. In its more elaborate form, determining an algorithm is similar to receiving the pieces of a puzzle (the inputs) and deciding how to arrange them to form a completed structure (the desired output). Unlike a jigsaw puzzle, however, the pieces of a program design puzzle can be arranged in many different ways depending on the algorithm chosen for transforming the inputs into the desired outputs. In this regard, the program designer is similar to an architect who must draw up the plans for a house.

The general purpose of using a top-down development procedure to design programs is to create a modular program structure. To achieve this goal, the description of the algorithm starts from the highest level requirement and proceeds to the parts that must be constructed to achieve this requirement. To make this more meaningful, consider that a computer program is required to track the number of parts in inventory. The required output for this program is a description of all parts carried in inventory and the number of units of each item in stock: the given inputs are the initial inventory quantity of each part, the number of items sold, the number of items returned, and the number of items purchased.

For these I/O specifications, a designer could initially organize the requirements for the program into the three sections illustrated in Figure 1-18. This is called a *first-level structure diagram* because it represents the first overall structure of the program selected by the designer.

In top-down algorithm design, the lower boxes in the structure diagram are refined until the tasks indicated in the boxes are small enough to be programmed as individual C functions. For example, both the data entry and report subsections shown in Figure 1-18 would be further refined into suitable modules. The data entry section certainly must include provisions for entering the data. Since it is the system designer's responsibility to plan for contingencies and human error, provisions must also be made for changing incorrect data after an entry has been made and for deleting a previously entered value altogether. Similar subdivisions for the report section can also be made. Figure 1-19 illustrates a second-level structure diagram for an inventory tracking system that includes these further refinements.

The process of refinement continues until the last level of tasks can be coded using individual functions. Notice that the design produces a tree-like structure where the levels branch out as we move from the top of the structure to the bottom. When the design is complete it specifies both how many functions are needed and the calling sequence of each unit (that is, lower level modules in the diagram are called from higher level ones). The individual tasks required for each box in the final structure diagram, which are coded as separate C functions, are frequently described using either flowcharts or pseudocode.

FIGURE 1–18   First-Level Structure Diagram

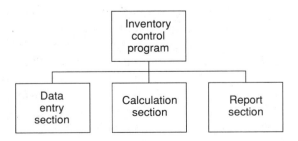

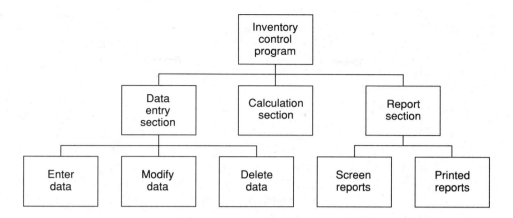

FIGURE 1–19 Second-Level Refinement Structure Diagram

Exercises 1-5

Note: In each of these exercises, a programming problem is given. Read the problem statement first and then answer the questions pertaining to the problem.

1. Consider the following programming problem: A C program is desired that calculates the amount, in dollars, contained in a piggybank. The bank contains Half dollars, Quarters, Dimes, Nickels, and Pennies.
   a. For this programming problem how many outputs are required?
   b. How many inputs does this problem have?
   c. Determine an algorithm for converting the input items into output items.
   d. Test the algorithm written for Exercise 1c using the following sample data: Half dollars = 0, Quarters = 17, Dimes = 24, Nickels = 16, Pennies = 12.

2. Consider the following programming problem: A C program is required to calculate the value of Distance, in miles, given the relationship

$$Distance = Rate * Elapsed\ Time$$

   a. For this programming problem how many outputs are required?
   b. How many inputs does this problem have?
   c. Determine an algorithm for converting the input items into output items.
   d. Test the algorithm written for Exercise 2c using the following sample data: Rate is 55 miles per hour and Elapsed Time is 2.5 hours.
   e. How must the algorithm you determined in Exercise 2c be modified if the elapsed time was given in minutes instead of hours.

3. a. Consider the following programming problem: A C program is required to determine the value of Ergies, given the relationships

$$Ergies = Fergies * \sqrt{Lergies}$$

a. For this programming problem how many outputs are required?
b. How many inputs does this problem have?
c. Determine an algorithm for converting the input items into output items.
d. Test the algorithm written for Exercise 4c using the following sample data:
Fergies = 14.65, and Lergies = 4.

4. Consider the following programming problem: A C program is required to display the following name and address:

> Mr. J. Knipper
> 63 Seminole Way
> Dumont, N.J. 07030

a. For this program problem how many lines of output are required?
b. How many inputs does this problem have?
c. Determine an algorithm for converting the input items into output items.

5. Consider the following program problem: A C program is required to determine how far a car has traveled after 10 seconds assuming the car is initially traveling at 60 miles per hour and the driver applies the brakes to uniformly decelerate at a rate of 12 miles/sec^2. Use the fact that distance = st – (1/2)dt^2, where s is the initial speed of the car, d is the deceleration, and t is the elapsed time.
a. For this programming problem how many outputs are required?
b. How many inputs does this problem have?
c. Determine an algorithm for converting the input items into output items.
d. Test the algorithm written for Exercise 5c using the data given in the problem.

6. Consider the following programming problem: In 1627, Manhattan Island was sold to the Dutch settlers for approximately $24. If the proceeds of that sale had been deposited in a Dutch bank paying 5 percent interest, compounded annually, what would the principal balance be at the end of 1990. A display is required as follows: Balance as of December 31, 1990, is: xxxxxx, where xxxxx is the amount calculated by your program.
a. For this programming problem how many outputs are required?
b. How many inputs does this problem have?
c. Determine an algorithm for converting the input items into output items.
d. Test the algorithm written for Exercise 6c using the data given in the problem statement.

7. Consider the following programming problem: A C program is required that calculates and displays the weekly gross pay and net pay of two individuals. The first individual is paid an hourly rate of $8.43 and the second individual is paid an hourly rate of $5.67. Both individuals have 20 percent of their gross pay withheld for income tax purposes and both pay 2 percent of their gross pay, before taxes, for medical benefits.
a. For this programming problem how many outputs are required?
b. How many inputs does this problem have?
c. Determine an algorithm for converting the input items into output items.
d. Test the algorithm written for Exercise 7c using the following sample data: The first person works 40 hours during the week and the second person works 35 hours.

8. Consider the following programming problem: The formula for the standard normal deviate, z, used in statistical applications is

$$z = \frac{X - \mu}{\sigma}$$

where μ refers to a mean value and σ to a standard deviation. Using this formula, write a program that calculates and displays the value of the standard normal deviate when $X = 85.3$, $\mu = 80$, and $\sigma = 4$.

   a. For this programming problem how many outputs are required?
   b. How many inputs does this problem have?
   c. Determine an algorithm for converting the input items into output items.
   d. Test the algorithm written for Exercise 8c using the data given in the problem.

9. Consider the following programming problem: The equation of an exponential curve used in statistical applications is:

$$y = e^x$$

Using this equation, a C program is required to calculate the value of y.

   a. For this programming problem how many outputs are required?
   b. How many inputs does this problem have?
   c. Determine an algorithm for converting the input items into output items.
   d. Test the algorithm written for Exercise 9c assuming $e = 2.718$ and $x = 10$.

1.6 Common Programming Errors

Part of learning any programming language is making the elementary mistakes commonly encountered as you begin to use the language. These mistakes tend to be quite frustrating, since each language has its own set of common programming errors waiting for the unwary. The more common errors made when initially programming in C are:

1. Omitting the parentheses after `main`.

2. Omitting or incorrectly typing the opening brace { that signifies the start of a function body.

3. Omitting or incorrectly typing the closing brace } that signifies the end of a function.

4. Misspelling the name of a function; for example, typing `print()` instead of `printf()`.

5. Forgetting to close the message to `printf()` with a double quote symbol.

6. Omitting the semicolon at the end of each statement.

7. Forgetting the `\n` to indicate a new line.

Our experience is that the third, fifth, sixth, and seventh errors in this list tend to be the most common. We suggest that you write a program and specifically introduce each of these errors, one at a time, to see what error messages are produced by your compiler. Then, when these error messages appear due to inadvertent errors, you will have had experience in understanding the messages and correcting the errors.

On a more fundamental level, a major programming error made by all beginning programmers is the rush to code and run a program before the programmer fully understands what is required and the algorithms and procedures that will be used to produce the desired result. A symptom of this haste to get a program entered into the computer is the lack of either an outline of the proposed program or a written program itself. Many problems can be caught just by checking a copy of the program, either handwritten or listed from the computer, before it is ever compiled.

1.7   Chapter Summary

1. A C program consists of one or more modules called functions. One of these functions must be called `main()`. The `main()` function identifies the starting point of a C program.
2. Many functions, like `printf()`, are supplied in a standard library of functions provided with each C compiler.
3. The simplest C program consists of the single function `main()`.
4. Following the function name, the body of a function has the general form:

```
{
    All program statements in here;
}
```

5. All C statements must be terminated by a semicolon.
6. The `printf()` function is used to display text or numerical results. The first argument to `printf()` can be a message, which is enclosed in double quotes. The text in the message is displayed directly on the screen and may include new line escape sequences for format control.

Data Types, Declarations, and Displays

Chapter Two

We continue our introduction to the fundamentals of C in this chapter by presenting C's elementary data types, variables, declarations, and additional information on using the `printf()` function. These new concepts and tools enable us to both expand our programming abilities and gain useful insight into how data is stored in a computer.

Before reading this chapter, you should have an understanding of basic computer storage concepts and terms. If you are unfamiliar with the terms *bit*, *byte*, and *memory address*, read the supplement at the end of this chapter for an introduction to these terms.

2.1 Data Types

There are four basic *data types* used in C: integer, floating point, double precision, and character data. Each data type is described below.

Integer Values

An *integer value*, which is called an integer constant in C, is any positive or negative number without a decimal point. Examples of valid integer constants are:

$$5 \quad -10 \quad +25 \quad 1000 \quad 253 \quad -26351 \quad +36$$

As these examples show, integers may be signed (have a leading + or − sign) or unsigned (no leading + or − sign). No commas, decimal points, or special symbols, such as the dollar sign, are allowed. Examples of invalid integer constants are:

$$\$255.62 \quad 2,523 \quad 3. \quad 6,243,892 \quad 1,492.89 \quad +6.0$$

Each computer has its own internal limit on the largest (most positive) and smallest (most negative) integer values that can be used in a program. These limits depend on how much storage each computer sets aside for an integer. The more common storage allocations are listed in Table 2-1. By referring to your computer's reference manual or using the `sizeof` operator introduced in Section 2.5, you can determine the actual number of bytes allocated by your computer for each integer value. (Review Section 2.8 if you are unfamiliar with the concept of a byte.)

TABLE 2-1   Integer Values and Byte Storage

Storage Area Reserved	Maximum Integer Value	Minimum Integer Value
1 byte	127	−128
2 bytes	32767	−32768
4 bytes	2147483647	−2147483648

Floating Point and Double Precision Numbers

Floating point and *double precision* numbers are any signed or unsigned numbers having a decimal point. Examples of floating point and double precision numbers are:

+10.625   5.   −6.2   3251.92   0.0   0.33   −6.67   +2.

As with integers, special symbols, such as the dollar sign and the comma, are not permitted in floating point or double precision numbers. Examples of invalid floating point and double precision constants are:

5,326.25   24   123   6,459 $10.29

The difference between floating point and double precision numbers is how much storage a computer uses for each type. Most computers use twice the amount of storage for double precision numbers than for floating point numbers, which allows a double precision number to have approximately twice the precision of a floating point number (for this reason floating point numbers are sometimes called *single precision* numbers). The actual storage allocation for each data type, however, depends on the particular computer. In computers that use the same amount of storage for double precision and floating point numbers, these two data types become identical. The `sizeof` operator introduced in Section 2.5 will allow you to determine the amount of storage reserved by your computer for each of these data types.

Exponential Notation

Floating point and double precision numbers can be written in exponential notation, which is commonly used to express either very large or very small numbers in a compact form. The following examples illustrate how numbers with decimal points can be expressed in exponential notation.

Decimal Notation	Exponential Notation
1625.	1.625e3
63421.	6.3421e4
.00731	7.31e–3
.000625	6.25e–4

In exponential notation the letter *e* stands for *exponent*. The number following the *e* represents a power of 10 and indicates the number of places the decimal point should be moved to obtain the standard decimal value. The decimal point is moved to the right if the number after the *e* is positive, or moved to the left if the number after the *e* is negative. For example, the *e*3 in the number 1.625*e*3 means move the decimal place three places to the right, so that the number becomes 1625. The *e*–3 in the number 7.31*e*–3 means move the decimal point three places to the left, so that 7.31*e*–3 becomes .00731.

Character Type

The fourth basic data type recognized by C is the *character type*. Characters are the letters of the alphabet, the ten digits 0 through 9, and special symbols such as + $. , – ! . A single character constant is any one letter, digit, or special symbol enclosed by single quotes. Examples of valid character constants are:

'A'   '$'   'b'   '7'   'y'   '!'   'M'   'q'

Character constants are typically stored in a computer using either the ASCII or EBCDIC codes. ASCII, pronounced AS-KEY, is an acronym for American Standard Code for Information Interchange. EBCDIC, pronounced EBB-SAH-DICK, is an acronym for Extended Binary Coded Decimal Interchange Code. Each of these codes assigns individual characters to a specific pattern of 0s and 1s. Table 2-2 lists the correspondence between byte patterns and the letters of the alphabet used by the ASCII code.

Using Table 2-2, we can determine how the character constants 'J', 'O', 'N', 'E', and 'S', for example, are stored inside a computer that uses the ASCII character code. Using the ASCII code, this sequence of characters requires five bytes of storage (one byte for each letter) and would be stored as illustrated in Figure 2-1.

FIGURE 2–1 The Letters JONES Stored Inside a Computer

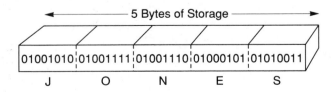

TABLE 2-2   The ASCII Uppercase Letter Codes

Letter	Computer Code	Letter	Computer Code
A	01000001	N	01001110
B	01000010	O	01001111
C	01000011	P	01010000
D	01000100	Q	01010001
E	01000101	R	01010010
F	01000110	S	01010011
G	01000111	T	01010100
H	01001000	U	01010101
I	01001001	V	01010110
J	01001010	W	01010111
K	01001011	X	01011000
L	01001100	Y	01011001
M	01001101	Z	01011010

Escape Sequences

When a backslash (\) is used in front of a select group of characters, the backslash tells the computer to escape from the way these characters would normally be interpreted. For this reason, the combination of a backslash and these specific characters are called *escape sequences*. We have already encountered an example of this in the newline escape sequence, \n. Table 2-3 lists other common escape sequences.

TABLE 2-3   Escape Sequences

Escape Sequence	Meaning
\b	move back one space
\f	move to next page
\n	move to next line
\r	carriage return
\t	move to next tab setting
\\	backslash character
\'	single quote
\nnn	treat nnn as an octal number

Although each escape sequence listed in Table 2-3 is made up of two distinct characters, the combination of the two characters with no intervening white space causes the computer to store one character code. Table 2-4 lists the ASCII code byte patterns for the escape sequences listed in Table 2-3.

TABLE 2-4   The ASCII Escape Sequence Codes

C Escape Sequence	Meaning	Computer Code
\b	backspace	00001000
\f	form feed	00001100
\n	newline	00001010
\r	carriage return	00001101
\\	backslash	01011100
\'	single quote	00100111

Exercises 2.1

1. Determine data types appropriate for the following data:
   a. the average of four grades
   b. the number of days in a month
   c. the length of the Golden Gate Bridge
   d. the numbers in a state lottery
   e. the distance from Brooklyn, N.Y. to Newark, N.J.

2. Convert the following numbers into standard decimal form:

$$6.34 \ e5 \qquad 1.95162 \ e2 \qquad 8.395 \ e1 \qquad 2.95 \ e-3 \qquad 4.623 \ e-4$$

3. Convert the following decimal numbers into exponential notation:

$$126. \qquad 656.23 \qquad 3426.95 \qquad 4893.2 \qquad .321 \qquad .0123 \qquad .006789$$

4. Using the system reference manuals for your computer, determine the character code used by your computer.

5. Using elementary computer science textbooks, construct a table similar to Table 2-2 for the EBCDIC code.

6. a. Using the ASCII code, determine the number of bytes required to store the letters KINGSLEY.
   b. Show how the letters KINGSLEY would be stored inside a computer that uses the ASCII code. That is, draw a figure similar to Figure 2-1 for the letters KINGSLEY.

7. a. Repeat Exercise 6a using the letters of your own last name.
   b. Repeat Exercise 6b using the letters of your own last name.

8. Since most computers use different amounts of storage for integer, floating point, double precision, and character values, discuss how a program might alert the computer to the amount of storage needed for the various values in the program.

9. Although the total number of bytes varies from computer to computer, memory sizes of 65,536 to more than 1 million bytes are not uncommon. In computer language, the letter K is used to represent the number 1024, which is 2 raised to the 10th power. Thus, a memory size of 64K is really 64 times 1024, or 65,536 bytes, and a memory size of 512K consists of 512 times 1024, or 524,288 bytes. Using this information, calculate the actual number of bytes in:

    a. a memory containing 64K bytes
    b. a memory containing 128K bytes
    c. a memory containing 192 bytes
    d. a memory containing 256 bytes
    e. a memory consisting of 64K words, where each word consists of 2 bytes
    f. a memory consisting of 64K words, where each word consists of 4 bytes
    g. a floppy diskette that can store 360K bytes

2.2 Arithmetic Operators

Integers, floating point numbers, and double precision numbers may be added, subtracted, divided, and multiplied. Although it is better not to mix integers with the other two numerical data types when performing arithmetic operations, predictable results are obtained when different data types are used in the same arithmetic expression. Somewhat surprising is the fact that character data can also be added and subtracted with both character and integer data to produce useful results.

The operators used for these arithmetic operations are called *arithmetic operators:*

Operation	Operator
Addition	+
Subtraction	−
Multiplication	*
Division	/

Each of these arithmetic operators is a binary operator that requires two operands. A simple arithmetic expression consists of an arithmetic operator connecting two arithmetic operands. Examples of arithmetic expressions are:

$$3 + 7$$
$$18 - 3$$
$$12.62 + 9.8$$
$$.08 * 12.2$$
$$12.6 / 2.$$

The spaces around the arithmetic operators in these examples are inserted strictly for clarity and may be omitted without affecting the value of the expression. When evaluating arithmetic expressions, the data type of the result is determined by the following rules:

1. If all operands are integers, the result is an integer.
2. If any operand is a floating point or double precision value, the result is a double precision number.

Notice that the result of an arithmetic expression is never a floating point number because the computer temporarily converts all floating point numbers to double precision numbers when arithmetic is being done.

Integer Division

The division of two integers can produce rather strange results for the unwary. For example, dividing the integer 15 by the integer 2 yields an integer result. Since integers cannot contain a fractional part, the correct result, 7.5, is not obtained. In C, the fractional part of the result obtained when dividing two integers is dropped *(truncated)*. Thus, the value of 15/2 is 7, the value of 9/4 is 2, and the value of 17/5 is 3.

There are times when we would like to retain the remainder of an integer division. To do this C provides an arithmetic operator that captures the remainder when two integers are divided. This operator, called the modulus operator, has the symbol %. The *modulus operator* can be used only with integers. For example,

9 % 4 is 1
17 % 3 is 2
14% 2 is 0

A Unary Operator (Negation)

Besides the binary operators for addition, subtraction, multiplication, and division, C also provides *unary operators*. One of these unary operators uses the same symbol that is used for binary subtraction (−). The minus sign used in front of a single numerical operand negates (reverses the sign of) the number.

Table 2-5 summarizes the six arithmetic operations we have described so far and lists the data type of the result produced by each operator based on the data type of the operands involved.

Operator Precedence and Associativity

Besides such simple expressions as 5 + 12 and .08 * 26.2, we frequently need to create more complex arithmetic expressions. C, like most other programming

TABLE 2-5   Summary of Arithmetic Operators

Operation	Operator	Type	Operand	Result
Addition	+	Binary	Both integers	Integer
			One operand not an integer	Double precision
Subtraction	–	Binary	Both integers	Integer
			One operand not an integer	Double precision
Multiplication	*	Binary	Both integers	Integer
			One operand not an integer	Double precision
Division	/	Binary	Both integers	Integer
			One operand not an integer	Double precision
Remainder	%	Binary	Both integers	Integer
Negation	–	Unary	One integer	Integer
			One floating point or double precision operand	Double precision

languages, requires that certain rules be followed when writing expressions containing more than one arithmetic operator. These rules are:

1. Two binary arithmetic operator symbols must never be placed side by side.

   For example, 5 * %6 is invalid because the two operators * and % are placed next to each other.

2. Parentheses may be used to form groupings, and all expressions enclosed within parentheses are evaluated first.

   For example, in the expression (6 + 4) / (2 + 3), the 6 + 4 and 2 + 3 are evaluated first to yield 10 / 5. The 10 / 5 is then evaluated to yield 2.

   Sets of parentheses may also be enclosed by other parentheses. For example, the expression (2 * (3 + 7)) / 5 is valid. When parentheses are used within parentheses, the expressions in the innermost parentheses are always evaluated first. The evaluation continues from innermost to outermost parentheses until the expressions of all parentheses have been evaluated. The number of right-facing parentheses, (, must always equal the number of left-facing parentheses,), so that there are no unpaired sets.

3. Parentheses cannot be used to indicate multiplication. The multiplication operator, *, must be used.

For example, the expression (3 + 4) (5 + 1) is invalid. The correct expression is (3 + 4) * (5 + 1).

As a general rule, parentheses should be used to specify logical groupings of operands and to indicate clearly to both the computer and programmers the intended order of arithmetic operations. In the absence of parentheses, expressions containing multiple operators are evaluated by the priority, or *precedence*, of each operator. Table 2-6 lists both the precedence and associativity of the operators considered in this section.

TABLE 2-6 Operator Precedence
and Associativity

Operator	Associativity
unary −	right to left
* / %	left to right
+ −	left to right

The precedence of an operator establishes its priority relative to all other operators. Operators at the top of Table 2-6 have a higher priority than operators at the bottom of the table. In expressions with multiple operators, the operator with the higher precedence is used before an operator with a lower precedence. For example, in the expression 6 + 4 / 2 + 3, the division is done before the addition, yielding an intermediate result of 6 + 2 + 3. The additions are then performed to yield a final result of 11.

Expressions containing operators with the same precedence are evaluated according to their *associativity*. This means that evaluation is either from left to right or from right to left as each operator is encountered. For example, in the expression 8 + 5 * 7 % 2 * 4, the multiplication and modulus operator are of higher precedence than the addition operator and are evaluated first. Both of these operators, however, are of equal priority. Therefore, these operators are evaluated according to their left-to-right associativity, yielding

$$8 + 5 * 7 \% 2 * 4 =$$
$$8 + 35 \% 2 * 4 =$$
$$8 + 1 * 4 =$$
$$8 + 4 = 12$$

Exercises 2.2

1. Listed on the following page are algebraic expressions and incorrect C expressions corresponding to them. Find the errors and write corrected C expressions.

Algebra	C Expression
a. (2)(3) + (4)(5)	(2)(3) + (4)(5)
b. $\dfrac{6+18}{2}$	6 + 18 / 2
c. $\dfrac{4.5}{12.2-3.1}$	4.5 / 12.2 – 3.1
d. 4.6(3.0 + 14.9)	4.6(3.0 + 14.9)
e. (12.1 + 18.9)(15.3 – 3.8)	(12.1 + 18.9)(15.3 – 3.8)

2. Assuming that amount = 1, $m = 50$, $n = 10$, and $p = 5$, evaluate the following expressions.

a. $n / p + 3$

b. $m / p + n - 10 * $ amount

c. $m - 3 * n + 4 *$ amount

d. amount / 5

e. 18 / p

f. 18 % p

g. $-p * n$

h. $-m$ / 20

i. $-m$ % 20

j. $(m + n) / (p + $ amount)

k. $m + n / p + $ amount

3. Repeat Exercise 2 assuming that amount = 1.0, $m = 50.0$, $n = 10.0$, and $p = 5.0$.

4. Determine the value of the following integer expressions:

a. 3 + 4 * 6

b. 3 * 4 / 6 + 6

c. 2 * 3 / 12 * 8 / 4

d. 10 * (1 + 7 * 3)

e. 20 – 2 / 6 + 3

f. 20 – 2 / (6 + 3)

g. (20 – 2) / 6 + 3

h. (20 – 2) / (6 + 3)

5. Determine the value of the following floating point expressions:

a. 3.0 + 4.0 * 6.0

b. 3.0 * 4.0 / 6.0 + 6.0

c. 2.0 * 3.0 / 12.0 * 8.0 / 4.0

d. 10.0 * (1.0 + 7.0 * 3.0)

e. 20.0 – 2.0 / 6.0 + 3.0

f. 20.0 – 2.0 / (6.0 + 3.0)

g. (20.0 – 2.0) / 6.0 + 3.0

h. (20.0 – 2.0) / (6.0 + 3.0)

6. Evaluate the following expressions and list the data type of the result. In evaluating the expressions be aware of the data types of all intermediate calculations.

a. 10.0 + 15 / 2 + 4.3

b. 10.0 + 15 % 2 + 4.3

c. 10.0 + 15.0 / 2 + 4.3

d. 3.0 * 4 / 6 + 6

e. 3.0 * 4 % 6 + 6

f. 3 * 4.0 / 6 + 6

g. 20.0 – 2 / 6 + 3

h. 10 + 17 % 3 + 4

i. 10 + 17 % 3 + 4.

j. 10 + 17 / 3. + 4

7. Although we have concentrated on only integer, floating point, and double precision numbers, C allows characters and integers to be added or subtracted. This can be done because C always converts a character to an equivalent integer value whenever a character is used in an arithmetic expression. Thus, characters and integers can be freely mixed in such expressions. For example, if your computer uses the ASCII code, the expression 'a' + 1 equals 'b', and 'z' – 1 equals 'y'. Similarly, 'A' + 1 is 'B', and 'Z' – 1 is 'Y'. With this as background, determine the character results of the following expressions (assume that all characters are stored using the ASCII code).

a. 'm' – 5

b. 'm' + 5

c. 'G' + 6

d. 'G' – 6

e. 'b' – 'a'

f. 'g' – 'a' + 1

g. 'G' – 'A' + 1

8. *a.* The table in Appendix B lists the integer values corresponding to each letter stored using the ASCII code. Using this table, notice that the uppercase letters consist of con-

tiguous codes starting with an integer value of 65 for A and ending with 90 for the letter Z. Similarly, the lowercase letters begin with the integer value of 97 for the letter a and end with 122 for the letter z. With this as background, determine the character value of the expressions 'A' + 32 and 'Z' + 32.

b. Using Appendix B, determine the integer value of the expression 'a' − 'A'.

c. Using the results of Exercises 8a and 8b, determine the character value of the following expression, where *uppercase letter* can be any uppercase letter from A to Z:

$$uppercase\ letter + 'a' - 'A'$$

2.3   Displaying Numerical Results

In addition to displaying messages, the printf() function allows us to evaluate arithmetic expressions and display their results. To do this we must pass at least two items to printf(): a control string that tells the function where and in what form the result is to be displayed, and the value that we wish to be displayed. Recall that items passed to a function are always placed within the function name parentheses, and are called arguments. Arguments must be separated from one another with commas, so that the function knows where one argument ends and the next begins. For example, in the statement

```
printf("The total of 6 and 15 is %d", 6 + 15);
```

the first argument is the message The total of 6 and 15 is %d, and the second argument is the expression 6 + 15.

The first argument passed to printf() must always be a *message*. A message that also includes a *control sequence*, such as %d, is termed a *control string*. Control sequences have a special meaning to the printf() function. They tell the function what type of value is to be displayed and where to display it.

The percent sign % in a control sequence tells printf() that we wish to print a number at the place in the message where the % is located. The d, placed immediately after the %, tells printf() that the number should be printed as an integer.

When printf() sees the control sequence in its control string, it substitutes the value of the next argument in place of the control sequence. Since this next argument is the expression 6 + 15, which has a value of 21, it is this value that is displayed. Thus, the statement

```
printf("The total of 6 and 15 is %d.", 6 + 15);
```

causes the printout

```
The total of 6 and 15 is 21.
```

Just as the %d control sequence alerts printf() that an integer value is to be displayed, the control sequence %f (the f stands for floating point) indicates that a number with a decimal point is to be displayed. For example, the statement

```
printf("The sum of %f and %f is %f.", 12.2, 15.754, 12.2 + 15.754);
```

causes the display

```
     The sum of 12.200000 and 15.754000 is 27.954000.
```

As this display shows, the %f control sequence causes printf() to display six digits to the right of the decimal place. If the number does not have six decimal digits, zeros are added to the number to fill the fractional part. If the number has more than six decimal digits, the fractional part is rounded to six decimal digits.

One caution should be mentioned here. The printf() function does *not* check the values it is given. If an integer control sequence is used (%d, for example) and the value given the function is either a floating point or double precision number, there is no telling what value will be displayed. Similarly, if a floating point control sequence is used and the corresponding number is an integer, an unanticipated result will occur.

Character data is displayed using the %c control sequence. For example, the statement

```
printf("The first letter of the alphabet is an %c.",'a');
```

causes the display

```
     The first letter of the alphabet is an a.
```

Program 2-1 illustrates using printf() to display the results of an expression within the statements of a complete program.

 Program 2-1

```
main()
{

    printf("%f plus %f equals %f\n", 15.0, 2.0, 15.0 + 2.0);
    printf("%f minus %f equals %f\n",15.0, 2.0, 15.0 - 2.0);
    printf("%f times %f equals %f\n",15.0, 2.0, 15.0 * 2.0);
    printf("%f divided by %f equals %f",15.0, 2.0, 15.0 / 2.0);

}
```

The output of Program 2-1 is:

```
15.000000 plus 2.000000 equals 17.000000
15.000000 minus 2.000000 equals 13.000000
15.000000 times 2.000000 equals 30.000000
15.000000 divided by 2.000000 equals 7.500000
```

Formatted Output

Besides displaying correct results, it is important that a program presents its results attractively. Most programs are judged, in fact, on the perceived ease of data entry and the style and presentation of their output. For example, displaying a monetary result as 1.897000 is not in keeping with accepted report conventions. The display should be either $1.90 or $1.89, depending on whether rounding or truncation is used.

The format of numbers displayed by `printf()` can be controlled by *field width specifiers* included as part of each control sequence. For example, the statement

```
printf("The sum of%3d and%4d is%5d.", 6, 15, 21);
```

causes the printout

```
The sum of  6 and  15 is  21.
```

The numbers 3, 4, and 5 in the control string are the field width specifiers. The 3 causes the first number to be printed in a total field width of three spaces, in this case two blank spaces followed by the number 6. The field width specifier for the second control sequence, `%4d`, causes two blank spaces and the number 15 to be printed for a total field width of four spaces. The last field width specifier causes the 21 to be printed in a field of five spaces, which includes three blanks and the number 21. As illustrated, each integer is right-justified within the specified field.

Field width specifiers are useful in printing columns of numbers so that the numbers in each column align correctly. For example, Program 2-2 illustrates how a column of integers would align in the absence of field width specifiers.

 Program 2-2

```
main()
{
  printf("\n%d", 6);
  printf("\n%d", 18);
  printf("\n%d", 124);
  printf("\n---");
  printf("\n%d", 6+18+124);
}
```

The output of Program 2-2 is

```
        6
       18
      124
      ---
      148
```

Since no field widths are given, the `printf()` function allocates enough space for each number as it is received. To force the numbers to align on the units digit requires a field width wide enough for the largest displayed number. For Program 2-2, a width of three suffices. The use of this field width is illustrated in Program 2-3.

 Program 2-3

```
main()
{
  printf("\n%3d", 6);
  printf("\n%3d", 18);
  printf("\n%3d", 124);
  printf("\n---");
  printf("\n%3d", 6+18+124);
}
```

The output of Program 2-3 is

```
        6
       18
      124
      ---
      148
```

Formatted floating point numbers require two field width specifiers. The first specifier determines the total display width, including the decimal point; the second determines how many digits are printed to the right of the decimal point. For example, the statement

```
printf("|%10.3f|",25.67);
```

causes the printout

```
|    25.670|
```

The bar symbol, |, in the example is used to mark the beginning and end of the display field. The field width specifier 10.3 tells `printf()` to display the number in a total field of 10, which includes one decimal point and three digits to the right of the decimal point. Since the number contains only two digits to the right of the decimal point, the decimal part of the number is padded with a trailing zero.

For all numbers (integers, floating point, and double precision), `printf()` ignores the specified field width if the total field width is too small, and allocates enough space for the integer part of the number to be printed. The fractional part of both floating point and double precision numbers is always displayed with the number of specified digits. If the fractional part contains fewer digits than specified, the number is padded with trailing zeros; if the fractional part contains more digits than called for in the specifier, the number is rounded to the indicated number of decimal places. Table 2-7 illustrates the effect of various field width specifiers.

Other Number Bases*

When outputting integers, several display conversions are possible. As we have seen, the control sequence %d, with or without a field width specifier, causes integers to be displayed in decimal (base 10) form. To have the value of an integer displayed as either a base 8 (octal) or a base 16 (hexadecimal) number requires the use of the control sequences %o and %x, respectively. Program 2-4 illustrates each of these control sequences.

TABLE 2-7 Effect of Field Width Specifiers

Specifier	Number	Display	Comments
|%2d|	3	| 3|	Number fits in field
|%2d|	43	|43|	Number fits in field
|%2d|	143	|143|	Field width ignored
|%2d|	2.3	Unpredictable	Floating point in an integer field
|%5.2f|	2.366	| 2.37|	Field of 5 with 2 decimal digits
|%5.2f|	42.3	|42.30|	Number fits in field
|%5.2f|	142.364	|142.36|	Field width ignored but fractional specifier used
|%5.2f|	142	Unpredictable	Integer in a floating point field

* This topic may be omitted on a first reading without loss of subject continuity.

Program 2-4

```
main()   /* a program to illustrate output conversions */
{
  printf("The decimal (base 10) value of 15 is %d.", 15);
  printf("\nThe octal (base 8) value of 15 is %o.", 15);
  printf("\nThe hexadecimal (base 16) value of 15 is %x.", 15);
}
```

The output produced by Program 2-4 is:

```
The decimal (base 10) value of 15 is 15.
The octal (base 8) value of 15 is 17.
The hexadecimal (base 16) value of 15 is f.
```

The display of integer values in one of the three possible number systems (decimal, octal, and hexadecimal) does not affect how the number is stored inside a computer. All numbers are stored using the computer's internal codes. The control sequences used in printf() simply tell the function how to convert the internal code for output display purposes.

Besides displaying integers in octal or hexadecimal form, integer constants can also be written in a program in these forms. To designate an octal integer constant, the number must have a leading zero. The number 023, for example, is an octal number in C. Hexadecimal numbers are denoted using a leading 0x. The use of octal and hexadecimal integer constants is illustrated in Program 2-5.

Program 2-5

```
main()
{
  printf("The decimal value of 025 is %d.\n",025);
  printf("The decimal value of 0x37 is %d.\n",0x37);
}
```

When Program 2-5 is run, the following output is obtained:

```
The decimal value of 025 is 21.
The decimal value of 0x37 is 55.
```

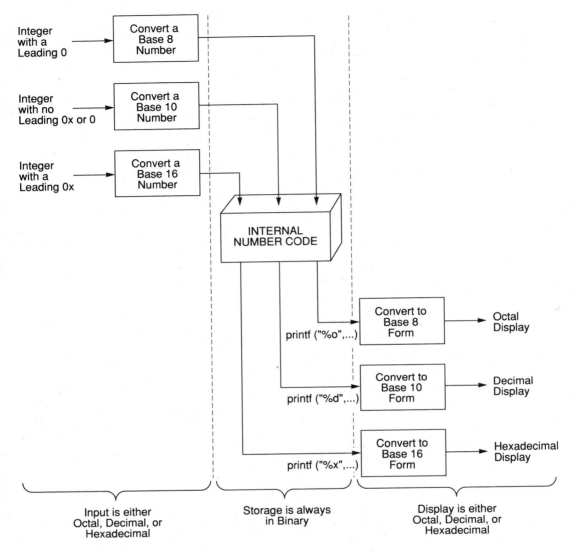

FIGURE 2–2 Input, Storage, and Display of Integers

The relationship between the input, storage, and display of integers is illustrated in Figure 2-2.

The same display conversions available for integers can also be used to display characters. In addition to the %c control sequence, the %d control sequence displays the value of the internal character code as a decimal number and the %o and %x control sequences cause the character code to be displayed in octal and hexadecimal form, respectively. These display conversions are illustrated in Program 2-6.

Program 2-6

```
main()
{

    printf("The decimal value of the letter %c is %d.", 'a', 'a');
    printf("\nThe octal value of the letter %c is %o.", 'a', 'a');
    printf("\nThe hex value of the letter %c is %x.", 'a', 'a');

}
```

When Program 2-6 is run, the following output is produced:

```
The decimal value of the letter a is 97.
The octal value of the letter a is 141.
The hex value of the letter a is 61.
```

The display conversions for character data are illustrated in Figure 2-3.

FIGURE 2–3 Character Display Options

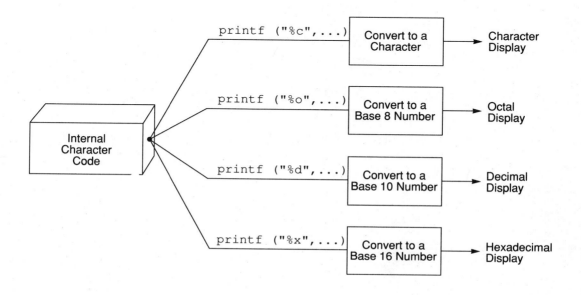

Exercises 2.3

1. Determine the output of the following program:

```
main()   /* a program illustrating integer truncation */
{

   printf("answer1 is the integer %d", 9/4);
   printf("\nanswer2 is the integer %d", 17/3);


}
```

2. Determine the output of the following program:

```
main()   /* a program illustrating the % operator */
{

   printf("The remainder of 9 divided by 4 is %d", 9 % 4);
   printf("\nThe remainder of 17 divided by 3 is %d", 17 % 3);


}
```

3. Write a C program that displays the results of the expressions 3.0 * 5.0, 7.1 * 8.3 – 2.2, and 3.2 / (6.1 * 5). Calculate the value of these expressions manually to verify that the displayed values are correct.

4. Write a C program that displays the results of the expressions 15 / 4, 15 % 4, and 5 * 3 – (6 * 4). Calculate the value of these expressions manually to verify that the display produced by your program is correct.

5. Determine the errors in each of the following statements:
  a. `printf("%d," 15)`
  b. `printf("%f", 33);`
  c. `printf("%5d", 526.768);`
  d. `printf("a b c", 26, 15, 18);`
  e. `printf("%3.6f", 47);`
  f. `printf("%3.6", 526.768);`
  g. `printf(526.768, 33,"%f %d");`

6. Determine and write out the display produced by the following statements:
  a. `printf("|%d|",5);`
  b. `printf("|%4d|",5);`
  c. `printf("|%4d|",56829);`
  d. `printf("|%5.2f|",5.26);`
  e. `printf("|%5.2f|",5.267);`
  f. `printf("|%5.2f|",53.264);`
  g. `printf("|%5.2f|",534.264);`
  h. `printf("|%5.2f|",534.);`

7. Write out the display produced by the following statements.

   a. `printf("The number is %6.2f\n",26.27);`
     `printf("The number is %6.2f\n",682.3);`
     `printf("The number is %6.2f\n",1.968);`

   b. `printf("$%6.2f\n",26.27);`
     `printf(" %6.2f\n",682.3);`
     `printf(" %6.2f\n",1.968);`
     `printf("--------\n");`
     `printf("$%6.2f\n", 26.27 + 682.3 + 1.968);`

   c. `printf("$%5.2f\n",26.27);`
     `printf(" %5.2f\n",682.3);`
     `printf(" %5.2f\n",1.968);`
     `printf("--------\n");`
     `printf("$%5.2f\n", 26.27 + 682.3 + 1.968);`

   d. `printf("%5.2f\n",34.164);`
     `printf("%5.2f\n",10.003);`
     `printf("-----\n");`
     `printf("%5.2f\n", 34.164 + 10.003);`

8. *a.* Rewrite the `printf()` function calls in the following program to produce the display:

```
                 The sales tax is $ 1.80
                 The total bill is $37.80
```

```
main()
{
   printf("The sales tax is %f", .05 * 36);
   printf("The total bill is %f", 37.80);
}
```

   b. Run the program written for Exercise 8a to verify the output display.

9. The following table lists the correspondence between the decimal numbers 1 through 15 and their octal and hexadecimal representation.

Decimal:	1	2	3	4	5	6	7	8	9	10	11	12	13	14	15
Octal:	1	2	3	4	5	6	7	10	11	12	13	14	15	16	17
Hexadecimal:	1	2	3	4	5	6	7	8	9	A	B	C	D	E	F

Using the above table, determine the output of the following program.

```
main()
{

   printf("The value of 14 in octal is %o.\n",14);
   printf("The value of 14 in hexadecimal is %x.\n",14);
   printf("The value of 0xA in decimal is %d.\n",0xA);
   printf("The value of 0xA in octal is %o.\n",0xA);

}
```

10. a. Write a program that uses the %d control sequence to display the integer values of the lowercase letters a, m, and n, respectively. Do the displayed values for these letters match the values listed in Appendix B?

b. Expand the program written for Exercise 10a to display the integer value corresponding to the internal computer code for a newline escape sequence.

2.4 Variables and Declarations

All data used in a computer program must be stored and retrieved from the computer's memory. Consider the four bytes of memory storage illustrated in Figure 2-4. For purposes of illustration assume that the two bytes with addresses 1321 and 1322 are used to store one integer number and that the bytes with addresses 2649 and 2450 are used to store a second integer.

Before high-level languages such as C existed, actual memory addresses were used to store and retrieve data. For example, storing the number 62 in the first set of bytes illustrated in Figure 2-4 and 17 in the next set of bytes required instructions equivalent to

> put a 62 in location 1321
> put a 17 in location 2649

Notice that only the address of the first byte in each set of locations was given. The computer needed only this first address to locate the starting point for storage or retrieval. Adding the two numbers just stored and saving the result in another set of memory locations, for example at location 45, required a statement comparable to

> add the contents of location 1321
> to the contents of location 2649
> and store the result into location 45

Clearly this method of storage and retrieval was a cumbersome process. In high-level languages like C, symbolic names are used in place of actual memory addresses. These symbolic names are called *variables*. A variable is simply a

FIGURE 2–4 Enough Storage for Two Integers

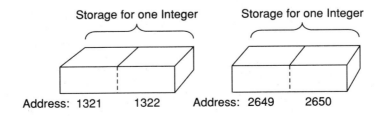

Storage for one Integer   Storage for one Integer

Address: 1321   1322   Address: 2649   2650

name given by the programmer to computer storage locations. The term, variable, is used because the value stored in the variable can change, or vary. For each name that the programmer uses, the computer keeps track of the actual addresses. Naming a variable is equivalent to putting a name on the door of a hotel room and referring to the room (or suite of rooms) by this name, such as the Blue Room, rather than using the actual room number.

The selection of variable names is left to the programmer, as long as the following rules are observed:

1. The variable name must begin with a letter or underscore (_), and may contain only letters, underscores, or digits. It cannot contain any blanks, commas, or special symbols, such as ( ) & , $ # . ! \ ? .

2. A variable name cannot be a reserved word (see Table 1-2).

3. The variable name consists of at the most, eight characters (although most computers now permit 31 characters).

These rules are similar to those used to name functions. As with function names, variable names should be mnemonics that give some indication of the variable's use. For example, a variable named `total` indicates that this variable will probably be used to store a value that is the total of some other values. As with function names, all variable names are typed in lowercase letters. This again is traditional in C, although not required.

Now assume that the two bytes previously illustrated in Figure 2-4 starting at address 1321 are given the variable name `num1`. Also assume that the two bytes starting at address 2649 are given the variable name `num2` and that the two bytes starting at address 45 have been given the name `result`, as illustrated in Figure 2-5.

Using these variable names, storing 62 in location 1321, 17 in location 2649, and adding the contents of these two locations is accomplished by the C statements

```
num1 = 62;
num2 = 17;
result = num1 + num2;
```

These statements are called *assignment statements* because they tell the computer to assign (store) a value into a variable. Assignment statements always

FIGURE 2–5 Giving Storage Locations Names

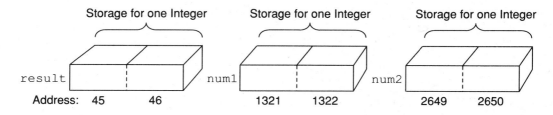

have an equal (=) sign and one variable name immediately to the left of this sign. The value on the right of the equal sign is determined first and this value is assigned to the variable on the left of the equal sign. The blank spaces in the assignment statements are inserted for readability. We will have much more to say about assignment statements in the next chapter, but for now we can use them to store values in variables.

A variable name is useful because it frees the programmer from concern over where data is physically stored inside the computer. We simply use the variable names and let the computer worry about where in memory the data is actually stored. Before storing values into variables, however, C requires that we clearly define the type of data that will be stored in each variable. We must tell the computer in advance the names of the variables that will be used for characters, the names that will be used for integers, and the names that will be used to store the other data types supported by C. Then, when the variable name is used, the computer will know how many bytes of storage to access.

Naming and defining the data type that can be stored in each variable is accomplished by using *declaration statements*. Declaration statements within a function appear immediately after the opening brace of a function, and like all C statements must end with a semicolon. A C function containing declaration statements has the general form

```
function name()
{
    declaration statements;

    other statements;
}
```

Declaration statements, in their simplest form, provide a data type and variable name. For example, the declaration statement

```
int total;
```

declares `total` as the name of a variable capable of storing an integer value.

Variables used to hold floating point values are declared using the reserved word `float`, while variables that will be used to hold double precision values are declared using the reserved word `double`. For example, the statement

```
float firstnum;
```

declares `firstnum` as a variable that can be used to store a floating point number. Similarly, the statement

```
double secnum;
```

declares that the variable will be used to store a double precision number.

Program 2-7 illustrates the declaration and use of four floating point variables. The printf() function is then used to display the contents of one of these variables.

 Program 2-7

```
main()
{
    float grade1;   /* declare grade1 as a float variable */
    float grade2;   /* declare grade2 as a float variable */
    float total;    /* declare total as a float variable */
    float average;  /* declare average as a float variable */

    grade1 = 85.5;
    grade2 = 97.0;
    total = grade1 + grade2;
    average = total/2.0;   /* divide the total by 2.0 */

    printf("The average grade is %f\n",average);
}
```

The placement of the declaration statements in Program 2-7 is straightforward, although we will shortly see that the four individual declarations can be combined into a single declaration. When Program 2-7 is run, the following output is displayed:

        The average grade is 91.250000

Two comments with respect to the printf() function call made in Program 2-7 should be mentioned here. If a variable name is one of the arguments passed to a function, as it is to printf() in Program 2-7, the function only receives a copy of the value stored in the variable. It does not receive the variable's name. When the program sees a variable name in the function parentheses, it first goes to the variable and retrieves the value stored. This value is then passed to the function. Thus, when a variable is included in the printf() argument list, printf() receives the value stored in the variable and then displays this value. Internally, printf() does not know where the value it receives came from or the variable name under which the value was stored.

Although this procedure for passing data into a function may seem surprising, it is really a safety procedure for ensuring that a called function does not have access to the original variable. This guarantees that the called function cannot inadvertently change data in a variable declared outside itself. We will have more to say about this in Chapter 6 when we examine and begin writing our own called functions.

The second comment concerns using the %f control sequence in Program 2-7. Although this control sequence works for both floating point and double precision numbers, the control sequence %lf may also be used for displaying the values of double precision variables. The l indicates that the number is a long floating point number, which is what a double precision number really is. Omitting the l control character has no effect on the printf() function when double precision values are displayed. As we shall see, however, it is essential in entering double precision values when the input function scanf() is used. This function is presented in the next chapter.

Just as integers, floating point, and double precision variables must be declared before they can be used, a variable used to store a character must also be declared. Character variables are declared using the reserved word char. For example, the declaration

```
char ch;
```

declares ch to be a character variable. Program 2-8 illustrates this declaration and the use of printf() to display the value stored in a character variable.

 Program 2-8

```
main()
{
  char ch;       /* this declares a character variable */

  ch = 'a';      /* store the letter a into ch */
  printf("\nThe character stored in ch is %c.", ch);
  ch = 'm';      /* now store the letter m into ch */
  printf("\nThe character now stored in ch is %c.", ch);
}
```

When Program 2-8 is run, the output produced is:

```
The character stored in ch is a.
The character now stored in ch is m.
```

Notice in Program 2-8 that the first letter stored in the variable ch is a and the second letter stored is m. Since a variable can only store one value at a time, the assignment of m to the variable automatically causes a to be erased.

Variables having the same data type can always be grouped together and declared using a single declaration statement. For example, the four separate declarations used in Program 2-7,

```
float grade1;
float grade2;
float total;
float average;
```

can be replaced by the single declaration statement

```
float grade1, grade2, total, average;
```

Similarly, the two character declarations,

```
char ch;
char key;
```

can be replaced with the single declaration statement

```
char ch, key;
```

Notice that declaring multiple variables in a single declaration requires that the data type of the variables be given only once, that all the variables be separated by commas, and that only one semicolon be used to terminate the declaration. The space after each comma is inserted for readability, and is not required.

Declaration statements can also be used to store an initial value into declared variables. For example, the declaration statement

```
int num1 = 15;
```

both declares the variable num1 as an integer variable and sets the value of 15 into the variable. Similarly, the declaration statement

```
float grade1 = 87.0, grade2 = 93.5, total;
```

declares three floating point variables and initializes two of them. Constants, expressions using only constants (such as 87.0 + 12.2), and expressions using constants and previously initialized variables can all be used as initializers within a function. For example, Program 2-8 with initialization would appear as:

```
main()
{
  char ch = 'a';   /* declaration and initialization */

  printf("\nThe character stored in ch is %c.", ch);
  ch = 'm';        /* now store the letter m into ch */
  printf("\nThe character now stored in ch is %c.", ch);
}
```

Declaration Statements as Definition Statements

The declaration statements we have introduced have performed both software and hardware tasks. From a software perspective, declaration statements always provide a convenient, up-front list of all variables and their data types. In this software role, variable declarations also eliminate an otherwise common and troublesome error caused by the misspelling of a variable's name within a program. For example, assume that a variable named `distance` is declared and initialized using the statement

```
int distance = 26;
```

Now assume that this variable is inadvertently misspelled in the statement

```
mpg = distnce / gallons;
```

In languages that do not require variable declarations, the program would treat `distnce` as a new variable and either assign an initial value of zero to the variable or use whatever value happened to be in the variable's storage area. In either case, a value would be calculated and assigned to `mpg`, and finding the error or even knowing that an error occurred could be extremely troublesome. Such errors are impossible in Ç, because the compiler will flag `distnce` as an undeclared variable. The compiler cannot, of course, detect when one declared variable is typed in place of another declared variable.

In addition to their software role, declaration statements can also perform a distinct hardware task. Since each data type has its own storage requirements, the computer can only allocate sufficient storage for a variable after knowing the variable's data type. Because variable declarations provide this information, they can be used to force the computer to reserve sufficient physical memory storage for each variable. Declaration statements used for this hardware purpose are also called *definition statements,* because they define or tell the computer how much memory is needed for data storage.

All the declaration statements we have encountered so far have also been definition statements. Later, we will see declaration statements that do not cause any new storage to be allocated and are used simply to declare or alert the program to the data types of previously created and existing variables.

Figure 2-6 illustrates the series of operations set in motion by declaration statements that also perform a definition role. The figure shows that definition statements (or, if you prefer, declaration statements that also cause memory to be allocated) "tag" the first byte of each set of reserved bytes with a name. This name is, of course, the variable's name and is used by the computer to correctly locate the starting byte of each variable's reserved memory area.

After a variable has been declared within a program, it is typically used by a programmer to refer to the contents of the variable (that is, the variable's

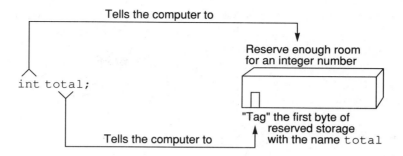

FIGURE 2–6a Defining the Integer Variable Named `total`

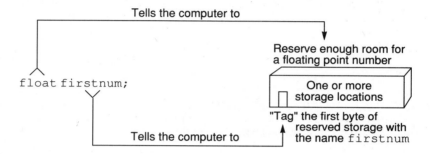

FIGURE 2–6b Defining the Floating Point Variable Named `firstnum`

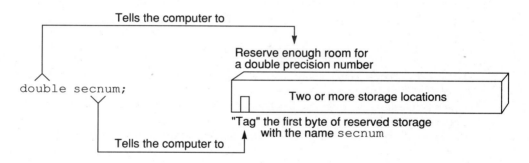

FIGURE 2–6c Defining the Double Precision Variable Named `secnum`

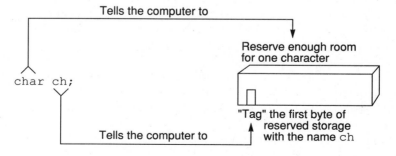

FIGURE 2–6d Defining the Character Variable Named `ch`

value). Where in memory this value is stored is generally of little concern to the programmer. The computer, however, must know where each value is stored and be able to locate each variable. In this task, the computer uses the variable name to locate the first byte of storage previously allocated to the variable. Knowing the variable's data type then allows the computer to store or retrieve the correct number of bytes.

Exercises 2.4

1. State whether the following variable names are valid or not. If they are invalid, state the reason why.

prod_a	c1234	abcd	_c3	12345
newbal	while	$total	new bal	a1b2c3d4
9ab6	sum.of	average	grade1	fin_grad

2. State whether the following variable names are valid or not. If they are invalid, state the reason why. Also indicate which of the valid variable names should not be used because they convey no information about the variable.

salestax	a243	r2d2	first_num	cc_a1
harry	sue	c3p0	average	sum
maximum	okay	a	awesome	goforit
3sum	for	tot.a1	c$five	netpay

3. a. Write a declaration statement to declare that the variable count will be used to store an integer.
b. Write a declaration statement to declare that the variable grade will be used to store a floating point number.
c. Write a declaration statement to declare that the variable yield will be used to store a double precision number.
d. Write a declaration statement to declare that the variable initial will be used to store a character.

4. Write declaration statements for the following variables.
a. num1, num2, and num3 used to store integer numbers
b. grade1, grade2, grade3, and grade4 used to store floating point numbers
c. tempa, tempb, and tempc used to store double precision numbers
d. ch, let1, let2, let3, and let4 used to store character types

5. Write declaration statements for the following variables.
a. firstnum and secnum used to store integers
b. price, yield, and coupon used to store floating point numbers
c. maturity used to store a double precision number

6. Rewrite each of these declaration statements as three individual declarations.
a. int month, day = 30, year;
b. double hours, rate, otime = 15.62;
c. float price, amount, taxes;
d. char in_key, ch, choice = 'f';

7. a. Determine what each statement causes to happen in the following program.

```
main()
{
    int num1;
    int num2;
    int total;

    num1 = 25;
    num2 = 35;
    total = num1 + num2;
    printf("The total of %d and %d is %d\n.",num1,num2,total);
}
```

b. What is the output that will be printed when the program listed in Exercise 7a is run?

8. Write a C program that stores the sum of the integer numbers 12 and 33 in a variable named sum. Have your program display the value stored in sum.

9. Write a C program that stores the integer value 16 in the variable length and the integer value 18 in the variable width. Have your program calculate the value assigned to the variable perimeter, using the assignment statement

```
perimeter = 2 * length + 2 * width;
```

and print out the value stored in the variable perimeter. Make sure to declare all the variables as integers at the beginning of the main() function.

10. Write a C program that stores the integer value 16 in the variable num1 and the integer value 18 in the variable num2. (Make sure to declare the variables as integers.) Have your program calculate the total of these numbers and their average. The total should be stored in the variable named total and the average in the variable named average. (Use the statement average = total/2.0; to calculate the average.) Use the printf() function to display the total and average.

11. Repeat Exercise 10, but store the number 15 in num1 instead of 16. With a pencil, write down the average of num1 and num2. What do you think your program will store in the integer variable that you used for the average of these two numbers? How can you ensure that the correct answer will be printed for the average?

12. Write a program that stores the number 105.62 in the variable firstnum, 89.352 in the variable secnum, and 98.67 in the variable thirdnum. (Make sure to declare the variables first as either float or double.) Have your program calculate the total of the three numbers and their average. The total should be stored in the variable total and the average in the variable average. (Use the statement average = total /3.0; to calculate the average.) Use the printf() function to display the total and average.

13. Every variable has at least three items associated with it. What are these three items?

14. a. A statement used to clarify the relationship between squares and rectangles is "All squares are rectangles but not all rectangles are squares." Write a similar statement that describes the relationship between definition and declaration statements.
b. Why must definition statements be placed before any other C statements using the defined variable?

Address:	159	160	161	162	163	164	165	166

Address:	167	168	169	170	171	172	173	174

Address:	175	176	177	178	179	180	181	182

Address:	183	184	185	186	187	188	189	190

FIGURE 2–7 Memory Bytes for Exercises 15, 16, and 17

Note for Exercises 15 through 17:

Assume that a character requires one byte of storage, an integer two bytes, a floating point number four bytes, a double precision number eight bytes, and that variables are assigned storage in the order they are declared.

15. *a.* Using Figure 2-7 and assuming that the variable name rate is assigned to the byte having memory address 159, determine the addresses corresponding to each variable declared in the following statements. Also fill in the appropriate bytes with the initialization data included in the declaration statements (use letters for the characters, not the computer codes that would actually be stored).

```
float rate;
char ch1 = 'w', ch2 = 'o', ch3 = 'w', ch4 = '!';
double taxes;
int num, count = 0;
```

b. Repeat Exercise 15a, but substitute the actual byte patterns that a computer using the ASCII code would use to store the characters in the variables ch1, ch2, ch3, and ch4. *(Hint:* Use Table 2-2.)

16. *a.* Using Figure 2-7 and assuming that the variable named cn1 is assigned to the byte at memory address 159, determine the addresses corresponding to each variable declared in the following statements. Also fill in the appropriate bytes with the initial-

ization data included in the declaration statements (use letters for the characters and not the computer codes that would actually be stored).

```
char cn1 = 'a', cn2 = ' ', cn3 = 'b', cn4 = 'u', cn5 = 'n';
char cn6 = 'c', cn7 = 'h', key = '\\', sch = '\'', inc = 'o';
char incl = 'f';
```

b. Repeat Exercise 16a, but substitute the actual byte patterns that a computer using the ASCII code would use to store the characters in each of the declared variables. (*Hint:* Use Table 2-2.)

17. Using Figure 2-7 and assuming that the variable name `miles` is assigned to the byte at memory address 159, determine the addresses corresponding to each variable declared in the following statements.

```
float miles;
int count, num;
double dist, temp;
```

2.5   Integer Qualifiers

Integer numbers are generally used in programs as counters to keep track of the number of times that something has occurred. For most applications, the counts needed are less than 32,767, which is the maximum integer value that can be stored in two bytes. Since most computers allocate at least two bytes for integers, there is usually no problem.

Sometimes, however, larger integer numbers are needed. In financial applications, for example, dates such as 7/12/89 are typically converted to the number of days from the turn of the century. This conversion makes it possible to store and sort dates using a single number for each date. Unfortunately, for dates after 1987, the number of days from the turn of the century is larger than the maximum value of 32,767 allowed when only two bytes are allocated for each integer variable. For financial programs dealing with mortgages and bonds maturing after 1987 that are run on computers allocating only two bytes per integer (PCs, for example), the limitation on the maximum integer value must be overcome.

To accommodate real application requirements such as this, C provides *long integer, short integer,* and *unsigned integer* data types. These three additional integer data types are obtained by adding the *qualifiers* long, short, or unsigned, respectively, to the normal integer declaration statements. For example, the declaration statement

```
long int days;
```

declares the variable `days` to be a long integer. The word `int` in a long integer declaration statement is optional, so the previous declaration statement can also be written as `long days;`. The amount of storage allocated for a long integer depends on the computer being used. Although you would expect that a long integer variable would be allocated more space than a standard integer, this may not be the case, especially for computers that reserve more than two bytes for normal integer variables. About all that can be said is that long integers will provide no less space than regular integers. The actual amount of storage allocated by your computer should be checked using the `sizeof` operator described at the end of this section.

Once a variable is declared as a long integer, integer values may be assigned as usual for standard integers, or an optional letter L (either uppercase or lowercase, with no space between the number and letter) may be appended to the integer. For example, the declaration statement

```
long days = 38276L;
```

declares days to be of type long integer and assigns the long integer constant 38276 to the variable days.

Printing long integer values using the `printf()` function requires the use of a lowercase l. Thus, to display a long integer, the control sequence `%ld` must be used.

In addition to the long qualifier, C also provides for a short qualifier. Although you would expect a short integer to conserve computer storage by reserving fewer bytes than used for an integer, this is not always the case. Some computers use the same amount of storage for both integers and short integers. Again, the amount of memory space allocated for a short integer data type depends on your computer, and can be checked using the `sizeof` operator (described at the end of this section). As with long integers, short integers may be declared using the terms `short` or `short int` in a declaration statement.

Once a variable is declared as a short integer, values are assigned as normally done with integers. Printing short integers using the `printf()` function requires no modifications to any of the control sequences used for integers.

The final integer data type is the unsigned integer. This data type is obtained by prefixing the reserved word `int` with the qualifier `unsigned`. For example, the declaration statement

```
unsigned int days;
```

declares the variable `days` to be of type unsigned.

The unsigned integer data type is used to store positive integers only and effectively doubles the positive value that can be stored without increasing the number of bytes allocated to an integer. This is accomplished by treating all unsigned integers as positive numbers, as illustrated in Figure 2-8.

Printing unsigned integers using the `printf()` function requires the use of the `%u` control sequence in place of the `%d` normally used for integers. The `%u`

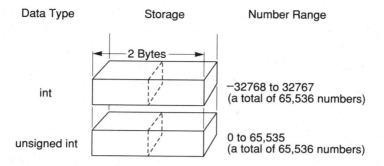

FIGURE 2–8 Unsigned Integers Can Only Be Positive Numbers

control sequence is especially convenient for displaying memory addresses, which is the topic of Section 3.2.

Determining Storage Size

C provides an operator to determine how much storage your computer allocates for each data type. This operator, called the sizeof operator, returns the number of bytes of the object or data type following it. Unlike a function, which is made of C statements, the sizeof operator is an integral part of the C language itself.

If the item following the reserved word, sizeof, is a variable, sizeof returns the number of bytes of storage that the computer reserved for the variable. If the item following the word, sizeof, is a data type, such as int or char, sizeof will return the number of bytes of storage that the computer uses for the given data type. Using either approach, we can use sizeof to determine the amount of storage used by different data types. Consider Program 2-9:

Program 2-9

```
main()
{
  char ch;
  int num1;

  printf("Bytes of storage used by a character: %d ",sizeof(ch));
  printf("\nBytes of storage used by an integer: %d",sizeof(num1));
}
```

Program 2-9 declares that the variable ch is used to store a character and that the variable num1 is used to store an integer. From our discussion in the last section, we know that each of these declaration statements is also a definition statement. As such, the first declaration statement instructs the computer to reserve enough storage for a character, and the second declaration statement instructs the computer to reserve enough storage for an integer. The `sizeof` operator is then used to tell us how much room the computer really set aside for these two variables. The `sizeof` operator itself is used as an argument to the `printf()` function. When Program 2-9 is run on an IBM personal computer the following output is obtained:

```
Bytes of storage used by a character: 1
Bytes of storage used by an integer: 2
```

In using the `sizeof` operator, one caution should be noted. The number of bytes given by the `sizeof` operator is in terms of the storage reserved for one character. Since almost all computers store one character in one byte, the value given by `sizeof` is normally a true byte count. If, however, a computer used two bytes to store one character (possible, but not very likely), the number given by the `sizeof` operator would represent the number of double bytes reserved for each data type. The true byte count would then be obtained by multiplying the number given by `sizeof` by two.

Exercises 2.5

1. *a.* Run Program 2-9 to determine how many bytes your computer uses to store character and integer data types.
   b. Expand Program 2-9 to determine how many bytes your computer uses for short integers, long integers, and unsigned integers.

2. After running the program written for Exercise 1, use Table 2-1 (see Section 2.1) to determine the maximum and minimum numbers that can be stored in integer, short integer, and long integer variables for your computer.

3. Program 2-9 did not actually store any values into the variables `ch` and `num1`. Why was this not necessary?

4. *a.* Expand Program 2-9 to determine how many bytes your computer uses to store floating point and double precision numbers.
   b. Although there is no long float data class, double precision numbers are sometimes considered as the equivalent long form for floating point numbers. Why is this so? Does the output of the program written for Exercise 4a support this statement?

2.6   Common Programming Errors

The common programming errors associated with the material presented in this chapter are:

1. Forgetting to declare all the variables used in a program. This error is detected by the compiler and an error message is generated for all undeclared variables.

2. Storing an incorrect data type in a declared variable. This error is not detected by the compiler. Here, the assigned value is converted to the data type of the variable it is assigned to.

3. Using a variable in an expression before a value has been assigned to the variable. Here, whatever value happens to be in the variable will be used when the expression is evaluated, and the result will be meaningless.

4. Dividing integer values incorrectly. This error is usually disguised within a larger expression and can be a very troublesome error to detect. For example, the expression

$$3.425 + 2/3 + 7.9$$

yields the same result as the expression

$$3.425 + 7.9$$

because the integer division of 2/3 is 0.

5. Mixing data types in the same expression without clearly understanding the effect produced. Since C allows expressions with "mixed" data types, it is important to be clear about the order of evaluation and the data type of all intermediate calculations. As a general rule it is better never to mix data types in an expression unless a specific effect is desired.

6. Not including the correct control sequence in `printf()` function calls for the data types of the remaining arguments.

7. Not closing off the control string in `printf()` with a double quote symbol followed by a comma when additional arguments are passed to `printf()`.

8. Forgetting to separate all arguments passed to `printf()` with commas.

2.7   Chapter Summary

1. The four basic types of data recognized by C are integer, floating point, double precision, and character data. Each of these types of data is typically stored in a computer using different amounts of memory.

2. The `printf()` function can be used to display all of C's data types. The control sequences for displaying integer, floating point, double precision, and character values are `%d`, `%f`, `%lf`, and `%c`, respectively. The `%f` control sequence can be used in place of the `%lf` sequence for double precision values. Additionally, field control specifiers can be used to format displays.

3. Every variable in a C program must be declared as to the type of value it can store. Declarations within a function must be placed as the first statements after a left brace. Variables may also be initialized when they are declared. Additionally, variables of the same type may be declared using a single declaration statement.

4. A simple C program containing declaration statements has the form:

```
main()
{
    declaration statements;

    other statements;
}
```

5. Declaration statements always play a software role of informing the compiler of a function's valid variable names. When a variable declaration also causes the computer to set aside memory locations for the variable, the declaration statement is also called a definition statement. (All the declarations we have encountered have also been definition statements.)

6. The `sizeof` operator can be used to determine the amount of storage reserved for variables.

2.8 Chapter Supplement: Bits, Bytes, Addresses and Number Codes

It would have been convenient if computers stored numbers and letters the way that people do. The number 126, for example, would then be stored as 126, and the letter A stored as the letter A. Unfortunately, due to the physical components used in building a computer, this is not the case.

The smallest, and most basic storage unit in a computer, is called a *bit*. Physically, a bit is really a switch that can be either open or closed. By convention, the open and closed positions of each switch are represented as a 0 and a 1, respectively.

A single bit that can represent the values 0 and 1, by itself, has limited usefulness. All computers, therefore, group a set number of bits together. The grouping of eight bits to form a larger unit is an almost universal computer standard. Such groups are commonly referred to as *bytes*. A single byte consisting of eight bits, where each bit can be 0 or 1, can represent any one of 256 different bit patterns. These consist of the pattern 00000000 (all eight switches open) to the pattern 11111111 (all eight switches closed), and all possible combinations of 0s and 1s in between. Each of these patterns can be used to represent either a letter of the alphabet, other single characters, such as a dollar sign, comma, etc., a single digit, or numbers containing more than one digit. The patterns of 0s and 1s used to represent letters, single digits, and other single characters are called *character codes* (one such code, called the ASCII code, is presented in Section 2.1). The patterns used to store numbers are called number codes (one such code, called two's complement, is presented at the end of this section).

Words and Addresses

One or more bytes may be grouped into larger units called *words.* The advantage of combining bytes into words is that multiple bytes are stored or retrieved by the computer for each word access. For example, retrieving a word consisting of four bytes results in more information than that obtained by retrieving a word consisting of a single byte. Such a retrieval is also considerably faster than individual retrievals of four single bytes. The increase in speed, however, is achieved by an increase in cost and complexity of the computer.

Personal computers, such as the Apple and Commodore machines, have words consisting of single bytes. AT&T and IBM personal computers, as well as Digital Equipment, Data General, and Prime minicomputers, have words consisting of two bytes each. Mainframe computers and advanced microprocessors have four-byte words.

The arrangement of words in a computer's memory can be compared to the arrangement of suites in a very large hotel, where each suite is made up of rooms of the same size. Just as each suite has a unique room number to locate and identify it, each word has a unique numeric address. In computers that allow each byte to be individually accessed, each byte has its own address. Like room numbers, word and byte addresses are always positive, whole numbers that are used for location and identification purposes. Also, like hotel rooms with connecting doors for forming larger suites, words can be combined to form larger units for the accommodation of different size data types.

Two's Complement Numbers

The most common integer code using bit patterns is called the *two's complement* representation. Using this code, the integer equivalent of any bit pattern, such as 10001101, is easy to determine and can be found for either positive or negative numbers with no change in the conversion method. For convenience we will assume words consisting of a single byte, although the procedure carries directly over to larger size words.

The easiest way to determine the integer represented by each bit pattern is to first construct a simple device called a value box. Figure 2-9 illustrates such a box for a single byte.

Mathematically, each value in the box illustrated in Figure 2-9 represents an increasing power of two. Since two's complement numbers must be capable of representing both positive and negative integers, the leftmost position, in addition to having the largest absolute magnitude, also has a negative sign.

−128	64	32	16	8	4	2	1

FIGURE 2–9 An Eight-Bit Value Box

Conversion of any binary number, for example 10001101, simply requires inserting the bit pattern in the value box and adding the values having ones under them. Thus, as illustrated in Figure 2-10, the bit pattern 10001101 represents the integer number −115.

Reviewing the value box shows that any binary number with a leading 1 represents a negative number, and any bit pattern with a leading 0 represents a positive number. The value box can also be used in reverse, to convert a base 10 integer number into its equivalent binary bit pattern. Some conversions, in fact, can be made by inspection. For example, the base 10 number −125 is obtained by adding 3 to −128. Thus, the binary representation of −125 is 10000011, which equals −128 + 2 + 1. Similarly, the two's complement representation of the number 40 is 00101000, which is 32 plus 8.

Although the value box conversion method is deceptively simple, the method is directly related to the mathematical basis of two's complement binary numbers. The original name of the two's complement binary code was the weighted-sign binary code, which correlates directly to the value box. As the name weighted sign implies, each bit position has a weight, or value, of two raised to a power and a sign. The signs of all bits except the leftmost bit are positive and the sign of the leftmost or most significant bit is negative.

FIGURE 2–10 Converting 10001101 to a Base 10 Number

−128	64	32	16	8	4	2	1
1	0	0	0	1	1	0	1

−128 + 0 + 0 + 0 + 8 + 4 + 0 + 1 = −115

Assignments, Addresses, and Interactive Input

Chapter Three

In Chapter 2 we explored how data is stored, introduced variables and their associated declaration statements, and became more comfortable using the `printf()` function. This chapter completes our introduction to C by discussing the proper use of both constants and variables in constructing expressions, presenting assignment expressions, and introducing addresses and the `scanf()` function for entering data interactively while a program is running.

Almost all of C's processing statements, except for function calls, use expressions, so it is important to have a clear understanding of what an expression is before proceeding. In its most general form, an *expression* is any combination of variables and constants that can be evaluated to yield a result. The simplest expressions consist of a single constant or variable, such as:

$$12.62 \quad 'a' \quad 5 \quad -10 \quad rate \quad total$$

Here, each constant or variable yields a result; for individual constants, the result is the constant itself, while for individual variables, the result is the value stored in the variable.

Slightly more complex expressions involve combining both constants and variables using the arithmetic operators introduced in the last chapter. Examples of such expressions are:

1. 10 + amount
2. count + 1
3. 16.3 + total
4. 0.08 * purchase
5. rate * total
6. grade1 + grade2 + grade3 + grade4

If an expression used in a program contains one or more variables, as in these examples, the variables must first be declared and have values stored in them before the expression can be evaluated to yield a useful result. For example, if you are asked to multiply rate times total (Example 5), you could not do it unless you first knew the values of rate and total. However, if you are told that rate is 5 and total is 10, you can multiply the two variables to yield 50. Expressions using both constants and variables are evaluated according to the rules presented in Chapter 2.

3.1   Assignment

We have already encountered simple assignment statements in Chapter 2. An assignment statement is simply an assignment expression that is terminated by a semicolon. In C, the equal sign, =, used in assignment statements is itself a binary operator. This differs from the way most other high-level languages process this symbol. The = symbol is called the *assignment operator* and is used in assignment expressions having the general form

variable = operand

The operand to the right of the assignment operator can be a constant, a variable, or another valid C expression. The assignment operator causes the value of the operand to the right of the equal sign to be stored in the variable to the left of the equal sign. Examples of valid assignment expressions are:

```
    year = 1988
   value = 3000
     sum = 90.2 + 80.3 + 65.0
    rate = prime
  inches = 12 * feet
   total = total + newvalue
     tax = salestax * amount
interest = principal * interest
     sum = (grade1 + grade2 + grade3) * factor
```

The assignment operator has the lowest precedence of all binary and unary arithmetic operators (see Table A-1 in Appendix A). Thus, any other operators contained in an expression using an assignment operator are always evaluated first. For example, in the expression `tax = salestax * amount`, the expression `salestax * amount` is first evaluated to yield a value. This value is then stored in the variable `tax`.

Like all expressions, assignment expressions themselves have a value. The value of the complete assignment expression is the value assigned to the variable on the left of the assignment operator. For example, the expression a = 5 both assigns a value of 5 to the variable a and results in the expression itself having a value of 5. The value of the expression can always be verified using a statement such as

```
printf("The value of the expression is %d", a = 5);
```

Here, the value of the expression itself is displayed and not the contents of the variable a. Although both the contents of the variable and the expression have the same value, it is worthwhile realizing that we are dealing with two distinct entities.

From a programming perspective, it is the actual assignment of a value to a variable that is significant in an assignment expression; the final value of the assignment expression itself is of little consequence. However, the fact that assignment expressions have a value has implications that must be considered when C's relational operators are presented.

When writing assignment expressions, you must be aware of two important considerations. Since the assignment operator has a lower precedence than any other arithmetic operator, the value of the operand to the right of the equal sign is always obtained first. For this value to have any meaning, all variables used in an expression to the right of the equal sign must have known values. For example, the expression interest = principal * rate will cause a valid number to be stored in interest only if the programmer first takes care to put valid numbers in principal and rate.

The second consideration to keep in mind is that since the value of an expression is stored in the variable to the left of the equal sign, there must be one variable listed immediately to the left of the equal sign. For example, the expression

$$\text{amount} + 1892 = 1000 + 10 * 5$$

is invalid. The right-side expression evaluates to the integer 1050, which can only be stored in a variable. Since amount + 1892 is not a valid variable name, the computer does not know where to store the calculated value.

Any expression that is terminated by a semicolon becomes a C statement. The most common example of this is the assignment statement, which is simply an assignment expression terminated with a semicolon. For example, terminating the assignment expression a = 33 with a semicolon results in the assignment statement a = 33; , which can be used in a program on a line by itself.

Since the equal sign is an operator in C, multiple assignments are possible in the same expression or its equivalent statement. For example, in the expression a = b = c = 25 all the assignment operators have the same precedence. Since the assignment operator has a right-to-left associativity, the final evaluation proceeds in the sequence

$$c = 25$$

$$b = c$$

$$a = b$$

This has the effect of assigning the number 25 to each of the variables individually, and can be represented as

$$a = (b = (c = 25))$$

Appending a semicolon to the original expression results in the multiple assignment statement

$$a = b = c = 25;$$

This latter statement is equivalent to the three individual statements

$$c = 25;$$

$$b = 25;$$

$$a = 25;$$

Program 3-1 illustrates the use of assignment statements in calculating the area of a rectangle.

 Program 3-1

```
main()
{
    float length, width, area;

    length = 27.2;
    width = 13.6;
    area = length * width;
    printf("The length of the rectangle is %f",length);
    printf("\nThe width of the rectangle is %f",width);
    printf("\nThe area of the rectangle is %f",area);
}
```

When Program 3-1 is run, the output obtained is:

```
The length of the rectangle is 27.200000
The width of the rectangle is 13.600000
The area of the rectangle is 369.920000
```

Notice the flow of control that the computer uses in executing Program 3-1. The program begins with the reserved word main and continues sequentially, statement by statement, until the closing brace is encountered. This flow of control is true for all programs. The computer works on one statement at a time, executing that statement with no knowledge of what the next statement will be. This explains why all operands used in an expression must have values assigned to them before the expression is evaluated.

When the computer executes the statement area = length * width; in Program 3-1, it uses whatever value is stored in the variables length and width at the time the assignment is executed. If no values have been specifically assigned to these variables before they are used in the expression length * width, the computer uses whatever values happen to occupy these variables when they are referenced. The computer does not "look ahead" to see that you might assign values to these variables later in the program.

Assignment Operators

Although only one variable is allowed immediately to the left of the equal sign in an assignment expression, the variable on the left of the equal sign can also be used on the right of the equal sign. For example, the assignment expression sum = sum + 10 is valid. Clearly, as an algebra equation sum could never be equal to itself plus 10. But in C, the expression sum = sum + 10 is not an equation—it is an expression that is evaluated in two major steps. The first step is to calculate the value of sum + 10. The second step is to store the computed value in sum. See if you can determine the output of Program 3-2.

 Program 3-2

```
main()
{
    int sum;

    sum = 25;
    printf("\nThe number stored in sum is %d.",sum);
    sum = sum + 10;
    printf("\nThe number now stored in sum is %d.",sum);
}
```

The assignment statement sum = 25; tells the computer to store the number 25 in sum, as shown in Figure 3-1. The first call to printf() causes the value stored in sum to be displayed by the message The number stored in sum is 25. The second assignment statement in Program 3-2, sum = sum + 10; causes the computer to retrieve the 25 stored in sum and add 10 to this number, yielding the number 35. The number 35 is then stored in the variable on the left side of the equal sign, which is the variable sum. The 25 that was

FIGURE 3–1 The Integer 25 Is Stored in sum

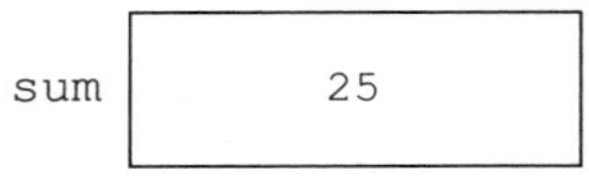

sum	25

FIGURE 3-2 sum = sum + 10; Causes a New Value to be Stored in sum

that was in sum is simply erased and replaced with the new value of 35, as shown in Figure 3-2.

Assignment expressions like sum = sum + 25, which use the same variable on both sides of the assignment operator, can be written using the following assignment operators:

$$+= \qquad -= \qquad *= \qquad /= \qquad \%=$$

For example, the expression sum = sum + 10 can be written as sum += 10. Similarly, the expression price *= rate is equivalent to the expression price = price * rate.

In using these new assignment operators it is important to note that the variable to the left of the assignment operator is applied to the complete expression on the right. For example, the expression price *= rate + 1 is equivalent to the expression price = price * (rate + 1), not price = price * rate + 1.

Accumulating

Assignment expressions like sum += 10 or its equivalent, sum = sum + 10, are common in programming. These expressions are required in accumulating subtotals when data is entered one number at a time. For example, if we want to add the numbers 96, 70, 85, and 60 in calculator fashion, the following statements could be used:

Statement	Value in sum
sum = 0;	0
sum = sum + 96;	96
sum = sum + 70;	166
sum = sum + 85;	251
sum = sum + 60;	311

The first statement clears sum by storing 0 in the variable. This removes any number ("garbage" value) in sum that would invalidate the final total. As each number is added, the value stored in sum is increased accordingly. After completion of the last statement, sum contains the total of all the added numbers.

Program 3-3 illustrates the effect of these statements by displaying sum's contents after each addition is made.

Program 3-3

```
main()
{
    int sum;

    sum = 0;
    printf("\nThe value of sum is initially set to %d.", sum);
    sum = sum + 96;
    printf("\n   sum is now %d.", sum);
    sum = sum + 70;
    printf("\n   sum is now %d.", sum);
    sum = sum + 85;
    printf("\n   sum is now %d.", sum);
    sum = sum + 60;
    printf("\n   The final sum is %d.", sum);
}
```

The output displayed by Program 3-3 is:

```
The value of sum is initially set to 0.
    sum is now 96.
    sum is now 166.
    sum is now 251.
    The final sum is 311.
```

Although Program 3-3 is not a practical program (it is easier to add the numbers by hand), it does illustrate the subtotaling effect of repeated use of statements having the form

variable = variable + new_value;

We will find many uses for this type of statement when we become more familiar with the repetition statements introduced in Chapter 5.

Counting

An assignment statement that is very similar to the accumulating statement is the counting statement. Counting statements have the form

variable = variable + fixed_number;

Examples of counting statements are:

```
i = i + 1;
n = n + 1;
count = count + 1;
j = j + 2;
m = m + 2;
kk = kk + 3;
```

In each of these examples, the same variable is used on both sides of the equal sign. After the statement is executed the value of the respective variable is increased by a fixed amount. In the first three examples the variables i, n, and count have all been increased by one. In the next two examples the respective variables have been increased by two, and in the final example the variable kk has been increased by three.

For the special case in which a variable is either increased or decreased by one, C provides two unary operators. Using the *increment operator,* ++, the expression *variable* = *variable* + 1 can be replaced by the expression ++*variable*. Examples of the increment operator are:

Expression	Alternative
i = i + 1	++i
n = n + 1	++n
count = count + 1	++count

Program 3-4 illustrates the use of the increment operator.

 Program 3-4

```
main()
{
  int count;

  count = 0;
  printf("\nThe initial value of count is %d.", count);
  ++count;
  printf("\n    count is now %d.", count);
  ++count;
  printf("\n    count is now %d.", count);
  ++count;
  printf("\n    count is now %d.", count);
  ++count;
  printf("\n    count is now %d.", count);
}
```

The output displayed by Program 3-4 is:

```
The initial value of count is 0.
     count is now 1.
     count is now 2.
     count is now 3.
     count is now 4.
```

In addition to the increment operator, C also provides a *decrement operator*, --. As you might expect, the expression *--variable* is equivalent to the expression *variable = variable - 1*. Examples of the decrement operator are:

Expression	Alternative
i = i - 1	--i
n = n - 1	--n
count = count - 1	--count

When ++ appears before a variable, it is called a *prefix increment operator*. Besides appearing before (pre) a variable, the increment operator can also be applied after a variable; for example, the expression n++. When the increment appears after a variable it is called a *postfix increment*. Both of these expressions, ++n and n++, correspond to the longer expression n = n + 1. The distinction between a prefix and postfix increment operator occurs when the variable being incremented is used in an assignment expression. For example, the expression k = ++n does two things in one expression. Initially the value of n is incremented by one and then the new value of n is assigned to the variable k. Thus, the statement k = ++n; is equivalent to the two statements

```
n = n + 1;    /* increment n first      */
k = n;        /* assign n's value to k  */
```

The assignment expression k = n++, which uses a postfix increment operator, reverses this procedure. A postfix increment operates after the assignment is completed. Thus, the statement k = n++; first assigns the current value of n to k and then increments the value of n by one. This is equivalent to the two statements

```
k = n;        /* assign n's value to k */
n = n + 1;    /* and then increment n   */
```

Just as there are prefix and postfix increment operators, C also provides *prefix* and *postfix decrement operators*. For example, both of the expressions --n and n-- reduce the value of n by one. These expressions are equivalent to the longer expression n = n – 1. As with the increment operator, however, the prefix and postfix decrement operators produce different results when used in assignment expressions. For example, the expression k = --n first decrements the value of n by one before assigning the value of n to k. But the expression k = n-- first assigns the current value of n to k and then reduces the value of n by one.

The increment and decrement operators can often be used advantageously to significantly reduce program storage requirements and increase execution speed. For example, consider the following three statements:

```
count = count + 1;
count += 1;
++count;
```

All perform the same function; however, when these instructions are compiled for execution on an IBM personal computer the storage requirements for the instructions are 9, 4, and 3 bytes, respectively. Using the assignment operator, =, instead of the increment operator results in using three times the storage space for the instruction, with an accompanying decrease in execution speed.

Exercises 3.1

1. Determine and correct the errors in the following programs.

a.
```
main ()
{

    width = 15
    area = length * width;
    printf("The area is %d",area
}
```

b.
```
main ()
{
    int length, width, area;

    area = length * width;
    length = 20;
    width = 15;
    printf("The area is %d",area);
```

c.
```
main ()
{
    int length = 20; width = 15, area;

    length * width = area;
    printf("The area is %d",area);
}
```

2. *a.* Write a C program to calculate and display the average of the numbers 32.6, 55.2, 67.9, and 48.6.
b. Run the program written for Exercise 2a on a computer.

3. *a.* Write a C program to calculate the circumference of a circle. The equation for determining the circumference of a circle is *circumference = 2 * 3.1416 * radius.* Assume that the circle has a radius of 3.3 inches.
b. Run the program written for Exercise 3a on a computer.

4. *a.* Write a C program to calculate the area of a circle. The equation for determining the area of a circle is *area = 3.1416 * radius * radius.* Assume that the circle has a radius of 5 inches.
b. Run the program written for Exercise 4a on a computer.

5. *a.* Write a C program to calculate the volume of a pool. The equation for determining the volume is *volume = length * width * depth.* Assume that the pool has a length of 25 feet, a width of 10 feet, and a depth of 6 feet.
b. Run the program written for Exercise 5a on a computer.

6. *a.* Write a C program to convert temperature in degrees Fahrenheit to degrees Celsius. The equation for this conversion is *Celsius = 5.0/9.0 * (Fahrenheit – 32.0).* Have your program convert and display the Celsius temperature corresponding to 98.6 degrees Fahrenheit.
b. Run the program written for Exercise 6a on a computer.

7. *a.* Write a C program to calculate the dollar amount contained in a piggy bank. The bank currently contains 12 half-dollars, 20 quarters, 32 dimes, 45 nickels, and 27 pennies.
b. Run the program written for Exercise 7a on a computer.

8. *a.* Write a C program to calculate the distance, in feet, of a trip that is 2.36 miles long. One mile is equal to 5,280 feet.
b. Run the program written for Exercise 8a on a computer.

9. *a.* Write a C program to calculate the elapsed time it took to make a 183.67 mile trip. The equation for computing elapsed time is *elapsed time = total distance / average speed.* Assume that the average speed during the trip was 58 miles per hour.
b. Run the program written for Exercise 9a on a computer.

10. *a.* Write a C program to calculate the sum of the numbers from 1 to 100. The formula for calculating this sum is *sum = (n/2) * (2*a + (n-1)*d),* where *n* = number of terms to be added, *a* = the first number, and *d* = the difference between each number.
b. Run the program written for Exercise 10a on a computer.

11. Determine why the expression a – b = 25 is invalid but the expression a – (b = 25) is valid.

3.2 Addresses

Two major items associated with every variable are: the value stored in the variable and the address of the variable. In C, the value stored in a variable is formally referred to as the variable's *rvalue,* and the address of the variable is called the variable's *lvalue.* These two terms make more sense when a typical illustration of a variable is considered, as illustrated in Figure 3-3. As shown in this figure, the address of the variable is typically written on the left of the figure and the variable's contents (the value in the box) on the right.

Programmers are usually concerned only with the value assigned to a variable (its contents, or rvalue) and give little attention to where the value is stored (its address, or lvalue). For example, consider Program 3-5.

 Program 3-5

```
main()
{
   int num;

   num = 22;
   printf("The value stored in num is %d.",num);
   printf("\nThe computer uses %d bytes to store this value",sizeof(num));

}
```

The output displayed when Program 3-5 is run is:

```
The value stored in num is 22.
The computer uses 2 bytes to store this value
```

Program 3-5 displays both the number 22, which is the value stored in the integer variable num (its rvalue), and the amount of storage used for this number. The information provided by Program 3-5 is illustrated in Figure 3-4.

We can go further and obtain the address, or lvalue, corresponding to the variable num. The address that is displayed corresponds to the address of the first byte set aside in the computer's memory for the variable.

FIGURE 3–3 A Typical Variable

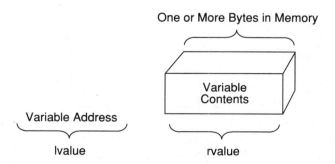

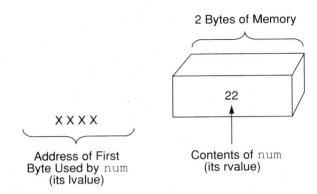

Address of First
Byte Used by num
(its lvalue)

Contents of num
(its rvalue)

FIGURE 3–4 Somewhere in Memory

To determine the address of num, we must use the address operator, &, which means *the address of,* directly in front of the variable name (no space between & and the variable). For example, &num means the *address of num,* &total means *the address of total,* and &price means *the address of price.* Program 3-6 uses the address operator to display the address of the variable num.

 Program 3-6

```
main()
{
    int num;

    num = 22;
    printf("num = %d   The address of num = %u.", num, &num);
}
```

The output of Program 3-6 is

num = 22   The address of num = 65460.

Figure 3-5 illustrates the additional address information provided by the output of Program 3-5.

Clearly, the address output by Program 3-6 depends on the computer used to run the program. Every time Program 3-6 is executed, however, it displays a representation of the address of the first byte used to store the variable num. Note also that the address is printed using the unsigned conversion sequence %u. The use of the control sequence %u in the call to printf() forces the address to be treated as an unsigned integer data type, and what is displayed

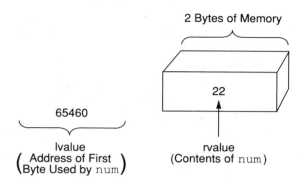

2 Bytes of Memory

22

65460

lvalue
$\left(\begin{array}{c}\text{Address of First} \\ \text{Byte Used by num}\end{array}\right)$

rvalue
(Contents of num)

FIGURE 3–5 A More Complete Picture of the Variable num

is printf()'s representation of the address in this format. An address, however, is not an unsigned integer data type—it is a unique data type that may
or may not require the same amount of storage as an unsigned integer. Using
the %u control sequence simply provides a convenient way of displaying an
address, since no specific control sequence exists for its display. The display has
no impact on how addresses are used internally to the program and merely
provides us with a useful representation that is helpful in understanding what
addresses are.

As we shall see, using addresses as opposed to only displaying them
provides the C programmer with an extremely powerful programming tool.
They provide the ability to enter directly into the computer's inner workings
and access its basic storage structure. This gives the C programmer capabilities and programming power that are not available in most other computer
languages.

Storing Addresses

Besides displaying the address of a variable, as was done in Program 3-6, we
can also store addresses in suitably declared variables. For example, the
statement

```
num_addr = &num;
```

stores the address corresponding to the variable num in the variable num_addr,
as illustrated in Figure 3-6. Similarly, the statements

```
d = &m;

tab_point = &list;

chr_point = &ch;
```

Variable   Contents

num_addr   Address of num

FIGURE 3–6 Storing num's Address into num_addr

store the addresses of the variables m, list, and ch in the variables d, tab_point, and chr_point, respectively, as illustrated in Figure 3-7.

The variables num_addr, d, tab_point, and chr_point are all called *pointer variables,* or *pointers.* Pointers are simply variables that are used to store the addresses of other variables.

Using Addresses*

To use a stored address, C provides us with an *indirection operator,* *. The * symbol, when followed immediately by a pointer (no space allowed between the * and the pointer), means *the variable whose address is stored in.* Thus, if num_addr is a pointer (remember that a pointer is a variable that contains an address), *num_addr means *the variable whose address is stored in* num_addr. Similarly, *tab_point means *the variable whose address is stored in* tab_point and *chr_point means *the variable whose address is stored in* chr_point. Figure 3-8 shows the relationship between the address contained in a pointer variable and the variable ultimately addressed.

Although *d literally means *the variable whose address is stored in* d, this is commonly shortened to *the variable pointed to by* d. Similarly, referring to Figure 3-8, *y can be read as *the variable pointed to by* y. The value ultimately obtained, as shown in Figure 3-8, is qqqq.

* This topic may be omitted on first reading without loss of subject continuity.

FIGURE 3–7 Storing More Addresses

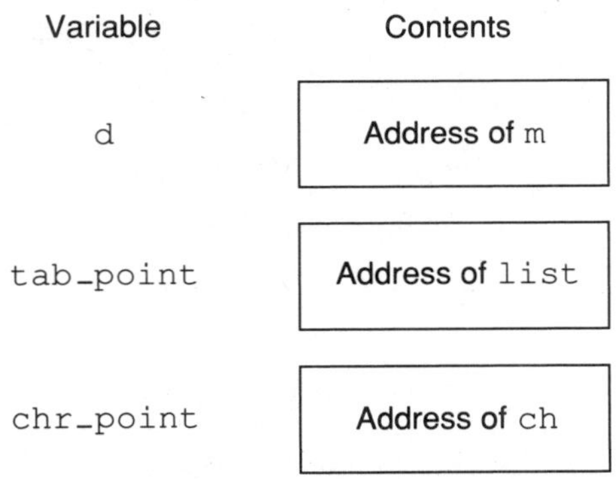

Variable   Contents

d   Address of m

tab_point   Address of list

chr_point   Address of ch

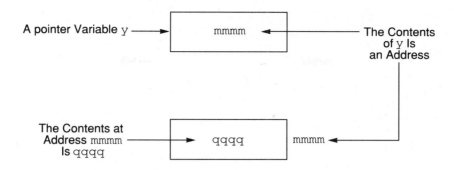

FIGURE 3–8 Using a Pointer Variable

When using a pointer variable, the value that is obtained is always found by first going to the pointer variable (or pointer, for short) for an address. The address contained in the pointer is then used to get the desired contents. Certainly, this is a rather indirect way of getting to the final value and, not unexpectedly, the term *indirect addressing* is used to describe this procedure.

Since using a pointer requires the computer to do a double lookup (first the address is retrieved, then the address is used to retrieve the actual data), a worthwhile question is, why would you want to store an address in the first place? The answer to this question must be deferred until we get to real applications, when the use of pointers becomes invaluable. However, given what was previously presented for a variable's storage locations, the idea of storing an address should not seem overly strange.

Declaring Pointers*

Like all variables, pointers must be declared before they can be used. In declaring a pointer variable, C requires that we also specify the type of variable that is pointed to. For example, if the address in the pointer num_addr is the address of an integer, the correct declaration for the pointer is

```
int *num_addr;
```

This declaration is read as *the variable pointed to by* num_addr (from the *num_addr in the declaration) *is an integer.*

Notice that the declaration int *num_addr; specifies two things: first, that the variable pointed to by num_addr is an integer; second, that num_addr must be a pointer (because it is used with the indirection operator *). Similarly, if the pointer tab_point points to (contains the address of) a floating point number and chr_point points to a character variable, the required declarations for these pointers are

```
float *tab_point;
```

```
char *chr_point;
```

*This topic may be omitted on first reading without loss of subject continuity.

These last two declarations can be read as *the variable pointed to by* tab_point *is a float* and *the variable pointed to by* chr_point *is a char.* Consider Program 3-7.

 Program 3-7

```
main()
{
 int *num_addr;        /* declare a pointer to an int    */
 int miles,dist;       /* declare two integer variables  */

 dist = 158;           /* store the number 158 into dist */
 miles = 22;           /* store the number 22 into miles */
 num_addr = &miles;    /* store the 'address of miles' in num_addr */

 printf("The address stored in num_addr is %u\n",num_addr);
 printf("The value pointed to by num_addr is %d\n\n",*num_addr);

 num_addr = &dist; /* now store the address of dist in num_addr */
 printf("The address now stored in num_addr is %u\n",num_addr);
 printf("The value now pointed to by num_addr is %d\n",*num_addr);

}
```

The output of Program 3-7 is:

```
The address stored in num_addr is 65460
The value pointed to by num_addr is 22

The address now stored in num_addr is 65462
The value now pointed to by num_addr is 158
```

The only value of Program 3-7 is in helping us understand "what gets stored where." Let's review the program to see how the output was produced.

The declaration statement int *num_addr; declares num_addr to be a pointer variable used to store the address of an integer variable. The statement num_addr = &miles; stores the address of the variable miles into the pointer num_addr. The first call to printf() causes this address to be displayed. Notice that we have again used the control sequence %u to print out the address. The second call to printf() in Program 3-7 uses the indirection operator to retrieve and print out the *value pointed to by* num_addr, which is, of course, the value stored in miles.

Since num_addr has been declared as a pointer to an integer variable, we can use this pointer to store the address of any integer variable. The statement

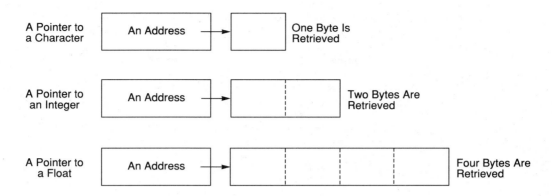

FIGURE 3–9 Addressing Different Data Types Using Pointers

num_addr = &dist illustrates this by storing the address of the variable dist in num_addr. The last two printf() calls verify the change in num_addr's value and that the new stored address does point to the variable dist. As illustrated in Program 3-7, only addresses should be stored in pointers.

It certainly would have been much simpler if the pointer used in Program 3-7 could have been declared as point num_addr;. Such a declaration, however, conveys no information as to the storage used by the variable whose address is stored in num_addr. This information is essential when the pointer is used with the indirection operator, as it is in the second printf() call in Program 3-7. For example, if the address of an integer is stored in num_addr, then only two bytes of storage are typically retrieved when the address is used. If the address of a character is stored in num_addr, only one byte of storage would be retrieved, and a float typically requires the retrieval of four bytes of storage. The declaration of a pointer must, therefore, include the type of variable being pointed to. Figure 3-9 illustrates this concept.

Exercises 3.2

1. If average is a variable, what does &average mean?

2. For the variables and addresses illustrated in Figure 3-10, determine &temp, &dist, &date, and &miles.

3. *a*. Write a program that includes the following declaration statements. Have the program use the address operator and the printf() function to display the addresses corresponding to each variable.

```
char key, choice;
int num, count;
long date;
float yield;
double price;
```

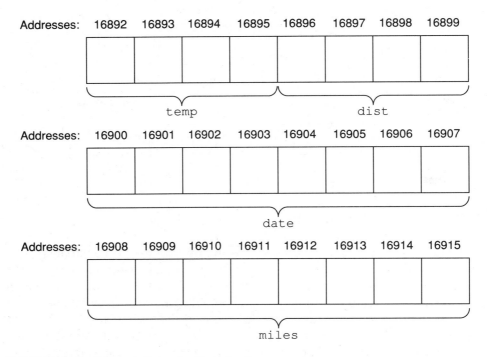

FIGURE 3–10 Memory Bytes for Exercise 2

b. After running the program written for Exercise 3a, draw a diagram of how your computer has set aside storage for the variables in the program. On your diagram, fill in the addresses displayed by the program.

c. Modify the program written in Exercise 3a to display the amount of storage your computer reserves for each data type (use the `sizeof` operator). With this information and the address information provided in Exercise 3b, determine if your computer set aside storage for the variables in the order they were declared.

4. If a variable is declared as a pointer, what must be stored in the variable?

5. Using the indirection operator, write expressions for the following:
   a. The variable pointed to by `x_addr`
   b. The variable whose address is in `y_addr`
   c. The variable pointed to by `pt_yld`
   d. The variable pointed to by `pt_miles`
   e. The variable pointed to by `mptr`
   f. The variable whose address is in `pdate`
   g. The variable pointed to by `dist_ptr`
   h. The variable pointed to by `tab_pt`
   i. The variable whose address is in `hours_pt`

6. Write declaration statements for the following:
   a. The variable pointed to by `y_addr` is an integer.
   b. The variable pointed to by `ch_addr` is a character.
   c. The variable pointed to by `pt_yr` is a long integer.
   d. The variable pointed to by `amt` is a double precision variable.
   e. The variable pointed to by `z` is an integer.

f. The variable pointed to by qp is a floating point variable.

g. date_pt is a pointer to an integer.

h. yld_addr is a pointer to a double precision variable.

i. amt_pt is a pointer to a floating point variable.

j. pt_chr is a pointer to a character.

7. *a.* What are the variables y_addr, ch_addr, pt_yr, amt, z, qp, date_ptr, yld_addr, amt_pt, and pt_chr used in Exercise 6 called?

b. Why are the variable names amt, z, and qp used in Exercise 6 not good choices for pointer variable names?

8. Write English sentences for the following declarations:

a. char *key_addr;   *d.* long *y_ptr;

b. int *m;   *e.* float *p_cou;

c. double *yld_addr;   *f.* int *pt_date;

9. Which of the following are declarations for pointers:

a. long a;   *f.* double w;

b. char b;   *g.* float *k;

c. char *c;   *h.* float l;

d. int x;   *i.* double *z;

e. int *p;

10. For the following declarations,

```
int *x_pt, *y_addr;

long *dt_addr, *pt_addr;

double *pt_z;

int a;

long b;

double c;
```

determine which of the following statements is valid.

a. y_addr = &a;	*h.* dt_addr = &b;	*o.* pt_addr = &c
b. y_addr = &b;	*i.* dt_addr = &c;	*p.* pt_addr = a;
c. y_addr = &c;	*j.* dt_addr = a;	*q.* pt_addr = b;
d. y_addr = a;	*k.* dt_addr = b;	*r.* pt_addr = c;
e. y_addr = b;	*l.* dt_addr = c;	*s.* y_addr = x_pt;
f. y_addr = c;	*m.* pt_z = &a;	*t.* y_addr = dt_addr;
g. dt_addr = &a;	*n.* pt_addr = &b;	*u.* y_addr = pt_addr;

11. For the variables and addresses illustrated in Figure 3-11, fill in the appropriate data as determined by the following statements:

a. pt_num = &m;   *e.* pt_day = z_addr;

b. amt_addr = &amt;   *f.* *pt_yr = 1987;

c. *z_addr = 25;   *g.* *amt_addr = *num_addr;

d. k = *num_addr;

Variable: `pt_num`
Address: 500

Variable: `amt_addr`
Address: 564

Variable: `z_addr`
Address: 8024

20492

Variable: `num_addr`
Address: 10132

18938

Variable: `pt_day`
Address: 14862

Variable: `pt_yr`
Address: 15010

694

Variable: `years`
Address: 694

Variable: `m`
Address: 8096

Variable: `amt`
Address: 16256

Variable: `firstnum`
Address: 18938

154

Variable: `balz`
Address: 20492

Variable: `k`
Address: 24608

FIGURE 3–11 Memory Locations for Exercise 11

12. Using the `sizeof` operator, determine the number of bytes used by your computer to store the address of an integer, character, and double precision number. (*Hint:* `sizeof (int*)` can be used to determine the number of memory bytes used for a *pointer to an integer*.) Would you expect the size of each address to be the same? Why or why not?

3.3   The `scanf()` Function

Data for programs that are only going to be executed once may be included directly in the program. For example, if we wanted to multiply the numbers 300.0 and .05, we could use Program 3-8.

Program 3-8

```
main()
{
    float num1,num2,product;

    num1 = 300.0;
    num2 = .05;
    product = num1 * num2;
    printf("%f times %f is %f", num1, num2, product);
}
```

The output displayed by Program 3-8 is:

```
300.000000 times .050000 is 15.000000
```

Program 3-8 can be shortened, as illustrated in Program 3-9. Both programs, however, suffer from the same problem: they must be rewritten in order to multiply different numbers. Both programs lack the facility for entering different numbers to be operated on.

 Program 3-9

```
main()
{
    printf("%f times %f is %f", 300.0, .05, 300.0*.05);
}
```

Except for the practice provided to the programmer of writing, entering, and running the program, programs that do the same calculation only once, on the same set of numbers, are clearly not very useful. After all, it is simpler to use a calculator to multiply two numbers than to enter and run either Program 3-8 or 3-9.

This section presents the scanf() function, which is used to enter data into a program while it is executing. Just as the printf() function displays a copy of the value stored inside a variable, the scanf() function allows the user to enter a value at the terminal. The value is then stored directly in a variable.

Like the printf() function, the scanf() function requires a control string as the first argument inside the function name parentheses. The control string tells the function the type of data being input and uses the same control sequences as the printf() function. Unlike the control string used in a printf() function, however, the control string passed to scanf() typically consists of control sequences only. Also, unlike printf() where a list of variable names can follow the control string, scanf() requires that a list of variable addresses follow the control string. For example, the statement scanf("%d", &num1); is a call to the scanf() function. The control sequence %d is identical to the control sequence used in printf() in that it tells the scanf() function that it will be dealing with an integer number. The address operator & in front of the variable num1 is required for scanf(). Recall from Section 3.2 that &num1 is read *the address of* num1.

When a statement such as scanf("%d", &num1); is encountered, the computer stops program execution and continuously scans the keyboard for data (scanf is short for scan function). When a data item is typed, the scanf() function stores the item using the address it was given. The program then continues execution with the next statement after the call to scanf(). To see this, consider Program 3-10.

 Program 3-10

```
main()
{
    float num1, num2, product;

    printf("Please type in a number: ");
    scanf("%f",&num1);
    printf("\nPlease type in another number: ");
    scanf("%f",&num2);
    product = num1 * num2;
    printf("\n%f times %f is %f",num1, num2, product);
}
```

FIGURE 3–12 scanf() Is Used to Enter Data; printf() Is Used to Display Data

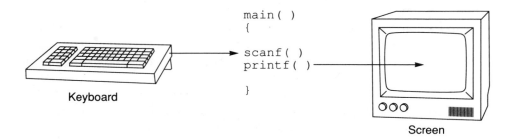

The first call to `printf()` in Program 3-10 produces a prompt, which is a message that tells the person at the terminal what should be typed. In this case the user is told to type a number. The computer then executes the next statement, which is a call to `scanf()`. The `scanf()` function puts the computer into a temporary pause (or wait) state for as long as it takes the user to type a value. Then the user signals the `scanf()` function by pressing the return key after the value has been typed. The entered value is stored in the variable whose address was passed to `scanf()`, and the computer is taken out of its paused state. Program execution then proceeds with the next statement, which in Program 3-10 is another call to `printf()`. This call causes the next message to be displayed. The second call to `scanf()` again puts the computer into a temporary wait state while the user types a second value. This second number is stored in the variable `num2`.

The following sample run was made using Program 3-10.

```
Please type in a number: 300.
Please type in another number: .05
300.000000 times .050000 is 15.000000
```

In Program 3-10, each call to `scanf()` is used to store one value into a variable. The `scanf()` function, however, can be used to enter and store as many values as there are control sequences in the control string. For example, the statement

```
scanf("%f %f",&num1,&num2);
```

results in two values being read from the terminal and assigned to the variables `num1` and `num2`. If the data entered at the terminal was

```
0.052 245.79
```

the variables `num1` and `num2` would contain the values `0.052` and `245.79`, respectively. The space in the control string between the two conversion sequences, `"%f %f"`, is strictly for readability. The control string `"%f%f"` would work equally well. When actually entering numbers such as `0.052` and `245.79`, however, you must leave at least one space between the numbers, regardless of which control string, `"%f %f"` or `"%f%f"`, is used. The space between the entered numbers clearly indicates where one number ends and the next begins. Inserting more than one space between numbers has no effect on `scanf()`.

The only time that a space can affect the value being entered is when `scanf()` is expecting a character data type. For example, the statement `scanf("%c%c%c",&ch1,&ch2,&ch3);` causes `scanf()` to store the next three characters typed in the variables `ch1`, `ch2`, and `ch3`, respectively. If you type x y z, the x is stored in `ch1`, a blank is stored in `ch2`, and y is stored in `ch3`. If, however, the statement `scanf("%c %c %c",&ch1,&ch2,&ch3);` was used, `scanf()` looks for three characters separated by exactly one space.

Any number of scanf() function calls may be made in a program, and any number of values may be input using a single scanf() function. Just be sure that a control sequence is used for each value to be entered and that the address operator is used in front of the variable name where the value is to be stored. The control sequences used in a scanf() control string are the same as those used in printf() calls, with one caution. In printing a double precision number using printf(), the control sequence for a floating point variable, %f, can be used. This is not true when using scanf(). If a double precision number is to be entered, the conversion sequence %lf must be used.

The scanf() function, again like the printf() function, does not test the data type of the values being entered. It is up to the user to ensure that all variables are declared correctly and that any numbers entered are of the correct type. However, scanf() is "clever" enough to make a few data type conversions. For example, if an integer is entered in place of a floating point or double precision number, the scanf() function automatically adds a decimal point at the end of the integer before storing the number. Similarly, if a floating point or double precision number is entered when an integer is expected, the scanf() function only uses the integer part of the number. For example, assume the following numbers are typed in response to the function call scanf("%f %d %f",&num1,&num2,&num3); :

                    56   22.879   33.923

scanf() converts the 56 to 56.0 and stores this value in the variable num1. The function continues scanning the input, expecting an integer value. As far as scanf() is concerned, the decimal point after the 22 in the number 22.879 indicates the end of an integer and the start of a decimal number. Thus, the number 22 is stored in num2. Continuing to scan the typed input, scanf() takes the .879 as the next floating point number and stores this value in num3. As far as scanf() is concerned, 33.923 is extra input and is ignored. If, though, you do not initially type enough data, the scanf() function will continue to make the computer pause until sufficient data has been entered.

Exercises 3.3

1. For the following declaration statements, write a scanf() function call that will cause the computer to pause while the appropriate data is typed by the user.
   a. int firstnum;
   b. float grade;
   c. double secnum;
   d. char keyval;
   e. int month,years;
      float average;

f. ```
char ch;
int num1, num2;
double grade1, grade2;
```
*g.* ```
float interest, principal, capital;
double price, yield;
```
h. ```
char ch, letter1, letter2;
int num1, num2, num3;
```
*i.* ```
float temp1, temp2, temp3;
double volts1, volts2;
```

2. For the following `scanf()` function calls, write appropriate declaration statements.
   a. `scanf("%d", &day);`
   b. `scanf("%c", &fir_char);`
   c. `scanf("%f", &grade);`
   d. `scanf("%lf", &price);`
   e. `scanf("%d %d %c", &num1, &num2, &ch1);`
   f. `scanf("%f %f %d", &firstnum, &secnum, &count);`
   g. `scanf("%c %c %d %lf", &ch1, &ch2, &flag, &average);`

3. Given the following declaration statements,

```
int num1, num2;
float firstnum, secnum;
double price, yield;
```

   determine and correct the errors in the following `scanf()` function calls.
   a. `scanf("%d", num1);`
   b. `scanf("%f %f %f", &num1, firstnum, &price);`
   c. `scanf("%c %lf %f", &num1, &secnum, &price);`
   d. `scanf("%d %d %lf", num1, num2, yield);`
   e. `scanf(&num1, &num2);`
   f. `scanf(&num1, "%d");`

4. *a.* Write a C program that displays the following prompt:

```
Enter the radius of a circle:
```

   After accepting a value for the radius, your program should calculate and display the circumference of the circle. *Note: circumference = 2 * 3.1416 * radius.*
   b. Check the value displayed by the program written for Exercise 4a by calculating the result manually.

5. *a.* Write a C program that first displays the following prompt:

```
Enter the temperature in degrees Fahrenheit:
```

   Have your program accept a value entered from the keyboard and convert the temperature entered to degrees Celsius, using the equation *Celsius = (5.0 / 9.0) * (Fahrenheit – 32.0).* Your program should then display the temperature in degrees Celsius, using an appropriate output message.
   b. Check the value displayed by the program written for Exercise 5a by calculating the result manually.

6. *a.* Write a C program that displays the following prompts:

```
Enter the length of the room:
Enter the width of the room:
```

After each prompt is displayed, your program should use a `scanf()` function call to accept data from the keyboard for the displayed prompt. After the width of the room is entered, your program should calculate and display the area of the room. The area displayed should be included in an appropriate message and calculated using the equation *area = length * width.*
b. Check the area displayed by the program written for Exercise 6a by calculating the result manually.

7. *a.* Write a C program that displays the following prompts:

```
Enter the miles driven:
Enter the gallons of gas used:
```

After each prompt is displayed, your program should use a `scanf()` function call to accept data from the keyboard for the displayed prompt. After the gallons of gas used has been entered, your program should calculate and display miles per gallon obtained. This value should be included in an appropriate message and calculated using the equation *miles per gallon = miles / gallons used.*
b. Check the value displayed by the program written for Exercise 7a by calculating the result manually.

8. *a.* Write a C program that displays the following prompts:

```
Enter the length of the swimming pool:
Enter the width of the swimming pool:
Enter the average depth of the swimming pool:
```

After each prompt is displayed, your program should use a `scanf()` function call to accept data from the keyboard for the displayed prompt. After the depth of the swimming pool is entered, your program should calculate and display the volume of the pool. The volume should be included in an appropriate message and calculated using the equation *volume = length * width * average depth.*
b. Check the volume displayed by the program written for Exercise 8a by calculating the result manually.

9. *a.* Write a C program that displays the following prompts:

```
Enter a number:
Enter a second number:
Enter a third number:
Enter a fourth number:
```

After each prompt is displayed, your program should use a `scanf()` function call to accept a number from the keyboard for the displayed prompt. After the fourth number has been entered, your program should calculate and display the average of the numbers. The average should be included in an appropriate message.
b. Check the average displayed for the program written in Exercise 9a by calculating the result manually.

c. Repeat Exercise 9a, making sure that you use the same variable name, `number`, for each number input. Also use the variable `sum` for the sum of the numbers. (*Hint:* To do this, you must use the statement `sum = sum + number;` after each number is accepted. Review the material on accumulating presented in Section 3.1.)

10. Write a C program that prompts the user to type a number. Have your program accept the number as an integer and immediately display the integer using a `printf()` function call. Run your program three times. The first time you run the program enter a valid integer number, the second time enter a floating point number, and the third time enter a character. Using the output display, see what number your program actually accepted from the data you entered.

11. Repeat Exercise 10 but have your program declare the variable used to store the number as a floating point variable. Run the program four times. The first time enter an integer, the second time enter a decimal number with less than six decimal places, the third time enter a number having more than six decimal places, and the fourth time enter a character. Using the output display, keep track of what number your program actually accepted from the data you typed in. What happened, if anything, and why?

12. Repeat Exercise 10 but have your program declare the variable used to store the number as a double precision variable. Run the program four times. The first time enter an integer, the second time enter a decimal number with less than six decimal places, the third time enter a number having more than six decimal places, and the fourth time enter a character. Using the output display, keep track of what number your program actually accepted from the data you typed in. What happened, if anything, and why?

13. *a.* Why do you think that most successful commercial applications programs contain extensive data input validity checks? (*Hint:* Review Exercises 10, 11, and 12.)
   b. What do you think is the difference between a data type check and a data reasonableness check?
   c. Assume that a program requests that a month, day, and year be entered by the user. What are some checks that could be made on the data entered?

14. Write a C program that uses the declaration statement `double num;`. Then use the function call `scanf("%f", &num);` to input a value into `num`. (Notice that we have used the wrong control sequence for the variable `num`.) Run your program and enter a decimal number. Using a `printf()` function call, have your program display the number stored in `num1`. Determine what problem you can run into when an incorrect control sequence is used in `scanf()`.

15. Program 3-10 prompts the user to input two numbers, where the first value entered is stored in `num1` and the second value is stored in `num2`. Using this program as a starting point, write a program that swaps the values stored in the two variables.

3.4   scanf() with Buffered Input*

Seemingly strange results are sometimes obtained when the `scanf()` function is used to accept characters. To see how this can occur, consider Program 3-11,

---

* This section contains supplementary material on the `scanf()` function and can be omitted on first reading without loss of subject continuity.

which uses `scanf()` to accept the next character entered at the keyboard and store the character in the variable `fkey`.

Program 3-11

```
main()
{
char fkey;

    printf("Type in a character: ");
    scanf("%c", &fkey);
    printf("The key just accepted is %d", fkey);
}
```

When Program 3-11 is run, the character entered in response to the prompt `Type in a character:` is stored in the character variable `fkey` and the decimal code for the character is displayed by the last `printf()` function call. The following sample run illustrates this:

```
Type in a character: m
The key just accepted is 109
```

At this point, everything seems to be working just fine, although you might be wondering why we displayed the decimal value of m rather than the character itself. The reason for this will soon become apparent.

In typing m, two keys are usually pressed, the m key and the ENTER key. On most computer systems these two characters are stored in a temporary holding area called a *buffer* immediately after they are pressed, as illustrated in Figure 3-13.

FIGURE 3–13 Typed Keyboard Characters Are First Stored in a Buffer

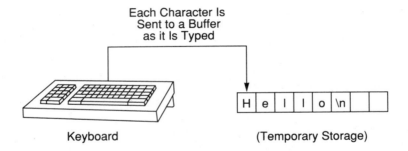

The first key pressed, m in this case, is taken from the buffer and stored in fkey. This, however, still leaves the code for the ENTER key in the buffer. Any subsequent call to `scanf()` for a character input will automatically pick up the code for the ENTER key as the next character. For example, consider Program 3-12.

 Program 3-12

```
main()
{
  char fkey, skey;

  printf("Type in a character: ");
  scanf("%c", &fkey);
  printf("The key just accepted is %d", fkey);
  printf("\nType in another character: ");
  scanf("%c", &skey);
  printf("The key just accepted is %d", skey);
}
```

The following is a sample run for Program 3-12.

```
Type in a character: m
The key just accepted is 109
Type in another character: The key just accepted is 10
```

Let us review what has happened. In entering m in response to the first prompt, the ENTER key is also pressed. From a character standpoint this represents the entry of two distinct characters. The first character is m, which is stored as 109. The second character also gets stored in the buffer with the numerical code for the ENTER key. The second call to `scanf()` picks up this code immediately, without waiting for any additional key to be pressed. The last call to `printf()` displays the code for this key. The reason for displaying the numerical code rather than the character itself is because the ENTER key has no printable character associated with it that can be displayed.

Remember that every key has a numerical code, including the ENTER, SPACE, ESCAPE, and CONTROL keys. These keys generally have no effect when entering numbers, because `scanf()` ignores them as leading or trailing input with numerical data. Nor do these keys affect the entry of a single character requested as the first user data to be input, as is the case in Program

3-11. Only when a character is requested after the user has already input some other data, as in Program 3-12, does the usually invisible ENTER key become noticeable.

There is a quick solution to avoid having the ENTER key accepted as a legitimate character input. All we have to do is accept the ENTER key, store it as a character variable, and then just not use it. Program 3-13 illustrates this technique. The ENTER key is accepted along with the first character typed. This clears the computer's buffer and prepares the way for the character input.

 Program 3-13

```
main()
{
  char fkey, skey;

  printf("Type in a character: ");
  scanf("%c%c", &fkey, &skey);     /* the enter code goes to skey */
  printf("The key just accepted is %d", fkey);
  printf("\nType in another character: ");
  scanf("%c", &skey);    /* accept another code */
  printf("The key just accepted is %d", skey);
}
```

In reviewing Program 3-13, observe that the first `scanf()` function call accepts two back-to-back characters. Now when the user types m and presses the ENTER key, the m is assigned to `fkey` and the code for the ENTER key is automatically assigned to `skey`. The next call to `scanf()` stores the code for the next key pressed in the variable `skey` also. This automatically erases the code for the ENTER key that was previously stored there. From the user's standpoint, the ENTER key has no effect except to signal the end of each character input. The following is a sample run for Program 3-13.

```
Type in a character: m
The key just accepted is 109
Type in another character: b
The key just accepted is 98
```

The solution to the "phantom" ENTER key used in Program 3-13 is not the only solution possible (there is never just one way of doing something in C).* All solutions, however, center on the fact that the ENTER key is a legitimate character input and must be treated as such when using a buffered system.

*Another solution, for example, is to replace the last `scanf()` call in Program 3-12 with the statement `scanf("\n%c",&skey);`.

3.5   Named Constants

Literal data is any data within a program that explicitly identifies itself. For example, the constants 2 and 3.1416 in the assignment statement

```
circum = 2 * 3.1416 * radius;
```

are also called literals because they are literally included directly in the statement. Additional examples of literals are contained in the following C assignment statements. See if you can identify them.

```
perimeter = 2 * length * width;
        y = (5 * p) / 7.2;
 salestax = 0.05 * purchase;
```

The literals are the numbers 2, 5 and 7.2, and 0.05 in the first, second, and third statements, respectively.

The same literal often appears many times in the same program. For example, in a program used to determine bank interest charges, the interest rate would typically appear in different places throughout the program. Similarly, in a program used to calculate taxes, the tax rate might appear in many individual instructions. If either the interest rate or sales tax rate change, the programmer would have the cumbersome task of changing the literal value everywhere it appears in the program. Multiple changes, however, are subject to error—if just one rate value is overlooked and not changed, the result obtained when the program is run will be incorrect. Literal values that appear many times in the same program are referred to by programmers as *magic numbers.* By themselves the numbers are quite ordinary, but in the context of a particular application they have a special ("magical") meaning.

To avoid the problem of having a magic number spread throughout a program in many places, C provides the programmer with the capability to define the value once, by equating the number to a *symbolic name.* Then, instead of using the number throughout the program, the symbolic name is used instead. If the number ever has to be changed, the change need only be made once at the point where the symbolic name is equated to the actual number value. Equating numbers to symbolic names is accomplished using a #define statement. Two such statements are:

```
#define SALESTAX 0.05 ←──────── no semicolon
#define PI 3.1416 ←──────── no semicolon
```

These two statements are called either #define or *equivalence* statements. The first #define statement equates the value 0.05 to the symbolic name SALESTAX, while the second #define statement equates the number 3.1416 to the symbolic name PI. Other terms for symbolic names are *named constants* or *symbolic constants*. We shall use these terms interchangeably.

Although we have typed the named constants in uppercase letters, lowercase letters could have been used. It is common in C, however, to use uppercase letters for named constants. Then, whenever a programmer sees uppercase letters in a program, he or she will know the name is a named constant defined in a #define statement, not a variable name declared in a declaration statement.

The named constants defined above can be used in any C statement in place of the numbers they represent. For example, the assignment statements

```
circum = 2 * PI * radius;
amount = SALESTAX * purchase;
```

are both valid. These statements must, of course, appear after the definitions of the named constants are made. Usually, all #define statements are placed at the top of a file, before any functions, including main(), are typed. Program 3-14 illustrates the use of such a #define statement.

 Program 3-14

```
#define SALESTAX 0.05
main()
{
   float amount, taxes, total;

   printf("\nEnter the amount purchased: ");
   scanf("%f", &amount);
   taxes = SALESTAX * amount;
   total = amount + taxes;
   printf("The sales tax is $%4.2f",taxes);
   printf("\nThe total bill is $%5.2f",total);
}
```

The following sample run was made using Program 3-14.

```
Enter the amount purchased: 36.00
The sales tax is $1.80
The total bill is $37.80
```

Whenever a named constant appears in an instruction it has the same effect as if the literal value it represents was used. Thus, SALESTAX is simply another way of representing the value 0.05. Since SALESTAX and the number 0.05 are equivalent, the value of SALESTAX may not be subsequently changed by the program. An instruction such as SALESTAX = 0.06; is meaningless, because SALESTAX is not a variable. Since SALESTAX is only a stand-in for the value 0.05, this statement is equivalent to writing the invalid statement 0.05 = 0.06;.

Notice also that #define statements do not end with a semicolon. The reason for this is that #define statements are not processed by the regular C compiler used to translate C statements into machine language. The # sign is a signal to a C *preprocessor*. This preprocessor screens all program statements when a C program is compiled. When the preprocessor encounters a # sign, it recognizes an instruction to itself. The word define tells the preprocessor to equate the symbolic constant in the statement with the information or data following it. In the case of a statement like #define SALESTAX 0.05, the word SALESTAX is equated to the value 0.05. The preprocessor then replaces each subsequent occurrence of the word SALESTAX in the C program with the value 0.05.

This explains why a #define statement does not end with a semicolon. If a semicolon followed the literal value 0.05, the preprocessor would equate the word SALESTAX with 0.05;. Then, when it replaced SALESTAX in the assignment statement taxes = SALESTAX * amount;, the statement would become taxes = 0.05; * amount;, which is the valid statement taxes = 0.05; followed by the invalid statement * amount;.

Realizing that #define statements simply relate two items allows us to use them to create individualized programming languages. For example, the #define statements

```
#define BEGIN {
#define END }
```

equate the first brace { to the word BEGIN and the closing brace } to the word END. Once these symbols are equated the words BEGIN and END can be used in place of the respective braces. This is illustrated in Program 3-15.

Program 3-15

```
#define SALESTAX 0.05
#define BEGIN {
#define END }
main()
BEGIN
   float amount, taxes, total;

   printf("\nEnter in the amount purchased: ");
   scanf("%f", &amount);
   taxes = SALESTAX * amount;
   total = amount + taxes;
   printf("\nThe sales tax is $%4.2f",taxes);
   printf("\nThe total bill is $%5.2f",total);
END
```

When Program 3-15 is compiled, the preprocessor faithfully replaces all occurrences of the words BEGIN and END with their equivalent symbols. Although using #define statements to create a new set of symbols equivalent to the standard C symbol set is usually not a good idea, Program 3-15 should give you an idea of the richness and diversity that C provides. Generally, the constructions that can be created in C are limited only by the imagination and good sense of the programmer.

Exercises 3.5

Determine the purpose of the programs given in Exercises 1 through 3. Then rewrite each program using #define statements for appropriate literals.

```
1. main()
   {
      float radius, circum;

      printf("\nEnter a radius: ");
      scanf("%f", &radius);
      circum = 2.0 * 3.1416 * radius;
      printf("\nThe circumference of the circle is %f", circum);
   }
```

```
2. main()
   {
      float prime, amount, interest;

      prime = .08;        /* prime interest rate */
      printf("\nEnter the amount: ");
      scant("%f", &amount);
      interest = prime * amount;
      printf("\nThe interest earned is %f dollars", interest);
   }
3. main()
   {
      float fahren, celsius;

      printf("\nEnter a temperature in degrees Fahrenheit: ");
      scanf("%f", &fahren);
      celsius = (5.0/9.0) * (fahren - 32.0);
      printf("\nThe equivalent Celsius temperature is %f", celsius);
   }
```

3.6 Common Programming Errors

In using the material presented in this chapter, be aware of the following possible errors:

1. Forgetting to assign initial values to all variables before the variables are used in an expression. Initial values can be assigned when the variables are declared, by explicit assignment statements, or by interactively entering values using the `scanf()` function.

2. Applying either the increment or decrement operator to an expression. For example, the expression

$$(count + n)++$$

   is incorrect. The increment and decrement operators can only be applied to individual variables.

3. Attempting to store an address in a variable that has not been declared as a pointer.

4. Forgetting to pass addresses to `scanf()`. Since `scanf()` treats all arguments following the control string as addresses, it is up to the programmer to ensure that addresses are passed correctly.

5. Including a message within the control string passed to scanf(). Unlike printf(), scanf()'s control string usually contains only control sequences.

6. Not including the correct control sequences in scanf() function calls for the data values that must be entered.

7. Not closing off the control string passed to scanf() with a double quote symbol followed by a comma, and forgetting to separate all arguments passed to scanf() with commas.

8. Terminating a #define command to the preprocessor with a semicolon. By now you probably end every line in your C programs with a semicolon, almost automatically. But there are cases, for example preprocessor commands, where a semicolon should not end a line.

A more exotic and less common error occurs when the increment and decrement operators are used with variables that appear more than once in the same expression. Although the cause of this error is explained later in Chapter 14, this error basically occurs because C does not specify the order in which operands are accessed within an expression. For example, the value assigned to result in the statement

```
result = i + i++;
```

is computer dependent. If your computer accesses the first operand, i, first, the above statement is equivalent to

```
result = 2 * i;
i++;
```

However, if your computer accesses the second operand, i++, first, the value of the first operand will be altered before it is used and a different value is assigned to result. As a general rule, therefore, do not use either the increment or decrement operator in an expression when the variable it operates on appears more than once in the expression.

3.7 Chapter Summary

1. An expression is a sequence of one or more operands separated by operators. An operand is a constant, a variable, or another expression. A value is associated with an expression.

2. Expressions are evaluated according to the precedence and associativity of the operators used in the expression.

3. The assignment symbol, =, is an operator. Expressions using this operator assign a value to a variable; additionally, the expression itself takes on a value. Since assignment is an operation in C, multiple uses of the assignment operator are possible in the same expression.

4. The increment operator, ++, adds one to a variable, while the decrement operator, −−, subtracts one from a variable. Both of these operators can be used as prefixes or postfixes. In prefix operation the variable is incremented (or decremented) before its value is used. In postfix operation the variable is incremented (or decremented) after its value is used.

5. All variables have an lvalue and an rvalue. The lvalue is the address of the variable and the rvalue is the contents of the variable. Programmers typically use variable names to reference the variable's contents (its rvalue) while computers typically use a variable's name to reference its address (lvalue). The address operator, &, can be used to obtain a variable's lvalue.

6. A pointer is a variable that is used to store the address of another variable. Pointers, like all C variables, must be declared. The indirection operator, *, is used both to declare a pointer variable and to access the variable whose address is stored in a pointer.

7. The `scanf()` function is a standard library function used for data input. `scanf()` requires a control string and a list of addresses. The general form of this function call is

```
scanf("control string", &arg1, &arg2, . . . , &argn);
```

The control string can only contain control sequences, such as %d, and must contain the same number of control sequences as argument addresses.

8. Each compiled C program is automatically passed through a preprocessor. Lines beginning with # in the first column are recognized as commands to this preprocessor. Preprocessor commands are not terminated with a semicolon.

9. Expressions can be made equivalent to a single identifier using the preprocessor define command. This command has the form

```
#define      identifier      expression
```

and allows the identifier to be used instead of the expression anywhere in the program after the command. Generally, a define command is placed at the top of a C program.

Flow of Control

Part Two

Selection

Chapter Four

The term *flow of control* refers to the order in which a program's statements are executed. Unless directed otherwise, the normal flow of control for all programs is *sequential*. This means that each statement is executed in sequence, one after another, in the order in which they are placed within the program.

Both selection and repetition statements allow the programmer to alter the normal sequential flow of control. As their names imply, *selection statements* provide the ability to select which statement will be executed next, while *repetition statements* provide the ability to go back and repeat a set of statements. In this chapter we present C's selection statements. Since selection requires choosing between alternatives, we begin this chapter with a description of C's selection criteria.

4.1 Relational Expressions

Besides providing addition, subtraction, multiplication, and division capabilities, all computers have the ability to compare numbers. Because many seemingly "intelligent" decision-making situations can be reduced to the level of choosing between two values, a computer's comparison capability can be used to create a remarkable intelligencelike facility.

The expressions used to compare operands are called *relational expressions*. A *simple* relational expression consists of a relational operator connecting two variable and/or constant operands, as shown in Figure 4-1. The relational operators available in C are given in Table 4-1. These relational operators may be used with integer, float, double, or character data, but must be typed exactly as given in Table 4-1. Thus, while the following examples are all valid:

```
age > 40        length <= 50      temp > 98.6
  3 < 4         flag == done      id_num == 682
day != 5        2.0 > 3.3         hours > 40
```

the following are invalid:

```
length =< 50       /* operator out of order  */
2.0 >> 3.3         /* invalid operator        */
flag = = done      /* spaces are not allowed */
```

FIGURE 4-1 Anatomy of a Simple Relational Expression

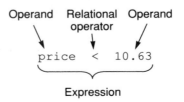

TABLE 4-1

Relational operator	Meaning	Example
<	less than	age < 30
>	greater than	height > 6.2
<=	less than or equal to	taxable <= 20000
>=	greater than or equal to	temp >= 98.6
==	equal to	grade == 100
!=	not equal to	number != 250

Relational expressions are sometimes called *conditions*, and we will use both terms to refer to these expressions. Like all C expressions, relational expressions are evaluated to yield a numerical result. In the case of relational expressions, the value of the expression can only be an integer value of 1 or 0. A condition that we would interpret as true evaluates to an integer value of 1, and a false condition results in an integer value of 0. For example, because the relationship 3 < 4 is always true, this expression has a value of 1, and because the relationship 2.0 > 3.3 is always false, the value of the expression itself is 0. This can be verified using the statements

```
printf("The value of 3 < 4 is %d", 3 < 4);
printf("\nThe value of 2.0 > 3.0 is %d", 2.0 > 3.3);
```

which results in the display

```
The value of 3 < 4 is 1
The value of 2.0 > 3.0 is 0
```

The value of a relational expression such as hours > 0 depends on the value stored in the variable hours.

In a C program, a relational expression's value is not as important as the interpretation C places on the value when the expression is used as part of a selection statement. In these statements, which are presented in the next section, we will see that a zero value is used by C to represent a false condition and any nonzero value is used to represent a true condition. The selection of which statement to execute next is then based on the value obtained.

In addition to numerical operands, character data can also be compared using relational operators. For example, in the ASCII code the letter 'A' is stored using a code having a lower numerical value than the letter 'B', the code for a 'B' is lower in value than the code for a 'C', and so on. For character sets coded in this manner, the following conditions are evaluated as listed.

Expression	Value	Interpretation
`'A' > 'C'`	0	False
`'D' <= 'Z'`	1	True
`'E' == 'F'`	0	False
`'G' >= 'M'`	0	False
`'B' != 'C'`	1	True

Comparing letters is essential in alphabetizing names or using characters to select a particular choice in decision-making situations.

Logical Operators

In addition to using simple relational expressions as conditions, more complex conditions can be created using the *logical operators* AND, OR, and NOT. These operators are represented by the symbols &&, ||, and !, respectively.

When the AND operator, &&, is used with two simple expressions, the condition is true only if both single expressions are true by themselves. Thus, the compound condition

$$age > 40 \text{ && } term < 10$$

is true (has a value of 1) only if age is greater than 40 and term is less than 10.

The logical OR operator, ||, is also applied between two expressions. When using the OR operator, the condition is satisfied if either one or both of the two expressions is true. Thus, the compound condition

$$age > 40 \text{ || } term < 10$$

will be true if either age is greater than 40, term is less than 10, or both conditions are true.

For the declarations

```
int i,j;
float a,b,complete;
```

the following represent valid conditions:

```
a > b
i == j || a < b || complete
a/b > 5 && i <= 20
```

Before these conditions can be evaluated, the values of a, b, i, j, and complete must be known. Assuming

a = 12.0, b = 2.0, i = 15, j = 30, and complete = 0.0

the previous expressions yield the following results:

Expression	Value	Interpretation
a > b	1	True
i == j || a < b || complete	0	False
a/b > 5 && i <= 20	1	True

The NOT operator is used to change an expression to its opposite state; that is, if the expression has any nonzero value (true), !*expression* produces a zero value (false). If an expression is false to begin with (has a zero value), !*expression* is true and evaluates to 1. For example, assuming the number 26 is stored in the variable age, the expression age > 40 has a value of zero (it is false), while the expression !(age > 40) has a value of 1. Since the NOT operator is used with only one expression, it is a unary operator.

The relational and logical operators have a hierarchy of execution similar to the arithmetic operators. Table 4-2 lists the precedence of these operators in relation to the other operators we have used.

TABLE 4-2

Operator	Associativity	Precedence
! unary - ++ --	right to left	highest
* / %	left to right	
+ -	left to right	
< <= > >=	left to right	
== !=	left to right	
&&	left to right	
||	left to right	
+= -= *= /=	right to left	lowest

The following example illustrates the use of an operator's precedence and associativity to evaluate relational expressions, assuming the following declarations:

```
char key = 'm';
int i = 5, j = 7, k = 12;
double x = 22.5;
```

Expression	Equivalent Expression	Value	Interpretation
i + 2 == k -1	(i + 2) == (k - 1)	0	False
3 * i - j < 22	((3 * i) - j) < 22	1	True
i + 2 * j > k	(i + (2 * j)) > k	1	True
k + 3 <= -j + 3 * i	(k + 3) <= ((-j) + (3*i))	0	False
'a' + 1 == 'b'	('a' + 1) == 'b'	1	True
key - 1 > 'p'	(key - 1) > 'p'	0	False
key + 1 == 'n'	(key + 1) == 'n'	1	True
25 >= x + 4.0	25 >= (x + 4.0)	0	False

As with all expressions, parentheses can be used to alter the assigned operator priority and improve the readability of relational expressions. By evaluating the expressions within parentheses first, the following compound condition is evaluated as:

```
(6 * 3 == 36 / 2)  ||  (13 < 3 * 3 + 4)  && !(6 - 2 < 5)
       (18 == 18)  ||      (13 < 9 + 4)  && !(4 < 5)
                1  ||         (13 < 13)  && !1
                1  ||             0       && 0
                1  ||             0
                1
```

Exercises 4.1

1. Determine the value of the following expressions. Assume a = 5, b = 2, c = 4, d = 6, and e = 3.

a. a > b
b. a != b
c. d % b == c % b
d. a * c != d * b
e. d * b == c * e

f. a * b
g. a % b * c
h. c % b * a
i. b % c * a

2. Using parentheses, rewrite the following expressions to correctly indicate their order of evaluation. Then evaluate each expression assuming a = 5, b = 2, and c = 4.

a. a % b * c && c % b * a
b. a % b * c || c % b * a

c. b % c * a && a % c * b
d. b % c * a || a % c * b

3. Write relational expressions to express the following conditions (use variable names of your own choosing):

a. a person's age is equal to 30
b. a person's temperature is greater than 98.6

    c. a person's height is less than 6 feet
    d. the current month is 12 (December)
    e. the letter input is *m*
    f. a person's age is equal to 30 and the person is taller than 6 feet
    g. the current day is the 15th day of the 1st month
    h. a person is older than 50 or has been employed at the company for at least 5 years
    i. a person's identification number is less than 500 and the person is older than 55
    j. a length is greater than 2 feet and less than 3 feet

4. Determine the value of the following expressions, assuming a = 5, b = 2, c = 4, and d = 5.

    a. `a == 5`
    b. `b * d == c * c`
    c. `d % b * c > 5 || c % b * d < 7`

4.2   The if-else Statement

The if-else statement directs the computer to select a sequence of one or more instructions based on the result of a comparison. For example, if a New Jersey resident's income is less than $20,000, the applicable state tax rate is 2 percent. If the person's income is greater than $20,000, a different rate is applied to the amount over $20,000. The if-else statement can be used in this situation to determine the actual tax based on whether the gross income is less than or equal to $20,000. The general form of the if-else statement is

```
if (expression) statement1;
else statement2;
```

The expression is evaluated first. If the value of the expression is nonzero, *statement1* is executed. If the value is zero the statement after the reserved word else is executed. Thus, one of the two statements (either *statement1* or *statement2*) is always executed depending on the value of the expression. Notice that the tested expression must be put in parentheses and a semicolon is placed after each statement.

    For clarity, the if-else statement may also be written on four lines using the form

```
if (expression)  ←──────── no semicolon here
    statement1;
else  ←──────────────────  no semicolon here
    statement2;
```

    The form of the if-else statement that is selected generally depends on the length of statements 1 and 2. However, when using the second form do not put a semicolon after the parentheses or the reserved word else. The semicolons go only after the ends of the statements.

As an example, let us write an income tax computation program containing an if-else statement. As previously described, a New Jersey state income tax is assessed at 2 percent of taxable income for incomes less than or equal to $20,000. For taxable income greater than $20,000, state taxes are 2.5 percent of the income that exceeds $20,000 plus a fixed amount of $400. The expression to be tested is whether taxable income is less than or equal to $20,000. An appropriate if-else statement for this situation is:

```
if (taxable <= 20000.0)
   taxes = .02 * taxable;
else
   taxes = .025 * (taxable - 20000.0) + 400.0;
```

Here we have used the relational operator <= to represent the relation "less than or equal to." If the value of taxable is less than or equal to 20000, the condition is true (has a value of 1) and the statement taxes = .02 * taxable; is executed. If the condition is not true, the value of the expression is zero, and the statement after the reserved word else is executed. Program 4-1 illustrates the use of this statement in a complete program.

 Program 4-1

```
main()
{
  float taxable, taxes;

  printf("Please type in the taxable income: ");
  scanf("%f",&taxable);

  if (taxable <= 20000.0)
    taxes = .02 * taxable;
  else
    taxes = .025 * (taxable - 20000.0) + 400.0;

  printf("Taxes are $%7.2f",taxes);
}
```

A blank line was inserted before and after the if-else statement to highlight it in the complete program. We will continue to do this throughout the text to emphasize the statement being presented.

To illustrate selection in action, Program 4-1 was run twice with different input data. The results are:

```
Please type in the taxable income: 10000.
Taxes are $ 200.00
```

and

```
Please type in the taxable income: 30000.
Taxes are $ 650.00
```

Observe that the taxable income input in the first run of the program was less than $20,000, and the tax was correctly calculated as 2 percent of the number entered. In the second run, the taxable income was more than $20,000, and the else part of the if-else statement was used to yield a correct tax computation of

```
.025 * ($30,000. - $20,000.) + $400. = $650.
```

Although any expression can be tested by an if-else statement, generally only relational expressions are used. However, statements such as

```
if (num)
   printf("Bingo!");
else
   printf("You lose!");
```

are valid. Since num, by itself, is a valid expression, the message Bingo! is displayed if num has any nonzero value and the message You lose! is displayed if num has a value of zero.

Compound Statements

Although only a single statement is permitted in both the if and else parts of the if-else statement, this statement can be a single compound statement. A *compound statement* is any number of single statements contained between braces, as shown in Figure 4-2. The use of braces to enclose a set of individual

FIGURE 4-2 A Compound Statement Consists of Individual Statements Enclosed Within Braces

```
{
   statement1;
   statement2;
   statement3;
       .
       .
       .
   last statement;
}
```

statements creates a single block of statements, which may be used anywhere in a C program in place of a single statement. The next example illustrates the use of a compound statement within the general form of an `if-else` statement.

```
if (expression)
{
   statement1;    /* as many statements as necessary  */
   statement2;    /* can be put within the braces      */
   statement3;    /* each statement must end with a ;  */
}
else
{
   statement4;
   statement5;
      .
      .
   statementn;
}
```

Program 4-2 illustrates the use of a compound statement in an actual program.

 Program 4-2

```
main()
{
  char temp_type;
  float temp, fahren, celsius;

  printf("Enter the temperature to be converted: ");
  scanf("%f",&temp);
  printf("Enter an f if the temperature is in Fahrenheit");
  printf("\n or a c if the temperature is in Celsius: ");
  scanf("\n%c",&temp_type);        \* see footnote on page 106 *\

  if (temp_type == 'f')
  {
    celsius = (5.0 / 9.0) * (temp - 32.0);
    printf("\nThe equivalent Celsius temperature is %6.2f", celsius);
  }
  else
  {
    fahren = (9.0 / 5.0) * temp + 32.0;
    printf("\nThe equivalent Fahrenheit temperature is %6.2f", fahren);
  }

}
```

Program 4-2 checks whether the value in temp_type is f. If the value is f, the compound statement corresponding to the if part of the if-else statement is executed. Any other letter results in execution of the compound statement corresponding to the else part. Following is a sample run of Program 4-2.

```
Enter the temperature to be converted: 212
Enter an f if the temperature is in Fahrenheit
   or a c if the temperature is in Celsius: f

The equivalent Celsius temperature is 100.00
```

One-Way Selection

A useful modification of the if-else statement involves omitting the else part of the statement altogether. In this case, the if statement takes the shortened and frequently useful form:

```
if (expression)
     statement;
```

The statement following the if (*expression*) is only executed if the expression has a nonzero value (a true condition). As before, the statement may be a compound statement.

This modified form of the if statement is called a *one-way* if *statement*. It is illustrated in Program 4-3, which checks a car's mileage and prints a message if the car has been driven more than 3000.0 miles.

 Program 4-3

```
#define LIMIT 3000.0
main()
{
  int id_num;
  float miles;

  printf("Please type in car number and mileage: ");
  scanf("%d %f", &id_num, &miles);

  if(miles > LIMIT)
    printf("  Car %d is over the limit.\n",id_num);

  printf("End of program output.\n");
}
```

To illustrate the one-way selection criteria in action, Program 4-3 was run twice, each time with different input data. Only the input data for the first run causes the message `Car 256 is over the limit` to be displayed.

```
Please type in car number and mileage: 256 3562.8
   Car 256 is over the limit.
End of program output.
```

and

```
Please type in car number and mileage: 23 2562.3
End of program output.
```

Exercises 4.2

1. Rewrite Program 4-1 using the following equivalence statements:

```
#define LIMIT 20000
#define REGRATE .02
#define HIGHRATE .025
#define FIXED 400
```

(If necessary, review Section 3.5 for the use of the `define` statement.)

2. a. If money is left in a particular bank for more than 5 years, the interest rate given by the bank is 9.5 percent, else the interest rate is 5.4 percent. Write a C program that uses the `scanf()` function to accept the number of years into the variable `num_yrs` and display the appropriate interest rate depending on the value input into `num_yrs`.
b. How many runs should you make for the program written in Exercise 2a to verify that it is operating correctly? What data should you input in each of the program runs?

3. a. In a pass/fail course, a student passes if the grade is greater than or equal to 70 and fails if the grade is lower. Write a C program that accepts a grade and prints the message `A passing grade` or `A failing grade`, as appropriate.
b. How many runs should you make for the program written in Exercise 3a to verify that it is operating correctly? What data should you input in each of the program runs?

4. a. Write a C program to compute and display a person's weekly salary as determined by the following expressions:

If the hours worked are less than or equal to 40, the person receives $8.00 per hour; else the person receives $320.00 plus $12.00 for each hour worked over 40 hours.

The program should request the hours worked as input and should display the salary as output.
b. How many runs should you make for the program written in Exercise 4a to verify that it is operating correctly? What data should you input in each of the program runs?

5. a. A senior salesperson is paid $400 a week and a junior salesperson $275 a week. Write a C program that accepts as input a salesperson's status in the character variable status. If status equals 's', the senior person's salary should be displayed, else the junior person's salary should be output.

b. How many runs should you make for the program written in Exercise 5a to verify that it is operating correctly? What data should you input in each of the program runs?

6. a. Write a program that displays either the message I feel great today! or I feel down today #$*! depending on the input. If the character u is entered in the variable ch, the first message should be displayed, else the second message should be displayed.

b. How many runs should you make for the program written in Exercise 6a to verify that it is operating correctly? What data should you input in each of the program runs?

7. a. Write a program to display the following two prompts:

```
Enter a month (use a 1 for Jan, etc.):
Enter a day of the month:
```

Have your program accept and store a number in the variable month in response to the first prompt, and accept and store a number in the variable day in response to the second prompt.

If the month entered is not between 1 and 12 inclusive, print a message informing the user that an invalid month has been entered.

If the day entered is not between 1 and 31, print a message informing the user that an invalid day has been entered.

b. What will your program do if the user types a number with a decimal point for the month? How can you insure that your if statements check for an integer number?

8. Write a C program that accepts a character using the scanf() function and determines if the character is a lowercase letter. A lowercase letter is any character that is greater than or equal to 'a' and less than or equal to 'z'. If the entered character is a lowercase letter, display the message The character just entered is a lowercase letter. If the entered letter is not lowercase, display the message The character just entered is not a lowercase letter.

9. Write a C program that first determines if an entered character is a lowercase letter (see Exercise 8). If the letter is lowercase, determine and print out its position in the alphabet. For example, if the entered letter is c, the program should print out 3, since c is the third letter in the alphabet. (*Hint:* If the entered character is in lowercase, its position can be determined by subtracting 'a' from the letter and adding 1.)

10. Repeat Exercise 8 to determine if the character entered is an uppercase letter. An uppercase letter is any character greater than or equal to 'A' and less than or equal to 'Z'.

11. Write a C program that first determines if an entered character is an uppercase letter (see Exercise 10). If the letter is uppercase, determine and print its position in the alphabet. For example, if the entered letter is G, the program should print out 7, since G is the seventh letter in the alphabet. (*Hint:* If the entered character is in uppercase, its position can be determined by subtracting 'A' from the letter and adding 1.)

12. Write a C program that accepts a character using the scanf() function. If the character is a lowercase letter (see Exercise 8), convert the letter to uppercase and display the letter in its uppercase form. (*Hint:* Subtracting the integer value 32 from a lowercase letter yields the code for the equivalent uppercase letter. Thus, 'A' = 'a' - 32.)

13. The following program displays the message `Hello there!` regardless of the letter input. Determine where the error is and, if possible, why the program always causes the message to be displayed.

```
main()
{
  char letter;

  printf("Enter a letter: ");
  scanf("%c",&letter);
  if (letter = 'm') printf("Hello there!");
}
```

14. Write a C program that asks the user to input two numbers. After your program accepts these numbers using one or more `scanf()` function calls, have your program check the numbers. If the first number entered is greater than the second number, print the message `The first number is greater`, else print the message `The first number is not greater than the second`. Test your program by entering the numbers 5 and 8 and then using the numbers 11 and 2. What will your program display if the two numbers entered are equal?

4.3   Nested `if` Statements

As we have seen, an `if-else` statement can contain simple or compound statements. Any valid C statement can be used, including another `if-else` statement. Thus, one or more `if-else` statements can be included within either part of an `if-else` statement. For example, substituting the one-way `if` statement

```
if (hours > 6)
    printf("snap");
```

for *statement1* in the following `if` statement

```
if (hours < 9)
    statement1;
else
    printf("pop");
```

results in the nested `if` statement

```
if (hours < 9)
{
  if (hours > 6)
    printf("snap");
}
else
    printf("pop");
```

The braces around the inner one-way if are essential, because in their absence C associates an else with the closest unpaired if. Thus, without the braces, the above statement is equivalent to

```
if (hours < 9)
   if (hours > 6)
      printf("snap");
   else
      printf("pop");
```

Here the else is paired with the inner if, which destroys the meaning of the original if-else statement. Notice also that the indentation is irrelevant as far as the compiler is concerned. Whether the indentation exists or not, the statement is compiled by associating the last else with the closest unpaired if, unless braces are used to alter the default pairing.

The process of *nesting* if statements can be extended indefinitely, so that the printf("snap"); statement could itself be replaced by either a complete if-else statement or another one-way if statement.

The if-else Chain

Generally, the case where the statement in the if part of an if-else statement is another if statement tends to be confusing and is best avoided. However, an extremely useful construction occurs when the else part of an if statement contains another if-else statement. This takes the form:

```
if (expression_1)
   statement1;
else
   if (expression_2)
      statement2;
   else
      statement3;
```

As with all C programs, the indentation we have used is not required. In fact, the above construction is so common that it is typically written using the following arrangement:

```
if (expression_1)
   statement1;
else if (expression_2)
   statement2;
else
   statement3;
```

This construction is called an if-else *chain*. It is used extensively in applications programs. Each condition is evaluated in order, and if any condition is true the corresponding statement is executed and the remainder of the chain is terminated. The final else statement is only executed if none of the previous conditions are satisfied. This serves as a default or catch-all case that is useful for detecting an impossible or error condition.

The chain can be continued indefinitely by repeatedly making the last statement another if-else statement. Thus, the general form of an if-else chain is:

```
if (expression_1)
   statement1;
else if (expression_2)
   statement2;
else if (expression_3)
   statement3;

      .

      .

      .

else if (expression_n)
   statement_n;
else
   last_statement;
```

As with all C statements, each individual statement can be a compound statement bounded by the braces { and }. To illustrate the if-else chain, Program 4-4 displays a person's marital status corresponding to a letter input. The following letter codes are used:

Marital Status	Input Code
Married	M
Single	S
Divorced	D
Widowed	W

 Program 4-4

```
main()
{
  char marcode;

    printf("Enter a marital code: ");
    scanf("%c", &marcode);

    if (marcode == 'M')
      printf("\nIndividual is married.");
    else if (marcode == 'S')
      printf("\nIndividual is single.");
```

continued

```
      else if (marcode == 'D')
        printf("\nIndividual is divorced.");
      else if (marcode == 'W')
        printf("\nIndividual is widowed.");
      else
        printf("An invalid code was entered.");
  }
```

As a final example illustrating the `if-else` chain, let us calculate the monthly income of a salesperson using the following commission schedule:

Monthly Sales	Income
greater than or equal to $50,000	$375 plus 16% of sales
less than $50,000 but greater than or equal to $40,000	$350 plus 14% of sales
less than $40,000 but greater than or equal to $30,000	$325 plus 12% of sales
less than $30,000 but greater than or equal to $20,000	$300 plus 9% of sales
less than $20,000 but greater than or equal to $10,000	$250 plus 5% of sales
less than $10,000	$200 plus 3% of sales

The following `if-else` chain can be used to determine the correct monthly income, where the variable `mon_sales` is used to store the salesperson's current monthly sales:

```
if (mon_sales >= 50000.00)
  income = 375.00 + .16 * mon_sales;
else if (mon_sales >= 40000.00)
  income = 350.00 + .14 * mon_sales;
else if (mon_sales >= 30000.00)
  income = 325.00 + .12 * mon_sales;
else if (mon_sales >= 20000.00)
  income = 300.00 + .09 * mon_sales;
else if (mon_sales >= 10000.00)
  income = 250.00 + .05 * mon_sales;
else
  income = 200.000 + .03 * mon_sales;
```

Notice that this example makes use of the fact that the chain is stopped once a true condition is found. This is accomplished by checking for the highest monthly sales first. If the salesperson's monthly sales are less than $50,000, the if-else chain continues checking for the next highest sales amount until the correct category is obtained.

Program 4-5 uses this if-else chain to calculate and display the income corresponding to the value of monthly sales input in the scanf() function.

 Program 4-5

```
main()
{
    float mon_sales, income;

    printf("Enter the value of monthly sales: ");
    scanf("%f", &mon_sales);

    if (mon_sales >= 50000.00)
        income = 375.00 + .16 * mon_sales;
    else if (mon_sales >= 40000.00)
        income = 350.00 + .14 * mon_sales;
    else if (mon_sales >= 30000.00)
        income = 325.00 + .12 * mon_sales;
    else if (mon_sales >= 20000.00)
        income = 300.00 + .09 * mon_sales;
    else if (mon_sales >= 10000.00)
        income = 250.00 + .05 * mon_sales;
    else
        income = 200.00 + .03 * mon_sales;
    printf("The income is $%7.2f",income);
}
```

A sample run using Program 4-5 is illustrated below.

```
Enter the value of monthly sales: 36243.89
The income is $4674.27
```

Exercises 4.3

1. A student's letter grade is calculated according to the following schedule. Write a C program that accepts a student's numerical grade, converts the numerical grade to an equivalent letter grade, and displays the letter grade.

Numerical grade	Letter grade
greater than or equal to 90	A
less than 90 but greater than or equal to 80	B
less than 80 but greater than or equal to 70	C
less than 70 but greater than or equal to 60	D
less than 60	F

2. The interest rate used on funds deposited in a bank is determined by the amount of time the money is left on deposit. For a particular bank, the following schedule is used. Write a C program that accepts the time that funds are left on deposit and displays the interest rate corresponding to the time entered.

Time on deposit	Interest rate
greater than or equal to 5 years	.095
less than 5 years but greater than or equal to 4 years	.09
less than 4 years but greater than or equal to 3 years	.085
less than 3 years but greater than or equal to 2 years	.075
less than 2 years but greater than or equal to 1 year	.065
less than 1 year	.058

3. Write a C program that accepts a number followed by one space and then a letter. If the letter following the number is `f`, the program is to treat the number entered as a temperature in degrees Fahrenheit, convert the number to the equivalent degrees Celsius, and print a suitable display message. If the letter following the number is `c`, the program is to treat the number entered as a temperature in Celsius, convert the number to the equivalent degrees Fahrenheit, and print a suitable display message. If the letter is neither `f` nor `c` the program is to print a message that the data entered is incorrect and terminate. Use an `if-else` chain in your program and make use of the conversion formulas:

$$\text{Celsius} = (5.0 \ / \ 9.0) * (\text{Fahrenheit} - 32.0)$$
$$\text{Fahrenheit} = (9.0 \ / \ 5.0) * \text{Celsius} + 32.0$$

4. Using the commission schedule from Program 4-5, the following program calculates monthly income:

```
main()
{
  float mon_sales, income;

  printf("Enter the value of monthly sales: ");
  scanf("%f", &mon_sales);

  if (mon_sales >= 50000.00)
    income = 375.00 + .16 * mon_sales;
  if (mon_sales >= 40000.00 && mon_sales < 50000.00)
    income = 350.00 + .14 * mon_sales;
  if (mon_sales >= 30000.00 && mon_sales < 40000.00)
    income = 325.00 + .12 * mon_sales;
  if (mon_sales >= 20000.00 && mon_sales < 30000.00)
    income = 300.00 + .09 * mon_sales;
  if (mon_sales >= 10000.00 && mon_sales < 20000.00)
    income = 250.00 + .05 * mon_sales;
  if (mon_sales < 10000.00)
    income = 200.00 + .03 * mon_sales;

  printf("\n\nThe income is $%7.2f",income);
}
```

a. Will this program produce the same output as Program 4-5?

b. Which program is better and why?

5. The following program was written to produce the same result as Program 4-5:

```
main()
{
  float mon_sales, income;

  printf("Enter the value of monthly sales: ");
  scanf("%f", &mon_sales);

  if (mon_sales < 10000.00)
    income = 200.00 + .03 * mon_sales;
  else if (mon_sales >= 10000.00)
    income = 250.00 + .05 * mon_sales;
  else if (mon_sales >= 20000.00)
    income = 300.00 + .09 * mon_sales;
  else if (mon_sales >= 30000.00)
    income = 325.00 + .12 * mon_sales;
  else if (mon_sales >= 40000.00)
    income = 350.00 + .14 * mon_sales;
  else if (mon_sales >= 50000.00)
    income = 375.00 + .16 * mon_sales;

  printf("\n\nThe income is $%7.2f",income);
}
```

a. Will this program run?

b. What does this program do?

c. For what values of monthly sales does this program calculate the correct income?

4.4   The switch Statement

The if-else chain is used in programming applications where one set of instructions must be selected from many possible alternatives. The switch statement provides an alternative to the if-else chain for cases that compare the value of an integer expression to a specific value. The general form of a switch statement is

```
switch (expression)
{                         /* start of compound statement */
   case value_1:     ◄─────────────── terminated with a colon
      statement1;
      statement2;
            .
            .
      break;
   case value_2:     ◄─────────────── terminated with a colon
      statementm;
      statementn;
            .
            .
      break;
            .
            .

   case value_n:     ◄─────────────── terminated with a colon
      statementw;
      statementx;
            .
            .

   default:          ◄─────────────── terminated with a colon
      statementaa;
      statementbb;
}                         /* end of switch and compound statement */
```

The switch statement uses four new reserved words: switch, case, default, and break. Let's see what each of these words does.

The reserved word switch identifies the start of the switch statement. The expression in parentheses following this word is evaluated and the result of the expression compared to various alternative values contained within the compound statement. The expression in the switch statement must evaluate to an integer result or a compilation error results.

Internal to the switch statement, the reserved word case is used to identify or label individual values that are compared to the value of the switch

137

expression. The `switch` expression's value is compared to each of these `case` values in the order that these values are listed until a match is found. When a match occurs, execution begins with the statement immediately following the match. Thus, as illustrated in Figure 4-3, the value of the expression determines where in the `switch` statement execution actually begins.

Any number of `case` labels may be contained within a `switch` statement, in any order. If the value of the expression does not match any of the `case` values, however, no statement is executed unless the reserved word `default` is encountered. The word `default` is optional and operates the same as the last `else` in an `if-else` chain. If the value of the expression does not match any of the `case` values, program execution begins with the statement following the word `default`.

Once an entry point has been located by the `switch` statement, no further `case` evaluations are done; all statements that follow within the braces are executed unless a `break` statement is encountered. This is the reason for the `break` statement, which identifies the end of a particular `case` and causes an immediate exit from the `switch` statement. Thus, just as the word `case` identifies possible starting points in the compound statement, the `break` state-

FIGURE 4-3 The Expression Determines an Entry Point

```
                              switch (expression) /* evaluate expression */
                              {
Start here if          ───▶   case value_1:
expression equals value_1            .

                                     .

                                 break;
Start here if          ───▶   case value_2:
expression equals value_2            .

                                     .

                                 break;
Start here if          ───▶   case value_3:
expression equals value_3            .

                                     .

                                 break;
                                 .
                                 .
                                 .
Start here if          ───▶   case value_n:
expression equals value_n            .

                                     .

                                 break;
Start here if no       ───▶   default:
previous match                       .

                                     .

                              }                    /* end of switch statement */
```

ment determines terminating points. If the break statements are omitted, all cases following the matching case value, including the default case, are executed.

When we write a switch statement, we can use multiple case values to refer to the same set of statements; the default label is optional. For example, consider the following:

```
switch (number)
{
  case 1:
    printf("Have a Good Morning");
    break;
  case 2:
    printf("Have a Happy Day");
    break;
  case 3: case 4: case 5:
    printf("Have a Nice Evening");
}
```

If the value stored in t̶h̶e̶ ̶v̶a̶r̶i̶a̶b̶le number is 1, the message Have a Good Morning is displayed. ̶S̶i̶m̶i̶l̶a̶r̶l̶y̶, the value of number is 2, the second message is displayed. Finally, ̶S̶i̶m̶i̶l̶a̶ ̶f̶ number is 3 or 4 or 5, the last message is displayed. Since the ̶i̶f̶ ̶t̶h̶e̶ be executed for these last three cases is the same, the cases ̶s̶t̶a̶t̶e̶ can be "stacked together" as shown in the example. Also, si̶ ̶r̶e̶ ̶i̶default, no message is printed if the value of number is no ̶o̶f̶ ̶t̶h̶e̶ case values. Although it is good programming practice ̶t̶o̶ ̶list case va̶l̶ increasing order, this is not required by the switch state̶m̶ent. A switchment may have any number of case values, in any orde̶r̶ only the values tested for need be listed.

Progra̶m̶ 4-6 uses a swit̶ch̶ statement to select the arithmetic operation (addition, ̶ ̶ ̶multiplication, or di̶v̶) to be performed on two numbers depending on th̶e̶ value of the variabl̶e̶ select.

Program 4-6

```
main ( )
{    int opselect;
  in double fnum, snum;
  d

    printf("Please type in two nu̶m̶bers: ");
    scanf("%lf %lf", &fnum, &snum)
    printf("Enter a select code:")
    printf("\n            1 for additi̶o̶n");
```

continued

```
printf("\n          2 for multiplication");
printf("\n          3 for division : ");
scanf("%d", &opselect);

switch (opselect)
{
   case 1:
     printf("The sum of the numbers entered is %6.3lf", fnum+snum);
     break;
   case 2:
     printf("The product of the numbers entered is %6.3lf",fnum*snum);
     break;
   case 3:
     printf("The first number divided by the second is %6.3lf",fnum/snum);
     break;
}     /* end of switch */

}   /* end of main() */
```

Program 4-6 was run twice. The result*play clearl*y identifies the case selected. The results are:

```
Please type in two numb 12 3
Enter a select code:
        1 for additio
        2 for multipli on
        3 for divisio 2
The product of the numb entered is  3
```

and

```
Please type in two numbe 12 3
Enter a select code:
        1 for addition
        2 for multipli on
        3 for division 3
The first number divided the second is   4.000
```

In reviewing Program 4-6, notice t break statement in the last case. Although this break is not necessary, it a good practice to terminate the case. last case in a switch statement with a brk. This prevents a possible progam last error later, if an additional case is subsecntly added to the switch statement ram With the addition of a new case, the eak between cases becomes necessary; having the break in place ensure ou will not forget to include it at the time of the modification.

Since character data types are always converted to integers in an expression, a `switch` statement can also be used to "switch" based on the value of a character expression. For example, assuming that `choice` is a character variable, the following `switch` statement is valid:

```
switch (choice)
{
  case 'a': case 'e': case 'i': case 'o': case 'u':
    printf("\nThe character in choice is a vowel");
    break;
  default:
    printf("\nThe character in choice is not a vowel");
    break;      /* this break is optional */
}    /* end of switch statement */
```

Exercises 4.4

1. Rewrite the following `if-else` chain using a `switch` statement:

```
if (let_grad == 'A')
  printf("The numerical grade is between 90 and 100");
else if (let_grad == 'B')
  printf("The numerical grade is between 80 and 89.9");
else if (let_grad == 'C')
  printf("The numerical grade is between 70 and 79.9");
else if (let_grad == 'D');
  printf("How are you going to explain this one");
else
{
  printf("Of course I had nothing to do with my grade.");
  printf("\nThe professor was really off the wall.");
}
```

2. Rewrite the following `if-else` chain using a `switch` statement:

```
if (bond_typ == 1)
  {
    in_data();
    check();
  }
else if (bond_typ == 2)
{
  dates();
  leap_yr();
}
```

continued

```
else if (bond_typ == 3)
{
  yield();
  maturity();
}
else if (bond_typ == 4)
{
  price();
  roi();
}
else if (bond_typ == 5)
{
  files();
  save();
}
else if (bond_typ == 6)
{
  retrieve();
  screen();
}
```

3. Rewrite Program 4-4 in Section 4.3 using a `switch` statement.

4. Determine why the `if-else` chain in Program 4-5 cannot be replaced with a `switch` statement.

5. Repeat Exercise 3 in Section 4.3 using a `switch` statement instead of an `if-else` chain.

6. Rewrite Program 4-6 using a character variable for the select code. (*Hint:* Review Section 3.4 if your program does not operate as you think it should.)

4.5 Common Programming Errors

There are four programming errors common to C's selection statements. The most common of these errors results from the fact that any expression in C can be tested by an `if` statement. Thus, if a relational expression is mistyped but results in some other legitimate C expression, the tested expression is valid even though unintended. A common example of this is the inadvertent substitution of the assignment operator, =, for the relational operator, ==. For example, the `if` statement

```
if (age = 40)
    printf("Happy Birthday!");
```

always causes the `Happy Birthday!` message to be displayed. Can you see why? The tested condition does not compare the value in `age` to the number 40, but assigns the number 40 to the variable `age`. The expression `age = 40` is not a relational expression at all, but an assignment expression. At the completion of the assignment, the expression itself has a value of 40. Since C treats any nonzero value as true, the call to printf() is made. Another way of looking at this is to realize that the if statement is equivalent to the following two statements:

```
age = 40;          /* assign 40 to age */
if (age)           /* test the value of age */
   printf("Happy Birthday!");
```

Since the C compiler has no means of knowing that the expression being tested is not the desired one, you must be especially careful when writing conditions.

A second common error is a typical debugging problem that can surface whenever an expression is evaluated and yields an unexpected result. Here the problem resides in the values assigned to the variables used in the expression rather than in the expression itself. With selection statements this takes the form of not executing the expected statement and the programmer concentrates on the selection statement as the source of the problem instead of the values assigned to the tested variables. For example, assume that the following one-way if statement is part of your program:

```
if (key == 'a') printf(" Got an a! ");
```

This statement will always display Got an a! when the variable key contains an a. Therefore, if the message is not displayed when you think it should be, investigation of key's value is called for. As a general rule, whenever a selection statement does not act as you think it should, make sure to test your assumptions about the values assigned to the tested variables. A useful method of doing this is to use printf() to display the values of all relevant variables. If an unanticipated value is displayed, you have at least isolated the source of the problem to the variables themselves, rather than the structure of the if statement. From there you will have to determine where and how the incorrect value was assigned.

A third source of error occurs when nested if statements are used and braces are not included to clearly indicate the desired structure. Without braces the compiler defaults to pairing elses with the closest unpaired ifs, which sometimes destroys the original intent of the selection statement. To avoid this problem and to create code that is readily adaptable to change it is useful to write all if-else statements as compound statements in the form

```
if (expression)
{
   one or more statements in here

}
else
{
   one or more statements in here
}
```

By using this form, no matter how many statements are added later, the original integrity and intent of the `if` statement is maintained.

The last error common to selection statements is a subtle one and is really a numerical accuracy problem relating to floating point and double precision numbers. Due to the way computers store these values, an expression such as `value == .1` should be avoided. Since decimal numbers like .1 cannot be represented perfectly in binary using a finite number of bits, testing for exact equality for such numbers can fail. To avoid the problem, the equality operator should not be used with floating point or double precision operands; an equivalent test requiring that the absolute value of the difference between operands be less than some small value should be used. This ensures that slight inaccuracies in representing floating point or double precision numbers in binary do not affect the evaluation of the tested expression.

4.6 Chapter Summary

1. Relational expressions are used to compare operands. If a relational expression is true, the value of the expression is the integer 1. If the relational expression is false, it has an integer value of 0.

2. `if-else` statements are used to select between two alternative statements based on the value of an expression. Although relational expressions are usually used for the tested expression, any valid expression can be used. In testing an expression, `if-else` statements interpret a nonzero value as true and a zero value as false.

3. `if-else` statements can contain other `if-else` statements. In the absence of braces, each `else` is associated with the closest unpaired `if`.

4. A compound statement consists of any number of individual statements enclosed within the brace pair { and }. Compound statements are treated as a single unit and can be used anywhere a single statement is called for.

5. The `switch` statement provides a multidirectional decision branch equivalent to an `if-else` chain. For this statement the value of an integer expression is compared to a number of integer or character constants or constant expressions. Program execution is transferred to the first matching `case` and continues through the end of the `switch` statement unless an optional `break` statement is encountered. `cases` in a `switch` statement can appear in any order and an optional `default` case can be included. The `default` case is executed if none of the other `cases` is matched.

4.7   Chapter Supplement: Errors, Testing, and Debugging

The ideal in programming is to efficiently produce readable, error-free programs that work correctly and can be modified or changed with minimum testing required for reverification. In this regard, it is useful to know the different errors that can occur, how to detect them, and how to correct them.

Compile-Time and Run-Time Errors

A program error can be detected in a variety of ways:

1. Before a program is compiled
2. While the program is being compiled
3. While it is being run
4. After the program has been executed and the output is being examined
5. Not at all.

Errors detected by the compiler are formally referred to as *compile-time* errors, and errors that occur while the program is being run are formally referred to as *run-time* errors.

There are methods for detecting errors both before a program is compiled and after it has been executed. The method for detecting errors after a program has been executed is called *program verification and testing*. The method for detecting errors before a program is compiled is called desk checking. *Desk checking* refers to the procedure of checking a program, by hand, at a desk or table for syntax and logic errors, which are described next.

Syntax and Logic Errors

Computer literature distinguishes between two primary types of errors, called syntax and logic errors. A *syntax* error is an error in the structure or spelling of a statement. For example the statement

```
if ( a lt b
{
   pintf("There are four syntax errors here\n")
   printf(" Can you find tem");
}
```

contains four syntax errors. These errors are:

1. The relational operator in the first line is incorrect, and should be the symbol <

2. The closing parenthesis is missing in line one

3. The function name `printf` is misspelled in the third line

4. The third line is missing the terminating semicolon (`;`)

All these errors will be detected by the compiler when the program is compiled. This is true of all syntax errors—since they violate the basic rules of C, if they are not discovered by desk checking, the compiler will detect them and display an error message indicating that a syntax error exists.* In some cases, the error message is clear and the error is obvious, and, in other cases, it takes a little detective work to understand the error message displayed by the compiler. Since all syntax errors are detected at compile time, the terms, compile-time and syntax errors, are often used interchangeably. Strictly speaking, however, compile-time refers to when the error was detected and syntax refers to the type of error detected.

Note that the misspelling of the word `tem` in the second `printf()` function call is not a syntax error. As far as the compiler is concerned, the second `printf()` statement satisfies all of the syntactical requirements for a valid `printf()` statement. This spelling error is a simple example of a logic error.

Logic errors are characterized by erroneous, unexpected, or unintentional errors resulting from a flaw in the program's logic. These errors, which are never caught by the compiler, may be detected by desk checking, by program testing, by accident when a user obtains an obviously erroneous output, or while the program is executing. In this latter case, a run-time error occurs that results in an error message being generated and/or abnormal and premature program termination.

Since logic errors may not be detected by the computer, they are always more difficult to detect than syntax errors. If not detected by desk checking, a logic error will reveal itself in two ways. In one instance, the program executes to completion but produces incorrect results. An example of this is the misspelling of the word `tem` in the code illustrated previously. Generally, logic errors of this type include:

No output. This is either caused by an omission of a `printf()` statement or a sequence of statements that inadvertently bypasses a `printf()` function call.

Unappealing or misaligned output. This is always caused by an error in a `printf()` statement.

Incorrect numerical results. This is caused either by incorrect values assigned to the variables used in an expression, the use of an incorrect arithmetic expression, an omission of a statement, roundoff error, or the use of an improper sequence of statements.

---

* They may not, however, all be detected at the same time. Frequently, one syntax error "masks" another error and the second error is only detected after the first error is corrected.

See if you can detect the logic error in Program 4-7.

 Program 4-7

```
#include <math.h>
main()     /* a compound interest program */
{
   int nyears;
   float capital, amount, rate
   printf("This program calculates the amount of money"\n);
   printf("in a bank account for an initial deposit\n");
   printf("invested for n years at an interest rate r.\n\n");
   printf("Enter the initial amount in the account: ");
   scanf("%f", &amount);
   printf("Enter the interest rate (ex. 5 for 5%): ");
   scanf("%f", &rate);
   capital = amount * pow( (1 + rate/100.), nyears)
   printf("\nThe final amount of money is $%8.2f", capital);
}
```

Following is a sample run of Program 4-7.

```
This program calculates the amount of money
in a bank account for an initial deposit
invested for n years at an interest rate r.

Enter the initial amount in the account: 1000.
Enter the interest rate (ex. 5 for 5%): 5

The final amount of money is $ 1000.00
```

As the output indicates, the final amount of money is the same as the initial amount input. Did you spot the error in Program 4-7 that produced this apparently erroneous output?

Unlike a misspelled output message, the error in Program 4-7 causes a computation mistake. Here, the error is that the program does not initialize the variable `nyears` before this variable is used in the calculation of `capital`. When the assignment statement that calculates `capital` is executed, the computer uses whatever value is stored in `nyears`. On those systems that initialize all variables to zero, the value, zero, will be used for `nyears`. However, on those systems that do not initialize all variables to zero, whatever "garbage" value that happens to occupy the storage locations corresponding to the variable `nyears` will be used (the manuals supplied with your compiler will show which of these two actions your compiler takes). In either case, an error is produced.

The second type of logic error is one that may cause the program to prematurely terminate execution and that almost always results in a system error message being displayed. Examples of this type of error are attempts to divide by zero or take the square root of a negative number. When this type of logic error occurs, it becomes a run-time error.

Testing and Debugging

In theory, a comprehensive set of test runs would reveal all logic errors and ensure that a program will work correctly for any and all combinations of input and computed data. In practice, this requires checking all possible combinations of statement execution. Due to the time and effort required, this is impossible, except for extremely simple programs. Let us see why this is so. Consider Program 4-8.

 Program 4-8

```
main()
{
   int num;

   printf("Enter a number:");
   scanf("%d", &num);
   if (num == 5) printf("Bingo!");
   else printf("Bongo!");
}
```

Program 4-8 has two paths that can be traversed from when the program is run to when the program reaches its closing brace. The first path, which is executed when the input number is 5, is in the sequence:

```
printf("Enter a number");
scanf("%d", &num);
printf("Bingo!");
```

The second path, which is executed whenever any number except 5 is input, includes the sequence of instructions:

```
printf("Enter a number");
scanf("%d", &num);
printf("Bongo!");
```

To test each possible path through Program 4-8 requires two runs of the program, with a judicious selection of test input data to ensure that both paths of the `if` statement are exercised. Adding one more `if` statement in the program increases the number of possible execution paths by a factor of two and requires four (2^2) runs of the program for complete testing. Similarly, two additional `if` statements increase the number of paths by a factor of four and require eight (2^3) runs for complete testing, and three additional `if` statements would produce a program that required sixteen (2^4) test runs.

Now consider an application program consisting of ten modules, each module containing five `if` statements. Assuming the modules are always called in the same sequence, there are thirty-two possible paths through each module (2 raised to the fifth power) and more than 1,000,000,000,000,000 (2 raised to the fiftieth power) possible paths through the complete program (all modules executed in sequence). The time needed to create individual test data to exercise each path and the actual computer run time required to check each path make the complete testing of such a program impossible.

The inability to fully test all combinations of statement execution sequences has led to the programming proverb that "There is no error-free program." It has also led to the realization that any testing that is done should be well thought out to maximize the possibility of locating errors. An important corollary to this is the realization that although a single test can reveal the presence of an error, it does not verify the absence of one. The fact that one error is revealed by testing does not indicate that another error is not lurking somewhere else in the program; the fact that one test revealed no errors does not indicate that there are no errors.

Once an error is discovered, however, the programmer must locate where the error occurred, and then fix it. In computer jargon, a program error is referred to as a *bug* and the process of isolating, correcting, and verifying the correction is called *debugging*.

Although there are no hard and fast rules for isolating the cause of an error, there are some techniques that you can use. The first is a preventive technique. Frequently, many errors are introduced by the programmer in the rush to code and run a program before fully understanding what is required and how to achieve the result. A symptom of this is the lack of an outline of the proposed program (pseudocode or flowchart) or a hand-written program. You can eliminate many errors by checking a copy of the program before it is ever entered or compiled by desk checking the program.

A second technique is to mimic the computer and execute each statement by hand. This means writing down each variable as it is encountered in the program and listing the value that should be stored in the variable as each input and assignment statement is encountered. Doing this also sharpens your programming skills, because it requires that you fully understand what each statement in your program causes to happen. Such a check is called *program tracing*.

A third and very powerful debugging technique is to use one or more diagnostic `printf()` function calls to display the values of selected variables. For example, since the program in Program 4-7 produced an incorrect value for capital, it is worthwhile placing a printf() statement immediately before the assignment statement for capital to display the value of all variables used in the computation. If the displayed values are correct, then the problem is the assignment statement. If the values are incorrect, we must determine where the incorrect values were actually obtained.

In this same manner, another use of printf() function calls in debugging is to display all input data values. This technique is called *echo printing* and is useful in establishing that the computer is correctly receiving and interpreting the input data.

Finally, no discussion of debugging is complete without mentioning the primary ingredient needed for successful isolation and correction of errors. This is the attitude and spirit you bring to the task. Since you wrote the program, your natural assumption is that it is correct or you would have changed it before it was compiled. It is extremely difficult to back away and honestly test and find errors in your own software. As a programmer, you must constantly remind yourself that just because you *think* your program is correct, does not make it so. Finding errors in your own programs is a sobering experience, but one that will help you become a master programmer. It can also be exciting and fun if approached as a detection problem with you as the master detective.

Repetition

Chapter Five

The programs examined so far have been useful in illustrating the correct structure of C programs and in introducing fundamental C input, output, assignment, and selection capabilities. By this time you should have gained enough experience to be comfortable with the concepts and mechanics of the C programming process. It is now time to move up a level in our knowledge and abilities.

The real power of most computer programs resides in their ability to repeat the same calculation or sequence of instructions many times over, each time using different data, without the necessity of rerunning the program for each new set of data values. In this chapter we explore the C statements that permit this. These statements are the `while`, `for`, and `do-while` statements.

5.1 The `while` Statement

The `while` statement is a general repetition statement that can be used in a variety of programming situations. The general form of the `while` statement is:

```
while (expression) statement;
```

The expression contained within the parentheses is evaluated in exactly the same manner as an expression contained in an `if-else` statement; the difference is how the expression is used. As we have seen, when the expression is true (has a nonzero value) in an `if-else` statement, the statement following the expression is executed once. In a `while` statement the statement following the expression is executed repeatedly as long as the expression retains a nonzero value. This naturally means that somewhere in the `while` statement there must be a statement that alters the value of the tested expression. As we will see, this is indeed the case. For now, however, considering just the expression and the statement following the parentheses, the process used by the computer in evaluating a while statement is:

1. test the expression
2. if the expression has a nonzero (true) value
   a. execute the statement following the parentheses
   b. go back to step 1
   `else`
   exit the `while` statement

Notice that step 2b forces program control to be transferred back to step 1. The transfer of control back to the start of a `while` statement in order to reevaluate the expression is called a *program loop*. The `while` statement literally loops back on itself to recheck the expression until it evaluates to zero (becomes false).

This looping process is illustrated in Figure 5-1. A diamond shape is used to show the two entry and two exit points required in the decision part of the `while` statement.

To make this a little more tangible, consider the relational expression `count <= 10` and the statement `printf("%d ",count);`. Using these, we can write the following valid `while` statement:

```
while (count <= 10)  printf("%d  ",count);
```

Although the above statement is valid, the alert reader will realize that we have created a situation in which the `printf()` function either is called forever (or until we stop the program) or is not called at all. Let us see why this happens.

If `count` has a value less than or equal to 10 when the expression is first evaluated, a call to `printf()` is made. The `while` statement then automatically loops back on itself and retests the expression. Since we have not changed the value stored in `count`, the expression is still true and another call to `printf()` is made. This process continues forever, or until the program containing this

FIGURE 5–1 Anatomy of a `while` Loop

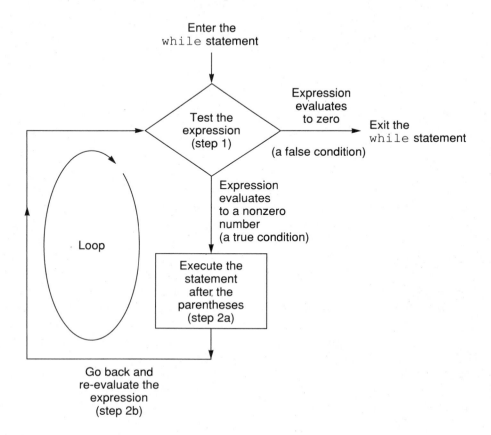

statement is prematurely stopped by the user. However, if count starts with a value greater than 10, the expression is false to begin with and the printf() function call is never made.

How do we set an initial value in count to control what the while statement does the first time the expression is evaluated? The answer, of course, is to assign values to each variable in the tested expression before the while statement is encountered. For example, the following sequence of instructions is valid:

```
count = 1;
while    (count <= 10)   printf("%d   ",count);
```

Using this sequence of instructions, we have ensured that count starts with a value of 1. We could assign any value to count in the assignment statement—the important thing is to assign *some* value. In practice, the assigned value depends on the application.

We must still change the value of count so that we can finally exit the while statement. To do this requires an expression such as ++count to increment the value of count each time the while statement is executed. The fact that a while statement provides for the repetition of a single statement does not prevent us from including an additional statement to change the value of count. All we have to do is replace the single statement with a compound statement. For example:

```
count = 1;                      /* initialize count */
while (count <= 10)
{
  printf("%d   ",count);
  ++count;                      /* increment count */
}
```

Note that, for clarity, we have placed each statement in the compound statement on a different line. This is consistent with the convention adopted for compound statements in the last chapter. Let us now analyze the above sequence of instructions.

The first assignment statement sets count equal to 1. The while statement is then entered and the expression is evaluated for the first time. Since the value of count is less than or equal to 10, the expression is true and the compound statement is executed. The first statement in the compound statement is a call to the printf() function to display the value of count. The next statement adds 1 to the value currently stored in count, making this value equal to 2. The while statement now loops back to retest the expression. Since count is still less than or equal to 10, the compound statement is again executed. This process continues until the value of count reaches 11. Program 5-1 illustrates these statements in an actual program.

Program 5-1

```
main()
{
  int count;

  count = 1;                 /* initialize count */
  while (count <= 10)
  {
    printf("%d  ",count);
    ++count;                 /* add 1 to count    */
  }
}
```

The output for Program 5-1 is:

       1 2 3 4 5 6 7 8 9 10

There is nothing special about the name count used in Program 5-1. Any valid integer variable could have been used.

Before we consider other examples of the while statement two comments concerning Program 5-1 are in order. First, the statement ++count can be replaced with any statement that changes the value of count. A statement such as count = count + 2, for example, would cause every second integer to be displayed. Second, it is the programmer's responsibility to ensure that count is changed in a way that ultimately leads to a normal exit from the while. For example, if we replace the expression ++count with the expression --count, the value of count will never reach 11 and an infinite loop will be created. An *infinite loop* is a loop that never ends. The computer will not reach out, touch you, and say, "Excuse me, you have created an infinite loop." It just keeps displaying numbers until you realize that the program is not working as you expected.

 Program 5-2

```
main()
{
  int i;

  i = 10;
  while (i >= 1)
  {
    printf("%d  ",i);
    --i;                  /* subtract 1 from i */
  }
}
```

Now that you have some familiarity with the while statement, see if you can read and determine the output of Program 5-2.

The assignment statement in Program 5-2 initially sets the int variable i to 10. The while statement then checks to see if the value of i is greater than or equal to 1. While the expression is true, the value of i is displayed by the call to printf() and the value of i is decremented by 1. When i finally reaches zero, the expression is false and the program exits the while statement. Thus, the following display is obtained when Program 5-2 is run:

10   9   8   7   6   5   4   3   2   1

To illustrate the power of the while statement, consider the task of printing a table of numbers from 1 to 10 with their squares and cubes. This can be done with a simple while statement as illustrated by Program 5-3.

 Program 5-3

```
main()
{
  int num;
  printf("NUMBER     SQUARE     CUBE\n");
  printf("------     ------     ----\n");

  num = 1;
  while (num < 11)
  {
    printf("%3d      %3d       %4d\n", num, num*num, num*num*num);
    ++num;          /* add 1 to num */
  }
}
```

When Program 5-3 is run, the following display is produced:

NUMBER	SQUARE	CUBE
1	1	1
2	4	8
3	9	27
4	16	64
5	25	125
6	36	216
7	49	343
8	64	512
9	81	729
10	100	1000

Note that the expression used in Program 5-3 is num < 11. For the integer variable num, this expression is exactly equivalent to the expression num <= 10. The choice of which to use is entirely up to you.

If we want to use Program 5-3 to produce a table of 1000 numbers, all we do is change the expression in the while statement from i < 11 to i < 1001. Changing the 11 to 1001 produces a table of 1000 lines—not bad for a simple five-line while statement.

All the program examples illustrating the while statement have checked for a fixed-count condition. Since any valid expression can be evaluated by a while statement, we are not restricted to constructing such loops. For example, consider the task of producing a Celsius to Fahrenheit temperature conversion table. Assume that Fahrenheit temperatures corresponding to Celsius temperatures ranging from 5 to 50 degrees are to be displayed in increments of five degrees. The desired display can be obtained with the series of statements:

```
celsius = 5;        /* starting Celsius value */
while (celsius <= 50)
{
    fahren = (9.0/5.0) * celsius + 32.0;
    printf("%5d%12.2f",celsius, fahren);
    celsius = celsius + 5;
}
```

As before, the while statement consists of everything from the word while through the closing brace of the compound statement. Prior to entering the while loop we have made sure to assign a value to the operand being evaluated, and there is a statement to alter the value of celsius to ensure an exit from the while loop. Program 5-4 illustrates the use of this code in a complete program.

 Program 5-4

```
main() /* program to convert Celsius to Fahrenheit */
{
    int celsius;
    float fahren;
    printf("DEGREES    DEGREES\n");
    printf("CELSIUS   FAHRENHEIT\n");
    printf("-------    ----------\n");

    celsius = 5;       /* starting Celsius value */
    while (celsius <= 50)
    {
        fahren = (9.0/5.0) * celsius + 32.0;
        printf("%5d%12.2f\n",celsius, fahren);
        celsius = celsius + 5;
    }
}
```

The display obtained when Program 5-4 is executed is:

```
DEGREES     DEGREES
CELSIUS    FAHRENHEIT
-------    ----------
   5          41.00
  10          50.00
  15          59.00
  20          68.00
  25          77.00
  30          86.00
  35          95.00
  40         104.00
  45         113.00
  50         122.00
```

Exercises 5.1

1. Rewrite Program 5-1 to print the numbers 2 to 10 in increments of two. The output of your program should be:

```
2   4   6   8   10
```

2. Rewrite Program 5-4 to produce a table that starts at a Celsius value of –10 and ends with a Celsius value of 60, in increments of ten degrees.

3. a. For the following program determine the total number of items displayed. Also determine the first and last numbers printed.

```
main()
{
  int num = 0;

  while (num <= 20)
  {
    ++num;
    printf("%d   ",num);
  }
}
```

b. Enter and run the program from Exercise 3a on a computer to verify your answers to the exercise.

c. How would the output be affected if the two statements within the compound statement were reversed (that is, if the printf() call were made before the ++num statement)?

4. Write a C program that converts gallons to liters. The program should display gallons from 10 to 20 in one-gallon increments and the corresponding liter equivalents. Use the relationship: liters = 3.785 * gallons.

5. Write a C program that converts feet to meters. The program should display feet from 3 to 30 in three foot increments and the corresponding meter equivalents. Use the relationship: meters = feet / 3.28.

6. A machine purchased for $28,000 is depreciated at a rate of $4,000 a year for seven years. Write and run a C program that computes and displays a depreciation table for seven years. The table should have the form:

YEAR	DEPRECIATION	END-OF-YEAR VALUE	ACCUMULATED DEPRECIATION
1	4000	24000	4000
2	4000	20000	8000
3	4000	16000	12000
4	4000	12000	16000
5	4000	8000	20000
6	4000	4000	24000
7	4000	0	28000

7. An automobile travels at an average speed of 55 miles per hour for four hours. Write a C program that displays the distance driven, in miles, that the car has traveled after .5, 1, 1.5, etc., hours until the end of the trip.

5.2   `scanf()` Within a `while` Loop

Combining the `scanf()` function with the repetition capabilities of the `while` statement produces very adaptable and powerful programs. To understand the concept involved, consider Program 5-5, where a `while` statement is used to accept and then display four user-entered numbers, one at a time. Although it uses a very simple idea, the program highlights the flow of control concepts needed to produce more useful programs.

Program 5-5

```
main()
{
    int count;
    float num;

    printf("\nThis program will ask you to enter some numbers.\n");
    count = 1;

    while (count <= 4)
    {
        printf("\nEnter a number: ");
        scanf("%f", &num);
        printf("The number entered is %f", num);
        ++count;
    }
}
```

Following is a sample run of Program 5-5. The underlined items were input in response to the appropriate prompts.

```
This program will ask you to enter some numbers.

Enter a number: 26.2
The number entered is 26.200000
Enter a number: 5
The number entered is 5.000000
Enter a number: 103.456
The number entered is 103.456000
Enter a number: 1267.89
The number entered is 1267.890000
```

Let us review the program to clearly understand how the output was produced. The first message displayed is caused by execution of the first `printf()` function call. This call is outside and before the `while` statement, so it is executed once before any statement in the `while` loop.

Once the `while` loop is entered, the statements within the compound statement are executed while the tested condition is true. The first time through the compound statement, the message `Enter a number:` is displayed. The program then calls `scanf()`, which forces the computer to wait for a number to be entered at the keyboard. Once a number is typed and the RETURN key is pressed, the call to `printf()` displaying the number is executed. The variable `count` is then incremented by one. This process continues until four passes through the loop have been made and the value of `count` is 5. Each pass causes

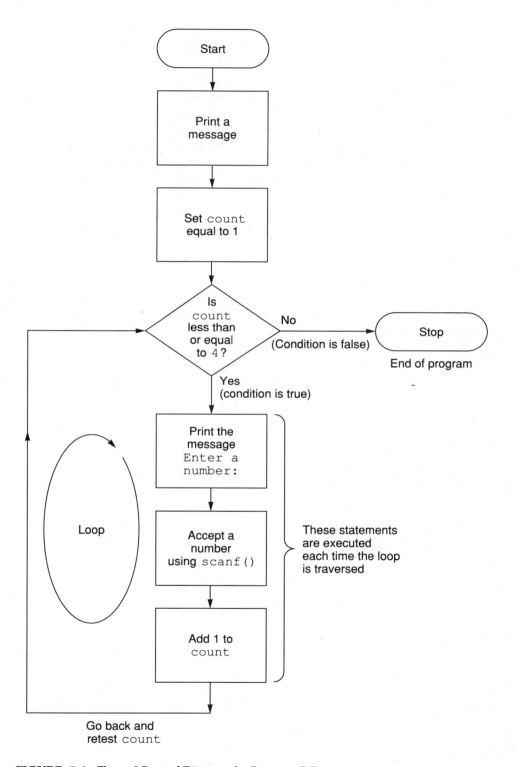

FIGURE 5–2 Flow of Control Diagram for Program 5-5

the message `Enter a number:` to be displayed, causes one call to `scanf()` to be made, and causes the message `The number entered is` to be displayed. Figure 5-2 illustrates this flow of control.

Rather than simply displaying the entered numbers, Program 5-5 can be modified in order to use the entered data. For example, let us add the numbers entered and display the total. To do this, we must be very careful in how we add the numbers, since the same variable, `num`, is used for each number entered. Because of this the entry of a new number in Program 5-5 automatically causes the previous number stored in `num` to be lost. Thus, each number entered must be added to the total before another number is entered. The required sequence is:

> Enter a number
> Add the number to the total

How do we add a single number to a total? A statement such as `total = total + num` does the job perfectly. This is the accumulating statement introduced in Section 3.1. After each number is entered, the accumulating statement adds the number into the total, as illustrated in Figure 5-3. The complete flow of control required for adding the numbers is illustrated in Figure 5-4.

FIGURE 5–3 Accepting and Adding a Number to a Total

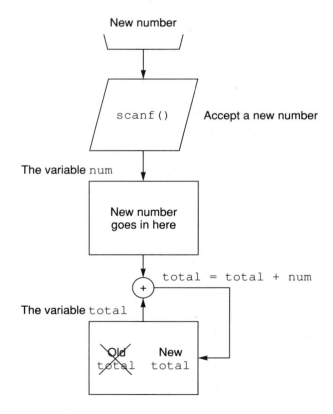

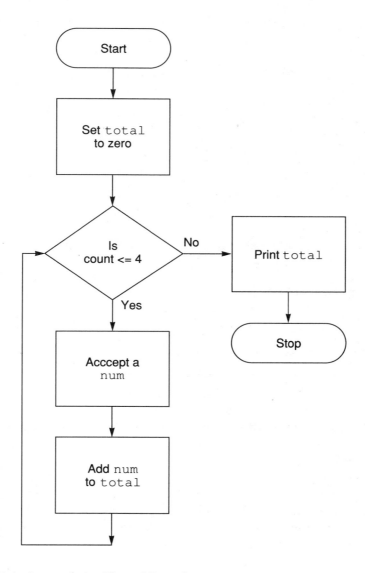

FIGURE 5–4 Accumulation Flow of Control

In reviewing Figure 5-4, observe that we have made a provision for initially setting the total to zero before the `while` loop is entered. If we were to clear the total inside the `while` loop, it would be set to zero each time the loop was executed and any value previously stored would be erased.

Program 5-6 incorporates the necessary modifications to Program 5-5 to total the numbers entered. As indicated in the flow diagram shown in Figure 5-4, the statement `total = total + num;` is placed immediately after the `scanf()` function call. Putting the accumulating statement at this point in the program ensures that the entered number is immediately "captured" into the total.

Program 5-6

```
main()
{
  int count;
  float num, total;

  printf("\nThis program will ask you to enter some numbers.\n");
  count = 1;
  total = 0;

  while (count <= 4)
  {
    printf("\nEnter a number: ");
    scanf("%f", &num);
    total = total + num;
    printf("The total is now %f", total);
    ++count;
  }
  printf("\n\nThe final total is %f",total);
}
```

Let us review Program 5-6. The variable `total` was created to store the total of the numbers entered. Prior to entering the `while` statement the value of `total` is set to zero. This ensures that any previous value present in the storage location(s) assigned to the variable `total` are erased. When the `while` loop is entered, the statement `total = total + num;` is used to add the value of the entered number into `total`. As each value is entered, it is added into the existing total to create a new total. Thus, `total` becomes a running subtotal of all the values entered. Only when all numbers are entered does `total` contain the final sum of all the numbers. After the `while` loop is finished, the last `printf()` function call is used to display this sum.

Using the same data that was entered in the sample run for Program 5-5, the following sample run of Program 5-6 was made:

```
This program will ask you to enter some numbers.

Enter a number: 26.2
The total is now 26.200000
Enter a number: 5
The total is now 31.200000
Enter a number: 103.456
The total is now 134.656000
Enter a number: 1267.89
The total is now 1402.546000

The final total is 1402.546000
```

Having used an accumulating assignment statement to add the numbers entered, we can now go further and calculate the average of the numbers. Where do we calculate the average—within the while loop or outside it?

In the case at hand, calculating an average requires that both a final sum and the number of items in that sum be available. The average is then computed by dividing the final sum by the number of items. At this point, we must ask, "At what point in the program is the correct sum available, and at what point is the number of items available?" In reviewing Program 5-6 we see that the correct sum needed for calculating the average is available after the while loop is finished. In fact, the whole purpose of the while loop is to ensure that the numbers are entered and added correctly to produce a correct sum. After the loop is finished, we also have a count of the number of items used in the sum. However, due to the way the while loop was constructed, the number in count (5) when the loop is finished is one more than the number of items (4) used to obtain the total. Knowing this, we simply subtract one from count before using it to determine the average. With this as background, see if you can read and understand Program 5-7.

 Program 5-7

```
main()
{
    int count;
    float num, total,average;

    printf("\nThis program will ask you to enter some numbers.\n");
    count = 1;
    total = 0;

    while (count <= 4)
    {
        printf("Enter a number: ");
        scanf("%f", &num);
        total = total + num;
        ++count;
    }
    --count;
    average = total / count;
    printf("\nThe average of the numbers is %f",average);
}
```

Program 5-7 is almost identical to Program 5-6, except for the calculation of the average. We have also removed the constant display of the total within and after the while loop. The loop in Program 5-7 is used to enter and add four numbers. Immediately after the loop is exited, the average is computed and displayed. Following is a sample run using Program 5-7:

```
This program will ask you to enter some numbers.

Enter a number: 26.2
Enter a number: 5
Enter a number: 103.456
Enter a number: 1267.89

The average of the numbers is 350.636500
```

Sentinels

In many situations the exact number of items to be entered is not known in advance or the items are too numerous to count beforehand. For example, when entering a large amount of market research data we might not want to take the time to count the number of actual data items that are to be entered. In cases like this we want to be able to enter data continuously and, at the end, type in a special data value to signal the end of data input.

In computer programming, data values used to signal either the start or end of a data series are called *sentinels*. The sentinel values must, of course, be selected so as not to conflict with legitimate data values. For example, if we were constructing a program that accepts a student's grades, and assuming that no extra credit is given that could produce a grade higher than 100, we could use any grade higher than 100 as a sentinel value. Program 5-8 illustrates this concept. In Program 5-8 data is continuously requested and accepted until a number larger than 100 is entered. Entry of a number higher than 100 alerts the program to exit the `while` loop and display the sum of the numbers entered.

 Program 5-8

```
main()
{
   float grade, total;
   grade = 0;
   total = 0;
   printf("\nTo stop entering grades, type in any number");
   printf("\n greater than 100.\n");
   while (grade <= 100)
   {
      printf("Enter a grade: ");
      scanf("%f", &grade);
      total = total + grade;
   }
   printf("\nThe total of the grades is %f",total-grade);
}
```

Following is a sample run using Program 5-8. As long as grades less than or equal to 100 are entered, the program continues to request and accept additional data. When a number greater than 100 is entered, the program adds this number to the total and exits the `while` loop. Outside of the loop and within the `printf()` function call, the value of the sentinel that was added to the total is subtracted and the sum of the legitimate grades that were entered is displayed.

```
To stop entering grades, type in any number
 greater than 100.

Enter a grade: 95
Enter a grade: 100
Enter a grade: 82
Enter a grade: 101

The total of the grades is 277.000000
```

One useful sentinel provided in C is the named constant EOF, which stands for End Of File. The actual value of EOF is compiler-dependent, but is always assigned a code that is not used by any other character. The way that EOF works is as follows:

Each computer operating system has its own code for an End Of File mark. In the UNIX operating systems this mark is generated whenever the `ctrl` and `D` keys are pressed simultaneously, while in the IBM-DOS operating system the mark is generated whenever the `ctrl` and `Z` keys are pressed simultaneously. When a C program detects this combination of keys as an input value, it converts the input value into its own EOF code, as illustrated in Figure 5-5.

The actual definition of the EOF constant, using the `#define` statement previously described in Section 3.5, is available in a compiler source file named `stdio.h`. Thus, to use the EOF named constant in a program, the `stdio.h` file must be included as part of the program. This is accomplished by adding the statement `#include <stdio.h>`, with no semicolon after the statement, at the top of the program. For example, consider Program 5-9.

FIGURE 5-5 Generation of the EOF Constant by the `scanf()` Function

Program 5-9

```c
#include <stdio.h>
main()
{
  float grade, total = 0;        /* note the initialization here */

  printf("\nTo stop entering grades, press either the F6 key");
  printf("\n or the ctrl and Z keys simultaneously on IBM computers");
  printf("\n or the ctrl and D keys for UNIX operating systems.\n\n");
  printf("Enter a grade: ");

  while ( scanf("%f", &grade) != EOF)
  {
    total = total + grade;
    printf("Enter a grade: ");
  }

  printf("\nThe total of the grades is %f",total);
}
```

Notice that the first line in Program 5-9 is the #include <stdio.h> statement. Since the stdio.h file contains the definition of EOF, this constant may now be referenced in the program.

EOF is used in Program 5-9 to control the while loop. The expression scanf("%f", &grades) != EOF makes use of the fact that the scanf() function returns an EOF value if an attempt is made to read an End Of File mark. From a user's viewpoint, assuming an IBM computer is being used, pressing both the ctrl and Z keys simultaneously generates an End Of File mark, which is converted to the EOF constant by scanf(). Following is a sample run using Program 5-9.

```
To stop entering grades, press either the F6 key
 or the ctrl and Z keys simultaneously on IBM computers
 or the ctrl and D keys for UNIX operating systems.

Enter a grade: 100
Enter a grade: 200
Enter a grade: 300
Enter a grade: ^Z

The total of the grades is 600.000000
```

One distinct advantage of Program 5-9 over Program 5-8 is that the sentinel value is never added into the total, so it does not have to be subtracted later. One disadvantage of Program 5-9, however, is that it requires the user to type in an unfamiliar combination of keys to terminate data input.

break and continue Statements

Two useful statements in connection with repetition statements are the break and continue statements. We have previously encountered the break statement in relation to the switch statement. The general form of this statement is:

break;

A break statement, as its name implies, forces an immediate break, or exit, from switch, while, for, and do-while statements only.

For example, execution of the following while loop is immediately terminated if a number greater than 76 is entered.

```
while(count <= 10)
{
  printf("Enter a number: ");
  scanf("%f", &num);
  if (num > 76)
  {
    printf("You lose!");
    break;          /* break out of the loop */
  }
  else
  printf("Keep on truckin!");
}
/* break jumps to here */
```

The break statement violates pure structured programming principles because it provides a second, nonstandard exit from a loop. Nevertheless, the break statement is extremely useful and valuable for breaking out of loops when an unusual condition is detected. The break statement is also used to exit from a switch statement, but this is because the desired case has been detected and processed.

The continue statement is similar to the break statement but applies only to loops created with while, do-while, and for statements. The general format of a continue statement is:

continue;

When `continue` is encountered in a loop, the next iteration of the loop is immediately begun. For `while` loops this means that execution is automatically transferred to the top of the loop and reevaluation of the tested expression is initiated. Although the `continue` statement has no direct effect on a `switch` statement, it can be included within a `switch` statement that itself is contained in a loop. Here the effect of `continue` is the same: the next loop iteration is begun.

As a general rule the `continue` statement tends to be less used than the `break` statement, but it is convenient for skipping over data that should not be processed while remaining in a loop. For example, invalid grades are simply ignored in the following section of code and only valid grades are added into the total:

```
while (count < 30)
{
   printf("Enter a grade: ");
   scanf("%f", &grade);
   if(grade < 0 || grade > 100) continue;
   total = total + grade;
   count = count + 1;
}
```

The Null Statement

Statements are always terminated by a semicolon. A semicolon with nothing preceding it is also a valid statement, called the *null statement*. Thus, the statement

```
;
```

is a null statement. This is a do-nothing statement that is used where a statement is syntactically required, but no action is called for. Null statements typically are used with either `while` or `for` statements. An example of a `for` statement using a null statement is found in Program 5-9c in the next section.

Exercises 5.2

1. Rewrite Program 5-6 to compute the total of eight numbers.

2. Rewrite Program 5-6 to display the prompt:

```
Please type in the total number of data values to be added:
```

In response to this prompt, the program should accept a user-entered number and then use this number to control the number of times the `while` loop is executed. Thus, if the user enters 5 in response to the prompt, the program should request the input of five numbers and display the total after five numbers have been entered.

3. a. Write a C program to convert Celsius degrees to Fahrenheit. The program should request the starting Celsius value, the number of conversions to be made, and the increment between Celsius values. The display should have appropriate headings and list the Celsius value and the corresponding Fahrenheit value. Use the relationship: Fahrenheit = (9.0 / 5.0) * Celsius + 32.0.

   b. Run the program written in Exercise 3a on a computer. Verify that your program starts at the correct starting Celsius value and contains the exact number of conversions specified in your input data.

4. a. Modify the program written in Exercise 3 to request the starting Celsius value, the ending Celsius value, and the increment. Thus, instead of the condition checking for a fixed count, the condition will check for the ending Celsius value.

   b. Run the program written in Exercise 4a on a computer. Verify that your output starts at the correct beginning value and ends at the correct ending value.

5. Rewrite Program 5-7 to compute the average of ten numbers.

6. Rewrite Program 5-7 to display the prompt:

```
Please type in the total number of data values to be averaged:
```

In response to this prompt, the program should accept a user-entered number and then use this number to control the number of times the while loop is executed. Thus, if the user enters 6 in response to the prompt, the program should request the input of six numbers and display the average of the next six numbers entered.

7. By mistake, a programmer put the statement average = total / count; within the while loop immediately after the statement total = total + num; in Program 5-7. Thus, the while loop becomes:

```
while (count <= 4)
{
  printf("\nEnter a number: ");
  scanf("%f", &num);
  total = total + num;
  average = total / count;
  ++count;
}
```

Will the program yield the correct result with this while loop? From a programming perspective, which while loop is better to use, and why?

8. a. Modify Program 5-8 to compute the average of the grades entered.

   b. Run the program written in Exercise 8a on a computer and verify the results.

9. a. A bookstore summarizes its monthly transactions by keeping the following information for each book in stock:

Book identification number
Inventory balance at the beginning of the month
Number of copies received during the month
Number of copies sold during the month

171

Write a C program that accepts this data for each book and then displays the book identification number and an updated book inventory balance using the relationship:

New Balance = Inventory balance at the beginning of the month
+ Number of copies received during the month
− Number of copies sold during the month

Your program should use a `while` statement with a fixed count condition so that information on only three books is requested.

b. Run the program written in Exercise 9a on a computer. Review the display produced by your program and verify that the output produced is correct.

10. Modify the program you wrote for Exercise 9 to keep requesting and displaying results until a sentinel identification value of 999 is entered. Run the program on a computer.

5.3   The `for` Statement

The `for` statement performs the same functions as the `while` statement, but uses a different form. In many situations, especially those that use a fixed count condition, the `for` statement format is easier to use than its `while` statement equivalent.

The general form of the `for` statement is:

```
for (initializing list; expression; altering list) statement;
```

Although the `for` statement looks a little complicated, it is really quite simple if we consider each of its parts separately.

Within the parentheses of the `for` statement are three items, separated by semicolons. Each of these items is optional and can be described individually, but the semicolons must be present. As we shall see, the items in parentheses correspond to the initialization, expression evaluation, and altering of expression values that we have already used with the `while` statement.

The middle item in the parentheses, the expression, is any valid C expression, and there is no difference in the way `for` and `while` statements use this expression. In both statements, as long as the expression has a nonzero (true) value, the statement following the parentheses is executed. This means that prior to the first check of the expression, initial values for the tested expression's variables must be assigned. It also means that before the expression is reevaluated, there must be one or more statements that alter these values. Recall that the general placement of these statements using a `while` statement follows the pattern:

```
initializing statements;
while (expression)
{
    loop statements;
            .

            .

            .
    expression-altering statements;
}
```

The need to initialize variables or make some other evaluations prior to entering a repetition loop is so common that the for statement allows all the initializing statements to be grouped together as the first set of items within the for's parentheses. The items in this initializing list are executed only once, before the expression is evaluated for the first time.

The for statement also provides a single place for all expression-altering statements. These items can be placed in the altering list, which is the last list contained within the for's parentheses. All items in the altering list are executed by the for statement at the end of the loop, just before the expression is reevaluated. Figure 5-6 illustrates the for statement's flow of control diagram.

The following section of code illustrates the correspondence between the for and while statements:

```
count = 1;
while (count <= 10)
{
    printf("%d", count);
    ++count:
}
```

The for statement corresponding to this section of code is:

```
for (count = 1; count <= 10; ++count)  printf("%d", count);
```

As seen in this example, the only difference between the for statement and the while statement is the placement of equivalent expressions. The grouping together of the initialization, expression test, and altering list in the for statement is very convenient, especially when they are used to create fixed-count loops. Consider the following for statement:

```
for (count = 2; count <= 20; count = count + 2)
    printf("%d  ",count);
```

For clarity, we have placed the statement following the parentheses on a line by itself. All the loop control information is contained within the parentheses. The loop starts with a count of 2, stops when the count exceeds 20, and increments the loop counter in steps of 2. Program 5-10 illustrates this for statement in an actual program.

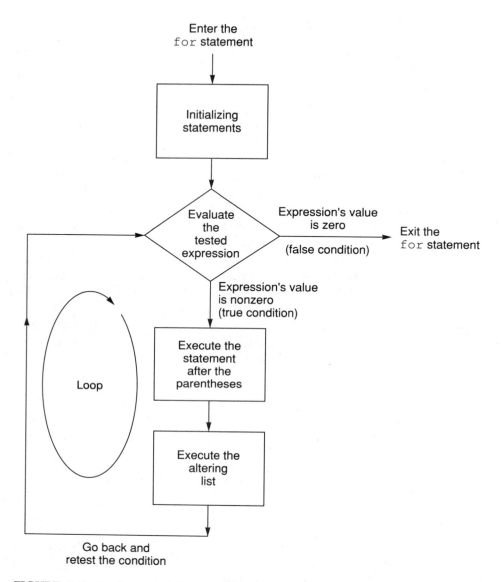

FIGURE 5–6 for Statement Flow of Control

 Program 5-10

```
main()
{
    int count;

    for (count = 2; count <= 20; count = count + 2)
        printf("%d  ",count);
}
```

The output of Program 5-10 is:

       2   4   6   8   10   12   14   16   18   20

The `for` statement does not require that any of the items in parentheses be present or that they be used for initializing or altering the values in the expression statements. However, the two semicolons must be present within the `for`'s parentheses. For example, the construction for (; count <= 20 ;) is valid.

If the initializing list is missing, the initialization step is omitted when the `for` statement is executed. This, of course, means that the programmer must provide the required initializations before the `for` statement is encountered. Similarly, if the altering list is missing, any expressions needed to alter the evaluation of the tested expression must be included directly within the statement part of the loop. The `for` statement only ensures that all expressions in the initializing list are executed once, before evaluation of the tested expression, and that all expressions in the altering list are executed at the end of the loop before the tested expression is rechecked. Thus, Program 5-10 can be rewritten in any of the three ways shown in Programs 5-10a, 5-10b, and 5-10c.

 Program 5-10a

```
main()
{
  int count;

  count = 2;     /* initializer outside for statement */
  for ( ; count <= 20; count = count + 2)
    printf("%d  ",count);
}
```

 Program 5-10b

```
main()
{
  int count;

  count = 2;     /* initializer outside for loop     */
  for( ; count <= 20; )
  {
    printf("%d  ",count);
    count = count + 2;     /* alteration statement */
  }
}
```

Program 5-10c

```
main()    /* all expressions within the for's parentheses */
{
  int count;

  for (count = 2; count <= 20; printf("%d  ",count), count = count + 2);
}
```

In Program 5-10a `count` is initialized outside the `for` statement and the first list inside the parentheses is left blank. In Program 5-10b, both the initializing list and the altering list are removed from within the parentheses. Program 5-10b also uses a compound statement within the `for` loop, with the expression-altering statement included in the compound statement. Finally, Program 5-10c has included all items within the parentheses, so there is no need for any useful statement following the parentheses. Here the null statement satisfies the syntactical requirement of one statement to follow the `for`'s parentheses. Observe also in Program 5-10c that the altering list (last set of items in parentheses) consists of two items, and that a comma has been used to separate these items. The use of commas to separate items in both the initializing and altering lists is required if either of these two lists contains more than one item. Last, note the fact that Programs 5-10a, 5-10b, and 5-10c are all inferior to Program 5-10. The `for` statement in Program 5-10 is much clearer since all the expressions pertaining to the tested expression are grouped together within the parentheses.

Although the initializing and altering lists can be omitted from a for statement, omitting the tested expression results in an infinite loop. For example, such a loop is created by the statement

```
for (count = 2; ; ++count) printf("%d",count);
```

As with the `while` statement, both `break` and `continue` statements can be used within a `for` loop. The `break` forces an immediate exit from the `for` loop, as it does in the `while` loop. The `continue`, however, forces control to be passed to the altering list in a `for` statement, after which the tested expression is reevaluated. This differs from the action of `continue` in a `while` statement, where control is passed directly to the reevaluation of the tested expression.

To understand the enormous power of the `for` statement, consider the task of printing a table of numbers from 1 to 10, including their squares and cubes, using this statement. Such a table was previously produced using a `while` statement in Program 5-3. You may wish to review Program 5-3 and compare it to Program 5-11 to get a further sense of the equivalence between the `for` and `while` statements.

Program 5-11

```
main()
{
    int num;
    printf("NUMBER      SQUARE      CUBE\n");
    printf("------      ------      ----\n");

    for (num = 1; num <= 10; ++num)
        printf("%3d       %3d       %4d\n", num, num*num, num*num*num);
}
```

When Program 5-11 is run, the display produced is:

```
        NUMBER      SQUARE      CUBE
        ------      ------      ----
          1           1           1
          2           4           8
          3           9          27
          4          16          64
          5          25         125
          6          36         216
          7          49         343
          8          64         512
          9          81         729
         10         100        1000
```

Simply changing the number 10 in the `for` statement of Program 5-11 to 1000 creates a loop that is executed 1000 times and produces a table of numbers from 1 to 1000. As with the `while` statement this small change produces an immense increase in the processing and output provided by the program.

scanf() Within a for Loop

Using a `scanf()` function call inside a `for` loop produces the same effect as when this function is called inside a `while` loop. For example, in Program 5-12 a `scanf()` function call is used to input a set of numbers. As each number is input, it is added to a total. When the `for` loop is exited, the average is calculated and displayed.

Program 5-12

```
main()
/* This program calculates the average */
/* of five user-entered numbers.       */
{
  int count;
  float num, total, average;

  total = 0.0;

  for ( count = 0; count < 5; ++count)
  {
    printf("\nEnter a number: ");
    scanf("%f", &num);
    total = total + num;
  }

  average = total / count;
  printf("\n\nThe average of the data entered is %f", average);
}
```

The `for` statement in Program 5-12 creates a loop that is executed five times. The user is prompted to enter a number each time through the loop. After each number is entered, it is immediately added to the total. Although, for clarity, `total` was initialized to zero before the `for` statement, this initialization could have been included with the initialization of `count`, as follows:

```
for (total = 0.0, count = 0; count < 5; ++count)
```

Nested Loops

There are many situations in which it is very convenient to have a loop contained within another loop. Such loops are called *nested loops*. A simple example of a nested loop is:

```
for(i = 1; i <= 5; ++i)          /* start of outer loop  <------+ */
{                                /*                             | */
  printf("\ni is now %d\n",i)    /*                             | */
  for(j = 1; j <= 4; ++j)        /* start of inner loop         | */
    printf("  j = %d", j);       /* end of inner loop           | */
}                                /* end of outer loop    <------+ */
```

The first loop, controlled by the value of i, is called the *outer loop*. The second loop, controlled by the value of j, is called the *inner loop*. Notice that all statements in the inner loop are contained within the boundaries of the outer loop and that we have used a different variable to control each loop. For each single trip through the outer loop, the inner loop runs through its entire sequence. Thus, each time the i counter increases by 1, the inner for loop executes completely. This situation is illustrated in Figure 5-7.

Program 5-13 includes the above code in a working program.

 Program 5-13

```
main()
{
  int i,j;

  for(i = 1; i <= 5; ++i)        /* start of outer loop <------+ */
  {                              /*                            | */
    printf("\ni is now %d\n",i)/*                              | */
    for(j = 1; j <= 4; ++j)      /* start of inner loop        | */
      printf("  j = %d", j);     /* end of inner loop          | */
  }                              /* end of outer loop  <-------+ */
}
```

Following is the output of a sample run of Program 5-13:

```
i is now 1
    j = 1  j = 2  j = 3  j = 4
i is now 2
    j = 1  j = 2  j = 3  j = 4
i is now 3
    j = 1  j = 2  j = 3  j = 4
i is now 4
    j = 1  j = 2  j = 3  j = 4
i is now 5
    j = 1  j = 2  j = 3  j = 4
```

Let us use a nested loop to compute the average grade for each student in a class of 20 students. Each student has taken four exams during the course of the semester. The final grade is calculated as the average of these examination grades.

The outer loop in our program will consist of 20 passes. Each pass through the outer loop is used to compute the average for one student. The inner loop will consist of 4 passes. One examination grade is entered in each inner loop

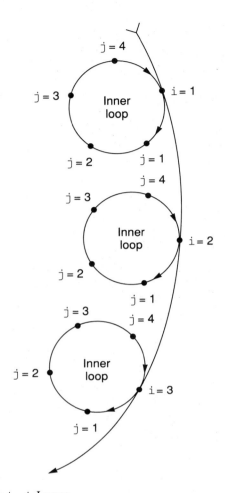

FIGURE 5–7 For Each i, j Loops

pass. As each grade is entered it is added to the total for the student, and at the end of the loop the average is calculated and displayed. Program 5-14 uses a nested loop to make the required calculations.

 Program 5-14

```
main()
{
   int i,j;
   float grade, total, average;
   for (i = 1; i <= 20; ++i)         /* start of outer loop */
   {
      total = 0;                     /* clear the total for this student */
      for (j = 1; j <= 4; ++j)       /* start of inner loop */
```
                                                                    continued

```
      {
        printf("Enter an examination grade for this student: ");
        scanf("%f", &grade);
        total = total + grade;      /* add the grade into the total  */
      }                             /* end of the inner for loop     */
      average = total / 4;          /* calculate the average         */
      printf("\nThe average for student %d is %f\n\n",i,average);
    }                    .          /* end of the outer for loop     */
  }
```

In reviewing Program 5-14, pay particular attention to the initialization of total within the outer loop, before the inner loop is entered. total is initialized 20 times, once for each student. Also notice that the average is calculated and displayed immediately after the inner loop is finished. Since the statements that compute and print the average are also contained within the outer loop, 20 averages are calculated and displayed. The entry and addition of each grade within the inner loop use techniques we have seen before, which should now be familiar to you.

Exercises 5.3

1. Determine the output of the following program.

```
main()
{
  int i;

  for (i = 20; i >= 0; i -= 4)
    printf("%d ",i);
}
```

2. Modify Program 5-11 to produce a table of the numbers 0 through 20 in increments of 2, with their squares and cubes.

3. Modify Program 5-11 to produce a table of numbers from 10 to 1, instead of 1 to 10 as it currently does.

4. Write and run a C program that displays a table of 20 temperature conversions from Fahrenheit to Celsius. The table should start with a Fahrenheit value of 20 degrees and be incremented in values of 4 degrees. Recall that Celsius = (5.0/9.0) * (Fahrenheit – 32.0).

5. Modify the program written for Exercise 4 to initially request the number of conversions to be displayed.

6. Write a C program that converts Fahrenheit to Celsius temperature in increments of 5 degrees. The initial value of Fahrenheit temperature and the total conversions to be made are to be requested as user input during program execution. Recall that Celsius = (5.0/9.0) * (Fahrenheit – 32.0).

7. Write and run a C program that accepts six Fahrenheit temperatures, one at a time, and converts each value entered to its Celsius equivalent before the next value is requested. Use a `for` loop in your program. The conversion required is Celsius = (5.0/9.0) * (Fahrenheit – 32.0).

8. Write and run a C program that accepts ten individual values of gallons, one at a time, and converts each value entered to its liter equivalent before the next value is requested. Use a `for` loop in your program. The conversion required is liters = 3.785 * gallons.

9. Modify the program written for Exercise 8 to initially request the number of data items that will be entered and converted.

10. Write and run a program that calculates and displays the amount of money available in a bank account that initially has $1,000 deposited in it and that earns 8 percent interest a year. Your program should display the amount available at the end of each year for a period of ten years. Use the relationship that the money available at the end of each year equals the amount of money in the account at the start of the year plus .08 times the amount available at the start of the year.

11. A machine purchased for $28,000 is depreciated at a rate of $4,000 a year for seven years. Write and run a C program that computes and displays a depreciation table for seven years. The table should have the form:

DEPRECIATION SCHEDULE

YEAR	DEPRECIATION	END-OF-YEAR VALUE	ACCUMULATED DEPRECIATION
1	4000	24000	4000
2	4000	20000	8000
3	4000	16000	12000
4	4000	12000	16000
5	4000	8000	20000
6	4000	4000	24000
7	4000	0	28000

12. a. Modify the program written for Exercise 10 to initially prompt the user for the amount of money initially deposited in the account.
 b. Modify the program written for Exercise 10 to initially prompt the user for both the amount of money initially deposited and the number of years that should be displayed.
 c. Modify the program written for Exercise 10 to initially prompt for the amount of money initially deposited, the interest rate to be used, and the number of years to be displayed.

13. A well-regarded manufacturer of widgets has been losing 4 percent of its sales each year. The annual profit for the firm is 10 percent of sales. This year the firm has had $10 million in sales and a profit of $1 million. Determine the expected sales and profit for the next 10 years. Your program should complete and produce a display as follows:

```
SALES AND PROFIT PROJECTION
---------------------------


YEAR               EXPECTED SALES             PROJECTED PROFIT
----               --------------             ----------------
  1                $10000000.00                 $1000000.00
  2                $ 9600000.00                 $ 960000.00
  3                      .                           .
  .                      .                           .
  .                      .                           .
  .                      .                           .
 10                      .                           .
-----------------------------------------------------------
Totals:            $      .                   $      .
```

14. Four experiments are performed, each experiment consisting of six test results. The results for each experiment are given below. Write a program using a nested loop to compute and display the average of the test results for each experiment.

1st experiment results:	23.2	31.5	16.9	27.5	25.4	28.6
2nd experiment results:	34.8	45.2	27.9	36.8	33.4	39.4
3rd experiment results:	19.4	16.8	10.2	20.8	18.9	13.4
4th experiment results:	36.9	39.5	49.2	45.1	42.7	50.6

15. Modify the program written for Exercise 14 so that the number of test results for each
experiment is entered by the user. Write your program so that a different number of test
results can be entered for each experiment.

16. a. A bowling team consists of five players. Each player bowls three games. Write a
   C program that uses a nested loop to enter each player's individual scores and then
   computes and displays the average score for each bowler. Assume that each bowler has
   the following scores:

1st bowler:	286	252	265
2nd bowler:	212	186	215
3rd bowler:	252	232	216
4th bowler:	192	201	235
5th bowler:	186	236	272

   b. Modify the program written for Exercise 16a to calculate and display the average
   team score. (*Hint:* Use a second variable to store the total of all the players' scores.)

17. Rewrite the program written for Exercise 16a to eliminate the inner loop. To do this,
you will have to input three scores for each bowler rather than one at a time. Each score
must be stored in its own variable name before the average is calculated.

18. Write a program that calculates and displays the yearly amount available if $1,000 is
invested in a bank account for 10 years. Your program should display the amounts available for interest rates from 6 percent to 12 percent inclusively, at 1 percent increments.
Use a nested loop, with the outer loop having a fixed count of 7 and the inner loop a fixed
count of 10. The first iteration of the outer loop should use an interest rate of 6 percent
and display the amount of money available at the end of the first 10 years. In each

subsequent pass through the outer loop, the interest rate should be increased by 1 percent. Use the relationship that the money available at the end of each year equals the amount of money in the account at the start of the year plus the interest rate times the amount available at the start of the year.

5.4   The do Statement

Both the while and for statements evaluate an expression at the start of the repetition loop. There are cases, however, where it is more convenient to test the expression at the end of the loop. For example, suppose we have constructed the following while loop to calculate sales taxes:

```
printf("Enter a price:");
scanf("%f", &price);
while (price != SENTINEL)
{
    salestax = RATE * price;
    printf("The sales tax is $%5.2f",salestax);
    printf("\nEnter a price: ");
    scanf("%f", &price);
}
```

Using this while statement requires either duplicating the prompt and scanf() function calls before the loop and then within the loop, as we have done, or resorting to some other artifice to force initial execution of the statements within the while loop.

The do statement, as its name implies, allows us to do some statements before an expression is evaluated. In many situations this can be used to eliminate the duplication illustrated in the previous example. The general form of the do statement is:

```
do
    statement;
while (expression);
```
◄─────────── don't forget the final ;

As with all C programs, the single statement in the do may be replaced with a compound statement. A flow-control diagram illustrating the operation of the do statement is shown in Figure 5-8.

As illustrated in Figure 5-8, all statements within the do statement are executed at least once before the expression is evaluated. Then, if the expression has a nonzero value, the statements are executed again. This process continues

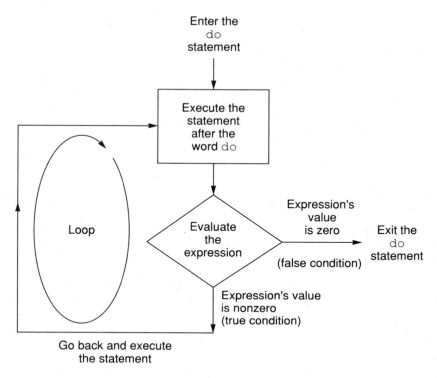

FIGURE 5–8 The do Statement's Flow of Control

until the expression evaluates to zero. For example, consider the following do statement:

```
do
{
    printf("\nEnter a price: ");
    scanf("%f", &price);
    salestax = RATE * price;
    printf("The sales tax is $%5.2f", salestax);
}
while (price != SENTINEL);
```

Observe that only one prompt and scanf() statement are required because the tested expression is evaluated at the end of the loop.

As with all repetition statements, the do statement can always replace or be replaced by an equivalent while or for statement. The choice of which statement to use depends on the application and the style preferred by the programmer. In general, the while and for statements are preferred because they clearly let anyone reading the program know what is being tested "right up front" at the top of the program loop.

Validity Checks

The do statement is particularly useful in filtering user-entered input and providing data validity checks. For example, assume that an operator is required to enter a valid customer identification number between the numbers 1000 and 1999. A number outside this range is to be rejected and a new request for a valid number made. The following section of code provides the necessary data filter to verify the entry of a valid identification number:

```
do
{
  printf("\nEnter an identification number: ");
  scanf("%f", &id_num);
}
while (id_num < 1000 || id_num > 1999);
```

Here, a request for an identification number is repeated until a valid number is entered. This section of code is "bare bones" in that it neither alerts the operator to the cause of the new request for data nor allows premature exit from the loop if a valid identification number cannot be found. An alternative removing the first drawback is:

```
do
{
  printf("\nEnter an identification number: ");
  scanf("%f", &id_num);
  if (id_num < 1000 || id_num > 1999)
  {
    printf("\n An invalid number was just entered");
    printf("\nPlease check the ID number and re-enter");
  }
  else
    break;    /* break if a valid id num was entered */
} while(1);   /* this expression is always true */
```

Here we have used a break statement to exit from the loop. Since the expression being evaluated by the do statement is always 1 (true), an infinite loop has been created that is only exited when the break statement is encountered.

Exercises 5.4

1. a. Using a do statement, write a program to accept a grade. The program should request a grade continuously as long as an invalid grade is entered. An invalid grade is any grade less than 0 or greater than 100. After a valid grade has been entered, your program should display the value of the grade entered.

b. Modify the program written for Exercise 1a so that the user is alerted when an invalid grade has been entered.

c. Modify the program written for Exercise 1b so that it allows the user to exit the program by entering the number 999.

d. Modify the program written for Exercise 1b so that it automatically terminates after five invalid grades are entered.

2. a. Write a program that continuously requests a grade to be entered. If the grade is less than 0 or greater than 100, your program should print an appropriate message informing the user that an invalid grade has been entered, else the grade should be added to a total. When a grade of 999 is entered the program should exit the repetition loop and compute and display the average of the valid grades entered.

b. Run the program written in Exercise 2a on a computer and verify the program using appropriate test data.

3. a. Write a program to reverse the digits of a positive integer number. For example, if the number 8735 is entered, the number displayed should be 5378. (*Hint:* Use a do statement and continuously strip off and display the units digit of the number. If the variable num initially contains the number entered, the units digit is obtained as (num % 10). After a units digit is displayed, dividing the number by 10 sets up the number for the next iteration. Thus, (8735 % 10) is 5 and (8735 / 10) is 873. The do statement should continue as long as the remaining number is not zero).

b. Run the program written in Exercise 3a on a computer and verify the program using appropriate test data.

4. Repeat any of the exercises in Section 5.3 using a do statement rather than a for statement.

5.5   Common Programming Errors

Five errors are commonly made by beginning C programmers when using repetition statements. Two of these pertain to the tested expression and have already been encountered with the if and switch statements. The first is the inadvertent use of the assignment operator, =, for the equality operator, ==, in the tested expression. An example of this error is typing the assignment expression a = 5 instead of the desired relational expression a == 5. Since the tested expression can be any valid C expression, including arithmetic and assignment expressions, this error is not detected by the compiler.

As with the if statement, repetition statements should not use the equality operator, ==, when testing floating point or double precision operands. For example, the expression fnum == .01 should be replaced by an equivalent test requiring that the absolute value of fnum - .01 be less than an acceptable amount. The reason for this is that all numbers are stored in binary form. Using a finite number of bits, decimal numbers such as .01 have no exact binary equivalent, so that tests requiring equality with such numbers can fail.

The next two errors are particular to the `for` statement. The most common is to place a semicolon at the end of the `for`'s parentheses, which frequently produces a do-nothing loop. For example, consider the statements

```
for(count = 0; count < 10; ++ count);
    total = total + num;
```

Here the semicolon at the end of the first line of code is a null statement. This has the effect of creating a loop that is traversed 10 times with nothing done except the incrementing and testing of `count`. This error tends to occur because C programmers are used to ending most lines with a semicolon.

The next error occurs when commas are used to separate the items in a `for` statement instead of the required semicolons. An example of this is the statement

```
for (count = 1, count < 10, ++count)
```

Commas must be used to separate items within the initializing and altering lists, and semicolons must be used to separate these lists from the tested expression.

The last error occurs when the final semicolon is omitted from the `do` statement. This error is usually made by programmers who have learned to omit the semicolon after the parentheses of a `while` statement and carry over this habit when the reserved word `while` is encountered at the end of a `do` statement.

5.6   Chapter Summary

1. The `while`, `for`, and `do` repetition statements create program loops. These statements evaluate an expression and, based on the resulting expression value, either terminate the loop or continue with it.

2. The `while` statement checks its expression before any other statement in the loop. This requires that any variables in the tested expression have values assigned before `while` is encountered. Within a `while` loop there must be a statement that alters the tested expression's value.

3. The `for` statement is extremely useful in creating loops that must be executed a fixed number of times. Initializing expressions, the tested expression, and expressions affecting the tested expression can all be included in parentheses at the top of a `for` loop. Additionally, any other loop statement can be included within the `for`'s parentheses as part of its altering list.

4. The `do` statement checks its expression at the end of the loop. This ensures that the body of a `do` loop is executed at least once. Within a `do` loop there must be at least one statement that alters the tested expression's value.

Functions

Part Three

Writing Your Own Functions

Chapter Six

In the programs we have written so far, the only two functions we have called have been `printf()` and `scanf()`. Although these two functions have been enormously helpful to us, it is now time to create our own useful functions, in addition to the `main()` function that is required in all programs.

In this chapter we learn how to write these functions, pass data to them, process the passed data, and return a result to the calling function.

6.1 Function and Argument Declarations

In creating our own functions, we must be concerned with the function itself and how it interfaces with other functions. This is true both in calling a function and in returning a value back from a function. In this section we describe the first part of the interface, passing data to a function and having the data correctly received and stored by the called function.

As we have already seen with the `printf()` and `scanf()` functions, a function is called, or used, by giving the function's name and passing any data to it in the parentheses following the function name (see Figure 6-1).

The called function must be able to accept the data passed to it by the function doing the calling. Only after the called function successfully receives the data can the data be manipulated to produce a useful result.

To clarify the process of sending and receiving data, consider Program 6-1, which calls a function named `find_max()`. The program, as shown, is not yet complete. Once the function `find_max()` is written and included in Program 6-1, the completed program, consisting of the functions `main()` and `find_max()`, can be run.

 Program 6-1

```
main()
{
   int firstnum, secnum;

   printf("Enter a number: ");
   scanf("%d", &firstnum);
   printf("\nGreat! Please enter a second number: ");
   scanf("%d", &secnum);

   find_max(firstnum, secnum);
}
```

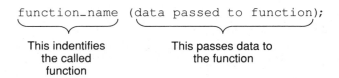

FIGURE 6-1 Calling and Passing Data to a Function

Let us review calling the function `find_max()` from the `main()` function. We will then write `find_max()` to accept the data passed to it and determine and display the largest or maximum value of the two passed values.

The function `find_max()` is referred to as the *called function,* since it is called or summoned into action by its reference in the `main()` function. The function that does the calling, in this case `main()`, is referred to as the *calling function.* The terms called and calling come from standard telephone usage, where one party calls the other on a telephone. The party initiating the call is referred to as the calling party, and the party receiving the call is referred to as the called party. The same terms describe function calls.

Calling a function is rather trivial. All that is required is that the name of the function be used and that any data passed to the function be enclosed within the parentheses following the function name. The items enclosed within the parentheses are called *actual arguments* of the called function (see Figure 6-2).

If a variable is one of the arguments in a function call, the called function receives a copy of the value stored in the variable. For example, the calling statement `find_max(firstnum,secnum);` causes the values or numbers currently residing in the variables `firstnum` and `secnum` to be passed to `find_max()`. The variable names in the calling statement are there to tell the calling function where to get the values that will be passed. After the values are passed, control is transferred to the called function.

As illustrated in Figure 6-3, the function `find_max()` does not receive the variable names `firstnum` and `secnum` and has no knowledge of these variable names. The function simply receives two values and must itself determine where to store these values before it does anything else. Although this procedure for passing data to a function may seem surprising, it is really a safety procedure for ensuring that a called function does not inadvertently change data stored in a variable. The function gets a copy of the data to use. It may change its copy and, of course, change any variables or arguments declared inside itself.

FIGURE 6-2 Calling and Passing Two Values to `find_max()`

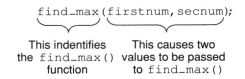

193

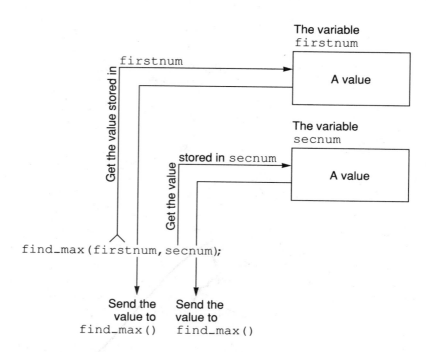

FIGURE 6-3 find_max() Receives Actual Values

However, unless specific steps are taken to do so, a function is not allowed to change the contents of variables declared in other functions.

Let us now begin writing the function find_max() to process the values passed to it.

Every function consists of two parts, a *function header* and a *function body*, as illustrated in Figure 6-4. One of the purposes of the function header is to ensure correct receipt and storage of any data passed to the function. The purpose of the function body is to operate on the passed data and return, at most, one value back to the calling function.

The function header itself consists of two parts, a *function header line* and *argument declarations*. The function header line is always the first line of a function and must include the name of the function and the names of the arguments that will be used by it. If the function returns a value, the function header line must also declare the type of value that will be returned. Since find_max() will not return any value, its function header line consists only

FIGURE 6-4 General Format of a Function

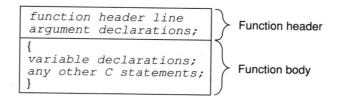

of the function name `find_max()` and a list of arguments. For example, the following header line can be used:

find_max(x,y)◄───────────── no semicolon

The names of the arguments in the function header line, in this case x and y, are chosen by the programmer. Any two names selected according to the rules used to choose variable names can be used.

The argument names in the header line are also called *formal arguments* and are used to store the values passed to the function when it is called. Thus, the argument x will be used to store the first value passed to `find_max()` and the argument y will be used to store the second value passed at the time of the function call. The function itself does not know where the values come from when the call is made from `main()`. The first part of the call procedure executed by the computer involves going to the variables `firstnum` and `secnum` and retrieving the values stored. These values are then passed to `find_max()` and ultimately stored in the formal arguments x and y (see Figure 6-5).

As far as the function `find_max()` is concerned, the arguments x and y are treated like variables. They must be declared and then can be used anywhere within the `find_max()` function. The declaration of these two arguments is given by an argument declaration statement that is placed immediately after the function header line.

Argument declarations, as the name implies, declare the data type of the arguments expected by the function. Since `find_max()` receives two integer values that will be stored in the arguments x and y, any of the following argument declaration statements can be used:

```
int x,y;      or    int y,x;      or    int x;      or    int y;
                                        int y;            int x;
```

As illustrated in these declarations, the order of the arguments is not important. The only requirement is that each argument be declared. Notice that

FIGURE 6–5 Storing Values into Arguments

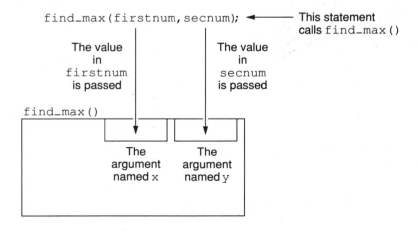

```
    {
        variable declarations (if any)
        other C statements
    }
```

FIGURE 6–6 Structure of a Function Body

these argument declarations are identical to variable declarations. The only difference between argument declarations and variable declarations is their placement in the function. Argument declarations always begin on the second line of the function immediately after the function header line, while variable declarations are placed within the function body. From a programming viewpoint, arguments can be considered as variables whose values are assigned outside the function and passed to the function when it is called. Variables are declared within a function body and have values assigned by statements within the function.

Putting all this together, a valid function header for the find_max() function is:

```
find_max(x,y)      /* this is the function header line */
int x,y;           /* argument declarations           */
```

Now that we have written the function header, we can construct the body of the function find_max(). You have already written many function bodies. A function body begins with an opening brace, {, contains any necessary variable declarations followed by any valid C statements, and ends with a closing brace, }. This is illustrated in Figure 6-6. You should recognize it as the same structure you have been using in all the main() functions you have written. This should not be a surprise, since main() is itself a function and must adhere to the rules required for constructing all legitimate functions.

In the body of the function find_max(), we will declare one variable that will store the maximum of the two numbers passed to find_max(). We will then use an if-else statement to find the maximum of the two numbers. Finally, the printf() function will be called to display the maximum. The complete function code is:

```
find_max(x,y)      /* function header line    */
int x,y;           /* argument declarations   */
{                  /* start of function body  */
  int max;         /* variable declaration    */

  if (x >= y)      /* find the maximum number */
    max = x;
  else
    max = y;

  printf("The maximum of the two numbers is %d.", max);
}        /* end of function body and end of function */
```

Notice that the argument declarations are made before the opening brace that starts the function body, and the variable declarations are made immediately after the opening brace. This is in keeping with the concept that argument values are passed to a function from outside the function, and that variables are declared and assigned values from within the function body.

Program 6-2 includes the `find_max()` function within the program code previously listed in Program 6-1.

 Program 6-2

```
main()
{
  int firstnum,secnum;

  printf("Enter a number: ");
  scanf("%d", &firstnum);
  printf("Great! Please enter a second number: ");
  scanf("%d", &secnum);

  find_max(firstnum, secnum);
}

/* following is the function find_max          */

find_max(x,y)          /* function header line     */
int  x,y;              /* argument declarations    */
{                      /* start of function body   */
  int max;             /* variable declaration     */

  if (x >= y)          /* find the maximum number  */
    max = x;
  else
    max = y;

  printf("\nThe maximum of the two numbers is %d.", max);
}        /* end of function body and end of function */
```

Program 6-2 can be used to select and print the maximum of any two integer numbers entered by the user. Following is a sample run using Program 6-2:

```
Enter a number: 25
Great! Please enter a second number: 5

The maximum of the two numbers is 25.
```

The placement of the `find_max()` function after the `main()` function in Program 6-2 is a matter of choice. Some programmers prefer to put all called

197

functions at the top of a program and make `main()` the last function listed. As we will see in the next section, putting `main()` last has some advantages when the other functions return noninteger values.

We prefer to list `main()` first because it is the driver function that should give anyone reading the program an idea of what the complete program is about before encountering the details of each function. Either placement approach is acceptable and you will encounter both styles in your programming work. In no case, however, can `find_max()` be placed inside `main()`. This is true for all C functions, which must be defined by themselves outside any other function. Each C function is a separate and independent entity with its own arguments and variables; nesting of functions is never permitted.

Exercises 6.1

---

1. For the following function headers, determine the number, type, and order (sequence) of the values that must be passed to the function:

   a. `factorial(n)`
      `int n;`
   b. `price(type,yield,maturity)`
      `int type;`
      `double yield, maturity;`
   c. `yield(type,price,maturity)`
      `int type;`
      `double price, maturity;`
   d. `interest(flag,price,time)`
      `char flag;`
      `float price,time;`
   e. `total(amount,rate)`
      `float amount, rate;`
   f. `roi(a,b,c,d,e,f,g)`
      `int a,d,f;`
      `char b,g;`
      `double c,e;`
   g. `get_val(item,iter,decflag,delim)`
      `int item,iter;`
      `char decflag,delim;`
   h. `tolower(c)`
      `char c;`
   i. `sin(val)`
      `double val;`

2. a. Write a function named `check`, which has three arguments. The first argument should accept an integer number, the second argument a floating point number, and the third argument a double precision number. The body of the function should just display the values of the data passed to the function when it is called. *Note:* When tracing errors in functions, it is very helpful to have the function display the values it has been passed. Quite frequently, the error is not in what the body of the function does with the data, but in the data received and stored. This type of error occurs when a different data type is passed to the function than the data type declared for the arguments.

b. Include the function written in Exercise 2a in a working program. Make sure your function is called from `main()`. Test the function by passing various data to it.

3. *a.* Write a function named `find_abs()` that accepts a double precision number passed to it, computes its absolute value, and displays the absolute value. The absolute value of a number is the number itself if the number is positive, and the negative of the number if the number is negative.

b. Include the function written in Exercise 3a in a working program. Make sure your function is called from `main()`. Test the function by passing various data to it.

4. *a.* Write a function called `mult()` that accepts two floating point numbers as arguments, multiplies these two numbers, and displays the result.

b. Include the function written in Exercise 4a in a working program. Make sure your function is called from `main()`. Test the function by passing various data to it.

5. *a.* Write a function named `sqr_it()` that computes the square of the value passed to it and displays the result. The function should be capable of squaring numbers with decimal points.

b. Include the function written in Exercise 5a in a working program. Make sure your function is called from `main()`. Test the function by passing various data to it.

6. *a.* Write a function named `powfun()` that raises an integer number passed to it to a positive integer power and displays the result. The positive integer should be the second value passed to the function. Declare the variable used to store the result as a long integer data type to insure sufficient storage for the result.

b. Include the function written in Exercise 6a in a working program. Make sure your function is called from `main()`. Test the function by passing various data to it.

7. *a.* Write a function that produces a table of the numbers from 1 to 10, their squares, and cubes. The function should produce the same display as that produced by Program 5-10.

b. Include the function written in Exercise 7a in a working program. Make sure your function is called from `main()`. Test the function by passing various data to it.

8. *a.* Modify the function written for Exercise 7 to accept the starting value of the table, the number of values to be displayed, and the increment between values. Name your function `sel_tab()`. A call to `sel_tab(6,5,2);` should produce a table of five lines, the first line starting with the number 6 and each succeeding number increasing by 2.

b. Include the function written in Exercise 8a in a working program. Make sure your function is called from `main()`. Test the function by passing various data to it.

6.2 Returning Values

As described in the last section, a function need not return any result back to the calling function. A function must, of course, process the data passed to it, or there would be no need for the function. In this section we see how the result produced can be returned directly to the calling function.

In keeping with our original definition of a function as a module that can accept data, operate on the data, and return a result, all C functions are restricted to returning at most one, and only one, "legitimate" value (see Figure 6-7). As you might expect, given C's flexibility, there is a way of returning more than a single value, but that is the topic of Section 6.6. Here we are only concerned with the return of a single value from a called function.

As with the initial calling of a function, returning a value requires that the interface between the called and calling functions be handled correctly. From its side of the return transaction, the called function must provide the following items:

the data type of the returned value
the actual value being returned

A function returning a value must specify, in its header line, the data type of the value that will be returned. Recall that the function header line is the first line of the function, which includes both the function's name and a list of argument names. As an example, consider the find_max() function written in the last section. It determined the maximum value of two numbers passed to the function. For convenience, the original code of find_max() is listed below.

```
find_max(x,y)         /* function header line   */
int x,y;              /* argument declarations  */
{                     /* start of function body */
  int max;            /* variable declaration   */
  if (x >= y)         /* find the maximum number */
    max = x;
  else
    max = y;
  printf("\n\nThe maximum of the two numbers is %d.", max);
}
```

As written, the function's header line is find_max(x,y), where x and y are the names chosen for the function's formal arguments.

FIGURE 6–7 A Function Returns at Most One Value

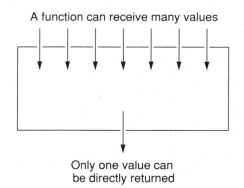

A function can receive many values

Only one value can
be directly returned

If `find_max()` is now to return a value, the function's header line must be amended to include the data type of the value being returned. For example, if an integer value is to be returned, the proper function header line is

```
int find_max(x,y)
```

Similarly, if the function is to return a floating point value the correct function header line is

```
float find_max(x,y)
```

If the function is to return a double precision value the header line would be

```
double find_max(x,y)
```

Let us now modify the function `find_max()` to return the maximum value of the two numbers passed to it. To do this, we must first determine the data type of the value that is to be returned and include this data type in the function's header line.

Since the maximum value determined by `find_max()` is stored in the integer variable `max`, it is the value of this variable that the function will return. Returning an integer value from `find_max()` requires that the function header line be `int find_max(x,y)`. Observe that this is the same as the original function header line for `find_max()` with the addition of the reserved word `int` to declare the data type of the returned value.

Having declared the data type that `find_max()` will return, all that remains is to include a statement within the function to cause the return of the correct value. To return a value, a function must use a `return` statement, which has the form:

```
return(expression);
```

When the `return` statement is encountered, the expression inside the parentheses is evaluated first. The value of the expression is then automatically converted to the data type declared in the function header line before being sent back to the calling function. After the value is returned, program control reverts to the calling function. Thus, to return the value stored in `max`, all we need to do is add the statement `return(max);` before the closing brace of the `find_max()` function. The complete function code is:

These must be the same data type

```
int find_max(x,y)        /* function header line     */
int x,y;                 /* argument   declaration   */
{                        /* start of function body   */
    int max;             /* variable declaration     */

    if (x >= y)
        max = x;
    else
        max = y;

    return(max);         /* return statement         */
}
```

In the new code for the function `find_max()`, note that the data type of the expression contained within the parentheses of the return statement correctly matches the data type in the function's header line. It is up to the programmer to ensure that this is so for every function returning a value. Failure to match the return value with the function's declared data type will not result in an error when your program is compiled, but it may lead to undesired results since the return value is always converted to the data type declared in the function declaration. Usually this is a problem only when the fractional part of a returned floating point or double precision number is truncated because the function was declared to return an integer value.

Having taken care of the sending side of the return transaction, we must now prepare the calling function to receive the value sent by the called function. On the calling (receiving) side, the calling function must:

> be alerted to the type of value to expect
> properly use the returned value

We will consider these items in reverse order.

To use a returned value we must either provide a variable to store the value or use the value directly in an expression. Storing the returned value in a variable is accomplished using a standard assignment statement. For example, the assignment statement

```
maxnum = find_max(firstnum,secnum);
```

can be used to store the value returned by `find_max()` in the variable named `maxnum`. This assignment statement does two things. First the right-hand side of the assignment statement calls `find_max()`, then the result returned by `find_max` is stored in the variable `maxnum`. Since the value returned by `find_max()` is an integer, the variable `maxnum` must also be declared as an integer variable within the calling function's variable declarations.

The value returned by a function need not be stored directly in a variable, but can be used wherever an expression is valid. For example, the expression `2 * find_max(firstnum,secnum)` multiplies the value returned by `find_max()` by two, and the statement

```
printf("%d", find_max (firstnum, secnum));
```

displays the returned value.

Finally, we must ensure that the calling function "knows" the data type of the function being called before a value is actually returned. This can always be taken care of by declaring the called function in the same way that a variable is declared. For example, including the declaration statement

```
int find_max();
```

with `main()`'s variable declarations is sufficient to alert `main()` that `find_max()` is a function that will return an integer value.

202

Program 6-3 illustrates the inclusion of both declaration and assignment statements for main() to correctly declare, call, and store a returned value from find_max(). As before, and in keeping with our convention of placing the main() function first, we have placed the find_max() function after main().

 Program 6-3

```
main()
{
   int find_max();           /* function declaration statement */
   int firstnum, secnum, maxnum;   /* variable declarations */

   printf("Enter a number: ");
   scanf("%d", &firstnum);
   printf("Great! Please enter a second number: ");
   scanf("%d", &secnum);

   maxnum = find_max(firstnum,secnum);

   printf("\nThe maximum of the two numbers is %d.",maxnum);
}


int find_max(x,y)                 /* function header line    */
int x,y;                          /* argument declarations   */
{
   int max;                       /* variable declarations   */

   if (x >= y)
     max = x;
   else
     max = y;

   return(max);                   /* return statement        */
}
```

In reviewing Program 6-3, it is important to note the four items we have introduced in this section. The first item is the declaration of find_max() within main(). This statement, which ends with a semicolon as all statements do, alerts main() to the data type that find_max() will be returning. The parentheses after the name find_max inform main() that find_max is a function rather than a variable. The second item to notice in main() is the use of an assignment statement to call find_max() and to store the returned value in the variable maxnum. We have also made sure to correctly declare maxnum as an integer within `main()`'s variable declarations so that it matches the data type of the returned value.

The last two items of note concern the coding of the `find_max()` function. The first line of `find_max()` declares that the function will return an integer value, and the expression in the return statement evaluates to a matching data type. Thus, `find_max()` is internally consistent in sending an integer value back to `main()`, and `main()` has been correctly alerted to receive and use the returned integer.

In writing your own functions you must always keep these four items in mind. For another example, see if you can identify these four items in Program 6-4.

 Program 6-4

```
main()
{
   int count;          /* start of declarations */
   double fahren;

   double tempvert();

   for(count = 1; count <= 4; ++count)
   {
     printf("Enter a Fahrenheit temperature: ");
     scanf("%lf", &fahren);
     printf("The Celsius equivalent is %6.2f\n\n", tempvert(fahren) );
   }
}

double tempvert(in_temp)            /* function header line */
double in_temp;                     /* argument declaration */
{
   return( (5.0/9.0) * (in_temp - 32.0) );
}
```

In reviewing Program 6-4 let us first analyze the function `tempvert()`. The complete definition of the function begins with the function's header line and ends with the closing brace after the return statement. The function is declared as a double, which means the expression in the function's return statement must evaluate to a double precision number. Since a function declaration is not a statement but the start of the code defining the function, the function declaration line does not end with a semicolon.

Within `tempvert()`, `in_temp` is declared as a double precision argument. Since an expression with a double precision number yields a double precision value, the correct data type, a double precision number, is returned by the function.

On the receiving side, `main()` has a declaration statement for the function `tempvert()` which agrees with `tempvert()`'s function definition. As with all declaration statements, multiple declarations of the same type may be made within the same statement. Thus, we could have used the same declaration statement to declare both the function `tempvert()` and the variable `fahren` as double precision data types. If we had done so, the single declaration statement

```
double fahren, tempvert();
```

could have been used to replace the two individual declarations for `tempvert()` and `fahren`. For clarity, however, we will always keep function declaration statements apart from variable declaration statements. No additional variable is declared in `main()` to store the returned value from `tempvert()` because the returned value is immediately passed to `printf()` for display.

One further point is worth mentioning here. One of the purposes of declarations, as we learned in Chapter 2, is to alert the computer to the amount of internal storage reserved for the data. The declaration statement within `main()` for `find_max()` performs this task and tells the computer how much storage area must be accessed by `main()` when the returned value is retrieved. Had we placed the `find_max()` function before `main()`, however, the function declaration line for `find_max()` would suffice to alert the computer to the type of storage needed for the returned value. In this case, the function declaration statement for `find_max()`, within `main()`, could be eliminated. Since we have chosen always to list `main()` as the first function in a file, we must include function declaration statements for all functions called by `main()`.

More on Returning Values (`void` Type)

From our discussion of returned data types, you might conclude that if no data type is listed in the function declaration line, no value is returned. Unfortunately, this conclusion is incorrect.

If a data type is omitted in a function header line, the function may return either an integer type or no type at all. That is, the default data type returned by a C function is an integer. Thus, the omission of a data type is no guarantee that the function will not return a value. More frequently it is a sign of poor programming practice in neglecting to clearly identify a returned integer value. In this text we will only omit the data type declaration if the function truly does not return a value. If a value is returned, its type will be explicitly included in the function's header line.

Newer versions of C have a data type called `void`. When the term `void` precedes the function's name in the function header line, both the computer and anyone reading the program are alerted to the fact that the function will not return any value to the calling function. If this data type is available on the version of C you are using, we recommend it for functions that do not return a value to the calling function.

Whether a function returns a value or not, it is good programming practice to include a return statement in the function. Although control is automatically returned to the calling program when the closing brace of a function is reached, this is considered "falling off the edge" of the called function. Using an explicit return statement is a better means of formally returning control to the calling function. If no value is to be returned, simply omit the parentheses and write the return statement as `return;`.

Finally, the fact that a function returns a value does not require that the calling function use the value. A function can be called without either using the returned value in an expression or assigning it to a variable. For example, the statement `tempvert(in_temp);` could be included in Program 6-4. This statement properly calls the function `tempvert()` without further using the returned value. Calling a user-written function without using the returned value is almost always a sign of an error on the part of the programmer, but the error will not be identified or indicated during program compilation.

Exercises 6.2

1. Rewrite Program 6-3 to have the function `find_max()` accept two floating point arguments and return a floating point value to `main()`. Make sure to modify `main()` in order to pass two floating point values to `find_max()` and accept and store the floating point value returned by `find_max()`.

2. For the following sections of code, write a variable declaration that should be included in the function for the returned variable.

 a. `float abs(a,b,c,d)`

```
        .
        .

     return(abs_num);
   }
```
 b. `double squar_rt(num);`

```
        .
        .

     return(squarval);
   }
```
 c. `char key_char()`

```
        .
        .

     return(in_key);
   }
```
 d. `int factorial(n)`

```
        .
        .

     return(factrn);
   }
```

3. For each section of code listed in Exercise 2, write a function declaration, assignment statement, and variable declaration that could be used by a calling function to correctly call the above functions and store the value returned by the function.

4. *a.* Write a function named `find_abs()` that accepts a double precision number passed to it, computes its absolute value, and returns the absolute value to the calling function. The absolute value of a number is the number itself if the number is positive, and the negative of the number if the number is negative.

   b. Include the function written in Exercise 4a in a working program. Make sure your function is called from `main()` and correctly returns a value to `main()`. Have `main()` use `printf()` to display the value returned. Test the function by passing various data to it.

5. *a.* Write a function called `mult()` that accepts two double precision numbers as arguments, multiplies these two numbers, and returns the result to the calling function.

   b. Include the function written in Exercise 5a in a working program. Make sure your function is called from `main()` and correctly returns a value to `main()`. Have `main()` use `printf()` to display the value returned. Test the function by passing various data to it.

6. *a.* Write a function named `powfun()` that raises an integer number passed to it to a positive integer power and returns the result to the calling function. Declare the variable used to return the result as a long integer data type to insure sufficient storage for the result.

   b. Include the function written in Exercise 6a in a working program. Make sure your function is called from `main()` and correctly returns a value to `main()`. Have `main()` use `printf()` to display the value returned. Test the function by passing various data to it.

7. A second-degree polynomial in x is given by the expression $ax^2 + bx + c$, where a, b, and c are known numbers and a is not equal to zero. Write a function named `poly_two(a,b,c,x)` that computes and returns the value of a second-degree polynomial for any passed values of a, b, c, and x.

8. *a.* Rewrite the function `tempvert()` in Program 6-4 to accept a temperature and a character as arguments. If the character passed to the function is the letter `f`, the function should convert the passed temperature from Fahrenheit to Celsius, else the function should convert the passed temperature from Celsius to Fahrenheit.

   b. Modify the `main()` function in Program 6-4 to call the function written for Exercise 8a. Your `main()` function should ask the user for the type of temperature being entered and pass the type (`f` or `c`) into `tempvert()`.

9. *a.* Write a function named `whole()` that returns the integer part of any number passed to the function. (*Hint:* Assign the passed argument to an integer variable.)

   b. Include the function written in Exercise 9a in a working program. Make sure your function is called from `main()` and correctly returns a value to `main()`. Have `main()` use `printf()` to display the value returned. Test the function by passing various data to it.

10. *a.* Write a function named `fracpart()` that returns the fractional part of any number passed to the function. For example, if the number 256.879 is passed to `fracpart()`, the number .879 should be returned. Have the function `fracpart()` call the function `whole()` that you wrote in Exercise 9. The number returned can then be determined as the number passed to `fracpart()` less the returned value when the same argument is passed to `whole()`. The completed program should consist of `main()` followed by `fracpart()` followed by `whole()`.

b. Include the function written in Exercise 10a in a working program. Make sure your function is called from `main()` and correctly returns a value to `main()`. Have `main()` use `printf()` to display the value returned. Test the function by passing various data to it.

6.3   Standard Library Functions

All C programs have access to a standard, preprogrammed set of functions for handling input and output of data, computing mathematical quantities, and manipulating strings of characters. These preprogrammed functions are stored in a system library that contains the collection of standard and tested functions available on your system.

Before using the functions available in the system library, you must know:

> the name of each available function
> the arguments required by each function
> the data type of the result (if any) returned by each function
> a description of what each function does

The first three items are provided by the function header. For example, consider the function named `sqrt()`, which calculates the square root of its argument. The function header for this function is:

```
double sqrt(num)
double num;      /* argument declaration */
```

This header lists all the information required to call the `sqrt()` function. `sqrt()` expects a double precision argument and returns a double precision value.

Many library functions require a standard set of common declarations and other information for proper operation. This information is always contained in a standard file named `stdio.h`. To include the information in this file in your program, the following statement must be included as the first statement of your program:

```
#include <stdio.h> ←———————— no semicolon
```

If you intend to use a library function in your program, placing the `#include` statement at the top of the program ensures proper access to the library function.

Input/Output Library Functions

We have already made extensive use of two input/output (I/O) library functions, `printf()` and `scanf()`. In this section we present two additional I/O library functions.

The `getchar()` function can be used for single character input. The function header for `getchar()` is:

```
char getchar()
```

This declaration is correct unless a noncharacter end-of-file sentinel must be detected. In this case, the declaration

```
int getchar();
```

is required (as described later in Section 9.1). The function `getchar()` expects no arguments to be passed to it and returns a character data type. The actual character returned by `getchar()` is the next single character entered at the terminal. For example, a statement such as

```
in_char = getchar();
```

causes the next character entered at the terminal to be stored in the variable `in_char`. This is equivalent to the longer statement

```
scanf("%c", &in_char);
```

The `getchar()` function is extremely useful when continuously inputting strings of characters, which is the topic of Chapter 10.

The output library function corresponding to `getchar()` is the `putchar()` function. The function header for `putchar()` is:

```
putchar(ch)
char ch;
```

Thus, `putchar()` expects a character argument and does not return any value. `putchar()` displays the character passed to it on the terminal. The statement `putchar('a')` is equivalent to the longer statement `printf("%c",'a')`.

Mathematical Library Functions

Table 6-1 lists the more commonly available system library mathematical functions. Before using these functions, check that they are available on your system.

As with all user-written functions, the arguments passed to a mathematical library function do not have to be numbers. The argument of a library function

TABLE 6-1 Commonly Available Mathematical Functions

Function Header	Description
`int abs (num)` `  int num;`	Returns the absolute value of an integer argument.
`long labs (num)` `  long num;`	Returns the absolute value of a long integer argument.
`double fabs (num)` `  double num;`	Returns the absolute value of a double precision argument.
`double pow (x, y)` `  double x, y;`	Returns *x* raised to the *y* power.
`int rand ()`	Returns a pseudorandom number.
`double sin (angle)` `  double angle;`	Returns the sine of an angle. The angle must be in radians.
`double cos (angle)` `  double angle;`	Returns the cosine of an angle. The angle must be in radians.
`double sqrt (num)` `  double num;`	Returns the square root of its argument. Returns a zero for negative arguments.

can be an expression, provided the expression can be evaluated to yield an argument of the required data type. For example, the following arguments are valid for the given functions:

```
sqrt (4.0 + 7 * 3)          abs (-24 % 3 + 6)
sqrt (25.0 * 3 - 1.04)      abs (a * b - m * n)
sqrt (a * b -  c/6.0)       pow (p*q, 5.0)
square (-32.0/8.0 - 6.0)    pow (2., n+3.)
```

The expressions in parentheses are evaluated first to yield a specific value. Thus, before the variables a, b, c, m, n, p, and q are used in the above expressions, actual values would have to be assigned to these variables. The value of the expression is then passed to the function. Table 6-2 lists the final value of selected expressions and the value returned by the listed function.

Like user-written functions, library functions can be included as part of a larger expression. The value returned by the function is computed before any other operation is performed. For example:

```
5 * square (2.0*7.0-4.0) - 200 = 5 * 100.0 - 200 = 300.0
3.0 * pow (2, 10) / 5.0 = 3 * 1024.0 / 5.0 = 614.4
36 / sqrt (3.0*4.0-3.0) = 36 / 3.0 = 12.0
```

TABLE 6-2   Selected Function Examples

Original Expression	Evaluated Expression	Returned Value
`sqrt(4.0+7.0*3.0)`	`sqrt(25.0)`	5.0
`sqrt(25.0*3.0-1.04)`	`sqrt(73.96)`	8.6
`square(-32.0/8.0 - 6.0)`	`square(-10.0)`	100
`abs(-24/3 + 6)`	`abs(-2)`	2

The step-by-step evaluation of the expression

$$4 \; * \; \text{sqrt}(5.0*20.0-3.96) \; / \; 7.0$$

is:

Step	Result
1. Perform multiplication in argument	`4*sqrt(100.0-3.96)/7.0`
2. Complete argument computation	`4*sqrt(96.04)/7.0`
3. Call the function	`4*9.8/7.0`
4. Perform the multiplication	`29.2/7`
5. Perform the division	`5.6`

Program 6-5 illustrates the use of the `sqrt()` function to determine the time it will take a ball to hit the ground after it has been dropped from a building. The mathematical formula used to calculate the time in seconds that it takes to fall a given distance in feet is:

$$time = \text{sqrt}(\, 2 * distance \, / \, g \,)$$

where g is the gravitational constant equal to 32.2 ft/sec^2.

 Program 6-5

```c
#include <stdio.h>
#define GRAV 32.2
main()
{
  double time, distance;
  double sqrt();              /* declare the sqrt() function */

  printf("Enter the distance (in feet): ");
  scanf("%lf", &distance);
  time = sqrt(2 * distance / GRAV);

  printf("\nIt will take %4.2lf seconds", time);
  printf("\nto fall %7.3lf feet.", distance);
}
```

Notice that Program 6-5 contains an `#include` statement and a `#define` statement that equates the value of the gravitational constant 32.2 to the symbolic name `GRAV`. Additionally, just as all functions that `main()` uses must be declared (unless they are physically located in the same file before `main()`), we have included a declaration for `sqrt()` with `main()`'s declaration statements. Although the actual code for the `sqrt()` function is contained within the standard system library, the proper declaration must be provided by the programmer. Alternatively, all compilers have a standard file named `math.h` that contains appropriate declaration statements for the supplied mathematical functions. Including the line `#include <math.h>` before `main()` removes the necessity for explicitly typing declarations for the mathematical functions as was done in Program 6-5. Following is a sample run using Program 6-5:

```
Enter the distance (in feet): 600

It will take 6.20 seconds
to fall 600.000 feet.
```

String Library Functions

Almost all C compilers have an extensive set of library functions for the input, comparison, manipulation, and output of strings of characters. A list and description of these functions is given in Table 6-3. We will describe these functions in Chapter 10, where character strings are presented.

TABLE 6-3 String Library Functions

Name	Description
`strcat(string1,string2)`	Concatenate `string2` to `string1`.
`strchr(string,character)`	Locate the position of the first occurrence of the character within the string.
`strcmp(string1,string2)`	Compare `string2` to `string1`.
`strcpy(string1,string2)`	Make `string1` equal to `string2`.
`strlen(string)`	Determine the length of the string.

Miscellaneous Routines

In addition to the input/output, mathematical, and string functions, all system libraries have an extensive collection of miscellaneous functions and other routines. Some of the more useful of these are listed in Table 6-4.

TABLE 6-4 **Miscellaneous Routines**

Name	Description
isalpha(character)	Returns a nonzero number if the character is a letter; otherwise it returns a zero.
isupper(character)	Returns a nonzero number if the character is uppercase; otherwise it returns a zero.
islower(character)	Returns a nonzero number if the character is lowercase; otherwise it returns a zero.
isdigit(character)	Returns a nonzero number if the character is a digit (0 through 9; otherwise it returns a zero.
toupper(character)	Returns the uppercase equivalent if the character is lowercase; otherwise it returns the character unchanged.
tolower(character)	Returns the lowercase equivalent if the character is uppercase; otherwise it returns the character unchanged.

These routines are included in a standard file named `ctype.h`. To access and use them in a program requires the following statement before `main()`:

```
#include <ctype.h>   ←———— no semicolon
```

The routines listed in Table 6-4 are particularly useful in checking characters input by a user. For example, Program 6-6 continuously requests that a user enter a character and determines if the character is a letter or a digit. The program exits the `while` loop when an `f` is typed. So that the user won't have to decide whether a lowercase or uppercase `f` must be entered to stop the program, the program converts all input to lowercase and just checks for a lowercase `f`.

A few remarks are in order in reviewing Program 6-6. First, the condition being tested in the `if-else` statement makes use of the fact that a condition is considered true if it evaluates to a nonzero value. Thus, the condition (`isalpha(in_char)`) could have been written as (`isalpha(in_char) != 0`), and the condition (`isdigit(in_char)`) could have been written (`isdigit(in_char) != 0`). The second call to `getchar()` in the `do-while` loop is used to remove the ENTER key.

Program 6-6

```c
#include <stdio.h>
#include <ctype.h>
main()
{
  char in_char;

  do
  {
    printf("\nPush any key (type an f to stop) ");
    in_char = getchar();          /* get the next character typed */
    in_char = tolower(in_char);        /* convert to lowercase */
    getchar();                    /* get and ignore the ENTER key */
    if ( isalpha(in_char) )    /* a nonzero value is true in C */
      printf("\nThe character entered is a letter.");
    else if ( isdigit(in_char) )
      printf("\nThe character entered is a digit.");
  } while (in_char != 'f');

}
```

Since functions return values, a function may itself be an argument to a function (including itself). For example, the two statements in Program 6-6:

```c
in_char = getchar();      /* get the next character typed */
in_char = tolower(in_char);        /* convert to lowercase */
```

may be combined into the single statement:

```c
in_char = tolower(getchar());
```

Exercises 6.3

1. Write a program that calculates the square root of a user-entered number. The program should keep prompting the user for a number until the number 999 is entered.

2. Write a program that calculates the absolute value of a user-entered integer number. The program should keep prompting the user for an integer number until the number 999 is entered. Determine what happens if a user types in a number with a decimal point rather than an integer.

3. Write a program that raises the first number input by a user to the power of the second number entered. The program should contain a `for` statement that causes four repetitions of the input prompts and calls to the `pow()` function.

4. Write a function named `root_4(m)` that returns the fourth root of its argument. In writing `root_4()` make use of the `sqrt()` library function.

5. Write a program using the `getchar()`, `toupper()`, and `putchar()` functions that echo back all letters entered in their uppercase form. The program should terminate when either an f or F is entered. (*Hint:* Convert all letters to uppercase and test only for an F.)

6. Rewrite Program 6-6 using a `while` statement in place of the `do-while` statement used in the program.

7. Write a C program that uses the `getchar()` function to input a character from the terminal into the variable `in_char`. Include the function call within a `do-while` loop that continues to prompt the user for an additional character until the + key is pressed. After each character is entered, print the decimal value used to store the character, using the `printf()` function call `printf("%d",in_char);`. From the output of your program, create a table by hand, listing all the characters on your keyboard and the internal code used by your computer to store them.

6.4 Variable Scope

Now that we have begun to write programs containing more than one function, we can look more closely at the variables declared within each function and their relationship to variables in other functions.

By their very nature, C functions are constructed to be independent modules. As we have seen, values are passed to a function using the function's argument list and a value is returned from a function using a return statement. Seen in this light, a function can be thought of as a closed box, with slots at the top to receive values and a single slot at the bottom of the box to return a value (see Figure 6-8).

The metaphor of a closed box is useful because it emphasizes the fact that what goes on inside the function, including all variable declarations within the function's body, are hidden from the view of all other functions. Since the variables created inside a function are available only to the function itself, they are said to be local to the function, or *local variables*. This term refers to the *scope* of a variable, where scope is defined as the section of the program where the variable is valid or "known." A variable can have either a local scope or a global scope. A variable with a *local scope* is simply one that has had storage locations set aside for it by a declaration statement made within a function body. Local variables are only meaningful when used in expressions or statements inside the function that declared them. This means that the same variable name can be declared and used in more than one function. For each function that declares the variable, a separate and distinct variable is created.

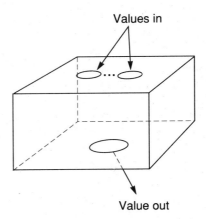

Values in

Value out

FIGURE 6–8 A Function Can Be Considered a Closed Box

All the variables we have used until now have been local variables. This is a direct result of placing our declaration statements inside functions and using them as definition statements that cause the computer to reserve storage for the declared variable. As we shall see, declaration statements can be placed outside functions and need not act as definitions that cause new storage areas to be reserved for the declared variable.

A variable with *global scope,* more commonly termed a *global variable,* is one whose storage has been created for it by a declaration statement located outside any function. Global variables are also referred to as *external* variables. These variables can be used by all functions in a program that are physically placed after the global variable declaration. This is shown in Program 6-7, where we have purposely used the same variable name inside both functions contained in the program.

 Program 6-7

```
int firstnum;     /* create a global variable named firstnum */
main()
{
  int secnum;     /* create a local variable named secnum */

  firstnum = 10;  /* store a value into the global variable */
  secnum = 20;    /* store a value into the local variable  */

  printf("\nFrom main(): firstnum = %d",firstnum);
  printf("\nFrom main(): secnum = %d\n",secnum);
  valfun();       /* call the function valfun */
  printf("\nFrom main() again: firstnum = %d",firstnum);
  printf("\nFrom main() again: secnum = %d",secnum);
}
```

continued

```
valfun()          /* no values are passed to this function */
{
  int secnum;    /* create a second local variable named secnum   */
  secnum = 30;   /* this only affects this local variable's value */
  printf("\nFrom valfun(): firstnum = %d",firstnum);
  printf("\nFrom valfun(): secnum = %d\n",secnum);
  firstnum = 40; /* this changes firstnum for both functions    */
  return;
}
```

The variable `firstnum` in Program 6-7 is a global variable because its storage is created by a declaration statement located outside a function. Since both functions, `main()` and `valfun()`, follow the declaration of `firstnum`, both of these functions can use this global variable with no further declaration needed.

Program 6-7 also contains two separate local variables, both named `secnum`. Storage for the `secnum` variable named in `main()` is created by the declaration statement located in `main()`. A different storage area for the `secnum` variable in `valfun()` is created by the declaration statement located in the `valfun()` function. Figure 6-9 illustrates the three distinct storage areas reserved by the three declaration statements found in Program 6-7.

Each of the variables named `secnum` are local to the function in which their storage is created, and each of these variables can only be used from within the appropriate function. Thus, when `secnum` is used in `main()`, the storage area reserved by `main()` for its `secnum` variable is accessed, and when `secnum` is used in `valfun()`, the storage area reserved by `valfun()` for its `secnum` variable is accessed. The following output is produced when Program 6-7 is run:

```
From main(): firstnum = 10
From main(): secnum = 20

From valfun(): firstnum = 10
From valfun(): secnum = 30

From main() again: firstnum = 40
From main() again: secnum = 20
```

FIGURE 6-9 The Three Storage Areas Created by Program 6-7

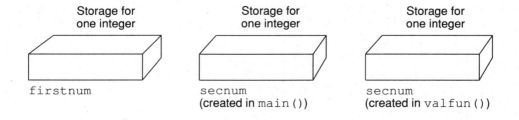

Let us analyze the output produced by Program 6-7. Since `firstnum` is a global variable, both the `main()` and `valfun()` functions can use and change its value. Initially, both functions print the value of `10` that `main()` stored in `firstnum`. Before returning, `valfun()` changes the value of `firstnum` to `40`, which is the value displayed when the variable `firstnum` is next displayed from within `main()`.

Since each function only "knows" its own local variables, `main()` can only send the value of its `secnum` to the `printf()` function, and `valfun()` can only send the value of its `secnum` to the `printf()` function. Thus, whenever `secnum` is obtained from `main()` the value of `20` is displayed, and whenever `secnum` is obtained from `valfun()` the value `30` is displayed.

C does not confuse the two `secnum` variables because only one function can execute at a given moment. Only the storage area for the variables created by the function currently being executed are accessed. If a variable that is not local to the function is used by the function, the program searches the global storage areas for the correct name.

The scope of a variable in no way influences or restricts the data type of the variable. Just as a local variable can be a character, integer, float, double, or any of the other data types (long/short) we have introduced, so can global variables be of these data types, as illustrated in Figure 6-10. The scope of a variable is determined solely by the placement of the declaration statement that reserves storage for it, while the data type of the variable is determined by using the appropriate reserved word (`char`, `int`, `float`, `double`, etc.) before the variable's name in a declaration statement.

Misuse of Globals

One caution should be mentioned here. Global variables allow the programmer to "jump around" the normal safeguards provided by functions. Rather than passing variables to a function, it is possible to make all variables global ones. *Do not do this.* By indiscriminately making all variables global you instantly destroy the safeguards C provides to make functions independent and insulated from each other, including the necessity of carefully designating the type of arguments needed by a function, the variables used in the function, and the value returned.

FIGURE 6–10 Relating the Scope and Type of a Variable

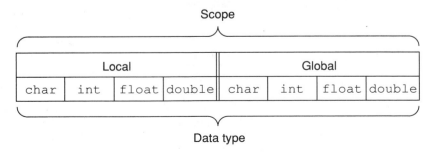

Using only global variables can be especially disastrous in larger programs that have many user-created functions. Since all variables in a function must be declared, creating functions that use global variables requires that you remember to write the appropriate global declarations at the top of each program using the function—they no longer come along with the function. More devastating than this, however, is the horror of trying to track down an error in a large program using global variables. Since a global variable can be accessed and changed by any function following the global declaration, it is a time-consuming and frustrating task to locate the origin of an erroneous value.

Global variables, however, are extremely useful in creating tables of data that must be shared between many functions. If many functions require access to a group of tables, global variables allow the functions to make efficient changes to the same table without the need for multiple table passing. We will see this when we explore arrays and data structures in the next three chapters.

Exercises 6.4

1. a. For the following section of code, determine the data type and scope of all declared variables. To do this use a separate sheet of paper and list the three column headings that follow (we have filled in the entries for the first variable):

Variable name	Data type	Scope
price	integer	global to `main()`, `roi()`, and `step()`

```
int price;
long int years;
double yield;
main()
{
  int bondtype;
  double interest, coupon;
      .
      .
      .
}

double roi(mat1,mat2)
int mat1, mat2;        /* these are arguments, not variables */
{
  int count;
  double eff_int;
      .
      .
      .
  return(eff_int);
}
```

```
int step(first,last)
float first, last;    /* these are arguments, not variables */
{
   int numofyrs;
   float fracpart;
       .
       .
       .
   return(10*numofyrs);
}
```

b. Draw boxes around the appropriate section of the above code to enclose the scope of each variable.

c. Determine the data type of the arguments that the functions roi() and step() expect, and the data type of the value returned by these functions.

2. *a.* For the following section of code, determine the data type and scope of all declared variables. To do this use a separate sheet of paper and list the three column headings that follow (we have filled in the entries for the first variable):

Variable name	Data type	Scope
key	char	global to main(), func1(), and func2()

```
char key;
long int number;
main()
{
   int a,b,c;
   double x,y;
       .
       .
       .
}
double secnum;
 int func1(num1, num2)
int num1, num2;       /* these are arguments, not variables */
{
   int o,p;
   float q;
       .
       .
       .
   return(p);
}
double func2(first,last)
float first, last;    /* these are arguments, not variables */
{
   int a,b,c,o,p;
   float r;
   double s,t,x;
       .
       .
       .
   return(s*t);
}
```

b. Draw a box around the appropriate section of the above code to enclose the scope of the variables `key`, `secnum`, `y`, and `r`.

c. Determine the data type of the arguments that the functions `func1()` and `func2()` expect, and the data type of the value returned by these functions.

3. Besides speaking about the scope of a variable, we can also apply the term to the arguments declared inside a function. What do you think is the scope of all function arguments?

4. Determine the values displayed by each call to `printf()` in the following program:

```
int firstnum = 10;   /* declare and initialize a global variable */
main()
{
  int firstnum = 20; /* declare and initialize a local variable  */

  printf("\nThe value of firstnum is %d",firstnum);
  display();
}

display()
{
  printf("\nThe value of firstnum is now %d",firstnum);
}
```

6.5 Variable Storage Class

The scope of a variable defines the location within a program where that variable can be used. Given a program, you could take a pencil and draw a box around the section of the program where each variable is valid. The space inside the box would represent the scope of a variable. From this viewpoint, the scope of a variable can be thought of as the space within the program where the variable is valid.

In addition to the space dimension represented by its scope, variables also have a time dimension. The time dimension refers to the length of time that storage locations are reserved for a variable. For example, all variable storage locations are released back to the computer when a program is finished running. However, while a program is still executing, interim variable storage areas are reserved and subsequently released back to the computer. Where and how long a variable's storage locations are kept before they are released can be determined by the storage class of the variable.

The four available storage classes are called `auto`, `static`, `extern`, and `register`. If one of these class names is used, it must be placed before the variable's data type in a declaration statement. Examples of declaration statements that include a storage class designation are:

```
auto int num;      /* auto storage class and int data type   */
static int miles;  /* static storage class and int data type   */
register int dist; /* register storage class and int data type */
extern int price;  /* extern storage class and int data type   */
auto float coupon; /* auto storage class and float data type   */
static double yrs; /* static storage class and double data type */
extern float yld;  /* extern storage class and float data type   */
auto char in_key;  /* auto storage class and char data type     */
```

To understand what the storage class of a variable means, we will first consider local variables (those variables created inside a function) and then global variables (those variables created outside a function).

Local Variable Storage Classes

Local variables can only be members of the `auto`, `static`, or `register` storage classes. If no class description is included in the declaration statement, the variable is automatically assigned to the `auto` class. Thus, auto is the default class used by C. All the local variables we have used, since the storage class designation was omitted, have been `auto` variables.

The term `auto` is short for *automatic.* Storage for automatic local variables is automatically reserved or created each time a function declaring automatic variables is called. As long as the function has not returned control to its calling function, all automatic variables local to the function are "alive"—that is, storage for the variables is available. When the function returns control to its calling function, its local automatic variables "die"—that is, the storage for the variables is released back to the computer. This process repeats itself each time a function is called. For example, consider Program 6-8, where the function `testauto()` is called three times from `main()`.

 Program 6-8

```
main()
{
  int count;  /* create the auto variable count */

  for(count = 1; count <= 3; ++count)
    testauto();
}
```

continued

```
testauto()
{
  int num = 0;   /* create the auto variable num */
                 /* and initialize to zero       */

  printf("\nThe value of the automatic variable num is %d", num);
  ++num;
  return;
}
```

The output produced by Program 6-8 is:

```
The value of the automatic variable num is 0
The value of the automatic variable num is 0
The value of the automatic variable num is 0
```

Each time `testauto()` is called, the automatic variable `num` is created and initialized to zero. When the function returns control to `main()` the variable `num` is destroyed along with any value stored in `num`. Thus, the effect of incrementing `num` in `testauto()`, before the function's return statement, is lost when control is returned to `main()`.

For most applications, the use of automatic variables works just fine. There are cases, however, where we would like a function to remember values between function calls. This is the purpose of the `static` storage class. A local variable that is declared as `static` causes the program to keep the variable and its latest value even when the function that declared it is through executing. Examples of `static` variable declarations are:

```
static int rate;
static float taxes;
static double amount;
static char in_key;
static long years;
```

A local `static` variable is not created and destroyed each time the function declaring the static variable is called. Once created, local static variables remain in existence for the life of the program. This means that the last value stored in the variable when the function is finished executing is available to the function the next time it is called.

Since local `static` variables retain their values, they are not initialized within a declaration statement in the same way as automatic variables. To see why, consider the automatic declaration `int num = 0;`, which causes the automatic variable `num` to be created and set to zero each time the declaration is encountered. This is called a *run-time initialization* because initialization occurs each time the declaration statement is encountered. This type of initialization would be disastrous for a `static` variable, because resetting the variable's value to zero each time the function is called would destroy the very value we are trying to save.

The initialization of static variables (both local and global) is done only once, when the program is first compiled. At compilation time the variable is created and any initialization value is placed in it. Thereafter, the value in the variable is kept without further initialization each time the function is called. To see how this works, consider Program 6-9.

 Program 6-9

```
main()
{
  int count;                /* count is a local auto variable */

  for(count = 1; count <= 3; ++count)
    teststat();
}

teststat()
{
  static int num = 0;      /* num is a local static variable */

  printf("\nThe value of the static variable num is now %d", num);
  ++num;
  return;
}
```

The output produced by Program 6-9 is:

```
The value of the static variable num is now 0
The value of the static variable num is now 1
The value of the static variable num is now 2
```

As illustrated by the output of Program 6-9, the static variable num is set to zero only once. The function teststat() then increments this variable just before returning control to main(). The value that num has when leaving the function teststat() is retained and displayed when the function is next called.

Unlike automatic variables that can be initialized by either constants or expressions using both constants and previously initialized variables, static variables can only be initialized using constants or constant expressions, such as 3.2 + 8.0. Also, unlike automatic variables, all static variables are set to zero when no explicit initialization is given. Thus, the specific initialization of num to zero in Program 6-9 is not required.

The remaining storage class available to local variables, the register class, is not used as extensively as either automatic or static variables. Examples of register variable declarations are:

```
register int time;
register double diffren;
register float coupon;
```

Register variables have the same time duration as automatic variables; that is, a local register variable is created when the function declaring it is entered, and is destroyed when the function completes execution. The only difference between register and automatic variables is where the storage for the variable is located.

Storage for all variables (local and global), except register variables, is reserved in the computer's memory area. Most computers have a few additional high-speed storage areas located directly in the computer's processing unit that can also be used for variable storage. These special high-speed storage areas are called *registers*. Since registers are physically located in the computer's processing unit, they can be accessed faster than the normal memory storage areas located in the computer's memory unit. Also, computer instructions that reference registers typically require less space than instructions that reference memory locations because there are fewer registers that can be accessed than there are memory locations.

For example, although the AT&T WE® 32100 Central Processing Unit has nine registers that can be used for local C program variables, it can be connected to memories that have more than four billion bytes. Most other computers have a similar set of user-accessible registers but millions of memory locations. When the compiler substitutes the location of a register for a variable during program compilation, less space in the instruction is needed than is required to address a memory having millions of locations.

Besides decreasing the size of a compiled C program, using register variables can also increase the execution speed of a C program, if the computer you are using supports this data type. Variables declared with the register storage class are automatically switched to the auto storage class if your computer does not support register variables or if the declared register variables exceed the computer's register capacity.

The only restriction in using the register storage class is that the address of a register variable, using the address operator &, cannot be taken. This is easily understood when you realize that registers do not have standard memory addresses.

Global Variable Storage Classes

Global variables, also referred to as external variables, are created by declaration statements external to a function. By their nature, these externally defined variables do not come and go with the calling of any function. Once an external (global) variable is created, it exists until the program in which it is declared is finished executing. Thus, external variables cannot be declared as either `auto` or `register` variables that are created and destroyed as the program is executing. Global variables may, however, be declared as members of the `static` or `extern` storage classes. Examples of declaration statements including these two class descriptions are:

```
extern int sum;
extern double price;
static double yield;
```

The `static` and `extern` classes affect only the scope, not the time duration, of global variables. As with `static` local variables, all global variables are initialized to zero at compile time if no explicit initialization is present.

The purpose of the `extern` storage class is to extend the scope of a global variable beyond its normal boundaries. To understand this, we must first make note of the fact that all of the programs we have written so far have always been contained together in one file. Thus, when you have saved or retrieved programs you have only needed to give the computer a single name for your program. This is not required by C.

Larger programs typically consist of many functions that are stored in multiple files. An example of this is shown in Figure 6-11, where the three

FIGURE 6–11 A Program May Extend Beyond One File

```
file1
┌────────────────────────┐
│ int price;             │
│ float yield;           │
│ static double coupon;  │
│ main()                 │
│ {                      │
│    func1();            │
│    func2();            │
│    func3();            │
│    func4();            │
│ }                      │
│ func1()                │
│ {                      │
│       .                │
│       .                │
│       .                │
│ }                      │
│ func2()                │
│ {                      │
│       .                │
│       .                │
│       .                │
│ }                      │
└────────────────────────┘
```

```
file2
┌────────────────────────┐
│ double interest;       │
│ func3()                │
│ {                      │
│       .                │
│       .                │
│       .                │
│ }                      │
│ func4()                │
│ {                      │
│       .                │
│       .                │
│       .                │
│ }                      │
└────────────────────────┘
```

functions `main()`, `func1()`, and `func2()` are stored in one file and the two functions `func3()` and `func4()` are stored in a second file.

For the files illustrated in Figure 6-11, the global variables `price`, `yield`, and `coupon` declared in `file1` can only be used by the functions `main()`, `func1()`, and `func2()` in this file. The single global variable, `interest`, declared in `file2` can only be used by the functions `func3()` and `func4()` in `file2`.

Although the variable `price` has been created in `file1`, we may want to use it in `file2`. Placing the declaration statement `extern int price;` in `file2`, as shown in Figure 6-12, allows us to do this. Putting this statement at the top of `file2` extends the scope of the variable `price` into `file2` so that it may be used by both `func3()` and `func4()`.

Similarly, placing the statement `extern float yield;` in `func4()` extends the scope of this global variable, created in `file1`, into `func4()`, and the scope of the global variable `interest`, created in `file2`, is extended into `func1()` and `func2()` by the declaration statement `extern double interest;` placed before `func1()`. Notice `interest` is not available to `main()`.

A declaration statement that specifically contains the word `extern` is different from every other declaration statement in that it does not cause the creation of a new variable by reserving new storage for the variable. An `extern` declaration statement simply informs the computer that the variable already exists and can now be used. The actual storage for the variable must

FIGURE 6–12 Extending the Scope of a Global Variable

```
file1                                file2
┌──────────────────────────┐   ┌──────────────────────────┐
│ int price;               │   │ double interest;         │
│ float yield;             │   │ extern int price;        │
│ static double coupon;    │   │ func3()                  │
│ main()                   │   │ {                        │
│ {                        │   │      .                   │
│    func1();              │   │      .                   │
│    func2();              │   │      .                   │
│    func3();              │   │ }                        │
│    func4();              │   │ func4()                  │
│ }                        │   │ {                        │
│ extern double interest;  │   │    extern float yield;   │
│ func1()                  │   │      .                   │
│ {                        │   │      .                   │
│      .                   │   │      .                   │
│      .                   │   │ }                        │
│      .                   │   │                          │
│ }                        │   │                          │
│ func2()                  │   │                          │
│ {                        │   │                          │
│      .                   │   │                          │
│      .                   │   │                          │
│      .                   │   │                          │
│ }                        │   │                          │
└──────────────────────────┘   └──────────────────────────┘
```

be created somewhere else in the program using one, and only one, global declaration statement in which the word extern has not been used. Initialization of the global variable can, of course, be made with the original declaration of the global variable. Initialization within an extern declaration statement is not allowed and will cause a compilation error.

The existence of the extern storage class is the reason we have been so careful to distinguish between the creation and declaration of a variable. Declaration statements containing the word extern do not create new storage areas; they only extend the scope of existing global variables.

The last global class, static global variables, is used to prevent the extension of a global variable into a second file. Global static variables are declared in the same way as local static variables, except that the declaration statement is placed outside any function.

The scope of a global static variable cannot be extended beyond the file in which it is declared. This provides a degree of privacy for static global variables. Since they are only "known" and can only be used in the file in which they are declared, other files cannot access or change their values. static global variables cannot be subsequently extended to a second file using an extern declaration statement. Trying to do so will result in a compilation error.

Exercises 6.5

1. *a.* List the storage classes available to local variables.
   b. List the storage classes available to global variables.

2. Describe the difference between a local auto variable and a local static variable.

3. What is the difference between the following functions:

```
init1()
{
  static int yrs = 1;

  printf("\nThe value of yrs is %d", yrs);
  yrs = yrs + 2;
}

init2()
{
  static int yrs;

  yrs = 1;
  printf("\nThe value of yrs is %d", yrs);
  yrs = yrs + 2;
}
```

4. *a.* Describe the difference between a static global variable and an extern global variable.
   b. If a variable is declared with an extern storage class, what other declaration statement must be present somewhere in the program?

```
file1                            file2
┌─────────────────────────┐  ┌─────────────────────────┐
│ char choice;            │  │ char b_type;            │
│ int flag;               │  │ double maturity;        │
│ long date, time;        │  │ roi()                   │
│ main()                  │  │ {                       │
│ {                       │  │      .                  │
│      .                  │  │      .                  │
│      .                  │  │      .                  │
│      .                  │  │ }                       │
│ }                       │  │ pduction()              │
│ double coupon;          │  │ {                       │
│ price()                 │  │      .                  │
│ {                       │  │      .                  │
│      .                  │  │      .                  │
│      .                  │  │ }                       │
│      .                  │  │ bid()                   │
│ }                       │  │ {                       │
│ yield()                 │  │      .                  │
│ {                       │  │      .                  │
│      .                  │  │      .                  │
│      .                  │  │ }                       │
│      .                  │  │                         │
│ }                       │  │                         │
└─────────────────────────┘  └─────────────────────────┘
```

FIGURE 6–13 Files for Exercise 6

5. The declaration statement `static double years;` can be used to create either a local or global `static` variable. What determines the scope of the variable `years`?

6. For the function and variable declarations illustrated in Figure 6-13, place an `extern` declaration to individually accomplish the following:

    a. Extend the scope of the global variable `choice` into all of `file2`.

    b. Extend the scope of the global variable `flag` into function `pduction()` only.

    c. Extend the scope of the global variable `date` into `pduction()` and `bid()`.

    d. Extend the scope of the global variable `date` into `roi()` only.

    e. Extend the scope of the global variable `coupon` into `roi()` only.

    f. Extend the scope of the global variable `b_type` into all of `file1`.

    g. Extend the scope of the global variable `maturity` into both `price()` and `yield()`.

6.6 Passing Addresses

In the normal course of operation, a called function receives values from its calling function, stores the passed values in its own local arguments, manipulates these arguments appropriately, and possibly returns a single value. This method of calling a function and passing values to it is referred to as a function *call by value.*

    This call by value procedure is a distinct advantage of C. It allows functions to be written as independent entities that can use any variable name without concern that other functions may also be using the same name. In writing a function, arguments can conveniently be thought of as either initialized variables or variables that will be assigned values when the function is executed. At no time, however, does the called function have direct access to any local variable contained in the calling function.

There are times when it is convenient to give a function access to local variables of its calling function. This allows the called function to use and change the value in the variable without the knowledge of the calling function, where the local variable is declared. To do this requires that the address of the variable be passed to the called function. Once the called function has the variable's address, it "knows where the variable lives," so to speak, and can access the variable using the address and the indirection operator.

Passing addresses is referred to as a function *call by reference,* since the called function can reference, or access, the variable using the passed address. In this section we describe the techniques required to pass addresses to a function and have the function accept and use the passed addresses.

Passing, Storing, and Using Addresses

To pass, store, and use addresses requires the use of the address operator (&), pointers, and the indirection operator (*). Let us review these topics before applying them to writing a function.

The address operator is the ampersand symbol, &. Recall that the ampersand followed immediately by a variable means "the address of" the variable. Examples of this are:

&firstnum means "the address of firstnum"
&secnum means "the address of secnum"

Addresses themselves are values that can be stored in variables. The variables that store addresses are called *pointers.* Again, recall that pointers, like all variables, must be declared. In declaring pointers, the data type corresponding to the contents of the address being stored must be included in the declaration. Since all addresses appear the same, this additional information is needed by the computer to know how many storage locations to access when it uses the address stored in the pointer. Examples of pointer declarations are:

```
char *in_addr;
int *num_pt;
float *dst_addr:
double *nml_addr;
```

To understand pointer declarations, read them "backwards," starting with the indirection operator, the asterisk, *. Again, recall that an asterisk followed immediately by a variable or argument can be translated as either "the variable (or argument) whose address is stored in "or" the variable (or argument) pointed to by." Thus, *in_addr can be read as either "the variable whose address is stored in in_addr" or "the variable pointed to by in_addr." Applying this to pointer declarations, the declaration char *in_key;, for example, can be read as either "the variable whose address is stored in in_key is a character" or "the variable pointed to by in_key is a character." Both of these statements are frequently shortened to the simpler statement that "in_key points to a character." As all three interpretations of the declaration statement are correct, select and use whichever description makes a pointer declaration meaningful to you.

We now put all this together to pass two addresses to a function named sortnum(). The function will be written to compare the values contained in the passed addresses and swap the values, if necessary, so that the smaller value is stored in the first address.

Passing addresses to a function should be familiar to you, because we have been using addresses each time we have called the scanf() function. Consider Program 6-10.

 Program 6-10

```
main()
{
    double firstnum, secnum;

    printf("Enter two numbers: ");
    scanf("%lf %lf", &firstnum, &secnum);

    sortnum(&firstnum, &secnum);

    printf("\nThe smaller number is %lf", firstnum);
    printf("\nThe larger number is %lf",secnum);
}
```

Observe in Program 6-10 that addresses are passed to both scanf() and sortnum() (also see Figure 6-14). Had just the values of firstnum and secnum been passed to sortnum(), the function could not swap them in the variables because it would not have access to firstnum and secnum.

One of the first requirements in writing sortnum() is to declare two arguments that can store the passed addresses. The following declarations can be used:

```
double *nm1_addr; /* nm1_addr points to a double precision variable*/
double *nm2_addr; /* nm2_addr points to a double precision variable*/
```

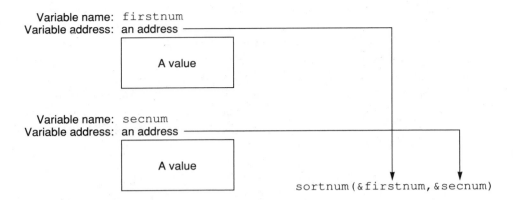

Variable name: `firstnum`
Variable address: an address

A value

Variable name: `secnum`
Variable address: an address

A value

`sortnum(&firstnum,&secnum)`

FIGURE 6–14 Passing Addresses to `sortnum()`

The choice of the argument names `nm1_addr` and `nm2_addr` is, as with all argument names, up to the programmer.

Putting what we have together, the function header for `sortnum()` is:

```
sortnum(nm1_addr,nm2_addr)      /* function declaration   */
double *nm1_addr, *nm2_addr;    /* argument declarations */
```

Notice that a single declaration is used to declare the two pointers, `nm1_addr` and `nm2_addr`.

Before writing the body of `sortnum()` to actually compare and swap values, let's first check that the values accessed using the addresses in `nm1_addr` and `nm2_addr` are correct. This is done in Program 6-11.

 Program 6-11

```
main()
{
   double firstnum = 20.0, secnum = 5.0;

   sortnum(&firstnum, &secnum);
}

sortnum(nm1_addr,nm2_addr)
double *nm1_addr, *nm2_addr;
{
   printf("The number whose address is in nm1_addr is %lf", *nm1_addr);
   printf("\nThe number whose address is in nm2_addr is %lf", *nm2_addr);

}
```

The output displayed when Program 6-11 is run is:

```
The number whose address is in nm1_addr is 20.000000
The number whose address is in nm2_addr is  5.000000
```

In reviewing Program 6-11, note two things. First, `sortnum()` is not declared in `main()` because it returns no direct value to `main()`. Second, within `sortnum()`, the indirection operator is used to access the values stored in `firstnum` and `secnum`. `sortnum()` itself has no knowledge of these variable names, but it does have the address of `firstnum` stored in `nm1_addr` and the address of `secnum` stored in `nm2_addr`. The expression `*nm1_addr` used in the first `printf()` call means "the variable whose address is in `nm1_addr`." This is of course the variable `firstnum`. Similarly, the second `printf()` call obtains the value stored in `secnum` as "the variable whose address is in `nm2_addr`." Thus, we have successfully used pointers to allow `sortnum()` to access variables in `main()`. Figure 6-15 illustrates the concept of storing addresses in arguments.

Having verified that `sortnum()` can access `main()`'s local variables `firstnum` and `secnum`, we can now expand `sortnum()` to compare the values in these variables with an `if` statement to see if they are in the desired order. Using pointers, the `if` statement takes the form

```
if (*nm1_addr > *nm2_addr)
```

This statement should be read: "if the variable whose address is in `nm1_addr` is larger than the variable whose address is in `nm2_addr`." If the condition is true, the values in `main()`'s variables `firstnum` and `secnum` can be interchanged from within `sortnum()` using the three-step interchange algorithm:

1. Store `firstnum`'s value in a temporary location.
2. Store `secnum`'s value in `firstnum`.
3. Store the temporary value in `secnum`.

FIGURE 6–15 Storing Addresses in Arguments

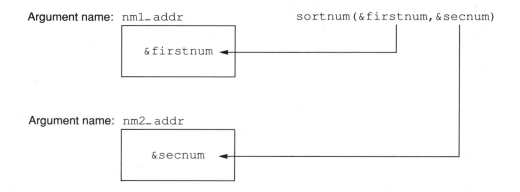

233

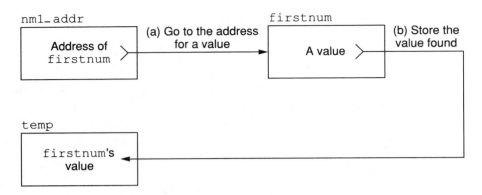

FIGURE 6-16 Indirectly Storing `firstnum`'s value

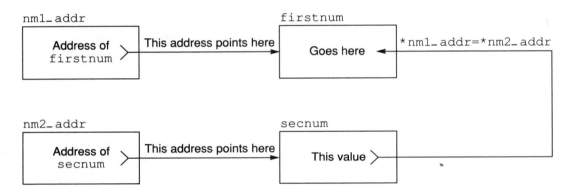

FIGURE 6-17 Indirectly Changing `firstnum`'s Value

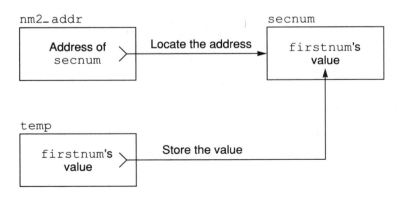

FIGURE 6-18 Indirectly Changing `secnum`'s Value

Using pointers from within `sortnum()`, this takes the form:

1. Store the variable pointed to by `nm1_addr` in a temporary location. The statement `temp = *nm1_addr;` does this (see Figure 6-16).

2. Store the variable whose address is in `nm2_addr` in the variable whose address is in `nm1_addr`. The statement `*nm1_addr = *nm2_addr;` does this (see Figure 6-17).

3. Move the value in the temporary location into the variable whose address is in `nm2_addr`. The statement `*nm2_addr = temp;` does this (see Figure 6-18).

Program 6-12 contains the final form of `sortnum()`, written according to our description.

 Program 6-12

```
main()
{
  double firstnum, secnum;

  printf("Enter two numbers: ");
  scanf("%lf %lf", &firstnum, &secnum);
  sortnum(&firstnum, &secnum);                    /* call sortnum() */
  printf("The smaller number is %6.2lf", firstnum);
  printf("\nThe larger number is %6.2lf",secnum);
}

sortnum(nm1_addr,nm2_addr)
double *nm1_addr, *nm2_addr;       /* declare two pointers */
{
  double temp;

  if (*nm1_addr > *nm2_addr)
  {
    temp = *nm1_addr;              /* save firstnum's value */
    *nm1_addr =  *nm2_addr;        /* move secnum's value in firstnum */
    *nm2_addr = temp;              /* change secnum's value */
  }
  return;
}
```

The following sample run was obtained using Program 6-12:

```
Enter two numbers: 20.6 3.9
The smaller number is  3.90
The larger number is  20.60
```

In reviewing Program 6-12, note that the sole reason for using pointers is to allow us to swap `firstnum`'s value if the values are not in the desired order.

Exercises 6.6

1. Write declaration statements for:

a. a formal argument named `price` that will be used to accept the address of a double precision number

b. a formal argument named `minutes` that will be used to accept the address of an integer number

c. a formal argument named `key` that will be used to accept the address of a character

d. a formal argument named `yield` that will be used to store the address of a double precision number

2. The addresses of the integer variables `sec`, `min`, and `hours` are to be passed to a function named `time(a,b,c)`. Write a suitable function header for `time()`.

3. Rewrite the `find_max()` function in Program 6-3 so that the variable `max` is declared in `main()` and the maximum value of the two passed numbers is written directly to `max`. (*Hint:* The address of `max` will also have to be passed to `find_max()`.)

4. Write a function named `change()` that accepts a floating point number and the addresses of the integer variables named `quarters`, `dimes`, `nickels`, and `pennies`. The function should determine the number of quarters, dimes, nickels, and pennies in the number passed to it and write these values directly into the respective variables declared in its calling function.

5. a. The time in hours, minutes, and seconds is to be passed to a function named `secs()`. Write `secs()` to accept these values and determine the total number of seconds in the passed data. Write this function so that the total number of seconds is returned by the function as an integer number.

b. Repeat Exercise 5a but also pass the address of the variable `tot_sec` to the function `secs()`. Using this passed address, have `secs()` directly alter the value of `tot_sec`.

6. Write a function named `time()` that accepts an integer number of seconds and the addresses of three variables named `hours`, `min`, and `sec`. The function is to convert the passed number of seconds into an equivalent number of hours, minutes, and seconds and directly alter the value of the respective variables using their passed addresses.

7. Write a function named `yr_calc()` that accepts a long integer representing the total number of days from the turn of the century and the addresses of the variables `year`, `month`, and `day`. The function is to calculate the current year, month, and day for the given number of days and write these values directly in the respective variables using the passed addresses. For this problem assume that each year has 365 days and each month has 30 days.

8. Write a function named `liquid()` that is to accept an integer number and the addresses of the variables `gallons`, `quarts`, `pints`, and `cups`. The passed integer represents the total number of cups and the function is to determine the number of gallons, quarts, pints, and cups in the passed value. Using the passed addresses, the function should directly alter the respective variables in the calling function. Use the relationships of two cups to a pint, four cups to a quart, and 16 cups to a gallon.

9. The following program uses the same variable names in both the calling and called function. Determine if this causes any problem for the computer. What problems might this code pose to a programmer? Also determine the type of data stored in each variable.

```
main()
{
  int min, hour;

  printf("Enter two numbers :");
  scanf("%d %d", &min, &hour);
  time(&min,&hour);
}

time(min,hour)
int *min, *hour;
{
  int sec;

  sec = ( (*hour) * 60 + *min ) * 60;
  printf("The total number of seconds is %d", sec);
}
```

10. Assume that the following declaration has been made:

```
int *pt1, *pt2;
```

Since the asterisk, *, is used for both multiplication and indirection, how is the expression

```
* pt1 * * pt2
```

evaluated by the computer? Why does the computer evaluate the expression in the order you have indicated? Rewrite this expression to make its meaning clearer to anyone reading it.

6.7 Common Programming Errors

The most common programming error related to functions is passing values to a function that is not prepared to receive them. The values passed to a function must correspond to the data types of the arguments declared within the function. The simplest way to verify that correct values have been received is to display all passed values within a function's body before any calculations are made. Once this verification has taken place, the display can be dispensed with.

The next common error occurs when the same variable is declared locally within both the calling and called functions. Even though the variable name is the same, a change to one local variable does not alter the value in the other local variable.

Related to this error is the error caused when a local variable has the same name as a global variable. Within the function declaring the local variable, the use of the variable name only affects the local contents. Thus, the value of the global variable can never be altered within the function.

Another common error is omitting the called function's declaration within the calling function. The called function must be alerted to the type of value that will be returned, and this information is provided by the function declaration. This declaration can only be omitted if the called function is physically placed in a program before its calling function or the called function returns an integer or void data type. The actual value returned by a function can be verified by displaying it both before and after it is returned.

The last two common errors are terminating a function's header line with a semicolon and forgetting to declare a function's arguments.

6.8   Chapter Summary

1. A function is called by giving its name and passing any data to it in the parentheses following the name. If a variable is one of the arguments in a function call, the called function receives a copy of the variable's value.

2. The general form of a user-written function is:

```
function_type function_name(argument list)
argument declarations;
{
   variable declarations;

   other C statements;
   return (expression);
}
```

The first two lines of the function are referred to as the function's header. The opening and closing braces of the function and all statements in between these braces constitute the function's body.

3. A function's type is the data type of the value returned by the function. If no type is declared the function is assumed to return an integer value. If the function does not return a value it should be declared as a void type.

4. Argument declarations declare the data type of the values passed to the function. They are placed before the opening brace that defines the function's body.

5. Functions can formally return only one value to their calling functions. This value is the value of the expression in the return statement.

6. A function that returns a value must be declared in the calling function. This can be done either by physically placing the called function above the calling function in the program or by including a function declaration within the calling program.

7. A set of preprogrammed functions for input, output, mathematical procedures, and string handling are included in the standard library provided with each C compiler. To use one of these functions you must obtain the name of the function, the arguments expected by the function, the data type of the returned value (if any), and a description of what the function does.

8. Every variable used in a program has a scope, which determines where in the program the variable can be used. The scope of a variable is either local or global and is determined by where the variable's definition statement is placed. A local variable is defined within a function and can only be used within its defining function. A global variable is defined outside a function and can be used in any function following the variable's definition. All global variables (which are formally called external variables) are initialized to zero and can be shared between files using the keyword extern.

9. Every variable has a class. The class of a variable determines how long the value in the variable will be retained. auto variables are local variables that exist only while their defining function is executing. register variables are similar to automatic variables but are stored in a computer's internal registers rather than in memory. static variables can be either global or local and retain their values for the duration of a program's execution. static variables are also set to zero when they are defined.

10. A function can also be passed the address of a variable. This address must be stored in a pointer of the proper type and can be used to directly alter the value stored at the passed address. By passing addresses, a function has the capability of effectively returning many values.

Complex Data Types

Part Four

Arrays

Chapter Seven

The variables used so far have all had a common characteristic: each variable could only be used to store a single value at a time. For example, although the variables in_key, counter, and price declared in the statements

```
char in_key;
int counter;
float price;
```

are of different data types, each variable can only store one value of the declared data type. These types of variables are called *scalar variables*. A scalar variable is a single variable that cannot be further subdivided or separated into a legitimate data type.

Frequently we may have a set of values, all of the same data type, that form a logical group. For example, Figure 7-1 illustrates three groups of items. The first group is a list of five integer grades, the second group is a list of four character codes, and the last group is a list of six floating point prices.

A simple list consisting of individual items of the same scalar data type is called a *single-dimensional array* in computer language. In this chapter we describe how single-dimensional arrays are declared, initialized, stored inside a computer, and used. We will explore the use of single-dimensional arrays with example programs and present the procedures for declaring and using multi-dimensional arrays.

7.1   Single-Dimensional Arrays

A single-dimensional array, also called a *one-dimensional array*, is a list of values of the same data type. For example, consider the list of grades illustrated in Figure 7-2. All the grades in the list are integer numbers and must be declared as such. However, the individual items in the list do not have to be declared separately. The items in the list can be declared as a single unit and stored under a common variable name called the *array name*. For convenience, we will choose grades as the name for the list shown in Figure 7-2. To declare that grades is to be used to store five individual integer values requires the

FIGURE 7–1   Three Lists of Items

Grades	Codes	Prices
98	x	10.96
87	a	6.43
92	m	2.58
79	n	.86
85		12.27
		6.39

Grade
98
87
92
79
85

FIGURE 7–2 A List of Grades

declaration statement `int grades[5];`. Notice that this declaration statement gives the data type of the items in the array, the array (or list) name, and the number of items in the array. Further examples of array declarations are:

```
char code[4];       /* an array of four character codes */
double prices[6];   /* an array of six double precision prices */
float amount[100];  /* an array of 100 floating point amounts */
```

Each array has sufficient memory reserved for it to hold the number of data items given in the declaration statement. Thus, the array named `code` has storage reserved for four characters, the `prices` array has storage reserved for six double precision numbers, and the array named `amount` has storage reserved for 100 floating point numbers. Figure 7-3 illustrates the storage reserved for the `code` and `grades` arrays. For illustrative purposes, we have assumed that each character is stored using one byte and that each integer requires two bytes of storage.

Each item in a list is officially called an *element* or *component* of the array. The individual elements stored in the arrays illustrated in Figure 7-3 are stored sequentially, with the first array element stored in the first reserved location,

FIGURE 7–3 The `code` and `grades` Arrays in Memory

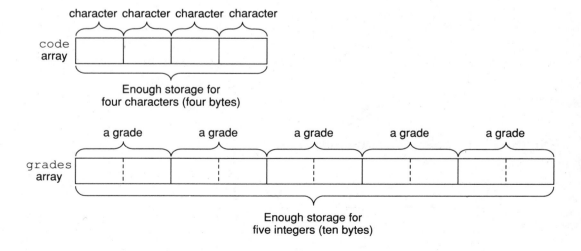

245

the second element stored in the second reserved location, and so on until the last element is stored in the last reserved location.

To access individual elements in a one-dimensional array requires some unique means of identifying each element. Fortunately, each item in the list is stored sequentially. Any single item can be accessed by giving the name of the array and the position of the item in the array. The element's position is called its *index* or *subscript value*. The first element has an index of 0, the second element has an index of 1, and so on. The index gives the number of elements to move over, starting from the beginning of the array, to locate the desired element. In C, the array name and index are combined by listing the index in square brackets after the array name. For example:

grades[0] refers to the first grade stored in the grades array
grades[1] refers to the second grade stored in the grades array
grades[2] refers to the third grade stored in the grades array
grades[3] refers to the fourth grade stored in the grades array
grades[4] refers to the fifth grade stored in the grades array

Figure 7-4 illustrates the grades array in memory with the correct designation for each array element. Each individual element is called an *indexed variable* or a *subscripted variable,* since both a variable name and an index or subscript value must be used to reference the element. Remember that the index or subscript value gives the position of the element in the array. When we read a subscripted variable such as grades[0], we read the variable as "grades sub zero." This is a shortened way of saying "the grades array subscripted by zero," and distinguishes the first element in an array from a scalar variable that could be declared as grades0. Similarly, grades[1] is read as "grades sub one" and grades[4] is read as "grades sub four."

Although it may seem unusual to reference the first element with an index of zero, doing so increases the computer's speed of accessing array elements. Internally, unseen by the programmer, the computer uses the index as an offset from the array's starting position. As illustrated in Figure 7-5, the index tells the computer how many elements to skip over, starting from the beginning of the array, to get to the desired element.

FIGURE 7–4 Identifying Individual Array Elements

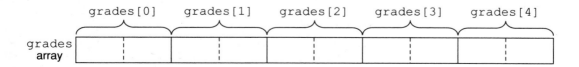

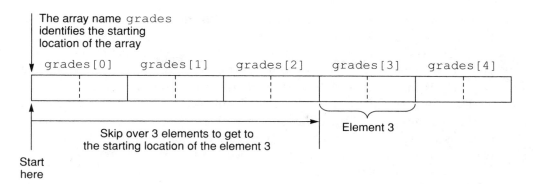

FIGURE 7–5 Accessing an Individual Element—Element 3

Subscripted variables can be used anywhere that scalar variables are valid. Examples using the elements of the grades array are:

```
grades[0] = 98;
grades[1] = grades[0] - 11;
grades[2] = 2 * (grades[0] - 6);
grades[3] = 79;
grades[4] = (grades[2] + grades[3] - 3)/2;
total = grades[0] + grades[1] + grades[2] + grades[3] + grades[4];
```

The index contained within square brackets need not be an integer. Any expression that evaluates to an integer may be used as an index. For example, assuming that i and j are integer variables, the following subscripted variables are valid:

```
grades[i]
grades[2*i]
grades[j-i]
```

One extremely important advantage of using integer expressions as subscripts is that it allows sequencing through an array using a for loop. This makes statements like

```
total = grades[1] + grades[2] + grades[3] + grades[4] + grades[5];
```

unnecessary. The index value in each of the subscripted variables in this statement can be replaced by the counter in a for loop to access each element in the array sequentially. For example, the code

```
  total = 0;                 /* initialize total to zero */
  for (i = 0; i <= 4; ++i)
  total += grades[i];        /* add in a grade */
```

sequentially retrieves each array element and adds the element to the total. Here the variable i is used both as the counter in the for loop and as a subscript. As i increases by one each time through the for loop, the next element in the array is referenced. The procedure for adding the array elements within the for loop is the same procedure we have used many times before.

The advantage of using a for loop to sequence through an array becomes apparent when you work with larger arrays. For example, if the grades array contains 100 values rather than just 5, simply changing the number 4 to 99 in the for statement is sufficient to sequence through the 100 grades and add each grade to the total.

As another example of using a for loop to sequence through an array, assume that we want to locate the maximum value in an array of 1000 elements named price. The procedure we will use to locate the maximum value is to assume initially that the first element in the array is the largest number. Then, as we sequence through the array, the maximum is compared to each element. When an element with a higher value is located, that element becomes the new maximum.

```
maximum = price[0];        /* set the maximum to element zero       */
for(i = 1; i <= 999; ++i)  /* cycle through the rest of the array */
   if (price[i] > maximum)  /* compare each element to the maximum */
      maximum = price[i];   /* capture the new high value            */
```

In this code, the for statement consists of one if statement. The search for a new maximum value starts with element 1 of the array and continues through the last element. In a thousand-element array, the last element is element 999.

Input and Output of Array Values

Individual array elements can be assigned values using individual assignment statements or, interactively, using the scanf() function. Examples of individual data entry statements are:

```
price[5] = 10.69;
scanf("%d %lf", &grades[0], &price[2])
scanf("%c", &code[0]);
scanf("%d %d %d", &grades[0], &grades[1], &grades[2]);
```

Alternatively, a for statement can be used to cycle through the array for interactive data input. For example, the code

```
for(i = 0; i <= 4; ++i)
{
  printf("Enter a grade: ");
  scanf("%d", &grades[i]);
}
```

prompts the user for five grades. The first grade input is stored in `grades[0]`, the second grade input in `grades[1]`, and so on until all five grades are entered.

One caution should be mentioned about storing data in an array. C does not check the value of the index being used (called a *bounds check*). If an array has been declared as consisting of 10 elements, for example, and you use an index of 12, which is outside the bounds of the array, C will not notify you of the error when the program is compiled. The program will attempt to access element 12 by skipping over the appropriate number of bytes from the start of the array. Usually this results in a program crash—but not always. If the referenced location itself contains a data value, the program will simply access the value in the referenced memory locations. This leads to more errors, which are particularly troublesome to locate when the variable legitimately assigned to the storage location is used at a different point in the program.

During output, individual array elements can be displayed using the `printf()` function or complete sections of the array can be displayed by including a `printf()` function call within a `for` loop. Examples of this are:

```
printf("%lf," price[6]);
printf("The value of element %d is %d", i, grades[i]);
for( n = 5; n <= 20; ++n)
  printf("%d %lf", n, price[n]);
```

The first call to `printf()` displays the value of the double precision subscripted variable `price[6]`. The second call to `printf()` displays the value of `i` and the value of `grades[i]`. Before this statement can be executed, `i` would have to have an assigned value. Finally, the last example includes `printf()` within a `for` loop. Both the value of the index and the value of the elements from 5 to 20 are displayed.

Program 7-1 illustrates these input and output techniques using an array named `grades` that is defined to store five integer numbers. Included in the program are two `for` loops. The first `for` loop is used to cycle through each array element and allows the user to input individual array values. After five values have been entered, the second `for` loop is used to display the stored values.

Program 7-1

```
main()
{
  int i, grades[5];

  for (i = 0; i <= 4; ++i)        /* Enter five grades */
  {
    printf("Enter a grade: ");
    scanf("%d", &grades[i]);
  }
  for (i = 0; i <= 4; ++i)        /* Print five grades */
    printf("\ngrades %d is %d", i, grades[i]);
}
```

Following is a sample run using program 7-1.

```
                    Enter a grade: 85
                    Enter a grade: 90
                    Enter a grade: 78
                    Enter a grade: 75
                    Enter a grade: 92

                    grades 0 is 85
                    grades 1 is 90
                    grades 2 is 78
                    grades 3 is 75
                    grades 4 is 92
```

In reviewing the output produced by Program 7-1, pay particular attention to the difference between the index value displayed and the numerical value stored in the corresponding array element. The index value refers to the location of the element in the array, while the subscripted variable refers to the value stored in the designated location.

In addition to simply displaying the values stored in each array element, the elements can also be processed by appropriately referencing the desired element. For example, in Program 7-2, each element's value is accumulated in a total, which is displayed upon completion of the individual display of each array element.

Program 7-2

```
main()
{
  int i, grades[5], total = 0;

  for (i = 0; i <= 4; ++i)          /* Enter five grades */
  {
    printf("Enter a grade: ");
    scanf("%d", &grades[i]);
  }

  printf("\nThe total of the grades ");
  for (i = 0; i <= 4; ++i)          /* Display and total the grades */
  {
    printf("%d   ", grades[i]);
    total += grades[i];
  }
  printf("is   %d",total);
}
```

Following is a sample run using Program 7-2:

```
Enter a grade: 85
Enter a grade: 90
Enter a grade: 78
Enter a grade: 75
Enter a grade: 92

The total of the grades 85  90   78   75   92   is   420
```

Notice that in Program 7-2, unlike Program 7-1, only the numerical value stored in each array element is displayed and not their index values. Although the second for loop was used to accumulate the total of each element, the accumulation could also have been accomplished in the first loop by placing the statement total += grades[i]; after the scanf() call used to enter a value. Also notice that the printf() call used to display the total is made outside of the second for loop, so that the total is displayed only once, after all values have been added to the total. If this printf() call were placed inside of the for loop five totals would be displayed, with only the last displayed total containing the sum of all of the array values.

Exercises 7.1

1. Write array declarations for the following:
   a. a list of 60 double precision interest rates
   b. a list of 30 floating point temperatures
   c. a list of 25 characters, each representing a code
   d. a list of 100 integer years
   e. a list of 26 double precision coupon rates
   f. a list of 1000 floating point distances
   g. a list of 20 integer code numbers

2. a. Write a program to input the following values into an array named `prices`: 10.95, 16.32, 12.15, 8.22, 15.98, 26.22, 13.54, 6.45, 17.59. After the data has been entered, have your program output the values.
   b. Repeat Exercise 2a, but after the data has been entered, have your program display it in the following form:

10.95	16.32	12.15
8.22	15.98	26.22
13.54	6.45	17.59

3. a. Write a program to input 15 integer numbers into an array named `temp`. As each number is input, add the numbers into the total. After all numbers are input, display the numbers and their average.
   b. Repeat Exercise 3a, but locate the maximum number in the array (do not add the numbers) as the values are being input. (*Hint:* Set the maximum equal to zero before the `for` loop used to input the numbers.)
   c. Repeat Exercise 3b, keeping track of both the maximum element in the array and the index number for the maximum. After displaying the numbers, print the two messages

   ```
   The maximum value is: ____
   This is element number ____  in the list of numbers
   ```

   Have your program display the correct values in place of the underlines in the messages.
   d. Repeat Exercise 3c, but have your program locate the minimum of the data entered.

4. a. Write a program to input the following integer numbers into an array named `grades`: 89, 95, 72, 83, 99, 54, 86, 75, 92, 73, 79, 75, 82, 73. As each number is input, add the numbers to the total. After all numbers are input and the total is obtained, calculate the average of the numbers and use the average to determine the deviation of each value from the average. Store each deviation in an array named `deviation`. Each deviation is obtained as the element value less the average of all the data. Have your program display each deviation alongside its corresponding element from the grades array.
   b. Calculate the variance of the data used in Exercise 4a. The variance is obtained by squaring each individual deviation and dividing the sum of the squared deviations by the number of deviations.

5. Write a program that declares three single-dimensional arrays named `price`, `quantity`, and `amount`. Each array should be capable of holding ten elements. Using a `for` loop, input values for the `price` and `quantity` arrays. The entries in the `amount` array should be the product of the corresponding values in the `price` and `quantity` arrays

(thus, amount[i] = quantity[i] * price[i];). After all of the data has been entered, display the following output:

```
        Quantity          Price          Amount
        --------          -----          ------
```

Under each column heading display the appropriate value.

6. a. Write a program that inputs ten double precision numbers into an array named raw. After ten user-input numbers are entered into the array, your program should cycle through raw ten times. During each pass through the array, your program should select the lowest value in raw and place the selected value in the next available slot in an array named sorted. Thus, when your program is complete, the sorted array should contain the numbers in raw sorted order from lowest to highest. (*Hint:* Make sure to reset the lowest value selected during each pass to a very high number so that it is not selected again. You will need a second for loop within the first for loop to locate the minimum value for each pass.)

b. The method used in Exercise 6a to sort the values in the array is very inefficient. Can you determine why? What might be a better method of sorting the numbers in an array?

7.2   Array Initialization

Arrays, like scalar variables, can be declared either inside or outside a function. Arrays declared inside a function are *local arrays* and arrays declared outside a function are *global arrays*. For example, consider the following section of code:

```
int gallons[20];            /* a global array */
static double dist[25];      /* a static global array */
main()
{
  int i;

  for (i = 1; i <= 10; ++i)
    mpg(i);                   /* call mpg() ten times */
    .
    .
}
mpg(car_no)                   /* function declaration */
int car_no;                   /* argument declaration */
{
  int miles[15];              /* an automatic local array */
  static course[15];          /* a static local array    */
    .
    .
  return;
}
```

As indicated in the code, both the `dist` and `gallons` arrays are globally declared arrays, `miles` is an automatic local array, and `course` is a `static` local array. As with scalar variables, all global arrays and local `static` arrays are created once, at compilation time, and retain their values until `main()` finishes executing. `auto` arrays are created and destroyed each time the function they are local to is called. Thus, the `dist`, `gallons`, and `course` arrays are created once, and the `miles` array is created and destroyed ten times.

Creating and destroying individual scalar variables does not typically affect the time it takes to run a program. This is also true for small automatic arrays. The creation and destruction of large arrays, however, might have an impact on system performance. If automatic arrays could be initialized each time they are created, the effect on total program execution time could be significant. It is for this reason that the temporary automatic arrays are not allowed to be initialized within the declaration statement creating them (they can of course be initialized using a `for` loop, as can local `static` and globally declared arrays). The case is different for global arrays and local `static` arrays.

Global and local `static` arrays can be initialized from within their declaration statements by listing the desired values within braces and separating these by commas. Examples of this for `static` arrays (local and global) are:

```
static int grades[5] = {98, 87, 92, 79, 85};
static char codes[6] = {'s', 'a', 'm', 'p', 'l', 'e'};
static double prices[10] = {10.96, 6.43, 2.58, .86};
```

Examples of external global array declarations, including initializers, are:

```
int gallons[20] = {19, 16, 14, 19, 20, 18,   /* initializing values */
                   12, 10, 22, 15, 18, 17,   /* may extend across    */
                   16, 14, 23, 19, 15, 18,   /* multiple lines       */
                   21, 5 }

double yield[6] = {9.05, 9.10, 9.15, 9.20, 9.25, 9.30};
```

If the number of initializers is less than the formally declared maximum number of elements listed in square brackets, the initializers are applied starting with array element zero. Thus, in the initialization of the `static prices` array, only `prices[0]`, `prices[1]`, `prices[2]`, and `prices[3]` are initialized with the listed values.

If no specific initializers are given in the declaration statement, all local `static` and global (both `static` and `extern`) array elements are set to zero (this is also true for local `static` and global scalar variables). For example, the declaration `static int dist[100];` sets all elements of the `dist` array equal to zero at compilation time. Similarly, since `prices[4]` through `prices[9]` were not specifically initialized when the `prices` array was declared, these elements are also set to zero. Unfortunately, there is no method of either indicating repetition of an initialization value or initializing later array elements without first specifying values for earlier elements.

A unique feature of initializers is that the size of an array may be omitted when initializing values are included in the declaration statement. For example, the declaration

```
static int gallons[] = {16, 12, 10, 14, 11};
```

reserves enough storage room for five elements. Similarly, the following two declarations are equivalent:

```
static char codes[6] = {'s', 'a', 'm', 'p', 'l', 'e'};
static char codes[] = {'s', 'a', 'm', 'p', 'l', 'e'};
```

Both of these declarations set aside six character locations for an array named codes. An interesting and useful simplification can also be used when initializing character arrays. For example, the declaration

```
static char codes[] = "sample";    /* no braces or commas */
```

uses the string "sample" to initialize the codes array. Recall that a string is any sequence of characters enclosed in double quotes. This last declaration creates an array named codes having seven elements and fills the array with the seven characters illustrated in Figure 7-6. The first six characters, as expected, consist of the letters s, a, m, p, l, and e. The last character, which is the escape sequence \0, is called the *null character*. The null character is automatically appended to all strings by the C compiler. This character has an internal storage code that is numerically equal to zero (the storage code for the zero character has a numerical value of 48, so the two cannot be confused by the computer), and is used as a marker, or sentinel, to mark the end of a string. As we shall see in Chapter 9, this marker is invaluable when manipulating strings of characters.

Exercises 7.2

1. Write static array declarations, including initializers, for the following:
   a. a list of ten integer grades: 89, 75, 82, 93, 78, 95, 81, 88, 77, 82
   b. a list of five double precision amounts: 10.62, 13.98, 18.45, 12.68, 14.76
   c. a list of 100 double precision interest rates; the first six rates are 6.29, 6.95, 7.25, 7.35, 7.40, 7.42
   d. a list of 64 floating point temperatures; the first ten temperatures are 78.2, 69.6, 68.5, 83.9, 55.4, 67.0, 49.8, 58.3, 62.5, 71.6
   e. a list of 15 character codes; the first seven codes are f, j, m, q, t, w, z

2. The string of characters "Good Morning" is to be stored in a static character array named goodstr1. Write the declaration for this array in three different ways.

FIGURE 7–6 A String Is Terminated with a Special Sentinel

codes[0] codes[1] codes[2] codes[3] codes[4] codes[5] codes[6]

s	a	m	p	l	e	\0

3. *a.* Write declaration statements to store the string of characters "Input the Following Data" in a `static` character array named `messag1`, the string "----------------" in the `static` array named `messag2`, the string "Enter the Date: " in the `static` array named `messag3`, and the string "Enter the Account Number: " in the `static` array named `messag4`.

b. Include the array declarations written in Exercise 3a in a program that uses the `printf()` function to display the messages. For example, the statement `printf("%s", messag1);` causes the string stored in the `messag1` array to be displayed. Your program will require four such statements to display the four individual messages. Using the `printf()` function with the `%s` control sequence to display a string requires that the end of string marker `\0` is present in the character array used to store the string.

4. *a.* Write a declaration to store the string "This is a test" into a `static` array named `strtest`. Include the declaration in a program to display the message using the following loop:

```
for (i = 0; i <= 14; ++i) printf("%c", strtest[i]);
```

b. Modify the `for` statement in Exercise 4a to display only the array characters `t, e, s,` and `t`.

c. Include the array declaration written in Exercise 4a in a program that uses the `printf()` function to display characters in the array. For example, the statement `printf("%s", strtest);` will cause the string stored in the `strtest` array to be displayed. Using this statement requires that the last character in the array is the end of string marker `\0`.

d. Repeat Exercise 4a using a `while` loop. (*Hint:* Stop the loop when the `\0` escape sequence is detected. The expression `while (strtest[i] != '\0')` can be used.)

5. *a.* Write a declaration to store the following values in a `static` array named `prices`: 16.24, 18.98, 23.75, 16.29, 19.54, 14.22, 11.13, 15.39. Include the declaration in a program that displays the values in the `static` array.

b. Repeat Exercise 5a, but make the array a nonstatic global array.

6. Write a program that uses a declaration statement to store the following numbers in a `static` array named `rates`: 17.24, 25.63, 5.94, 33.92, 3.71, 32.84, 35.93, 18.24, 6.92. Your program should then locate and display both the maximum and minimum values in the array.

7. Write a program that stores the following prices in a global array: 9.92, 6.32, 12.63, 5.95, 10.29. Your program should also create two automatic arrays named `units` and `amounts`, each capable of storing five double precision numbers. Using a `for` loop and a `scanf()` function call, have your program accept five user-input numbers into the units array when the program is run. Your program should store the product of the corresponding values in the `prices` and `units` arrays in the `amounts` array (for example, `amounts[1] = prices[1] * units[1]`) and display the following output (fill in the table appropriately):

```
       Price        Units        Amount
       -----        -----        ------
        9.92          .            .
        6.32          .            .
       12.63          .            .
        5.95          .            .
       10.29          .            .
                                  ------
       Total:                       .
```

7.3 Passing Arrays

Individual array elements are passed to a function by simply including them as subscripted variables in the function call argument list. For example, the function call `find_min(grades[2], grades[6]);` passes the values of the elements `grades[2]` and `grades[6]` to the function `find_min()`.

Passing a complete array to a function is in many respects an easier operation than passing individual elements. The called function receives access to the actual array, rather than a copy of the values in the array. For example, if `grades` is an array, the function call `find_max(grades);` makes the complete `grades` array available to the `find_max()` function. This is different from passing a single variable to a function.

When passing a single scalar or single array element, the called function always receives a copy of the value stored in the variable. Passing an array this way requires making a complete and separate copy of all array values. For large arrays, making duplicate copies of the array for each function call would be wasteful of computer storage, consume large amounts of execution time, and frustrate the effort to return multiple element changes made by the called program. To avoid these problems, the called function is given direct access to the original array. Thus, any changes made by the called function are made directly to the array itself. For the following specific examples of function calls, assume that the arrays `nums`, `keys`, `units`, and `prices` are declared as:

```
int nums[5];                    /* an array of five integers   */
char keys[256];                 /* an array of 256 characters  */
double units[500], prices[500]; /* two arrays of 500 doubles   */
```

For these arrays, the following function calls can be made:

```
find_max(nums);
find_ch(keys);
calc_tot(nums, units, prices);
```

In each case, the called function receives direct access to the named array.

On the receiving side, the called function must be alerted that an array is being made available. For example, suitable function declarations for the previous functions are:

```
find_max(vals)    find_ch(in_keys)    calc_tot(arr1,arr2,arr3)
int vals[5];      char in_keys[256];  int arr1[5];
                                      double arr2[500],arr3[500];
```

In each of these function declarations, the names in the argument list are chosen by the programmer and are local to the function. However, the internal local names used by the functions still refer to the original array created outside the function. This is made clear in Program 7-3.

Program 7-3

```
main()
{
   static int nums[5] = {2, 18, 1, 27, 16};

   find_max(nums);
}

find_max(vals)        /* find the maximum value */
int vals[5];
{
   int i, max = vals[0];

   for (i = 1; i <= 4; ++i)
      if (max < vals[i]) max = vals[i];

printf("The maximum value is %d", max);
}
```

Only one array is created in Program 7-3. In main() this array is known as nums, and in find_max() the array is known as vals. As illustrated in Figure 7-7, both names refer to the same array. Thus, in Figure 7-7 vals[3] is the same element as nums[3].

FIGURE 7-7 Only One Array Is Created

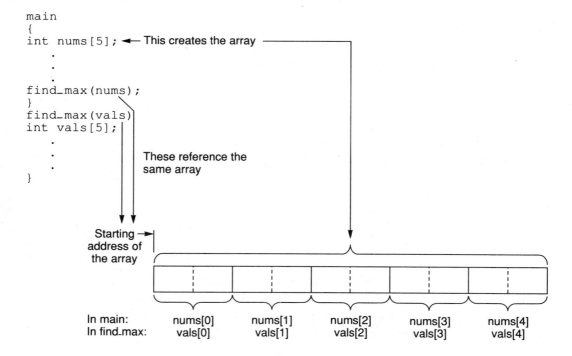

The argument declaration in find_max() actually contains extra information that is not required by the function. All that find_max() must know is that the argument vals references an array of integers. Since the array has been created in main() and no additional storage space is needed in find_max(), the declaration for vals can omit the size of the array. Thus, an alternative function declaration is:

```
find_max(vals)
int vals[];
```

This form of the function declaration makes more sense when you realize that only one item is actually passed to find_max when the function is called. As you might have suspected, the item passed is the starting address of the nums array. This is illustrated in Figure 7-8.

Since only one item is passed to find_max, the number of elements in the array need not be included in the declaration for vals. In fact, it is generally advisable to omit the size of the array in the argument declaration. For example, consider the more general form of find_max(), which can be used to find the maximum value of an integer array of arbitrary size.

```
int find_max(vals,num_els)      /* find the maximum value */
int vals[], num_els;
{
  int i, max = vals[0];

  for (i = 1; i <= (num_els - 1); ++i)
   if (max < vals[i]) max = vals[i];

  return(max);
}
```

FIGURE 7–8 The Starting Address of the Array Is Passed

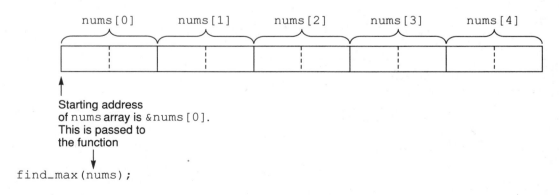

find_max(nums);

The more general form of find_max() declares that the function returns an integer value. The function expects the starting address of an integer array and the number of elements in the array as arguments. Then, using the number of elements as the boundary for its search, the function's for loop causes each array element to be examined in sequential order to locate the maximum value. Since the highest subscript allowed is always one less than the total number of elements in the array, the expression (num_els - 1) is used to terminate the loop. Program 7-4 illustrates the use of find_max() in a complete program.

 Program 7-4

```
main()
{
    static int nums[5] = {2, 18, 1, 27, 16};
    int find_max();

    printf("The maximum value is %d", find_max(nums,5));
}

int find_max(vals,num_els)
int vals[], num_els;
{
    int i, max = vals[0];

    for (i = 1; i <= (num_els - 1); ++i)
      if (max < vals[i]) max = vals[i];

    return(max);
}
```

The output displayed when Program 7-4 is executed is:

```
The maximum value is 27
```

Exercises 7.3

1. The following declaration was used to create the prices array:

```
double prices[500];
```

Write two different declarations for a function named `sort_arr()` that accepts the `prices` array as an argument named `in_array`.

2. The following declaration was used to create the `keys` array:

```
char keys[256];
```

Write two different declarations for a function named `find_key()` that accepts the `keys` array as an argument named `select`.

3. The following declaration was used to create the `rates` array:

```
float rates[256];
```

Write two different declarations for a function named `prime()` that accepts the `rates` array as an argument named `rates`.

4. *a.* Modify the `find_max()` function in Program 7-3 to locate the minimum value of the passed array.
   b. Include the function written in Exercise 4a in a complete program and run the program on a computer.

5. Write a program that has a declaration in `main()` to store the following numbers into a `static` array named `rates`: 6.5, 7.2, 7.5, 8.3, 8.6, 9.4, 9.6, 9.8, 10.0. There should be a function call to `show()` that accepts the `rates` array as an argument named `rates` and then displays the numbers in the array.

6. *a.* Write a program that has a declaration in `main()` to store the string "Vacation is near" into a `static` array named `message`. There should be a function call to `display()` that accepts `message` in an argument named `strng` and then displays the message.
   b. Modify the `display()` function written in Exercise 6a to display the first eight elements of the `message` array.

7. Write a program that declares three single-dimensional arrays named `price`, `quantity`, and `amount`. Each array should be declared in `main()` and should be capable of holding ten double precision numbers. The numbers that should be stored in `price` are 10.62, 14.89, 13.21, 16.55, 18.62, 9.47, 6.58, 18.32, 12.15, 3.98. The numbers that should be stored in `quantity` are 4, 8.5, 6, 7.35, 9, 15.3, 3, 5.4, 2.9, 4.8. Your program should pass these three arrays to a function called `extend()`, which should calculate the elements in the `amount` array as the product of the equivalent elements in the `price` and `quantity` arrays (for example, `amount[1] = price[1] * quantity[1]`). After `extend()` has put values into the `amount` array, the values in the array should be displayed from within `main()`.

8. Write a program that includes two functions named `calc_avg()` and `variance()`. The `calc_avg()` function should calculate and return the average of the values stored in a `static` array named `testvals`. The array should be declared in `main()` and include the values 89, 95, 72, 83, 99, 54, 86, 75, 92, 73, 79, 75, 82, 73. The `variance()` function should calculate and return the variance of the data. The variance is obtained by subtracting the average from each value in `testvals`, squaring the values obtained, adding them, and dividing by the number of elements in `testvals`. The values returned from `calc_avg()` and `variance` should be displayed using `printf()` function calls in `main()`.

7.4 Two-Dimensional Arrays

A *two-dimensional array* consists of both rows and columns of elements. For example, the array of numbers

$$8 \quad 16 \quad 9 \quad 52$$
$$3 \quad 15 \quad 27 \quad 6$$
$$14 \quad 25 \quad 2 \quad 10$$

is called a two-dimensional array of integers. This array consists of three rows and four columns. To reserve storage for this array, both the number of rows and the number of columns must be included in the array's declaration. Calling the array `val`, the appropriate declaration for this two-dimensional array is

```
int val[3][4];
```

Similarly, the declarations

```
double prices[10][5];
char code[6][26];
```

declare that the array `prices` consists of 10 rows and 5 columns of double precision numbers and that the array `code` consists of 6 rows and 26 columns of characters.

In order to locate each element in a two-dimensional array, an element is identified by its position in the array. As illustrated in Figure 7-9, the term `val[1][3]` uniquely identifies the element in row 1, column 3. As with single-dimensional array variables, double-dimensional array variables can be used anywhere that scalar variables are valid. Examples using elements of the `val` array are:

```
num = val[2][3];
val[0][0] = 62;
new_num = 4 * (val[1][0] - 5);
sum_row0 = val[0][0] + val[0][1] + val[0][2] + val[0][3];
```

FIGURE 7–9 Each Array Element Is Identified by Its Row and Column

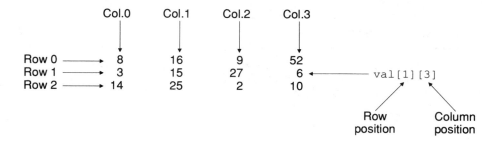

The last statement causes the values of the four elements in row 0 to be added and the sum to be stored in the scalar variable sum_row0.

As with single-dimensional arrays, two-dimensional arrays can be declared either inside or outside a function. Arrays declared inside a function are local arrays; arrays declared outside a function are global arrays. For example, consider the following section of code:

```
int bingo[2][3];
main()
{
   static double lotto[104][6];
   double pick_six[52][6];
           .
           .
           .
}
```

The bingo array is a globally declared two-dimensional array consisting of 2 rows and 3 columns; the lotto array is a local static two-dimensional array consisting of 104 rows and 6 columns; and the pick_six array is a local automatic array of 52 rows and 6 columns.

As with single-dimensional arrays, all global and local static two-dimensional arrays can be initialized from within their declaration statements. This is done by listing the initial values within braces and separating them by commas. Additionally, braces can be used to separate individual rows. For example, the declaration

```
static int val[3][4] = { {8,16,9,52},
                         {3,15,27,6},
                         {14,25,2,10} };
```

declares val to be an array of integers with three rows and four columns, with the initial values given in the declaration. The first set of internal braces contains the values for row 0 of the array, the second set of internal braces contains the values for row 1, and the third set of braces the values for row 2.

Although the commas in the initialization braces are always required, the inner braces can be omitted. Thus, the initialization for val may be written as

```
static int val[3][4] = {8,16,9,52,
                        3,15,27,6,
                        14,25,2,10};
```

The separation of initial values into rows in the declaration statement is not necessary since the compiler assigns values beginning with the [0][0] element and proceeds row by row to fill in the remaining values. Thus, the initialization

```
static int val[3][4] = {8,16,9,52,3,15,27,6,14,25,2,10};
```

is equally valid but does not clearly illustrate to another programmer where one row ends and another begins.

Passing two-dimensional arrays into functions is a process identical to passing single-dimensional arrays. The called function receives access to the entire array. For example, the function call `display(val);` makes the complete `val` array available to the function named `display()`. Thus, any changes made by `display()` will be made directly to the `val` array. Assuming that the following two-dimensional arrays named `test`, `code`, and `stocks` are declared as:

```
int test[7][9];
char code[26][10];
float stocks[256][52];
```

the following function calls are valid:

```
find_max(test);
obtain(code);
price(stocks);
```

On the receiving side, the called function must be alerted that a two-dimensional array is being made available. For example, suitable function declarations for the previous functions are:

```
find_max(nums)        obtain(key)          price(names)
int nums[7][9];       char key[26][10];    float names[256][52];
```

In each of these function declarations, the argument names chosen are local to the function. However, the internal local names used by the function still refer to the original array created outside the function. If the array is a global one, there is no need to pass the array because the function could reference the array by its global name. Program 7-5 illustrates passing a local, two-dimensional array into a function that displays the array's values.

 Program 7-5

```
main()
{
   static int val[3][4] = {8,16,9,52,
                           3,15,27,6,
                           14,25,2,10};

   display(val);
}

display(nums)
int nums[3][4];
```

continued

```
      {
        int row_num, col_num;
        for (row_num = 0; row_num < 3; ++row_num)
        {
          for(col_num = 0; col_num < 4; ++col_num)
            printf("%4d",nums[row_num][col_num]);
          printf("\n");
        }
      }
```

Only one array is created in Program 7-5. This array is known as `val` in `main()` and as `nums` in `display()`. Thus, `val[0][2]` refers to the same element as `nums[0][2]`.

Notice the use of the nested `for` loop in Program 7-5. Nested `for` statements are especially useful when dealing with multidimensional arrays because they allow the programmer to cycle through each element. In Program 7-5, the variable `row_num` controls the outer loop and the variable `col_num` controls the inner loop. For each pass through the outer loop, which corresponds to a row, the inner loop makes one pass through the column elements. After a complete column is printed, the `\n` escape sequence causes a new line to be started for the next row. The effect is a display of the array in a row-by-row fashion:

```
     8    16     9    52
     3    15    27     6
    14    25     2    10
```

The argument declaration for `nums` in `display()` contains extra information that is not required by the function. The declaration for `nums` can omit the row size of the array. Thus, an alternative function declaration is:

```
       display(nums)
       int nums[][4];
```

The reason why the column size must be included while the row size is optional becomes obvious when you consider how the array elements are stored in memory. Starting with element `val[0][0]`, each succeeding element is stored consecutively, row by row, as `val[0][0]`, `val[0][1]`, `val[0][2]`, `val[0][3]`, `val[1][0]`, `val[1][1]`, etc., as illustrated in Figure 7-10.

FIGURE 7-10 Storage of the `val` Array

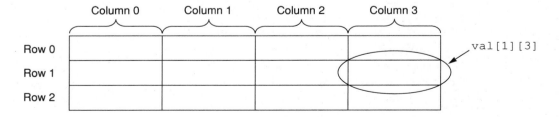

As with all array accesses, an individual element of the `val` array is obtained by adding an offset to the starting location of the array. For example, the element `val[1][3]` is located at an offset of 14 bytes from the start of the array. Internally, the computer uses the row index, column index, and column size to determine this offset using the following calculation:

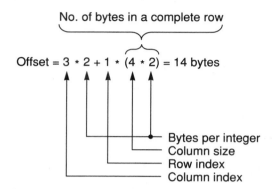

No. of bytes in a complete row

Offset = 3 * 2 + 1 * (4 * 2) = 14 bytes

Bytes per integer
Column size
Row index
Column index

The number of columns is necessary in the offset calculation so that the computer can determine the number of positions to skip over in order to get to the desired row.

Larger-Dimensional Arrays

Although arrays with more than two dimensions are not commonly used, C does allow any size array to be declared. This is done by listing the maximum size of all indices for the array. For example, the declaration `int response[4][10][6];` declares a three-dimensional array. The first element in the array is designated as `response[0][0][0]` and the last element as `response[3][9][5]`. Similarly, arrays with four, five, six, or more dimensions can be declared. In declaring these higher-dimensional arrays as function arguments, all but the first index size must be included in the argument declaration.

Exercises 7.4

1. Write appropriate declaration statements for:
   a. an array of integers with 6 rows and 10 columns
   b. an array of integers with 2 rows and 5 columns
   c. an array of characters with 7 rows and 12 columns
   d. an array of characters with 15 rows and 7 columns
   e. an array of double precision numbers with 10 rows and 25 columns
   f. an array of double precision numbers with 16 rows and 8 columns

2. Write a function that multiplies each element of a 7 by 10 array of integers by a scalar number. Both the array name and the number by which each element is to be multiplied are to be passed into the function as arguments. Assume the array is an array of integers.

3. Write a function that adds the values of all elements in a two-dimensional array that is passed to the function. Assume that the array is an array of double precision numbers having four rows and five columns.

4. Write a function that adds respective values of two double-dimensional arrays named first and second, respectively. Both arrays have two rows and three columns. For example, element [1] [2] of the resulting array should be the sum of first [1] [2] and second [1] [2]. Assume the arrays are arrays of integers.

5. a. Write a function that finds and displays the maximum value in a two-dimensional array of integers. The array should be declared as a 10 row by 20 column array of integers in main () and the starting address of the array should be passed to the function.
b. Modify the function written in Exercise 5a so that it also displays the row and column number of the element with the maximum value.
c. Can the function you wrote for Exercise 5a be generalized to handle any size two-dimensional array?

6. Write a function that can be used to sort the elements of a 10 by 20 two-dimensional array of integers. (*Hint:* Use the sortnum () function in Program 6-12 to swap array elements.)

7. a. A professor has constructed a two-dimensional array of floating point numbers having 35 rows and 4 columns. This array currently contains the numerical grades of the students in the professor's four classes. Write a C program that determines the total number of grades in the ranges less than 60, greater than or equal to 60 and less than 70, greater than or equal to 70 and less than 80, greater than or equal to 80 and less than 90, and greater or equal to 90.
b. How might the function you wrote for Exercise 7a be modified to include the case where no grade is present? That is, what grade could be used to indicate an invalid grade and how would your function have to be modified to exclude counting such a grade?

7.5   Common Programming Errors

The most common programming error associated with arrays is the use of a subscript to reference a nonexistent array element. As the C compiler does no bounds checking on arrays, this error is never caught when the program is compiled. This is always a run-time error that results in either a program "crash" or a value that has no relation to the intended element being accessed from memory. In either case it is usually an extremely troublesome error to locate. The only solution to this problem is to make sure, either by specific programming statements or by careful coding, that each subscript references a valid array element.

A second error occurs when an attempt is made to initialize a nonstatic local array (all global arrays can be initialized). This error, however, will be found by the compiler.

7.6 Chapter Summary

1. A single-dimensional array is a data structure that can be used to store a list of values of the same data type. Such arrays must be declared by giving the data type of the values that are stored in the array and the array size. For example, the declaration

```
int num[100];
```

creates an array of 100 integers.

2. Array elements are stored in contiguous locations in memory and referenced using the array name and a subscript, for example, num[22]. Any nonnegative integer-value expression can be used as a subscript and the subscript 0 always refers to the first element in an array.

3. Arrays can be declared either as global or local arrays. Global array elements are automatically initialized to zero if no other explicit initialization is given. Global static arrays and local static arrays are also initialized to zero if no other explicit initialization is given. Automatic local arrays cannot be initialized when they are declared and contain "garbage" values when they are created.

4. Two-dimensional arrays are declared by specifying both a row and a column size. For example, the declaration

```
float rates[12][20];
```

reserves memory space for a table of 12 by 20 floating point values. Individual elements in a two-dimensional array are identified by providing both a row and a column index. The element in the first row and first column has row and column subscripts of 0.

5. Automatic two-dimensional arrays cannot be initialized and contain "garbage" values when they are created. All static arrays (local or global) and all global two-dimensional array elements are set to zero unless explicitly initialized.

6. Arrays are passed to a function by passing the name of the array as an argument. The value actually passed is the address of the first array storage location. Thus, the called function receives direct access to the original array and not a copy of the array elements. Within the called function a formal argument must be declared to receive the passed array name. The declaration of the formal argument can omit the row size of the array.

7.7   Chapter Supplement: Sorting Methods

Most programmers need to sort a list of data items at some time in their careers. For example, experimental results might have to be arranged in either increasing (ascending) or decreasing (descending) order for statistical analysis, lists of names may have to be sorted in alphabetical order, or a list of dates rearranged in ascending date order.

For sorting data, two major categories of sorting techniques exist, called internal and external sorts, respectively. *Internal sorts* are used when the data list is not too large and the complete list can be stored within the computer's memory, usually in an array. *External sorts* are used for much larger data sets that are stored in large external disk or tape files, and cannot be accommodated within the computer's memory as a complete unit.

In this section, we present two common internal sorts, called the selection and exchange sort, respectively. Although the exchange sort, also known as a "bubble sort," is the more common of the two, we will see that the selection sort is easier and frequently more efficient.

Selection Sort

In a selection sort the smallest (or largest) value is initially selected from the complete list of data and exchanged with the first element in the list. After this first selection and exchange, the next smallest (or largest) element in the revised list is selected and exchanged with the second element in the list. Since the smallest element is already in the first position in the list, this second pass need only consider the second through last elements. For a list consisting of n elements this process is repeated $n-1$ times, with each pass through the list requiring one less comparison than the previous pass.

For example, consider the list of numbers illustrated in Figure 7-11. The first pass through the initial list results in the number 32 being selected and exchanged with the first element in the list. The second pass, made on the reordered list, results in the number 155 being selected from the second through

FIGURE 7-11   A Sample Selection Sort

Initial List	Pass 1	Pass 2	Pass 3	Pass 4
690	32	32	32	32
307	307	155	144	144
32	690	690	307	307
155	155	307	690	426
426	426	426	426	690

fifth elements. This value is then exchanged with the second element in the list. The third pass selects the number 307 from the third through fifth elements in the list and exchanges this value with the third element. Finally, the fourth and last pass through the list selects the remaining minimum value and exchanges it with the fourth list element. Although each pass in this example resulted in an exchange, no exchange would have been made in a pass if the smallest value were already in the correct location.

Program 7-6 implements a selection sort for a list of ten numbers that are stored in an array named nums. For later comparison to an exchange sort, the number of actual moves made by the program to get the data into sorted order is counted and displayed.

 Program 7-6

```
main()
{
  static int nums[10] = {22,5,67,98,45,32,101,99,73,10};
  int i, j, temp, moves, min, minind;
  moves = 0;
  for ( i = 0; i < 10; ++i)
  {
    min = nums[i];
    minind = i;
    for ( j = i + 1; j < 10; ++j)
      if (nums[j] < min)
      {
        min = nums[j];
        minind = j;
      }
    /* perform the switch */
    if (min < nums[i])
    {
      temp = nums[i];
      nums[i] = nums[minind];
      nums[minind] = temp;
      ++moves;
    }
  }
  printf("The sorted list, in ascending order, is:\n");
  for (i = 0; i < 10; ++i)
    printf("%d  ",nums[i]);
  printf("\n %d moves were made to sort this list\n", moves);
}
```

Program 7-6 uses a nested `for` loop to perform the selection sort. The outer `for` loop causes nine passes to be made through the data, which is one less than the total number of data items in the list. For each pass the variable `min` is initially assigned the value `nums[i]`, where i is the outer `for` loop's counter variable. Since i begins at 0 and ends at 8, each element in the list is successively designated as the next exchange element.

The inner loop is used in Program 7-6 to cycle through the elements below the designated exchange element to select the next smallest value. Thus, this loop begins at the index value `I+1` and continues through the end of the list. When a new minimum is found its value and position in the list are stored in the variables named `min` and `minind`, respectively. Upon completion of the inner loop, the program will make an exchange only if it finds a value less than the one in the designated exchange position.

Following is the output produced by Program 7-6.

```
The sorted list, in ascending order, is:
5   10   22   32   45   67   73   98   99   101
   8 moves were made to sort this list
```

Clearly the number of moves displayed depends on the initial order of the values in the list. An advantage of the selection sort is that the maximum number of moves that must be made is $n-1$, where n is the number of items in the list. Further, each move is a final move that results in an element residing in its final location in the sorted list.

A disadvantage of the selection sort is that $n(n-1)/2$ comparisons are always required, regardless of the initial arrangement of the data. This number of comparisons is obtained as follows: the last pass always requires one comparison, the next-to-last pass requires two comparisons, and so on, to the first pass, which requires $n-1$ comparisons. Thus, the total number of comparisons is

$$1 + 2 + 3 + \ \ldots \ n-1 = n(n-1)/2.$$

Exchange Sort

In an exchange sort successive values in the list are compared, beginning with the first two elements. If the list is to be sorted in ascending (from smallest to largest) order, the smaller value of the two being compared is always placed before the larger value. For lists sorted in descending (from largest to smallest) order, the smaller of the two values being compared is always placed after the larger value.

For example, assuming that a list of values is to be sorted in ascending order, if the first element in the list is larger than the second, the two elements are interchanged. Then, the second and third elements are compared. Again, if the second element is larger than the third, these two elements are interchanged.

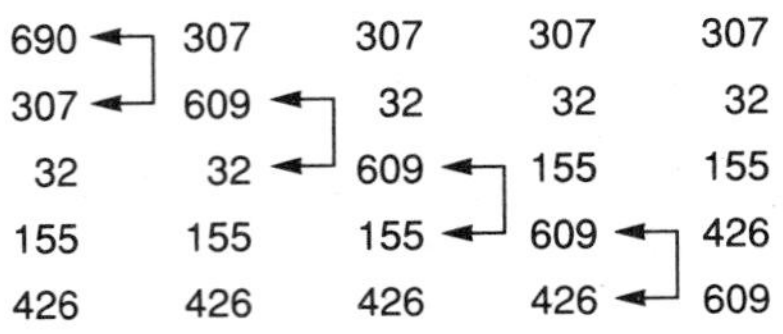

```
690 ◄┐  307    307    307    307
307 ◄┘  609 ◄┐  32     32     32
 32      32 ◄┘  609 ◄┐  155    155
155     155    155 ◄┘  609 ◄┐  426
426     426    426    426 ◄┘  609
```

FIGURE 7-12 The First Pass of an Exchange Sort

This process continues until the last two elements have been compared and exchanged, if necessary. If no exchanges were made during this initial pass through the data, the data is in the correct order and the process is finished; otherwise a second pass is made through the data, starting from the first element and stopping at the next-to-last element. The reason for stopping at the next-to-last element on the second pass is that the first pass always results in the most positive value "sinking" to the bottom of the list.

As a specific example of this process, consider the list of numbers illustrated in Figure 7-12. The first comparison results in the interchange of the first two element values, 690 and 307. The next comparison, between elements two and three in the revised list, results in the interchange of values between the second and third elements, 609 and 32. This comparison and possible switching of adjacent values is continued until the last two elements have been compared and possibly switched. This process completes the first pass through the data and results in the largest number moving to the bottom of the list. As the largest value sinks to its resting place at the bottom of the list, the smaller elements slowly rise, or "bubble," to the top of the list. This bubbling effect of the smaller elements gave rise to the name "bubble sort" for this sorting algorithm.

As the first pass through the list ensures that the largest value always moves to the bottom of the list, the second pass stops at the next-to-last element. This process continues with each pass stopping at one higher element than the previous pass, until either $n-1$ passes through the list have been completed or no exchanges are necessary in any single pass. In both cases the resulting list is in sorted order.

Program 7-7 implements an exchange sort for the same list of ten numbers used in Program 7-6. For comparison to the earlier selection sort, the number of exchanges made by the program is also counted and displayed.

Program 7-7

```
#define TRUE 1
#define FALSE 0
main()
{
   static int nums[10] = {22,5,67,98,45,32,101,99,73,10};
```

continued

```
int i, temp, moves, npts, outord;
moves = 0;
npts = 10;
outord = TRUE;
while (outord && npts > 0)
{
  outord = FALSE;
  for ( i = 0; i < npts - 1; ++i)
    if (nums[i] > nums[i+1])
      {
        temp = nums[i+1];
        nums[i+1] = nums[i];
        nums[i] = temp;
        outord = TRUE;
        ++moves;
      }
  --npts;
  }
printf("The sorted list, in ascending order, is:\n");
for (i = 0; i < 10; ++i)
  printf("%d ",nums[i]);
printf("\n %d moves were made to sort this list\n", moves);
}
```

As illustrated in Program 7-7, the exchange sort requires a nested loop. The outer loop in Program 7-7 is a while loop that checks if any exchanges were made in the last pass. It is the inner for loop that does the actual comparison and exchanging of adjacent element values.

Immediately before the inner loop's for statement is encountered, the value of the variable outord is set to TRUE, to indicate that the list is initially out of order (not sorted) and force the first pass through the list. If the inner loop then detects an element is out of order outord is again set to TRUE, which indicates that the list is still unsorted. The outord variable is then used by the outer loop to determine whether another pass through the data is to be made. Thus, the sort is stopped either because outord is FALSE after at least one pass has been completed or $n–1$ passes through the data have been made. In both cases the resulting list is in sorted order.

Following is the output produced by Program 7-7.

```
The sorted list, in ascending order, is:
5   10   22   32   45   67   73   98   99   101
  18 moves were made to sort this list
```

As with the selection sort, the number of moves required by an exchange sort depends on the initial order of the values in the list.

An advantage of the exchange sort is that processing is terminated whenever a sorted list is encountered. In the best case, when the data is in sorted order to begin with, an exchange sort requires no moves (the same for the selection sort) and only $n-1$ comparisons (the selection sort always requires $n(n-1)/2$ comparisons). In the worst case, when the data is in reverse sorted order, the selection sort does better. Here both sorts require $n(n-1)/2$ comparisons but the selection sort needs only $n-1$ moves while the exchange sort needs $n(n-1)/2$ moves. The additional moves required by the exchange sort result from the intermediate exchanges between adjacent elements to "settle" each element into its final position. In this regard, the selection sort is superior because no intermediate moves are necessary. For random data, such as that used in Programs 7-6 and 7-7, the selection sort generally performs equal to or better than the exchange sort.

Arrays,
Addresses,
and Pointers

Chapter Eight

There is a direct and intimate relationship among arrays, addresses, and pointers. In fact, generally unknown to programmers of high-level languages such as FORTRAN, BASIC, and COBOL, addresses run rampant throughout the executable versions of their programs. These addresses are used by the computer to keep track of where data and instructions are kept.

One of C's advantages is that it allows the programmer access to the addresses used by the program. Although we have already used addresses in calling the scanf() function and in function calls by reference, the real power of pointers is in dealing with arrays, strings, and other data structure elements. In this chapter we explore the exceptionally strong connection that exists among arrays, addresses, and pointers. The programming techniques learned in this chapter are then extended in the following chapters on strings and data structures.

8.1 Array Names as Pointers

Figure 8-1 illustrates the storage of a single-dimensional array named grades, which contains five integers. Assume that each integer requires two bytes of storage.

Using subscripts, the fourth element in the grades array is referred to as grades[3]. The use of a subscript, however, conceals the extensive use of addresses by the computer. Internally, the computer immediately uses the subscript to calculate the address of the desired element based on both the starting address of the array and the amount of storage used by each element. Calling the fourth element grades[3] forces the computer, internally, into the address computation (assuming two bytes for each integer);

$$\&grades[3] = \&grades[0] + (3 * 2)$$

Remembering that the address operator, &, means "the address of," this last statement is read "the address of grades[3] equals the address of grades[0] plus 6." Figure 8-2 illustrates the address computation used to locate grades[3].

FIGURE 8–1 The grades Array in Storage

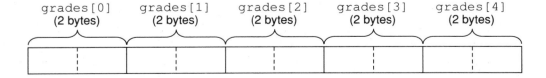

| grades[0]
(2 bytes) | grades[1]
(2 bytes) | grades[2]
(2 bytes) | grades[3]
(2 bytes) | grades[4]
(2 bytes) |

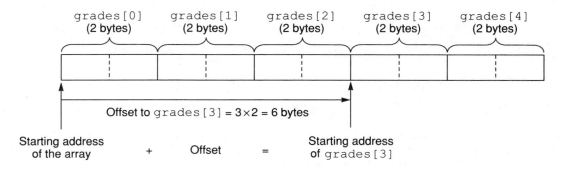

FIGURE 8-2 Using a Subscript to Obtain an Address

Recall that a pointer is a variable used to store addresses. If we create a pointer to store the address of the first element in the grades array, we can mimic the operation used by the computer to access the array elements. Before we do this, let us first consider Program 8-1.

 Program 8-1

```
main()
{
  int i;
  static int grades[] = {98, 87, 92, 79, 85};
  for (i = 0; i <= 4; ++i)
    printf("\nElement %d is %d", i, grades[i]);
}
```

When Program 8-1 is run, the following display is obtained:

```
Element 0 is 98
Element 1 is 87
Element 2 is 92
Element 3 is 79
Element 4 is 85
```

Program 8-1 displays the values of the static array grades using standard subscript notation. Now, let us store the address of array element 0 in a pointer. Then, using the indirection operator, *, we can use the address in the pointer to access each array element. For example, if we store the address of grades[0] into a pointer named g_ptr (using the assignment statement g_ptr = &grades[0];), then, as illustrated in Figure 8-3 the expression *g_ptr, which means "the variable pointed to by g_ptr," references grades[0].

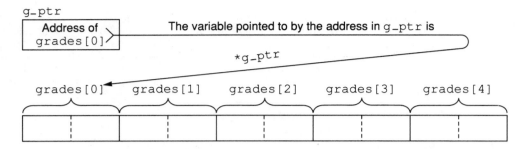

FIGURE 8-3 The Variable Pointed to by *g_ptr Is grades[0]

One unique feature of pointers is that *offsets* may be included in expressions using pointers. For example, the 1 in the expression *(g_ptr + 1) is an offset. The complete expression references the integer variable that is one beyond the variable pointed to by g_ptr. Similarly, as illustrated in Figure 8-4, the expression *(g_ptr + 3) references the variable that is three integers beyond the integer pointed to by g_ptr. This is the variable grades[3].

Table 8-1 lists the complete correspondence between elements referenced by subscripts and by pointers and offsets. The relationships listed in Table 8-1 are illustrated in Figure 8-5.

TABLE 8-1 Array Elements May Be Referenced in Two Ways

Array Element	Subscript Notation	Pointer Notation
Element 0	grades[0]	*g_ptr
Element 1	grades[1]	*(g_ptr + 1)
Element 2	grades[2]	*(g_ptr + 2)
Element 3	grades[3]	*(g_ptr + 3)
Element 4	grades[4]	*(g_ptr + 4)

FIGURE 8-4 An Offset of 3 from the Address in g_ptr

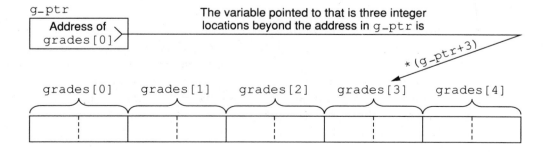

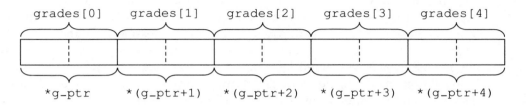

FIGURE 8–5   The Relationship Between Array Elements and Pointers

Using the correspondence between pointers and subscripts illustrated in Figure 8-5, the array elements previously accessed in Program 8-1 using subscripts can now be accessed using pointers. This is done in Program 8-2.

 Program 8-2

```
main()
{
  int *g_ptr;              /* declare a pointer to an int */
  int i;
  static int grades[] = {98, 87, 92, 79, 85};

  g_ptr = &grades[0];      /* store the starting array address */
  for (i = 0; i <= 4; ++i)
    printf("\nElement %d is %d", i, *(g_ptr + i) );
}
```

The following display is obtained when Program 8-2 is run:

```
Element 0 is 98
Element 1 is 87
Element 2 is 92
Element 3 is 79
Element 4 is 85
```

Notice that this is the same display produced by Program 8-1.

The method used in Program 8-2 to access *individual* array elements simulates how the computer internally references *all* array elements. Any subscript used by a programmer is automatically converted to an equivalent pointer expression by the computer. In our case, since the declaration of g_ptr included the information that integers are pointed to, any offset added to the address in g_ptr is automatically scaled by the size of an integer. Thus, *(g_ptr + 3), for example, refers to the address of grades[0] plus an offset of six bytes (3 * 2). This is the address of grades[3] illustrated in Figure 8-2.

The parentheses in the expression *(g_ptr + 3) are necessary to correctly reference the desired array element. Omitting the parentheses results in the expression *g_ptr + 3. This expression adds 3 to "the variable pointed to by g_ptr." Since g_ptr points to grades[0], this expression adds the value of grades[0] and 3 together. Note also that the expression *(g_ptr + 3) does not change the address stored in g_ptr. Once the computer uses the offset to locate the correct variable from the starting address in g_ptr, the offset is discarded and the address in g_ptr remains unchanged.

Although the pointer g_ptr used in Program 8-2 was specifically created to store the starting address of the grades array, this was, in fact, unnecessary. When an array is created, the compiler automatically creates an internal pointer constant for it and stores the starting address of the array in this pointer. In almost all respects, a pointer constant is identical to a pointer variable created by a programmer; but, as we shall see, there are some differences.

For each array created, the name of the array becomes the name of the pointer constant created by the compiler for the array, and the starting address of the first location reserved for the array is stored in this pointer. Thus, declaring the grades array in both Program 8-1 and Program 8-2 actually reserved enough storage for five integers, created an internal pointer named grades, and stored the address of grades[0] in the pointer. This is illustrated in Figure 8-6.

The implication is that every reference to grades using a subscript can be replaced by an equivalent reference using grades as a pointer. Thus, wherever the expression grades[i] is used, the expression *(grades + i) can also be

FIGURE 8-6 Creating an Array Also Creates a Pointer

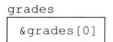

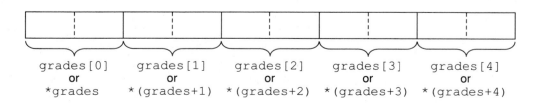

used. This is illustrated in Program 8-3, where grades is used as a pointer to reference all of its elements.

 Program 8-3

```
main()
{
  int i;
  static int grades[] = {98, 87, 92, 79, 85};
  for (i = 0; i <= 4; ++i)
    printf("\nElement %d is %d", i, *(grades + i) );
}
```

Executing Program 8-3 produces the same output previously produced by Program 8-1 and Program 8-2. However, using grades as a pointer made it unnecessary to declare and initialize the pointer g_ptr used in Program 8-2.

In most respects an array name and pointer can be used interchangeably. A true pointer, however, is a variable and the address stored in it can be changed. An array name is a pointer constant and the address stored in the pointer cannot be changed by an assignment statement. Thus, a statement such as grades = &grades[2]; is invalid. This should come as no surprise. Since the whole purpose of an array name is to correctly locate the beginning of the array, allowing a programmer to change the address stored in the array name would defeat this purpose and lead to havoc whenever array elements were referenced. Also, expressions taking the address of an array name are invalid because the pointer created by the compiler is internal to the computer, not stored in memory as are pointer variables. Thus, trying to store the address of grades using the expression &grades results in a compiler error.

An interesting sidelight to the observation that elements of an array can be referenced using pointers is that a pointer reference can always be replaced with a subscript reference. For example, if num_ptr is declared as a pointer variable, the expression *(num_ptr + i) can also be written as num_ptr[i]. This is true even though num_ptr is not created as an array. As before, when the compiler encounters the subscript notation, it replaces it internally with the pointer notation.

Exercises 8.1

1. Replace each of the following references to a subscripted variable with a pointer reference.

a. prices[5]   *d.* dist[9]   *g.* celsius[16]
b. grades[2]   *e.* mile[0]   *h.* num[50]
c. yield[10]   *f.* temp[20]   *i.* time[12]

2. Replace each of the following references using a pointer with a subscript reference.

  a. `* (message + 6)`   *c.* `* (yrs + 10)`   *e.* `* (rates + 15)`

  b. `*amount`   *d.* `* (stocks + 2)`   *f.* `* (codes + 19)`

3. *a.* List the three things that the declaration statement `double prices[5];` causes the compiler to do.

  b. If each double precision number uses four bytes of storage, how much storage is set aside for the `prices` array?

  c. Draw a diagram similar to Figure 8-6 for the `prices` array.

  d. Determine the byte offset relative to the start of the `prices` array, corresponding to the offset in the expression `* (prices + 3)`.

4. *a.* Write a declaration to store the string "This is a sample" into a static array named `samtest`. Include the declaration in a program that displays the values in `samtest` using a `for` loop and pointer references to each element in the array.

  b. Modify the program written in Exercise 4a to display only array elements 10 through 15 (these are the letters *s*, *a*, *m*, *p*, *l*, and *e*).

5. Write a declaration to store the following values into a static array named `rates`: 12.9, 18.6, 11.4, 13.7, 9.5, 15.2, 17.6. Include the declaration in a program that displays the values in the array using pointer notation.

6. Repeat Exercise 6 in Section 7.2, but use pointer references to access all array elements.

7. Repeat Exercise 7 in Section 7.2, but use pointer references to access all array elements.

8.2   Pointer Arithmetic

Pointer variables, like all variables, contain values. The value stored in a pointer is, of course, an address. Thus, by adding and subtracting numbers to pointers we can obtain different addresses. Additionally, the addresses in pointers can be compared using any of the relational operators (`==`, `!=`, `<`, `>`, etc.) that are valid for comparing other variables. In performing arithmetic on pointers we must be careful to produce addresses that point to something meaningful. In comparing pointers we must also make comparisons that make sense. Consider the declarations:

```
int nums[100];
int *n_pt;
```

To set the address of `nums[0]` into `n_pt`, either of the following two assignment statements can be used:

```
n_pt = &nums[0];
```

```
n_pt = nums;
```

The two assignment statements produce the same result because `nums` is a pointer constant that itself contains the address of the first location in the array.

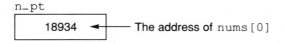

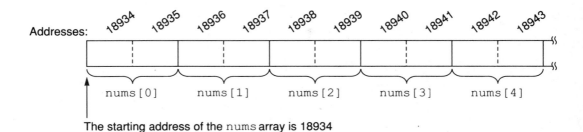

The starting address of the nums array is 18934

FIGURE 8-7 The nums Array in Memory

This is, of course, the address of nums[0]. Figure 8-7 illustrates the allocation of memory resulting from the previous declaration and assignment statements, assuming that each integer requires two bytes of memory and that the location of the beginning of the nums array is at address 18934.

Once n_pt contains a valid address, values can be added and subtracted from the address to produce new addresses. When adding or subtracting numbers to pointers, the computer automatically adjusts the number to ensure that the result still "points to" a value of the correct type. For example, the statement n_pt = n_pt + 4; forces the computer to scale the 4 by the correct number to ensure that the resulting address is the address of an integer. Assuming that each integer requires two bytes of storage, as illustrated in Figure 8-7, the computer multiplies the 4 by two and adds eight to the address in n_pt. The resulting address is 18942, which is the correct address of nums[4].

This automatic scaling by the computer ensures that the expression n_pt + i, where i is any positive integer, correctly points to the ith element beyond the one currently being pointed to by n_pt. Thus, if n_pt initially contains the address of nums[0], n_pt + 4 is the address of nums[4], n_pt + 50 is the address of nums[50], and n_pt + i is the address of nums[i]. Although we have used actual addresses in Figure 8-7 to illustrate the scaling process, the programmer need never know or care about the actual addresses used by the computer. The manipulation of addresses using pointers generally does not require knowledge of the actual address.

Addresses can also be incremented or decremented using both prefix and postfix increment and decrement operators. Adding one to a pointer causes the pointer to point to the next element of the type being pointed to. Decrementing a pointer causes the pointer to point to the previous element. For example, if the pointer variable p is a pointer to an integer, the expression p++ causes the address in the pointer to be incremented to point to the next integer. This is illustrated in Figure 8-8.

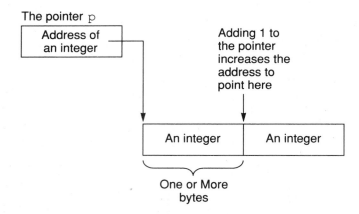

FIGURE 8-8 Increments Are Scaled When Used with Pointers

In reviewing Figure 8-8, notice that the increment added to the pointer is correctly scaled to account for the fact that the pointer is used to point to integers. It is, of course, up to the programmer to ensure that the correct type of data is stored in the new address contained in the pointer.

The increment and decrement operators can be applied as both prefix and postfix pointer operators. All of the following combinations using pointers are valid:

```
*pt_num++      /* use the pointer and then increment it */
*++pt_num      /* increment the pointer before using it */
*pt_num--      /* use the pointer and then decrement it */
*--pt_num      /* decrement the pointer before using it */
```

Of the four possible forms, the most commonly used is the form *pt_num++. This is because such an expression allows each element in an array to be accessed as the address is "marched along" from the starting address of the array to the address of the last array element. To see the use of the increment operator, consider Program 8-4. In this program each element in the nums array is retrieved by successively incrementing the address in n_pt.

 Program 8-4

```
main()
{
  static int nums[5] = {16, 54, 7, 43, -5};
  int i, total = 0, *n_pt;
  n_pt = nums;    /* store address of nums[0] in n_pt */
  for (i = 0; i <= 4; ++i)
    total = total + *n_pt++;
  printf("The total of the array elements is %d", total);
}
```

The output produced by Program 8-4 is:

```
The total of the array elements is 115
```

The expression `total = total + *n_pt++` used in Program 8-4 is a standard accumulating expression. Within this expression, the term `*n_pt++` first causes the computer to retrieve the integer pointed to by `n_pt`. This is done by the `*n_pt` part of the term. The postfix increment, `++`, then adds one to the address in `n_pt` so that `n_pt` now contains the address of the next array element. The increment is, of course, scaled by the computer so that the actual address in `n_pt` is the correct address of the next element.

Pointers may also be compared. This is particularly useful when dealing with pointers that point to elements in the same array. For example, rather than using a counter in a `for` loop to correctly access each element in an array, the address in a pointer can be compared to the starting and ending address of the array itself. The expression

```
n_pt <= &nums[4]
```

is true (nonzero) as long as the address in `n_pt` is less than or equal to the address of `nums[4]`. Since `nums` is a pointer constant that contains the address of `nums[0]`, the term `&nums[4]` can be replaced by the equivalent term `nums + 4`. Using either of these forms, Program 8-4 can be rewritten as Program 8-5 to continue adding array elements while the address in `n_pt` is less than or equal to the address of the last array element.

 Program 8-5

```
main()
{
   static int nums[5] = {16, 54, 7, 43, -5};
   int total = 0, *n_pt;

   n_pt = nums;    /* store address of nums[0] in n_pt */

   while (n_pt <= nums + 4)
     total += *n_pt++;

   printf("The total of the array elements is %d", total);
}
```

Notice that in Program 8-5 the compact form of the accumulating expression, `total += *n_pt++`, was used in place of the longer form, `total = total + *n_pt++`. Also, the expression `nums + 4` does not change the address in `nums`.

Since `nums` is an array name and not a pointer variable, its value cannot be changed. The expression `nums + 4` first retrieves the address in `nums`, adds 4 to this address (appropriately scaled) and uses the result for comparison purposes. Expressions such as `*nums++`, which attempt to change the address, are invalid. Expressions such as `*nums` or `*(nums + i)`, which use the address without attempting to alter it, are valid.

Pointer Initialization

Like all variables, pointers can be initialized when they are declared. When initializing pointers, however, you must be careful to set an address in the pointer. For example, an initialization such as

```
int *pt_num = &miles;
```

is only valid if `miles` itself were declared as an integer variable prior to `pt_num`. Here we are creating a pointer to an integer and setting the address in the pointer to the address of an integer variable. Notice that if the variable `miles` is declared subsequently to `pt_num`, as follows,

```
int *pt_num = &miles;
int miles;
```

an error occurs. This is because the address of `miles` is used before `miles` has even been defined. Since the storage area reserved for `miles` has not been allocated when `pt_num` is declared, the address of `miles` does not yet exist.

Pointers to arrays can be initialized within their declaration statements. For example, if `prices` has been declared an array of floating point numbers, either of the following two declarations can be used to initialize the pointer named `zing` to the address of the first element in `prices`:

```
float *zing = &prices[0];

float *zing = prices;
```

The last initialization is correct because `prices` is itself a pointer constant containing an address of the proper type. (The variable name `zing` was selected in this example to reinforce the idea that any variable name can be selected for a pointer.)

Exercises 8.2

---

1. Replace the `while` statement in Program 8-5 with a `for` statement.

2. a. Write a program that stores the following numbers in the `static` array named `rates`: 6.25, 6.50, 6.8, 7.2, 7.35, 7.5, 7.65, 7.8, 8.2, 8.4, 8.6, 8.8, 9.0. Display the values in the array by changing the address in a pointer called `disp_pt`. Use a `for` statement in your program.

b. Modify the program written in Exercise 2a to use a `while` statement.

3. *a.* Write a program that stores the string `Hooray for All of Us` into a `static` array named `strng`. Use the declaration `static char strng[] = "Hooray for All of Us";`, which ensures that the end-of-string escape sequence `\0` is included in the array. Display the characters in the array by changing the address in a pointer called `mess_pt`. Use a `for` statement in your program.
b. Modify the program written in Exercise 3a to use the `while` statement `while (*mess_pt++ != '\0')`.
c. Modify the program written in Exercise 3a to start the display with the word `All`.

4. Write a program that stores the following numbers in the static array named `miles`: 15, 22, 16, 18, 27, 23, 20. Have your program copy the data stored in `miles` to another array named `dist` and then display the values in the `dist` array.

5. Write a program that stores the following letters in the `static` array named `message`: `This is a test.` Have your program copy the data stored in `message` to another array named `mess2` and then display the letters in the `mess2` array.

6. Write a program that declares three single-dimensional arrays named `miles`, `gallons`, and `mpg`. Each array should be capable of holding ten elements. In the `miles` array store the numbers 240.5, 300.0, 189.6, 310.6, 280.7, 216.9, 199.4, 160.3, 177.4, 192.3. In the `gallons` array store the numbers 10.3, 15.6, 8.7, 14, 16.3, 15.7, 14.9, 10.7, 8.3, 8.4. Each element of the `mpg` array should be calculated as the corresponding element of the `miles` array divided by the equivalent element of the `gallons` array; for example, `mpg[0] = miles[0] / gallons[0]`. Use pointers when calculating and displaying the elements of the `mpg` array.

8.3   Passing and Using Array Addresses

When an array is passed to a function, its address is the only item actually passed. By this we mean the address of the first location used to store the array, as illustrated in Figure 8-9. Since the first location reserved for an array corresponds to element 0 of the array, the "address of the array" is also the address of element 0.

For a specific example in which an array is passed to a function, let us consider Program 8-6. In this program, the `nums` array is passed to the `find_max()` function using conventional array notation.

FIGURE 8–9   The Address of an Array Is the Address of the First Location Reserved for the Array

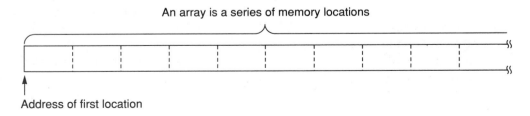

An array is a series of memory locations

Address of first location

Program 8-6

```
main()
{
   static int nums[5] = {2, 18, 1, 27, 16};
   int find_max();

   printf("The maximum value is %d", find_max(nums,5));
}

int find_max(vals,num_els)      /* find the maximum value */
int vals[], num_els;
{
   int i, max = vals[0];

   for (i = 1; i <= (num_els - 1); ++i)
    if (max < vals[i]) max = vals[i];

   return(max);
}
```

The output displayed when Program 8-6 is executed is:

The maximum value is 27

The argument named `vals` in the declaration line for `find_max()` actually receives the address of the array `nums`. As such, `vals` is really a pointer, since pointers are variables (or arguments) used to store addresses. Since the address passed into `find_max()` is the address of an integer, another suitable declaration for `find_max()` is:

```
find_max(vals,num_els)
int *vals;          /* vals declared as a pointer to an integer */
int num_els;
```

The declaration `int *vals;` declares that `vals` is used to store an address of an integer. The address stored is, of course, the location of the beginning of an array. Following is a rewritten version of the `find_max()` function that uses the new pointer declaration for `vals`, but retains the use of subscripts to refer to individual array elements:

```
int find_max(vals,num_els)              /* find the maximum value */
int *vals;              /* vals declared as a pointer to an integer */
int num_els;
{
  int i, max = vals[0];

  for (i = 1; i <= (num_els - 1); ++i)
   if (max < vals[i]) max = vals[i];

  return(max);
}
```

One further observation needs to be made. Regardless of how vals is declared in the function header or how it is used within the function body, it is truly a pointer variable. As such, the address in vals may be modified. This is not true for the name nums. Since nums is the name of the originally created array, it is a pointer constant. As described in Section 8.1, this means that the address in nums cannot be changed and that the expression &nums is invalid. No such restrictions, however, apply to the pointer variable named vals. All the address arithmetic that we learned in the previous section can be legitimately applied to vals.

We shall write two additional versions of find_max(), both using pointers instead of subscripts. In the first version we simply substitute pointer notation for subscript notation. In the second version we use address arithmetic to change the address in the pointer.

As previously stated, a reference to an array element using the subscript notation array_name[i] can always be replaced by the pointer notation *(array_name + i). In our first modification to find_max(), we make use of this correspondence by simply replacing all references to vals[i] by the equivalent expression *(vals + i).

```
int find_max(vals,num_els)              /* find the maximum value */
int *vals;              /* vals declared as a pointer to an integer */
int num_els;
{
  int i, max = *vals;

  for (i = 1; i <= (num_els - 1); ++i)
   if (max < *(vals + i) )   max = *(vals + i);

  return(max);
}
```

Our last version of find_max() makes use of the fact that the address stored in vals can be changed. After each array element is retrieved using the address in vals, the address itself is incremented by one in the altering list of the for statement. The expression *vals++ used initially to set max to the value of vals[0] also adjusts the address in vals to point to the second element in the array. The element obtained from this expression is the array element pointed to by vals before vals is incremented. The postfix increment, ++, does not change the address in vals until after the address has been used to retrieve the array element.

```
int find_max(vals,num_els)      /* find the maximum value     */
int *vals;                      /* vals declared as a pointer */
int num_els;
{
  int i, max = *vals++;    /* get the first element and increment */

  for (i = 1; i <= (num_els - 1); ++i, ++vals)
  {
    if (max < *vals)   max = *vals;
  }
  return(max);
}
```

Let us review this version of find_max(). Initially the maximum value is set to "the thing pointed to by vals." Since vals initially contains the address of the first element in the array passed to find_max(), the value of this first element is stored in max. The address in vals is then incremented by one. The one that is added to vals is automatically scaled by the number of bytes used to store integers. Thus, after the increment, the address stored in vals is the address of the next array element. This is illustrated in Figure 8-10. The value of this next element is compared to the maximum and the address is again incremented, this time from within the altering list of the for statement. This process continues until all the array elements have been examined.

FIGURE 8–10 Pointing to Different Elements

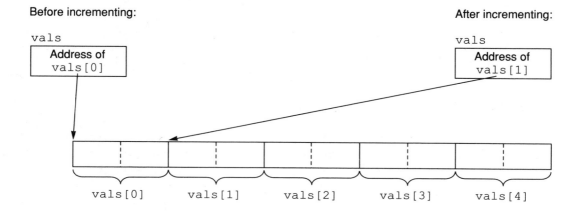

290

The version of `find_max()` that appeals to you is a matter of personal style and taste. Generally, beginning programmers feel more at ease using subscripts than using pointers. Also, if the program uses an array as the natural storage structure for the application and data at hand, an array reference using subscripts is more appropriate to clearly indicate the intent of the program. However, as we learn about strings and data structures, the use of pointers becomes an increasingly useful and powerful tool in its own right. In these instances there is no simple or easy equivalence using subscripts.

One further "neat trick" can be gleaned from our discussion. Since passing an array to a function really involves passing an address, we can just as well pass any valid address. For example, the function call

```
find_max(&nums[2],3)
```

passes the address of `nums[2]` to `find_max()`. Within `find_max()` the pointer `vals` stores the address and the function starts the search for a maximum at the element corresponding to this address. Thus, from `find_max()`'s perspective, it has received an address and proceeds appropriately.

Advanced Pointer Notation*

Access to multidimensional arrays can also be made using pointer notation, although the notation becomes more and more cryptic as the array dimensions increase. An extremely useful application of this notation occurs with two-dimensional character arrays, one of the topics of the next chapter. Here we consider pointer notation for two-dimensional numeric arrays. For example, consider the declaration

```
static int nums[2][3] = { {16,18,20},
                          {25,26,27} };
```

This declaration creates an array of elements and a set of pointer constants named `nums`, `nums[0]`, and `nums[1]`. The relationship between these pointer constants and the elements of the `nums` array are illustrated in Figure 8-11.

The availability of the pointer constants associated with a two-dimensional array allows us to reference array elements in a variety of ways. One way is to consider the two-dimensional array as an array of rows, where each row is itself

---

* This topic may be omitted with no loss of subject continuity.

FIGURE 8–11 Storage of the `nums` Array and Associated Pointer Constants

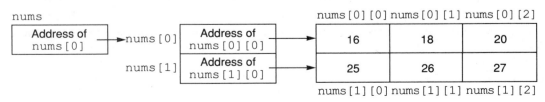

an array of three elements. Considered in this light, the address of the first element in the first row is provided by nums[0] and the address of the first element in the second row is provided by nums[1]. Thus, the variable pointed to by nums[0] is num[0][0] and the variable pointed to by nums[1] is num[1][0]. Once the nature of these constants is understood, each element in the array can be accessed by applying an appropriate offset to the appropriate pointer. Thus, the following notations are equivalent:

Pointer Notation	Subscript Notation	Value
*nums[0]	nums[0][0]	16
*(nums[0] + 1)	nums[0][1]	18
*(nums[0] + 2)	nums[0][2]	20
*nums[1]	nums[1][0]	25
*(nums[1] + 1)	nums[1][1]	26
*(nums[1] + 2)	nums[1][2]	27

We can now go even further and replace nums[0] and nums[1] with their respective pointer notations, using the address of nums itself. As illustrated in Figure 8-11, the variable pointed to by nums is nums[0]. That is, *nums is nums[0]. Similarly, *(nums + 1) is nums[1]. Using these relationships leads to the following equivalences:

Pointer Notation	Subscript Notation	Value
*(*nums)	nums[0][0]	16
*(*nums + 1)	nums[0][1]	18
*(*nums + 2)	nums[0][2]	20
((nums + 1))	nums[1][0]	25
((nums + 1) + 1)	nums[1][1]	26
((nums + 1) + 2)	nums[1][2]	27

The same notation applies when a two-dimensional array is passed to a function. For example, assume that the two-dimensional array nums is passed to the function calc() using the call calc(nums);. Here, as with all array passes, an address is passed. A suitable function header for the function calc() is:

```
calc(pt)
int pt[2][3];
```

As we have already seen, the argument declaration for pt can also be

```
int pt[][3];
```

Using pointer notation, another suitable declaration is

```
int (*pt)[3];
```

In this last declaration, the parentheses are required to create a single pointer to objects of three integers. Each object is, of course, equivalent to a single row of the nums array. By suitably offsetting the pointer, each element in the array can be accessed. Notice that without the parentheses the declaration becomes

```
int *pt[3];
```

which inappropriately creates an array of three pointers, each one pointing to a single integer.

Once the correct declaration for pt is made (any of the appropriate declarations), the following notations within the function calc() are all equivalent:

Pointer Notation	Subscript Notation	Value
*(*pt)	pt[0][0]	16
*(*pt+1)	pt[0][1]	18
*(*pt+2)	pt[0][2]	20
((pt+1))	pt[1][0]	25
((pt+1)+1)	pt[1][1]	26
((pt+1)+2)	pt[1][2]	27

The last two notations using pointers are encountered in more advanced C programs. The first of these occurs because functions can return any valid C scalar data type, including pointers to any of these data types. If a function returns a pointer, the data type being pointed to must be declared in the function's declaration. For example, the declaration

```
int *calc()
```

declares that calc() returns a pointer to an integer value. This means that *an address* of an integer variable is returned. Similarly, the declaration

```
float *taxes()
```

declares that taxes() returns a pointer to a floating point value. This means that *an address* of a floating point variable is returned.

In addition to declaring pointers to integers, floating point numbers, and C's other data types, pointers can also be declared that point to (contain the address of) a function. Pointers to functions are possible because function names, like array names, are themselves pointer constants. For example, the declaration

$$\text{int (*calc)()}$$

declares `calc` to be a pointer to a function that returns an integer. This means that `calc` will contain the address of a function, and the function whose address is in the variable `calc` returns an integer value. If, for example, the function `sum()` returns an integer, the assignment `calc = sum;` is valid.

Exercises 8.3

1. The following declaration was used to create the `prices` array:

```
double prices[500];
```

Write three different declarations for a function named `sort_arr()` that accepts the `prices` array as an argument named `in_array`.

2. The following declaration was used to create the `keys` array:

```
char keys[256];
```

Write three different declarations for a function named `find_key()` that accepts the `keys` array as an argument named `select`.

3. The following declaration was used to create the `rates` array:

```
float rates[256];
```

Write three different declarations for a function named `prime()` that accepts the `rates` array as an argument named `rates`.

4. Modify the `find_max()` function to locate the minimum value of the passed array. Write the function using only pointers.

5. In the last version of `find_max()` presented, `vals` was incremented inside the altering list of the `for` statement. Instead, suppose that the incrementing was done within the condition expression of the `if` statement, as follows:

```
find_max(vals,num_els)      /* incorrect version          */
int *vals;                  /* vals declared as a pointer */
int num_els;
{
  int i, max = *vals++;     /* get the first element and increment */
  for (i = 1; i <= (num_els - 1); ++i)
  {
    if (max < *vals++)   max = *vals;
  }
  return(max);
}
```

This version produces an incorrect result. Determine why.

6. a. Write a program that has a declaration in `main()` to store the following numbers into a `static` array named `rates`: 6.5, 7.2, 7.5, 8.3, 8.6, 9.4, 9.6, 9.8, 10.0. There should

be a function call to `show()` that accepts `rates` in an argument named `rates` and then displays the numbers using the pointer notation `*(rates + i)`.
b. Modify the `show()` function written in Exercise 6a to alter the address in `rates`. Always use the expression `*rates` rather than `*(rates + i)` to retrieve the correct element.

7. a. Write a program that has a declaration in `main()` to store the string `Vacation is near` into a `static` array named `message`. There should be a function call to `display()` that accepts `message` in an argument named `strng` and then displays the message using the pointer notation `*(strng + i)`.
b. Modify the `display()` function written in Exercise 7a to alter the address in `message`. Always use the expression `*strng` rather than `*(strng + i)` to retrieve the correct element.

8. Write a program that declares three single-dimensional arrays named `price`, `quantity`, and `amount`. Each array should be declared in `main()` and be capable of holding ten double precision numbers. The numbers to be stored in `price` are 10.62, 14.89, 13.21, 16.55, 18.62, 9.47, 6.58, 18.32, 12.15, 3.98. The numbers to be stored in `quantity` are 4, 8.5, 6, 7.35, 9, 15.3, 3, 5.4, 2.9, 4.8. Have your program pass these three arrays to a function called `extend()`, which calculates the elements in the `amount` array as the product of the equivalent elements in the `price` and `quantity` arrays (for example, `amount[1] = price[1] * quantity[1]`). After `extend()` has put values into the `amount` array, display the values in the array from within `main()`. Write the `extend()` function using pointers.

9. a. Determine the output of the following program:

```
main()
{
   static int nums[2][3] = { {33,16,29},
                             {54,67,99}};

   arr(nums);
}

arr(val)
int (*val)[3];
{
    printf("\n %d",*(*val) );
    printf("\n %d",*(*val + 1) );
    printf("\n %d",*(*(val + 1) + 2) );
    printf("\n %d",*(*val) + 1 );
}
```

b. Given the declaration for `val` in the `arr()` function, would the reference `val[1][2]` be valid within the function?

8.4 Common Programming Errors

A common programming error occurs when pointers are used to reference nonexistent array elements. For example, if `nums` is an array of ten integers, the expression *(nums + 15) points six integer locations beyond the last element of the array. As C does not do any bounds checking on array references, this type of error is not caught by the compiler. This is the same error as using a subscript to reference an out-of-bounds array element disguised in its pointer notation form.

The remaining errors are not specific to pointers used for array references, but are common whenever pointer notation is used. These errors result from incorrect use of the address and indirection operators. For example, if pt is a pointer variable, the expressions

```
pt = &45
pt = &(miles + 10)
```

are both invalid because they attempt to take the address of a value. Notice that the expression pt = &miles + 10, however, is valid. Here, 10 is added to the address of miles. Again, it is the programmer's responsibility to ensure that the final address "points to" a valid data element.

Addresses cannot be taken of any register variable. Thus, for the declarations

```
register int total;
int *pt_tot;
```

the assignment

```
pt_tot = &total;
```

is invalid. The reason for this is that register variables are stored in a computer's internal registers, and these storage areas do not have standard memory addresses.

Addresses of pointer constants also cannot be taken. For example, given the declarations

```
int nums[25];
int *pt;
```

the assignment

```
pt = &nums;
```

is invalid. nums is a pointer constant that is itself equivalent to an address. The correct assignment is pt = nums.

Another common mistake made by beginner programmers is to initialize pointer variables incorrectly. For example, the initialization

```
int *pt = 5;
```

is invalid. Since pt is a pointer to an integer, it must be initialized with a valid address.

A more confusing error results from using the same name as both a pointer and a nonpointer variable. For example, assume that `minutes` is declared as an integer variable in `main()` and that `main()` passes the address of `minutes` to the function `time()` using the function call `time(&minutes);`. Due to the scope of local variables, the same names used in `main()` can also be used in `time()` without causing the computer any confusion. Thus, a valid function header for `time()` could be

```
time(minutes)
int *minutes;
```

With these declarations, the value stored in `minutes` within `main()` is accessed using the variable's name, while the same value is accessed in `time()` using the notation `*minutes`. This can be very confusing to a programmer. To avoid this, most programmers usually develop their own systems for naming pointer arguments and variables. For example, prefixing pointer names by `pt_` or suffixing them with the characters `_addr` helps to indicate clearly that the arguments or variables are pointers.

The final error that occurs is one common to pointer usage in general. The situation always arises when the beginning C programmer becomes confused about whether a variable *contains* an address or *is* an address. Pointer variables and pointer arguments contain addresses. Although a pointer constant is synonymous with an address, it is useful to treat pointer constants as pointer variables with two restrictions:

1. The address of a pointer constant cannot be taken.
2. The address "contained in" the pointer constant cannot be altered.

Except for these two restrictions, pointer constants and variables can be used almost interchangeably. Therefore, when an address is required any of the following can be used:

> a pointer variable name
> a pointer argument name
> a pointer constant name
> a nonpointer variable name preceded by the address operator
> (e.g., `&variable`)
> a nonpointer argument name preceded by the address operator
> (e.g., `&argument`)

Some of the confusion surrounding pointers is caused by the cavalier use of the word *pointer*. For example, the phrase "a function requires a pointer argument" is more clearly understood when it is realized that the phrase really means "a function requires an address as an argument." Similarly, the phrase "a function returns a pointer" really means "a function returns an address."

If you are ever in doubt as to what is really contained in a variable, or how it should be treated, use the printf() function to display the contents of the variable, the "thing pointed to," or "the address of the variable." Seeing what is displayed frequently helps sort out what is really in the variable.

8.5 Chapter Summary

1. An array name is a pointer constant. The value of the pointer constant is the address of the first element in the array. Thus, if val is the name of an array, val and &val[0] can be used interchangeably.

2. Any reference to an array element using subscript notation can always be replaced using pointer notation. That is, the notation a[i] can always be replaced by the notation *(a + i). This is true whether a was initially declared explicitly as an array or as a pointer.

3. Arrays are passed to functions by reference. The called function always receives direct access to the originally declared array elements.

4. When a single-dimensional array is passed to a function, the argument declaration for the function can be either an array declaration or a pointer declaration. Thus, the following argument declarations are equivalent:

```
float a[];
float *a;
```

5. Pointers can be incremented, decremented, and compared. Numbers added to or subtracted from a pointer are automatically scaled. The scale factor used is the number of bytes required to store the data type originally pointed to.

Character Strings

Chapter Nine

On a fundamental level, strings are simply arrays of characters that can be manipulated using standard element-by-element array-processing techniques. On a higher level, string library functions are available for treating strings as complete entities. This chapter explores the input, manipulation, and output of strings using both approaches. We will also examine the particularly close connection between string-handling functions and pointers.

9.1 String Fundamentals

A *string constant*, informally referred to as a *string*, is any sequence of characters enclosed in double quotes. For example, "This is a string", "Hello World!", and "xyz 123 *!#@&" are all strings.

A string is stored as an array of characters terminated by a special end-of-string marker called the null character. The *null character*, represented by the escape sequence \0, is the sentinel marking the end of the string. For example, Figure 9-1 illustrates how the string "Good Morning!" is stored in memory. The string uses fourteen storage locations, with the last character in the string being the end-of-string marker \0. The double quotes are not stored as part of the string.

Since a string is stored as an array of characters, the individual characters in the array can be input, manipulated, or output using standard array-handling techniques utilizing either subscript or pointer notations. The end-of-string null character is useful for detecting the end of the string when handling strings in this fashion.

String Input and Output

Although the programmer has the choice of using either a library or a user-written function for processing a string already in memory, inputting a string from a keyboard or displaying a string always requires some reliance on standard library functions. Table 9-1 lists the commonly available library functions for both character-by-character and complete string input/output.

The gets() and puts() functions deal with strings as complete units. Both are written using the more elemental functions getchar() and putchar(). The getchar() and putchar() functions provide for the input and output of individual characters. Programs that access any of these four functions must

FIGURE 9–1 Storing a String in Memory

G	o	o	d		M	o	r	n	i	n	g	!	\0

Table 9-1 Standard String and
Character Library Functions

Input	Output
gets()	puts()
scanf()	printf()
getchar()	putchar()

contain an include instruction of the form #include <stdio.h>. The stdio.h file contains definitions required by the accessed library functions.

Program 9-1 illustrates the use of gets() and puts() to input and output a string entered at the user's terminal.

 Program 9-1

```
#include <stdio.h>
main()
{
  char message[81];    /* enough storage for a complete line */

  printf("Enter a string:\n");
  gets(message);
  printf("The string just entered is:\n");
  puts(message);
}
```

The following is a sample run of Program 9-1:

```
Enter a string:
This is a test input of a string of characters.
The string just entered is:
This is a test input of a string of characters.
```

The gets() function used in Program 9-1 continuously accepts and stores the characters typed at the terminal into the character array named message. Pressing the ENTER key at the terminal generates a newline character, \n, which is interpreted by gets() as the end-of-character entry. All the characters encountered by gets(), except the newline character, are stored in the message array. Before returning, the gets() function appends the null character to the stored set of characters, as illustrated in Figure 9-2a. The puts() function is then used to display the string. As illustrated in Figure 9-2b, the puts() function automatically sends a newline escape sequence to the display terminal after the string has been printed.

FIGURE 9-2a `gets()` Substitutes \0 for the Entered \n

FIGURE 9-2b `puts()` Substitutes \n when \0 is Encountered

In general, a `printf()` function call can always be used in place of a `puts()` function call. For example, the statement `printf("%s\n",message);` is a direct replacement for the statement `puts(message);` used in Program 9-1. The newline escape sequence in the `printf()` function call substitutes for the automatic newline generated by `puts()` after the string is displayed.

The one-to-one correspondence between the output functions `printf()` and `puts()` is not duplicated by the input functions `scanf()` and `gets()`. For example, `scanf("%s",message)` and `gets(message)` are not equivalent. The `scanf()` function reads a set of characters up to either a blank space or a newline character, whereas `gets()` stops accepting characters only when a newline is detected. Trying to enter the characters `This is a string` using the statement `scanf("%s",message);` results in the word `This` being assigned to the `message` array. Entering the complete line using a `scanf()` function call would require a statement such as

```
scanf("%s %s %s %s", message1, message2, message3, message4);
```

Here, the word `This` would be assigned to the string `message1`, the word `is` assigned to the string `message2`, and so on. The fact that a blank is used as a delimiter by `scanf()` makes this function not that useful for entering string data.

Note that if the `scanf()` function *is* used for inputting string data, the `&` is not used before the array name. Since an array name is a pointer constant equivalent to the address of the first storage location reserved for the array, `message` is the same as `&message[0]`. Thus, the function call `scanf("%s",&message[0])` can be replaced by `scanf("%s",message)`.

String Processing

Strings can be manipulated using either standard library functions or standard array-processing techniques. The library functions typically available for use are presented in the next section. For now we will concentrate on processing a string in a character-by-character fashion. This will allow us to understand how the standard library functions are constructed and to create our own library functions. For a specific example, consider the function `strcopy()` that copies the contents of `string1` to `string2`.

```
strcopy(string1, string2)      /* copy string1 to string2 */
char string1[], string2[];     /* two arrays are passed    */
{
  int i = 0;                   /* i will be used as a subscript  */

  while (string1[i] != '\0')   /* check for the end-of-string    */
  {
    string2[i] = string1[i];   /* copy the element to string2 */
    ++i;
  }
  string2[i] = '\0';           /* terminate the second string */
  return;
}
```

Although this string copy function can be shortened considerably and written more compactly, the function illustrates the main features of string manipulation. The two strings are passed to `strcopy()` as arrays. Each element of `string1` is then assigned to the equivalent element of `string2` until the end-of-string marker is encountered. The detection of the null character forces the termination of the `while` loop controlling the copying of elements. Since the null character is not copied from `string1` to `string2`, the last statement in `strcopy()` appends an end-of-string character to `string2`. Prior to calling `strcopy()`, the programmer must ensure that sufficient space has been allocated for the `string2` array to accommodate the elements of the `string1` array.

Program 9-2 includes the `strcopy()` function in a complete program.

 Program 9-2

```
#include <stdio.h>
main()
{
  char message[81];    /* enough storage for a complete line    */
  char new_mess[81];   /* enough storage for a copy of message */
  int i;

  printf("Enter a sentence:");
  gets(message);
  strcopy(message,new_mess);    /* pass two array addresses */
  puts(new_mess);

}
```

continued

```
strcopy(string1, string2)        /* copy string1 to string2 */
char string1[], string2[];       /* two arrays are passed    */
{
  int i = 0;                     /* i will be used as a subscript */

  while ( string1[i] != '\0')    /* check for the end-of-string   */
  {
    string2[i] = string1[i];     /* copy the element to string2 */
    ++i;
  }
  string2[i] = '\0';             /* terminate the second string */
  return;
}
```

The following is a sample run of Program 9-2:

```
Enter a sentence: How much wood could a woodchuck chuck.
How much wood could a woodchuck chuck.
```

Character-by-Character Input

Just as strings can be processed using character-by-character techniques, they can also be entered and displayed in this manner. For example, consider Program 9-3, which uses the character-input function `getchar()` to enter a string one character at a time. The shaded portion of Program 9-3 essentially replaces the `gets()` function previously used in Program 9-1.

 Program 9-3

```
#include <stdio.h>
main()
{
  char message[81],c;    /* enough storage for a complete line */
  int i;

  printf("Enter a string:\n");

  i = 0;
  while( i < 80 && (c = getchar()) != '\n')
  {
    message[i] = c;        /* store the character entered */
    ++i;
  }
  message[i] = '\0';       /* terminate the string */

  printf("The string just entered is:\n");
  puts(message);
}
```

The following is a sample run of Program 9-3:

```
Enter a string:
This is a test input of a string of characters.
The string just entered is:
This is a test input of a string of characters.
```

The `while` statement in Program 9-3 causes characters to be read providing the number of characters entered is less than 81 and the character returned by `getchar()` is not the newline character. The parentheses around the expression `c = getchar()` are necessary to assign the character returned by `getchar()` to the variable `c` prior to comparing it to the newline escape sequence. Otherwise, the comparison operator, `!=`, which takes precedence over the assignment operator, causes the entire expression to be equivalent to

```
c = (getchar() != '\n')
```

This has the effect of first comparing the character returned by `getchar` to `'\n'`. The value of the relational expression `getchar() != '\n'` is either 0 or 1, depending on whether or not `getchar()` received the newline character. The value assigned to `c` then would also be either 0 or 1, as determined by the comparison.

Program 9-3 also illustrates a very useful technique for developing functions. The shaded statements constitute a self-contained unit for entering a complete line of characters from a terminal. As such, these statements can be removed from `main()` and placed together as a new function. Program 9-4 illustrates placing these statements in a new function called `getline()`.

 Program 9-4

```c
#include <stdio.h>
main()
{
  char message[81];    /* enough storage for a complete line */
  int i;

  printf("Enter a string:\n");
  getline(message);
  printf("The string just entered is:\n");
  puts(message);
}
```

continued

```
getline(strng)
char strng[];
{
  int i = 0;
  char c;
  while( i < 80 && (c = getchar()) != '\n')
  {
    strng[i] = c;          /* store the character entered */
    ++i;
  }
  strng[i] = '\0';         /* terminate the string        */
  return;
}
```

Since the `getline()` function does not formally return a value to `main()`, it does not have to be declared in `main()`. However, if your C compiler supports the `void` data type, `getline()` should be declared in `main()` as `void getline();`. We can go further with `getline()` and write it more compactly by having the character returned by `getchar()` assigned directly to the `strng` array. This eliminates the need for the local variable `c` and results in the following version:

```
getline(strng)
char strng[];
{
  int i = 0;
  while( i < 80 && (strng[i++] = getchar()) != '\n')
    ;
  strng[i] = '\0';         /* terminate the string        */
  return;
}
```

Notice that in addition to assigning the returned character from `getchar()` directly to the `strng` array, the assignment statement

$$strng[i++] = getchar()$$

additionally increments the subscript `i` using the postfix operator, `++`. The null statement, `;`, then fulfills the requirement that a `while` loop contain at least one statement. Both versions of `getline()` are suitable replacements for `gets()`, and show the interchangeability between user-written and library functions.

C's enormous flexibility is shown by this ability to replace a library function with a user-written version and its ability to have functions written in various ways. Neither version of getline() is "more correct" from a programming standpoint. Each version presented (and more versions can be created) has its advantages and disadvantages. While the second version is more compact, the first version is clearer to beginning programmers. In creating your own C programs, select a style that is comfortable and remain with it until your growing programming expertise dictates modifications to your style.

Exercises 9.1

1. a. The following function can be used to select and display all vowels contained within a user-input string:

```c
vowels(strng)
char strng[];
{
   int i = 0;
   char c;

   while ((c = strng[i++]) != '\0')
     switch(c)
     {
        case 'a':
        case 'e':
        case 'i':
        case 'o':
        case 'u':
          putchar(c);
     } /* end of switch */
     putchar('\n');
}
```

Notice that the switch statement in vowels() uses the fact that selected cases "drop through" in the absence of break statements. Thus, all selected cases result in a putchar() function call. Include vowels() in a working program that accepts a user-input string and then displays all vowels in the string. In response to the input How much is the little worth worth?, your program should display ouieieoo.
b. Modify vowels() to count and display the total number of vowels contained in the string passed to it.

2. Modify the vowels() function given in Exercise 1a to count and display the individual numbers of each vowel contained in the string.

3. a. Write a C function to count the total number of characters, including blanks, contained in a string. Do not include the end-of-string marker in the count.
b. Include the function written for Exercise 3a in a complete working program.

4. Write a program that accepts a string of characters from a terminal and displays the hexadecimal equivalent of each character.

5. Write a C program that accepts a string of characters from a terminal and displays the string one word per line.

6. Write a function that reverses the characters in a string. (*Hint:* This can be considered as a string copy starting from the back end of the first string.)

7. Write a function named `del_char()` that can be used to delete characters from a string. The function should take three arguments: the string name, the number of characters to delete, and the starting position in the string where characters should be deleted. For example, the function call `del_char(strng,13,5)`, when applied to the string `all enthusiastic people`, should result in the string `all people`.

8. Write a function named `add_char()` to insert one string of characters into another string. The function should take three arguments: the string to be inserted, the original string, and the position in the original string where the insertion should begin. For example, the call `add_char("for all",message,6)` should insert the characters `for all` in `message` starting at `message[5]`.

9. *a.* Write a C function named `to_upper()` that converts individual lowercase letters into uppercase letters. The expression `ch - 'a' + 'A'` can be used to make the conversion for any lowercase character stored in `ch`.
b. Add a data input check to the function written in Exercise 9a to verify that a valid lowercase letter is passed to the function. A character is lowercase if it is greater than or equal to `a` and less than or equal to `z`. If the character is not a valid lowercase letter, have the function `to_upper()` return the passed character unaltered.
c. Write a C program that accepts a string from a terminal and converts all lowercase letters in the string to uppercase letters.

10. Write a C program that accepts a string from a terminal and converts all uppercase letters in the string to lowercase letters.

11. Write a C program that counts the number of words in a string. A word is encountered whenever a transition from a blank space to a nonblank character is encountered. Assume the string contains only words separated by blank spaces.

9.2 Pointers and Library Functions

Pointers are exceptionally useful in constructing string-handling functions. When pointer notation is used in place of subscripts to access individual characters in a string, the resulting statements are both more compact and more efficient. In this section, we describe the equivalence between subscripts and pointers when accessing individual characters in a string.

Consider the `strcopy()` function introduced in the previous section. This function was used to copy the characters of one string to a second string. For convenience, this function is repeated here.

```
strcopy(string1,string2)    /* copy string1 to string2 */
char string1[], string2[];
{
  int i = 0;

  while ( string1[i] != '\0')    /* check for the end-of-string */
  {
    string2[i] = string1[i];     /* copy the element to string2 */
    ++i;
  }
  string2[i] = '\0';             /* terminate the second string */
  return;
}
```

The function strcopy() is used to copy the characters from one array to another array, one character at a time. As currently written, the subscript i in the function is used successively to reference each character in the array named string1 by "marching along" the string one character at a time. Before we write a pointer version of strcopy(), we will make two modifications to the function to make it more efficient.

The while statement in strcopy() tests each character to ensure that the end of the string has not been reached. As with all relational expressions, the tested expression, string1[i] != '\0', is either true or false. Using the string this is a string illustrated in Figure 9-3 as an example, as long as string1[i] does not reference the end-of-string character the value of the expression is nonzero and is considered to be true. The expression is only false when the value of the expression is zero. This occurs when the last element in the string is accessed.

Recall that C defines false as zero and true as anything else. Thus, the expression string1[i] != '\0' becomes zero, or false, when the end of the string is reached. It is nonzero, or true, everywhere else. Since the null character has an internal value of zero by itself, the comparison to '\0' is not necessary. When string1[i] references the end-of-string character, the value of string1[i] is zero. When string1[i] references any other character, the value of string1[i] is the value of the code used to store the character and is nonzero. Figure 9-4 lists the ASCII codes for the string this is a string. As seen in the figure, each element has a nonzero value except for the null character.

Since the expression string1[i] is only zero at the end of a string and nonzero for every other character, the expression while (string1[i] != '\0') can be replaced by the simpler expression while (string1[i]). Although this may appear confusing at first, the revised test expression is certainly more compact than the longer version. Since end-of-string tests are frequently written by advanced C programmers in this shorter form, it is worthwhile being familiar with this expression. Including this expression in strcopy() results in the version of strcopy() shown below Figure 9-3 on the following page.

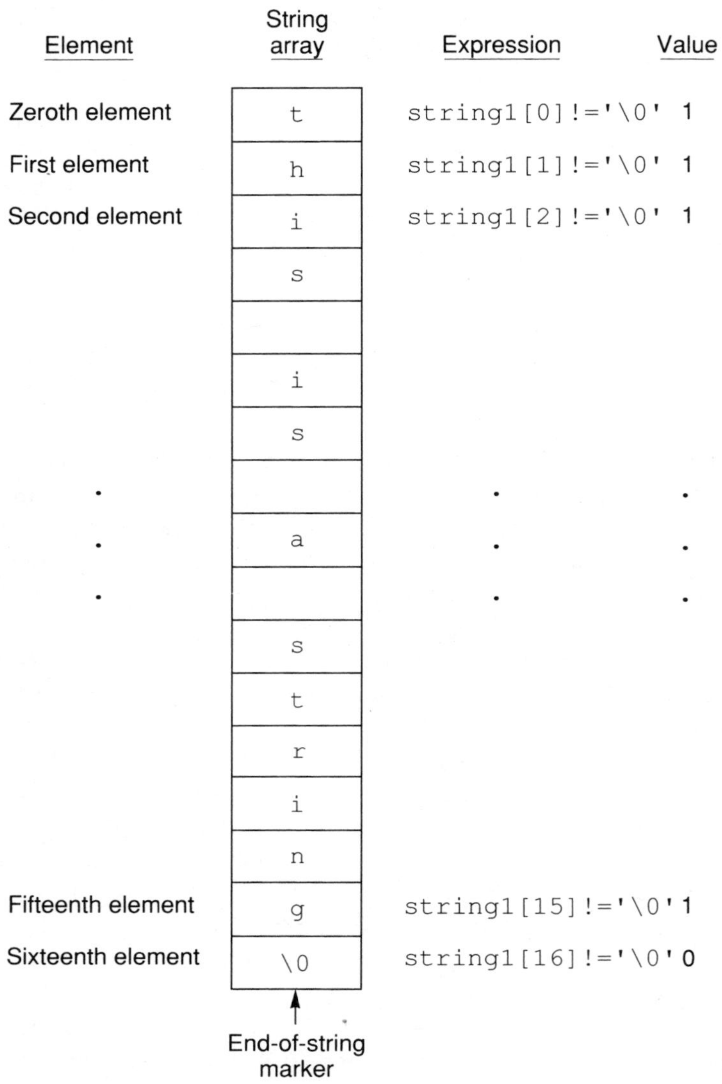

Element	String array	Expression	Value
Zeroth element	t	`string1[0]!='\0'`	1
First element	h	`string1[1]!='\0'`	1
Second element	i	`string1[2]!='\0'`	1
	s		
	i		
	s		
.		.	.
.	a	.	.
.		.	.
	s		
	t		
	r		
	i		
	n		
Fifteenth element	g	`string1[15]!='\0'`	1
Sixteenth element	\0	`string1[16]!='\0'`	0

End-of-string
marker

FIGURE 9–3 The `while` Test Becomes False at the End of the String

```
strcopy(string1,string2)    /* copy string1 to string2 */
char string1[], string2[];
{
  int i = 0;
  while (string1[i])
  {
    string2[i] = string1[i];   /* copy the element to string2 */
    ++i;
  }
  string2[i] = '\0';           /* terminate the second string */
  return;
}
```

String array	Stored codes	Expression	Value
t	116	string1[0]	116
h	104	string1[1]	104
i	105	string1[2]	105
s	115		
	32		
i	105		
s	115		
	32		
a	97		
	32		
s	115		
t	116		
r	114		
i	105		
n	110		
g	103	string1[15]	113
\0	0	string1[16]	0

FIGURE 9–4 The ASCII Codes Used to Store this is a string

The second modification that can be made to this string copy function is to include the assignment inside the test portion of the while statement. Our new version of the string copy function is:

```
strcopy(string1,string2)    /* copy string1 to string2 */
char string1[], string2[];
{
  int i = 0;

  while (string2[i] = string1[i])
     ++i;
  return;
}
```

Notice that including the assignment statement within the test part of the `while` statement eliminates the necessity of separately terminating the second string with the null character. The assignment within the parentheses ensures that the null character is copied from the first string to the second string. The value of the assignment expression only becomes zero after the null character is assigned to `string2`, at which point the `while` loop is terminated.

The conversion of `strcopy()` from subscript notation to pointer notation is now straightforward. Although each subscript version of `strcopy` can be rewritten using pointer notation, the following is the equivalent of our last subscript version:

```
strcopy(string1,string2)    /* copy string1 to string2 */
char *string1, *string2;
{

  while (*string2 = *string1)
  {
    string1++;
    string2++;
  }
  return;
}
```

In both subscript and pointer versions of `strcopy()`, the function receives the name of the array being passed. Recall that passing an array name to a function actually passes the address of the first location of the array. In our pointer version of `strcopy()` the two passed addresses are stored in the pointer arguments `string1` and `string2`, respectively.

The declarations `char *string1;` and `char *string2;` used in the pointer version of `strcopy()` indicate that `string1` and `string2` are both pointers containing the address of a character, and stress the treatment of the passed addresses as pointer values rather than array names. These declarations are equivalent to the declarations `char string1[]` and `char string2[]`, respectively.

Internal to `strcopy()`, the pointer expression `*string1`, which refers to "the element whose address is in `string1`," replaces the equivalent subscript expression `string1[i]`. Similarly, the pointer expression `*string2` replaces the equivalent subscript expression `string2[i]`. The expression `*string2 = *string1` causes the element pointed to by `string1` to be assigned to the element pointed to by `string2`. Since the starting addresses of both strings are passed to `strcopy()` and stored in `string1` and `string2`, respectively, the expression `*string1` initially refers to `string1[0]` and the expression `*string2` initially refers to `string2[0]`.

Consecutively incrementing both pointers in `strcopy()` with the expressions `string1++` and `string2++` simply causes each pointer to "point to" the next consecutive character in the respective string. As with the subscript version, the pointer version of strcopy steps along, copying element by element, until the end of the string is copied.

One final change to the string copy function can be made by including the pointer increments as postfix operators within the test part of the while statement. The final form of the string copy function is:

```
strcopy(string1,string2)    /* copy string1 to string2 */
char *string1, *string2;
{

  while ( *string2++ = *string1++ )
    ;
  return;
}
```

There is no ambiguity in the expression *string2++ = *string1++ even though the indirection operator, *, and the increment operator, ++, have the same precedence. These operators associate from left to right, so the character pointed to is accessed before the pointer is incremented. Only after completion of the assignment *string2 = *string1 are the pointers incremented to correctly point to the next characters in the respective strings.

Most C compilers include a string copy function in their standard library. This library function is typically written exactly like our pointer version of strcopy().

Library Functions

Extensive collections of string and character handling functions and routines are included with most C compilers. These were previously listed in Section 6.3, and for convenience are repeated in Table 9-2.

Library functions and routines are called in the same manner that all C functions are called. This means that if a library function returns a value the function must be declared within your program before it is called. For example, if a library function named strngfoo() returns a pointer to a character, the calling function must be alerted that an address is being returned. Thus, the statement char *strngfoo();, which declares that strngfoo() returns the address of a character (pointer to char), must be placed either as an external declaration or directly within the calling function's variable declarations.

Before attempting to use any standard library functions, check that they are included in the C compiler available on your computer system. Be careful to check the type of arguments expected by the function, the data type of any returned value, and if any standard header files, such as ctype.h, must be included in your program to access these routines.

TABLE 9-2   String and Character Library Functions and Routines

Name	Description
strcat(string1,string2)	Concatenates string2 to string1.
strchr(string,character)	Locates the position of the first occurrence of the character within the string. Returns the address of the character.
strcmp(string1,string2)	Compares string2 to string1.
strcpy(string1,string2)	Copies string2 to string1.
strlen(string)	Returns the length of the string.
isalpha(character)	Returns a nonzero number if the character is a letter; otherwise it returns a zero.
isupper(character)	Returns a nonzero number if the character is uppercase; otherwise it returns a zero.
islower(character)	Returns a nonzero number if the character is lowercase; otherwise it returns a zero.
isdigit(character)	Returns a nonzero number if the character is a digit (0 through 9); otherwise it returns a zero.
toupper(character)	Returns the uppercase equivalent if the character is lowercase; otherwise it returns the character unchanged.
tolower(character)	Returns the lowercase equivalent if the character is uppercase; otherwise it returns the character unchanged.

Exercises 9.2

1. Determine the value of *text, *(text + 3), and *(text + 10), assuming that text is an array of characters and the following has been stored in the array:

   a. now is the time
   b. rocky raccoon welcomes you
   c. Happy Holidays
   d. The good ship

2. a. The following function, `convert()`, "marches along" the string passed to it and sends each character in the string one at a time to the `to_upper()` function until the null character is encountered.

```
convert(strng)          /* convert a string to uppercase letters */
char strng[];
{
  int i = o;

  while (strng[i] != '\0')
  {
    strng[i] = to_upper(strng[i]);
    ++i;
  }
  return;
}

to_upper(letter)   /* convert a character to uppercase */
char letter;
{
  if( letter >= 'a' && letter <= 'z')
    return (letter - 'a' + 'A');
  else
    return (letter);
}
```

The `to_upper()` function takes each character passed to it and first examines it to determine if the character is a lowercase letter (a lowercase letter is any character between *a* and *z*, inclusive). Assuming that characters are stored using the standard ASCII character codes, the expression `letter - 'a' + 'A'` converts a lowercase letter to its uppercase equivalent. Rewrite the `convert()` function using pointers.
b. Include the `convert()` and `to_upper()` functions in a working program. The program should prompt the user for a string and echo the string back to the user in uppercase letters. Use `gets()` and `puts()` for string input and display.

3. Using pointers, repeat Exercise 1 from Section 9.1.

4. Using pointers, repeat Exercise 2 from Section 9.1.

5. Using pointers, repeat Exercise 3 from Section 9.1.

6. Write a function named `remove()` that deletes all occurrences of a character from a string. The function should take two arguments: the string name and the character to be removed. For example, if `message` contains the string `Happy Holidays`, the function call `remove(message,'H')` should place the string `appy olidays` into `message`.

7. Using pointers, repeat Exercise 6 from Section 9.1.

8. Write a program using the `getchar()`, `toupper()`, and `putchar()` library functions that echo back each letter entered in its uppercase form. The program should terminate when the digit 1 key is pressed.

9. Write a function that uses pointers to add a single character at the end of an existing string. The function should replace the existing \0 character with the new character and append a new \0 at the end of the string.

315

10. Write a function that uses pointers to delete a single character from the end of a string. This is effectively achieved by moving the \0 character one position closer to the start of the string.

11. Determine the string-handling functions that are available with your C compiler. For each available function list the data types of the arguments expected by the function and the data type of any returned value.

12. Write a function named `trimfrnt()` that deletes all leading blanks from a string. Write the function using pointers.

13. Write a function named `trimrear()` that deletes all trailing blanks from a string. Write the function using pointers.

14. Write a function named `strlen()` that returns the number of characters in a string. Do not include the \0 character in the returned count.

9.3 String Definitions and Pointer Arrays

The definition of a string automatically involves a pointer. For example, the definition `static char message1[81];` both reserves storage for 81 characters and automatically creates a pointer constant, `message1`, which contains the address of `message1[0]`. As a pointer constant, the address associated with the pointer cannot be changed—it must always "point to" the beginning of the created array.

Instead of initially creating a string as an array, however, it is also possible to create a string using a pointer. This is similar in concept to declaring a passed array as either an array or a pointer argument internal to the receiving function. For example, the definition `char *message2;` creates a pointer to a character. In this case, `message2` is a true pointer variable. Once a pointer to a character is defined, assignment statements, such as `message2 = "this is a string";`, can be made. In this assignment, `message2` receives the address of the first location used by the computer to store the string.

The main difference in the definitions of `message1` as an array and `message2` as a pointer is the way the pointer is created. Defining `message1` using the declaration `static char message1[81]` explicitly calls for a fixed amount of storage for the array. This causes the compiler to create a pointer constant. Defining `message2` using the declaration `char *message2` explicitly creates a pointer variable first. This pointer is then used to hold the address of a string when the string is actually specified. This difference in definitions has both storage and programming consequences.

From a programming perspective, defining `message2` as a pointer to a character allows string assignments, such as `message2 = "this is a string";`, to be made. Similar assignments are not allowed for strings defined as arrays. Thus, the statement `message1 = "this is a string";` is not valid.

Both definitions, however, allow initializations to be made using a string assignment. For example, both of the following initializations are valid:

```
static char message1[81] = "this is a string";
char *message2 = "this is a string";
```

As with all array initializations, the `static` designation is required for initializing local arrays; it is not required for initializing global arrays. The same is not true for `message2`. The initialization of `message2` consists of setting an initial address into a pointer variable. As such, the `static` designation required for local array initialization is not necessary.

From a storage perspective, the allocation of space for `message1` and `message2` is different, as illustrated in Figure 9-5. As shown in the figure, both initializations cause the computer to store the same string internally. In the case of `message1`, a specific set of 81 storage locations is reserved and the first 17 locations are initialized. For `message1`, different strings can be stored, but each string will overwrite the previously stored characters. The same is not true for `message2`.

The definition of `message2` reserves enough storage for one pointer. The initialization then causes the string to be stored and the starting storage address of the string to be loaded into the pointer. If a later assignment is made to

FIGURE 9–5 String Storage Allocation

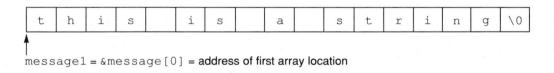

message1 = &message[0] = address of first array location

a. Storage allocation for a string defined as an array

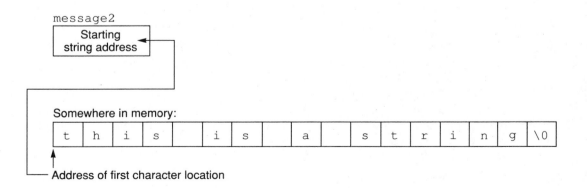

b. Storage of a string using a pointer

message2, the initial string remains in memory and new storage locations are allocated to the new string. Program 9-5 uses the message2 character pointer to successively "point to" two different strings.

 Program 9-5

```
main()
{
  char *message2 = "this is a string";

  printf("\nThe string is: %s", message2);
  printf("\n The first address of this string is %u", message2);

  message2 = "A new message";
  printf("\nThe string is now: %s", message2);
  printf("\n The first address of this string is %u", message2);
}
```

A sample output for Program 9-5 is:

```
The string is: this is a string
 The first address of this string is 1048672
The string is now: A new message
 The first address of this string is 1048727
```

In Program 9-5, the variable message2 is initially created as a pointer variable and loaded with the starting storage address of the first string. The printf() function is then used to display this string. When the %s conversion character is encountered by printf(), it alerts the function that a string is being referenced. The printf() function then expects either a string constant or a pointer containing the address of the first character in the string. This pointer can be either an array name or a pointer variable. The printf() function uses the address provided to correctly locate the string, and then continues accessing and displaying characters until it encounters a null character. As illustrated by the output, the address of the first character in the string is 1048672.

After the first string and its starting address is displayed, the next assignment statement in Program 9-5 causes the computer to store a second string and change the address in message2 to point to the starting location of this new string. The printf() function then displays this string and its starting storage address.

It is important to realize that the second string assigned to message2 does not overwrite the first string, but simply changes the address in message2 to point to the new string. As illustrated in Figure 9-6, both strings are stored inside the computer. Any additional string assignment to `message2` would result in the additional storage of the new string and a corresponding change in the address stored in `message2`.

Pointer Arrays

The declaration of an array of character pointers is an extremely useful extension to single string pointer declarations. For example, the declaration

```
static char *seasons[4];
```

creates an array of four elements, where each element is a pointer to a character. As individual pointers, each pointer can be assigned to point to a string using string assignment statements. Thus, the statements

```
seasons[0] = "Winter";
seasons[1] = "Spring";
seasons[2] = "Summer";
seasons[3] = "Fall";
```

set appropriate addresses into the respective pointers. Figure 9-7 illustrates the addresses loaded into the pointers for these assignments.

As illustrated in Figure 9-7, the `seasons` array does not contain the actual strings assigned to the pointers. These strings are stored elsewhere in the computer, in the normal data area allocated to the program. The array of pointers contains only the addresses of the starting location for each string.

FIGURE 9–6 Storage Allocation for Program 9-5

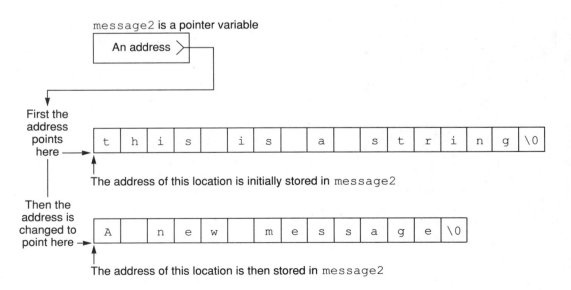

`message2` is a pointer variable

An address

First the address points here →

| t | h | i | s | | i | s | | a | | s | t | r | i | n | g | \0 |

The address of this location is initially stored in `message2`

Then the address is changed to point here →

| A | | n | e | w | | m | e | s | s | a | g | e | \0 |

The address of this location is then stored in `message2`

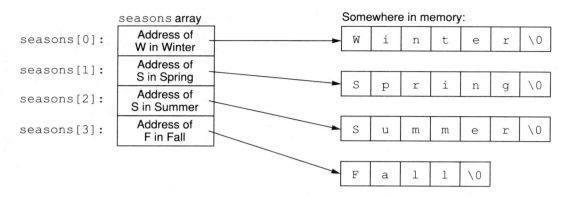

FIGURE 9-7 The Addresses Contained in the `seasons[]` Pointers

The initializations of the `seasons` array can also be incorporated directly within the definition of the array, as follows:

```
static char *seasons[4] = { "Winter", .
                            "Spring",
                            "Summer",
                            "Fall"};
```

This declaration both creates an array of pointers and initializes the pointers with appropriate addresses. Once addresses have been assigned to the pointers, each pointer can be used to access its corresponding string. Program 9-6 uses the `seasons` array to display each season using a `for` loop.

 Program 9-6

```
main()
{
   int n;
   static char *seasons[] = { "Winter",
                              "Spring",
                              "Summer",
                              "Fall"};


   for( n = 0; n < 4; ++n)
      printf("\nThe season is %s.",seasons[n]);
}
```

The output obtained for Program 9-6 is:

```
The season is Winter.
The season is Spring.
The season is Summer.
The season is Fall.
```

The advantage of using a list of pointers is that logical groups of data headings can be collected together and accessed with one array name. For example, the months in a year can be collectively grouped in one array called `months`, and the days in a week collectively grouped together in an array called `days`. The grouping of like headings allows the programmer to access and print an appropriate heading by simply specifying the correct position of the heading in the array. Program 9-7 uses the `seasons` array to correctly identify and display the season corresponding to a user-input month.

 Program 9-7

```
main()
{
  int n;
  static char *seasons[] = { "Winter",
                             "Spring",
                             "Summer",
                             "Fall"};

  printf("\nEnter a month (use 1 for Jan., 2 for Feb., etc.): ");
  scanf("%d", &n);
  n = (n % 12) / 3;    /* create the correct subscript */
  printf("The month entered is a %s month.",seasons[n]);
}
```

Except for the expression n = (n % 12) / 3, Program 9-7 is rather straightforward. The program requests the user to input a month and accepts the number corresponding to the month using a `scanf()` function call.

The expression n = (n % 12) / 3 uses a common program "trick" to scale a set of numbers into a more useful set. Using subscripts, the four elements of the `seasons` array must be accessed using a subscript from 0 through 3. Thus, the months of the year, which correspond to the numbers 1 through 12, must be adjusted to correspond to the correct season subscript. This is done using the expression n = (n % 12) / 3. The expression n % 12 adjusts the month entered to lie within the range 0 through 11, with 0 corresponding to December, 1 for January, etc. Dividing by 3 then causes the resulting number to range between 0 and 3, corresponding to the possible seasons elements. The result of the division by 3 is assigned to the integer variable n. The months 0, 1, and 2, when divided by 3, are set to 0; the months 3, 4, and 5 are set to 1; the months 6, 7, and 8 are set to 2; and the months 9, 10, and 11 are set to 3. This is equivalent to the following assignments:

Months	Season
December, January, February	Winter
March, April, May	Spring
June, July, August	Summer
September, October, November	Fall

The following is a sample output obtained for Program 9-7:

```
Enter a month (use 1 for Jan., 2 for Feb., etc.): 12
The month entered is a Winter month.
```

Exercises 9.3

1. Write two declaration statements that can be used in place of the declaration static char text[] = "Hooray!";.

2. Determine the value of *text, *(text + 3), and *(text + 7) for each of the following sections of code:

a.
```
char *text;
static char message[] = "the check is in the mail";
text = message;
```

b.
```
char *text;
static char formal[] = {'t','h','i','s',' ','i','s',' ','a','n',
                        'i','n','v','i','t','a','t','i','o','n','\0'};
text = &formal[0];
```

c.
```
char *test;
static char more[] = "Happy Holidays";
text = &more[4];
```

d.
```
char *text, *second;
char blip[] = "The good ship";
second = blip;
text = ++second;
```

3. Determine the error in the following program:

```
#include <stdio.h>
main()
{
    int i = 0;
    char message[] = {'H','e','l','l','o','\0'};

    for( ; i < 5; ++i)
        {putchar(*message); ++message;}
}
```

4. a. Write a C function that displays the day of the week corresponding to a user-entered input number between 1 and 7. That is, in response to an input of 2, the program displays the name `Monday`. Use an array of pointers in the function.

   b. Include the function written for Exercise 4a in a complete working program.

5. Modify the function written in Exercise 4a so that the function returns the address of the character string containing the proper month to be displayed.

6. Write a function that will accept ten lines of user-input text and store the entered lines as ten individual strings. Use a pointer array in your function.

9.4 Formatting Strings

Besides the special string-handling functions in the standard library provided with your C compiler, both the `printf()` and `scanf()` functions have string-formatting capabilities. Additionally, two related functions, `sprintf()` and `sscanf()`, provide further string-processing features. In this section we present the additional features that these functions provide when used with strings.

Field width specifiers can be included in a `printf()` control sequence to control the spacing of integers and decimal numbers. These specifiers can also be used with the `%s` control sequence to control the display of a string. For example, the statement

```
printf("|%25s|","Have a Happy Day");
```

displays the message `Have a Happy Day`, right justified, in a field of 25 characters, as follows:

```
|          Have a Happy Day|
```

We have placed a bar (|) at the beginning and end of the string field to delineate clearly the field being printed. Placing a minus sign (−) in front of the field width specifier forces the string to be left justified in the field. For example, the statement

```
printf("|%-25s|","Have a Happy Day");
```

causes the display:

```
|Have a Happy Day          |
```

If the field width specifier is too small for the string, the specifier is ignored and the string is displayed using sufficient space to accommodate the complete string.

The precision specifier used for determining the number of digits displayed to the right of a decimal number can also be used as a string specifier. When used with strings, the precision specifier determines the maximum number of characters that will be displayed. For example, the statement

```
printf("|%25.12s|","Have a Happy Day");
```

causes the first twelve characters in the string to be displayed, right justified, in a field of 25 characters. This produces the display:

```
|            Have a Happy|
```

Similarly, the statement

```
printf("|%-25.12s|","Have a Happy Day");
```

causes twelve characters to be left justified in a field of 25 characters. This produces the display:

```
|Have a Happy            |
```

When a precision specifier is used with no field width specifier, the indicated number of characters is displayed in a field sufficiently large to hold the designated number of characters. Thus, the statement

```
printf("|%.12s|","Have a Happy Day");
```

causes the first twelve characters in the string to be displayed in a field of 12 characters. If the string has less than the number of characters designated by the precision specifier, the display is terminated when the end-of-string is encountered.

In-Memory String Conversions

While `printf()` displays data to the standard device used by your computer for output and `scanf()` scans the standard device used for input, the `sprintf()` and `sscanf()` functions provide similar capabilities for writing and scanning strings to and from memory variables. For example, the statement

```
sprintf(dis_strn,"%d %d", num1, num2);
```

writes the numerical values of `num1` and `num2` into `dis_strn` rather than displaying the values on the standard output terminal. Here, `dis_strn` is a programmer-selected variable name that must be declared as either an array of characters, sufficiently large to hold the resulting string, or as a pointer to a string.

Typically, the `sprintf()` function is used to "assemble" a string from smaller pieces until a complete line of characters is ready to be written, either to the standard output device or to a file (writing data to a file is described in Chapter 11). For example, another string could be concatenated to `dis_strn` using the `strcat()` function and the complete string displayed using the `printf()` function.

In contrast to `sprintf()`, the string scan function `sscanf()` may be used to "disassemble" a string into smaller pieces. For example, if the string `"$23.45    10"` were stored in a character array named `data`, the statement

```
sscanf(data,"%c%lf %d",&dol,&price,&units);
```

would scan the string stored in the data array and "strip off" three data items. The dollar sign would be stored in the variable named `dol`, the `23.45` would be converted to a double precision number and stored in the variable named `price`, and the `10` would be converted to an integer value and stored in the variable named `units`. For a useful result, the variables `dol`, `price`, and `units` would have to be declared as the appropriate data types. In this way `sscanf()` provides a useful means of converting parts of a string into other data types. Typically, the string being scanned by `sscanf()` is used as a working storage area, or buffer, for storing a complete line from either a file or the standard input. Once the string has been filled, `sscanf()` disassembles the string into component parts and suitably converts each data item into the designated data type. For programmers familiar with COBOL, this is equivalent to first reading data into a working storage area before moving the data into smaller fields.

Format Strings

When you use any of the four functions, `printf()`, `scanf()`, `sprintf()`, or `sscanf()`, the control string containing the control sequences need not be explicitly contained within the function. For example, the control string `"$%5.2d  %d"` contained within the function call

```
printf("$%5.2d %f",num1,num2);
```

can itself be stored as a string and the address of the string can be used in the call to `printf()`. If either of the following declarations for `fmat` are made:

```
char *fmat = "$%5.2f %d";
```

or

```
char fmat[] = "$%5.2f %d";
```

the function call, `printf(fmat,num1,num2);` can be made in place of the previous call to `printf()`. Here, `fmat` is a pointer that contains the address of the control string used to determine the output display.

The technique of storing and using control strings in this manner is very useful for clearly listing format strings with other variable declarations at the beginning of a function. If a change to a format must be made, it is easy to find the desired control string without the necessity of searching through the complete function to locate the appropriate `printf()` or `scanf()` function call. Restricting the definition of a control string to one place is also advantageous when the same format control is used in multiple function calls.

Exercises 9.4

1. Determine the display produced by each of the following statements:
   a. `printf("!%10s!","four score and ten");`
   b. `printf("!%15s!","Home!");`
   c. `printf("!%-15s!","Home!");`
   d. `printf("!%15.2s!","Home!");`
   e. `printf("!%-15.2s!","Home!");`
2. a. Assuming that the following declaration has been made

   ```
   char *text = "Have a nice day!";
   ```

   determine the display produced by the statements

   ```
   printf("%s", text);
   printf("%c", *text);
   ```

   b. Since both `printf()` function calls in Exercise 2a display characters, determine why the indirection operator is required in the second call but not in the first.

3. Write a program that accepts three user-entered numbers as one string. Once the string has been accepted, have the program pass the string and the addresses of three floating point variables to a function called `separate()`. The `separate()` function should extract the three floating point values from the passed string and store them using the passed variable addresses.

4. Modify the program written for Exercise 3 to display the input string using the format `"%6.2f %6.2f %6.2f"`.

5. Write a program that accepts a string and two integer numbers from a user. Each of these inputs should be preceded by a prompt and stored using individual variable names. Have your program call a function that assembles the input data into a single string. Display the assembled string using a `puts()` call.

9.5 Common Programming Errors

Four errors are frequently made when pointers to strings are used. The most common is using the pointer to "point to" a nonexistent data element. This error is, of course, the same error we have already seen using subscripts. Since C compilers do not perform bounds checking on arrays, it is the programmer's responsibility to ensure that the address in the pointer is the address of a valid data element.

The second common error occurs when an attempt is made to initialize a local array of characters. Even though a local character pointer can be initialized without being declared as a `static` variable, only `static` local arrays can be initialized.

The third common error lies in not providing sufficient space for the end-of-string null character when a string is defined as an array of characters, and not including the `\0` character when the array is initialized.

Finally, the last error relates to a misunderstanding of terminology. For example, if `text` is defined as

```
char *text;
```

the variable `text` is sometimes referred to as a string. Thus, the terminology "store the characters `Hooray for the Hoosiers` into the `text` string" may be encountered. Strictly speaking, calling `text` a string or a string variable is incorrect. The variable `text` is a pointer that contains the address of the first character in the string. Nevertheless, referring to a character pointer as a string occurs frequently enough that you should be aware of it.

9.6 Chapter Summary

1. A string is an array of characters that is terminated by the null character.

2. Strings can always be processed using standard array-processing techniques. The input and display of a string, however, always require reliance on a standard library function.

3. The `gets()`, `scanf()`, and `getchar()` library functions can be used to input a string. The `scanf()` function tends to be of limited usefulness for string input because it terminates input when a blank is encountered.

4. The `puts()`, `printf()`, and `putchar()` functions can be used to display strings.

5. In place of subscripts, pointer notation and pointer arithmetic are especially useful for manipulating string elements.

6. Many standard library functions exist for processing strings as a complete unit. Internally, these functions manipulate strings in a character-by-character manner, usually using pointers.

7. String storage can be created by declaring an array of characters or a pointer to a character. A pointer to a character can be assigned a string directly. String assignment to an array of characters is invalid except when in a declaration statement.

8. As with all arrays, only `static` and external character arrays can be initialized. These arrays can be initialized using a string assignment of the form

```
char *arr_name[] = "text";
```

This initialization is equivalent to

```
char *arr_name[] = {'t','e','x','t','\0'};
```

Structures

In the broadest sense, *structure* refers to how individual elements of a group are arranged or organized. For example, a corporation's structure refers to the organization of the people and departments in the company and a government's structure refers to its form or arrangement. In programming, a structure refers to the way individual data items are arranged to form a cohesive and related unit. For example, consider the data items typically used in preparing mailing labels, as illustrated in Figure 10-1.

Each of the individual data items listed in the figure is an entity by itself. Taken together, all the data items form a single unit, representing a natural organization of the data for a mailing label. This larger grouping of related individual items is commonly called a *record*. In C, a record is referred to as a structure.

Although there could be thousands of names and addresses in a complete mailing list, the form of each mailing label, or its structure, is identical. In dealing with structures it is important to distinguish between the form of the structure and the data content of the structure.

The *form* of a structure consists of the symbolic names, data types, and arrangement of individual data items in the structure. The *content* of a structure refers to the actual data stored in the symbolic names. Figure 10-2 shows acceptable contents for the structure illustrated in Figure 10-1.

In this chapter, we describe the C statements required to create, fill, use, and pass structures between functions.

10.1 Single Structures

Using structures requires the same two steps needed for using any C variable. First the structure must be declared. Then specific values can be assigned to

FIGURE 10–1 Typical Mailing List Components

```
Name:
Street Address:
City:
State:
Zip Code:
```

FIGURE 10–2 The Contents of a Structure

```
Rhona Bronson-Karp
614 Freeman Street
Orange
NJ
07052
```

the individual structure elements. Declaring a structure requires listing the data types, data names, and arrangement of data items. For example, the definition

```
struct
{
    int month;
    int day;
    int year;
}   birth;
```

gives the form of a structure named `birth` and reserves storage for the individual data items listed in the structure. The `birth` structure consists of three data items, which are called *members of the structure.*

Assigning actual data values to the data items of a structure is called *populating the structure,* and is a relatively straightforward procedure. Each member of a structure is accessed by giving both the structure name and individual data item name, separated by a period. Thus, `birth.month` refers to the first member of the `birth` structure, `birth.day` refers to the second member of the structure, and `birth.year` refers to the third member. Program 10-1 illustrates assigning values to the individual members of the `birth` structure (observe that the `printf()` statement call has been continued across two lines).

 Program 10-1

```
main()
{
    struct
    {
        int month;
        int day;
        int year;
    }   birth;

    birth.month = 12;
    birth.day = 28;
    birth.year = 52;

    printf("My birth date is %d/%d/%d",
            birth.month,birth.day,birth.year);
}
```

The output produced by Program 10-1 is:

```
My birth date is 12/28/52
```

As in most C statements, the spacing of a structure definition is not rigid. For example, the `birth` structure could just as well have been defined

```
struct {int month; int day; int year;} birth;
```

Also, as with all C definition statements, multiple variables can be defined in the same statement. For example, the definition statement

```
struct {int month; int day; int year;} birth, current;
```

creates two structures having the same form. The members of the first structure are referenced by the individual names `birth.month`, `birth.day`, and `birth.year`, while the members of the second structure are referenced by the names `current.month`, `current.day`, and `current.year`. Notice that the form of this particular structure definition statement is identical to the form used in defining any program variable: the data type is followed by a list of variable names.

A useful modification of defining structures is listing the form of the structure with no following variable names. In this case, however, the list of structure members must be preceded by a *tag name*. For example, in the declaration

```
struct date
{
    int month;
    int day;
    int year;
};
```

the term `date` is a tag name. The declaration for the `date` structure provides a *template* for the structure without actually reserving any storage locations. As such it is not a definition statement. The template presents the form of a structure called `date` by describing how individual data items are arranged within the structure. Actual storage for the members of the structure is reserved only when specific variable names are assigned. For example, the definition statement

```
struct date birth, current;
```

reserves storage for two structures named `birth` and `current`, respectively. Each of these individual structures has the form previously declared for the `date` structure. In effect, the declaration for `date` creates a *structure type* named `date`. The variables `birth` and `current` are then defined to be of this structure type.

Like all variable declarations, a structure may be declared globally or locally. Program 10-2 illustrates the global declaration of a `date` structure. Internal to `main()`, the variable `birth` is defined using this global template.

Program 10-2

```
struct date
  {
    int month;
    int day;
    int year;
  };
main()
{
  struct date   birth;

  birth.month = 12;
  birth.day = 28;
  birth.year = 52;

  printf("My birth date is %d/%d/%d",
         birth.month,birth.day,birth.year);
}
```

The output produced by Program 10-2 is identical to the output produced by Program 10-1.

The initialization of structures follows the same rules as for the initialization of arrays: external and `static` structures may be initialized by following the definition with a list of initializers. For example, the definition statement

```
static struct date birth = {12, 28, 52};
```

can be used to replace the first four statements internal to `main()` in Program 10-2. Notice that the initializers are separated by commas, not semicolons.

The individual members of a structure are not restricted to integer data types, as illustrated by the `birth` structure. Any valid C data type can be used. For example, consider an employee record consisting of the following data items:

> Name:
> Identification Number:
> Regular Pay Rate:
> Overtime Pay Rate:

A suitable declaration for these data items is:

```
struct pay_rec
{
  char name[20];
  int id_num;
  float reg_rate;
  float ot_rate;
};
```

Once the template for `pay_rec` is declared, a specific structure using the `pay_rec` template can be defined and initialized. For example, the definition

```
struct pay_rec employee = {"H. Price",12387,15.89,25.50};
```

creates a structure named `employee` using the `pay_rec` template. The individual members of `employee` are initialized with the respective data listed between braces in the definition statement.

Notice that a single structure is simply a convenient method for combining and storing related items under a common name. Although a single structure is useful in explicitly identifying the relationship among its members, the individual members could be defined as separate variables. The real advantage to using structures is only realized when the same template is used in a list many times over. Creating lists with the same structure template is the topic of the next section.

Before leaving single structures, it is worth noting that the individual members of a structure can be any valid C data type, including both arrays and structures. An array of characters was used as a member of the `employee` structure defined previously. Accessing an element of a member array requires giving the structure's name, followed by a period, followed by the array designation. For example, `employee.name[4]` refers to the fifth character in the structure.

Including a structure within a structure follows the same rules for including any data type in a structure. For example, assume that a structure is to consist of a name and a date of birth, where a date structure has been declared as:

```
struct date
{
    int month;
    int date;
    int year;
};
```

A suitable definition of a structure that includes a name and a date structure is:

```
struct
{
    char name[20];
    struct date birth;
} person;
```

Notice that in declaring the date structure, the term `date` is a structure tag name. A tag name always appears before the braces in the declaration statement and identifies a structure template. In defining the `person` structure, `person` is the name of a specific structure, not a structure tag name. The same is true of the variable named `birth`. This is the name of a specific structure having the form of `date`. Individual members in the `person` structure are accessed by preceding the desired member with the structure name followed by a period. For example, `person.birth.month` refers to the `month` variable in the `birth` structure contained in the `person` structure.

Exercises 10.1

1. Declare a structure template named `s_temp` for each of the following records:

   a. a student record consisting of a student identification number, number of credits completed, and cumulative grade point average

   b. a student record consisting of a student's name, date of birth, number of credits completed, and cumulative grade point average

   c. a mailing list consisting of the items previously illustrated in Figure 10-1

   d. a stock record consisting of the stock's name, the price of the stock, and the date of purchase

   e. an inventory record consisting of an integer part number, part description, number of parts in inventory, and an integer reorder number

2. For the individual structure templates declared in Exercise 1, define a suitable structure variable name, and initialize each structure with the appropriate following data:

   a. `Identification Number: 4672`
   `Number of Credits Completed: 68`
   `Grade Point Average: 3.01`

   b. `Name: Rhona Karp`
   `Date of Birth: 8/4/60`
   `Number of Credits Completed: 96`
   `Grade Point Average: 3.89`

   c. `Name: Kay Kingsley`
   `Street Address: 614 Freeman Street`
   `City: Indianapolis`
   `State: IN`
   `Zip Code: 07030`

   d. `Stock: IBM`
   `Price Purchased: 134.5`
   `Date Purchased: 10/1/86`

   e. `Part Number: 16879`
   `Description: Battery`
   `Number in Stock: 10`
   `Reorder Number: 3`

3. *a.* Write a C program that prompts a user to input the current month, day, and year. Store the data entered in a suitably defined structure and display the date in an appropriate manner.

   b. Modify the program written in Exercise 3a to accept the current time in hours, minutes, and seconds.

4. Write a C program that uses a structure for storing the name of a stock, its estimated earnings per share, and its estimated price-to-earnings ratio. Have the program prompt the user to enter these items for five different stocks, each time using the same structure to store the entered data. When the data has been entered for a particular stock, have the program compute and display the anticipated stock price based on the entered earnings and price-per-earnings values. For example, if a user entered the data XYZ 1.56 12, the anticipated price for a share of XYZ stock is (1.56)*(12) = $18.72.

5. Write a C program that accepts a user-entered time in hours and minutes. Have the program calculate and display the time one minute later.

6. *a.* Write a C program that accepts a user-entered date. Have the program calculate and display the date of the next day. For purposes of this exercise, assume that all months consist of thirty days.

b. Modify the program written in Exercise 6a to account for the actual number of days in each month.

10.2   Arrays of Structures

The real power of structures is realized when the same structure is used for lists of data. For example, assume that the data shown in Figure 10-3 must be processed.

Clearly, the employee numbers can be stored together in an array of long integers, the names in an array of pointers, and the pay rates in an array of either floating point or double precision numbers. In organizing the data in this fashion, each column in Figure 10-3 is considered as a separate list, which is stored in its own array. Using arrays, the correspondence between items for each individual employee is maintained by storing an employee's data in the same array position in each array.

The separation of the complete list into three individual arrays is unfortunate, since all of the items relating to a single employee constitute a natural organization of data into records, as illustrated in Figure 10-4.

FIGURE 10–3 A List of Employee Data

Employee number	Employee name	Employee pay rate
32479	Abrams, B.	6.72
33623	Bohm, P.	7.54
34145	Donaldson, S.	5.56
35987	Ernst, T.	5.43
36203	Gwodz, K.	8.72
36417	Hanson, H.	7.64
37634	Monroe, G.	5.29
38321	Price, S.	9.67
39435	Robbins, L.	8.50
39567	Williams, B.	7.20

	Employee number	Employee name	Employee pay rate
1st record ———→	32479	Abrams, B.	6.72 |
2nd record ———→	33623	Bohm, P.	7.54 |
3rd record ———→	34145	Donaldson, S.	5.56 |
4th record ———→	35987	Ernst, T.	5.43 |
5th record ———→	36203	Gwodz, K.	8.72 |
6th record ———→	36417	Hanson, H.	7.64 |
7th record ———→	37634	Monroe, G.	5.29 |
8th record ———→	38321	Price, S.	9.67 |
9th record ———→	39435	Robbins, L.	8.50 |
10th record ———→	39567	Williams, B.	7.20 |

FIGURE 10–4 A List of Records

Using a structure, the integrity of the data organization as a record can be maintained and reflected by the program. Under this approach, the list illustrated in Figure 10-4 can be processed as a single array of ten structures.

Declaring an array of structures is the same as declaring an array of any other variable type. For example, if the template `pay_rec` is declared as

```
struct pay_rec {long idnum; char name[20]; float rate;};
```

then an array of ten such structures can be defined as

```
struct pay_rec employee[10];
```

This definition statement constructs an array of ten elements, each of which is a structure of the type `pay_rec`. Notice that the creation of an array of ten structures has the same form as the creation of any other array. For example, creating an array of ten integers named `employee` requires the declaration

```
int employee[10];
```

In this declaration the data type is integer, while in the former declaration for `employee` the data type is a structure using the `pay_rec` template.

Once an array of structures is declared, a particular data item is referenced by giving the position of the desired structure in the array followed by a period and the appropriate structure member. For example, the variable `employee[0].rate` references the `rate` member of the first `employee` structure in the `employee` array. Including structures as elements of an array permits a list of records to be processed using standard array programming techniques. Program 10-3 displays the first five employee records illustrated in Figure 10-4.

 Program 10-3

```
struct pay_rec
{
  long id;
  char name[20];
  float rate;
};          /* construct a global template */
main()
{
  int i;
  static struct pay_rec employee[5] =
              {
                { 32479, "Abrams, B.", 6.72 },
                { 33623, "Bohm, P.", 7.54},
                { 34145, "Donaldson, S.", 5.56},
                { 35987, "Ernst, T.", 5.43 },
                { 36203, "Gwodz, K.", 8.72 }
              };

for ( i = 0; i < 5; ++i)
  printf("%\nld %-20s %4.2f",employee[i].id,employee[i].name,employee[i].rate);
}
```

The output displayed by Program 10-3 is:

```
32479 Abrams, B.          6.72
33623 Bohm, P.            7.54
34145 Donaldson, S.       5.56
35987 Ernst, T.           5.43
36203 Gwodz, K.           8.72
```

In reviewing Program 10-3, notice the initialization of the array of structures. As with all array initializers, the array must be either global or static to be initialized. Although the initializers for each structure have been enclosed in inner braces, these are not strictly necessary because all members have been initialized. As with all external and static variables, in the absence of explicit initializers, the numeric elements of both static and external arrays or structures are initialized to zero and their character elements are initialized to nulls. The %-20s format included in the printf() function call forces each name to be displayed left justified in a field of 20 spaces.

Exercises 10.2

1. Define arrays of 100 structures for each of the structures described in Exercise 1 of Section 10.1.

2. a. Using the template

```
struct mon_days
{
  char name[10];
  int days;
};
```

define an array of 12 structures of type mon_days. Name the array convert[], and initialize the array with the names of the 12 months in a year and the number of days in each month.

b. Include the array created in Exercise 2a in a program that displays the names and number of days in each month.

3. Using the structure defined in Exercise 2a, write a C program that accepts a month from a user in numerical form and displays the name of the month and the number of days in the month. Thus, in response to an input of 3, the program would display March has 31 days.

4. a. Declare a single structure template suitable for an employee record of the type illustrated below:

Number	Name	Rate	Hours
3462	Jones	4.62	40
6793	Robbins	5.83	38
6985	Smith	5.22	45
7834	Swain	6.89	40
8867	Timmins	6.43	35
9002	Williams	4.75	42

b. Using the template declared in Exercise 4a, write a C program that interactively accepts the above data into an array of six structures. Once the data has been entered, the program should create a payroll report listing each employee's name, number, and gross pay. Include the total gross pay of all employees at the end of the report.

5. a. Declare a single structure template suitable for a car record of the type illustrated:

Car Number	Miles Driven	Gallons Used
25	1,450	62
36	3,240	136
44	1,792	76
52	2,360	105
68	2,114	67

b. Using the template declared for Exercise 5a, write a C program that interactively accepts the above data into an array of five structures. Once the data has been entered, the program should create a report listing each car number and the miles per gallon achieved by the car. At the end of the report include the average miles per gallon achieved by the complete fleet of cars.

10.3 Passing and Returning Structures

Individual structure members may be passed to a function in the same manner as any scalar variable. For example, given the structure definition

```
struct
{
  int id_num;
  double pay_rate;
  double hours;
} emp;
```

the statement

```
display(emp.id_num);
```

passes a copy of the structure member `emp.id_num` to a function named `display()`. Similarly, the statement

```
calc_pay(emp.pay_rate,emp.hours);
```

passes copies of the values stored in structure members `emp.pay_rate` and `emp.hours` to the function `calc_pay()`. Both functions, `display()` and `calc_pay()`, must declare the correct data types of their respective arguments.

On most compilers, complete copies of all members of a structure can also be passed to a function by including the name of the structure as an argument to the called function. For example, the function call

```
calc_net(emp);
```

passes a copy of the complete `emp` structure to `calc_net()`. Internal to `calc_net()`, an appropriate declaration must be made to receive the structure. Program 10-4 declares a global template for an employee record. This template is then used by both the `main()` and `calc_net()` functions to define specific structures with the names `emp` and `temp`, respectively.

 Program 10-4

```
struct   employee      /* declare a global template */
{
  int id_num;
  double pay_rate;
  double hours;
};
main()
{
  static struct employee emp = {6782, 8.93, 40.5};
  double net_pay, calc_net();
```

continued

```
    net_pay = calc_net(emp);        /* pass copies of the values in emp */
    printf("The net pay for employee %d is $%6.2f",emp.id_num,net_pay);
}


double calc_net(temp)
struct employee temp;     /* temp is of data type struct employee */
{
    return(temp.pay_rate * temp.hours);
}
```

The output produced by Program 10-4 is:

```
The net pay for employee 6782 is $361.66
```

In reviewing Program 10-4, observe that both `main()` and `calc_net()` use the same global template to define their individual structures. The structure defined in `main()` and the structure defined in `calc_net()` are two completely different structures. Any changes made to the local `temp` structure in `calc_net()` are not reflected in the `emp` structure of `main()`. In fact, since both structures are local to their respective functions, the same structure name could have been used in both functions with no ambiguity.

When `calc_net()` is called by `main()`, copies of `emp`'s structure values are passed to the `temp` structure. `calc_net()` then uses two of the passed member values to calculate a number, which is returned to `main()`. Since `calc_net()` returns a noninteger number, the data type of the value returned must be included in all declarations for `calc_net()`.

Although the structures in both `main()` and `calc_net()` use the same globally defined template, this is not strictly necessary. For example, the structure in `main()` could have been defined directly as:

```
static struct
{
  int id_num;
  double pay_rate;
  double hours;
} emp = {6782, 8.93, 40.5};
```

Similarly, the structure in `calc_net()` could have been defined as:

```
struct
{
  int id_num;
  double pay_rate;
  double hours;
} temp;
```

The global declaration of the employee template provided in Program 10-4 is highly preferable to these latter two individual structure specifications because the global template centralizes the declaration of the structure's organization. Any change that must subsequently be made to the structure need only be made once to the global template. Making changes to individual structure definitions requires that all occurrences of the structure definition be located, in every function defining the structure. For larger programs this usually results in an error when a change to one of the structure definitions is inadvertently omitted.

An alternative to passing a copy of a structure is to pass the address of the structure. This, of course, allows the called function to make changes directly to the original structure. For example, referring to Program 10-4, the call to calc_net() can be modified to

```
calc_net(&emp);
```

In this call, an address is passed. To correctly store this address calc_net() must declare the argument as a pointer. A suitable function definition for calc_net() is

```
calc net(pt)
struct employee *pt;
```

Here, the declaration for pt declares this argument as a pointer to a structure of type employee. The pointer variable, pt, receives the starting address of a structure whenever calc_net() is called. Within calc_net(), this pointer is used to directly reference any member in the structure. For example, (*pt).id_num refers to the id_num member of the structure, (*pt).pay_rate refers to the pay_rate member of the structure, and (*pt).hours refers to the hours member of the structure. These relationships are illustrated in Figure 10-5.

FIGURE 10–5 A Pointer Can Be Used to Access Structure Members

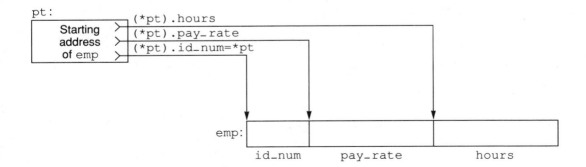

The parentheses around the expression *pt in Figure 10-5 are necessary to initially access "the structure whose address is in pt." This is followed by a reference to access the desired member within the structure. In the absence of the parentheses, the structure member operator . takes precedence over the indirection operator. Thus, the expression *pt.hours is another way of writing *(pt.hours), which would refer to "the variable whose address is in the pt.hours variable." This last expression clearly makes no sense because there is no structure named pt and hours does not contain an address.

As illustrated in Figure 10-5, the starting address of the emp structure is also the address of the first member of the structure. Thus, the expressions *pt and (*pt).id_num both refer to the id_num member of the emp structure.

The use of pointers is so common with structures that a special notation exists for them. The general expression (*pointer).member can always be replaced with the notation pointer->member, where the -> operator is constructed using a minus sign followed by a right-facing arrow (greater-than symbol). Either expression can be used to locate the desired member. For example, the following expressions are equivalent:

> (*pt).id_num   can be replaced by pt->id_num
> (*pt).pay_rate can be replaced by pt->pay_rate
> (*pt).hours   can be replaced by pt->hours

Program 10-5 illustrates passing a structure's address and using a pointer with the new notation to directly reference the structure.

 Program 10-5

```
struct employee        /* declare a global template */
{
  int id_num;
  double pay_rate;
  double hours;
};
main()
{
  static struct employee emp = {6782, 8.93, 40.5};
  double net_pay, calc_net();

  net_pay = calc_net(&emp);        /* pass an address */
  printf("The net pay for employee %d is $%6.2f",emp.id_num,net_pay);
}

double calc_net(pt)
struct employee *pt; /* pt is a pointer to a structure of employee type */
{
  return(pt->pay_rate * pt->hours);
}
```

The name of the pointer argument declared in Program 10-5 is, of course, selected by the programmer. When `calc_net()` is called, emp's starting address is passed to the function. Using this address as a reference point, individual members of the structure are accessed by including their names with the pointer.

As with all C expressions that reference a variable, the increment and decrement operators can also be applied to structure references. For example, the expression

```
++pt->hours
```

adds one to the `hours` member of the `emp` structure. Since the `->` operator has a higher priority than the increment operator, the `hours` member is accessed first and then the increment is applied.

Alternatively, the expression `(pt++)->hours` uses the postfix increment operator to increment the address in `pt` after the `hours` member is accessed. Similarly, the expression `(++pt)->hours` uses the prefix increment operator to increment the address in `pt` before the `hours` member is accessed. In both of these cases, however, there must be sufficient defined structures to ensure that the incremented pointers actually point to legitimate structures.

As an example, Figure 10-6 illustrates an array of three structures of type `employee`. Assuming that the address of `emp[1]` is stored in the pointer variable `pt`, the expression `++pt` changes the address in `pt` to the starting address of `emp[2]`, while the expression `--pt` changes the address to point to `emp[0]`.

Returning Structures

In practice, most structure-handling functions receive direct access to a structure by passing the address of the structure to the function. Then any changes can be made directly by the function using pointer references. If you want to have

FIGURE 10–6 Changing Pointer Addresses

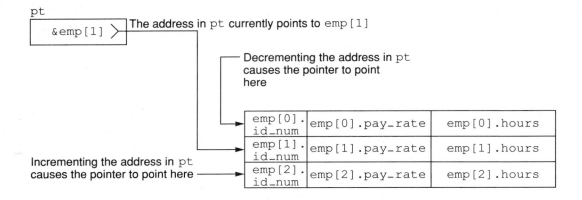

a function return a separate structure, however, and your compiler supports this option, you must follow the same procedures for returning complete structures as for returning scalar values. These include both declaring the function appropriately and alerting any calling function to the type of structure being returned. For example, the function `get_vals()` in Program 10-6 returns a complete structure to `main()`.

 Program 10-6

```
struct   employee        /* declare a global template */
{
  int id_num;
  double pay_rate;
  double hours;
};
main()
{
  struct employee emp;
  struct employee get_vals();

  emp = get_vals();
  printf("\nThe employee id number is %d", emp.id_num);
  printf("\nThe employee pay rate is $%5.2f", emp.pay_rate);
  printf("\nThe employee hours are %5.2f", emp.hours);
}

struct employee get_vals()
{
  struct employee new;

  new.id_num = 6789;
  new.pay_rate = 16.25;
  new.hours = 38.0;
  return(new);
}
```

The following output is displayed when Program 10-6 is run:

```
The employee id number is 6789
The employee pay rate is $16.25
The employee hours are 38.00
```

Since the `get_vals()` function returns a structure, the function header for `get_vals()` must specify the type of structure being returned. As get_vals() does not receive any arguments, the function header has no argument declarations and consists of the single line

```
struct employee get_vals()
```

Within get_vals(), the variable new is defined as a structure of the type to be returned. After values have been assigned to the new structure, the structure values are returned by including the structure name within the parentheses of the return statement.

On the receiving side, main() must be alerted that the function get_vals() will be returning a structure. This is handled by including a function declaration for get_vals() in main(). Notice that these steps for returning a structure from a function are identical to the normal procedures for returning scalar data types previously described in Chapter 6. Before attempting to pass or return a structure, however, be sure to check that the compiler you are using supports these options. Whether or not these options are available, structures can always be passed and directly altered using pointers.

Exercises 10.3

1. Write a C function named days() that determines the number of days from the turn of the century for any date passed as a structure. The date structure should use the template

```
struct date
{
    int month;
    int day;
    int year;
};
```

In writing the days() function, use the convention that all years have 360 days and each month consists of 30 days. The function should return the number of days for any date structure passed to it. Make sure to declare the returned variable a long integer to reserve sufficient room for dates such as 12/19/89.

2. Write a function named dif_days() that calculates and returns the difference between two dates. Each date is passed to the function as a structure using the following global template:

```
struct date
{
    int month;
    int day;
    int year;
};
```

The `dif_days()` function should make two calls to the `days()` function written for Exercise 1.

3. Rewrite the `days()` function written for Exercise 1 to receive a pointer to a date structure, rather than a copy of the complete structure.

4. *a.* Write a C function named `larger()` that returns the later date of any two dates passed to it. For example, if the dates 10/9/62 and 11/3/62 are passed to `larger()`, the second date would be returned.

   b. Include the `larger()` function that was written for Exercise 4a in a complete program. Store the date structure returned by `larger()` in a separate date structure and display the member values of the returned date.

5. *a.* Modify the function `days()` written for Exercise 1 to account for the actual number of days in each month. Assume, however, that each year contains 365 days (that is, do not account for leap years).

   b. Modify the function written for Exercise 5a to account for leap years.

10.4   Linked Lists

A classic data-handling problem is making additions or deletions to existing records that are maintained in a specific order. This is best illustrated by considering the alphabetical telephone list shown in Figure 10-7. Starting with this initial set of names and telephone numbers, we desire to add new records to the list in the proper alphabetical sequence, and to delete existing records in such a way that the storage for deleted records is eliminated.

Although the insertion or deletion of ordered records can be accomplished using an array of structures, these arrays are not efficient representations for adding or deleting records internal to the array. Arrays are fixed and prespecified in size. Deleting a record from an array creates an empty slot that requires either special marking or shifting up all elements below the deleted record to close

FIGURE 10–7   A Telephone List in Alphabetical Order

Acme, Sam
(201) 898-2392

Dolan, Edith
(213) 682-3104

Lanfrank, John
(415) 718-4581

Mening, Stephen
(914) 382-7070

Zemann, Harold
(718) 219-9912

the empty slot. Similarly, adding a record to the body of an array of structures requires that all elements below the addition be shifted down to make room for the new entry; or the new element could be added to the bottom of the existing array and the array then resorted to restore the proper order of the records. Thus, either adding or deleting records to such a list generally requires restructuring and rewriting the list—a cumbersome, time-consuming, and inefficient practice.

A *linked list* provides a convenient method for maintaining a constantly changing list, without the need to continually reorder and restructure the complete list. A linked list is simply a set of structures in which each structure contains at least one member whose value is the address of the next logically ordered structure in the list. Rather than requiring each record to be physically stored in the proper order, each new record is physically added either to the end of the existing list, or wherever the computer has free space in its storage area. The records are "linked" together by including the address of the next record in the record logically preceding it. From a programming standpoint, the current record being processed contains the address of the next record, no matter where the next record is actually stored.

The concept of a linked list is illustrated in Figure 10-8. Although the actual data for the Lanfrank structure illustrated in the figure may be physically stored anywhere in the computer, the additional member included at the end of the Dolan structure maintains the proper alphabetical order. This member provides the starting address of the location where the Lanfrank record is stored. As you might expect, this member is a pointer.

To see the usefulness of the pointer in the Dolan record, let us add a telephone number for June Hagar into the alphabetical list shown in Figure 10-7. The data for June Hagar is stored in a data structure using the same template as that used for the existing records. To ensure that the telephone number for Hagar is correctly displayed after the Dolan telephone number, the address in the Dolan record must be altered to point to the Hagar record, and the address in the Hagar record must be set to point to the Lanfrank record. This is illustrated in Figure 10-9.

Notice that the pointer in each structure simply points to the location of the next ordered structure, even if that structure is not physically located in the correct order. Removal of a structure from the ordered list is the reverse process of adding a record. The actual record is logically removed from the list by

FIGURE 10–8 Using Pointers to Link Structures

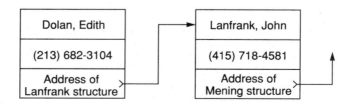

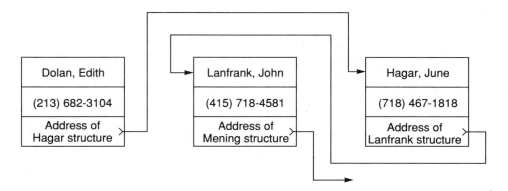

FIGURE 10–9   Adjusting Addresses to Point to Appropriate Records

simply changing the address in the structure preceding it to point to the structure immediately following the deleted record.

Each structure in a linked list has the same format; however, it is clear that the last record cannot have a valid pointer value that points to another record, since there is none. C provides a special pointer value called NULL that acts as a sentinel or flag to indicate when the last record has been processed. The NULL pointer value, like its end-of-string counterpart, has a numerical value of zero.

Besides an end-of-list sentinel value, a special pointer must also be provided for storing the address of the first structure in the list. Figure 10-10 illustrates the complete set of pointers and structures for a list consisting of three names.

The inclusion of a pointer in a structure should not seem surprising. As we discovered in Section 10.1, a structure can contain any C data type. For example, the structure declaration

```
struct test
{
  int id_num;
  double *pt_pay
};
```

declares a structure template consisting of two members. The first member is an integer variable named id_num, and the second variable is a pointer named pt_pay, which is a pointer to a double precision number. Program 10-7

FIGURE 10–10   Use of the Initial and Final Pointer Values

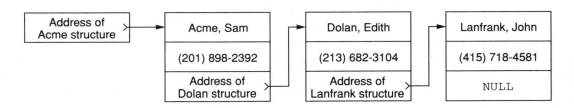

illustrates that the pointer member of a structure is used like any other pointer variable.

 Program 10-7

```
struct test
{
   int id_num;
   double *pt_pay;
};
main()
{
   struct test emp;
   double pay = 456.20;

   emp.id_num = 12345;
   emp.pt_pay = &pay;

   printf("Employee number %d was paid $%6.2f",
          emp.id_num, *emp.pt_pay);
}
```

The output produced by executing Program 10-7 is:

```
Employee number 12345 was paid $456.20
```

Figure 10-11 illustrates the relationship between the members of the emp structure defined in Program 10-7 and the variable named pay. The value assigned to emp.id_num is the number 12345 and the value assigned to pay is 456.20. The address of the pay variable is assigned to the structure member emp.pt_pay. Since this member has been defined as a pointer to a double precision number, placing the address of the double precision variable pay in it is a correct use of this member. Finally, since the member operator . has a higher precedence than the indirection operator *, the expression used in the printf() call in Program 10-7 is correct. The expression *emp.pt_pay is

FIGURE 10–11 Storing an Address in a Structure Member

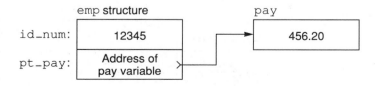

equivalent to the expression *(emp.pt_pay), which is translated as "the variable whose address is contained in the member emp.pt_pay."

Although the pointer defined in Program 10-7 has been used in a rather trivial fashion, the program does illustrate the concept of including a pointer in a structure. This concept can be easily extended to create a linked list of structures suitable for storing the names and telephone numbers previously listed in Figure 10-7. The following declaration creates a template for such a structure:

```
struct tele_typ
{
  char name[30];
  char phone_no[15];
  struct tele_typ *nextaddr;
};
```

The tele_typ template consists of three members. The first member is an array of 30 characters, suitable for storing names with a maximum of 29 letters and an end-of-string marker. The next member is an array of 15 characters, suitable for storing telephone numbers with their respective area codes. The last member is a pointer suitable for storing the address of a structure of the tele_typ type.

Program 10-8 illustrates the use of the tele_typ template by specifically defining three structures having this form. The three structures are named t1, t2, and t3, respectively, and the name and telephone members of each of these structures are initialized when the structures are defined, using the data previously listed in Figure 10-7.

 Program 10-8

```
#include <stdio.h>
struct tele_typ
{
  char name[30];
  char phone_no[15];
  struct tele_typ *nextaddr;
};
main()
{
  static struct tele_typ t1 = {"Acme, Sam","(201) 898-2392"};
  static struct tele_typ t2 = {"Dolan, Edith","(213) 682-3104"};
  static struct tele_typ t3 = {"Lanfrank, John","(415) 718-4581"};
  struct tele_typ *first;    /* create a pointer to a structure */

  first = &t1;               /* store t1's address in first */
  t1.nextaddr = &t2;         /* store t2's address in t1.nextaddr */
  t2.nextaddr = &t3;         /* store t3's address in t2.nextaddr */
  t3.nextaddr = NULL;        /* store the NULL address in t3.nextaddr */

  printf("\n%s %s %s",first->name,t1.nextaddr->name,t2.nextaddr->name);
}
```

The output produced by executing Program 10-8 is:

```
Acme, Sam
Dolan, Edith
Lanfrank, John
```

Program 10-8 demonstrates the use of pointers to access successive structure members. As illustrated in Figure 10-12, each structure contains the address of the next structure in the list.

The initialization of the names and telephone numbers for each of the structures defined in Program 10-8 is straightforward. Although each structure consists of three members, only the first two members of each structure are initialized. As both of these members are arrays of characters, they can be initialized with strings. The remaining member of each structure is a pointer. To create a linked list, each structure pointer must be assigned the address of the next structure in the list.

FIGURE 10–12 The Relationship Between Structures in Program 10-8

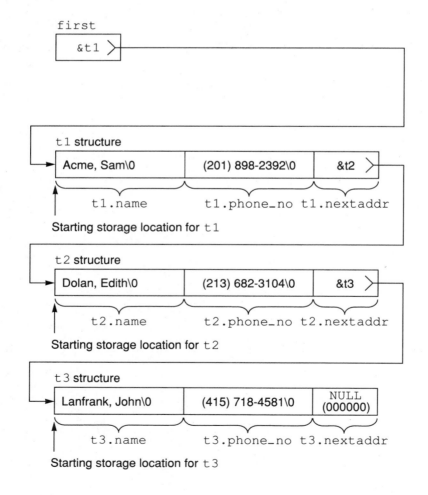

The four assignment statements in Program 10-8 perform the correct assignments. The expression `first = &t1` stores the address of the first structure in the list in the pointer variable named `first`. The expression `t1.nextaddr = &t2` stores the starting address of the `t2` structure into the pointer member of the `t1` structure. Similarly, the expression `t2.nextaddr = &t3` stores the starting address of the `t3` structure into the pointer member of the `t2` structure. To end the list, the value of the `NULL` pointer, which is zero, is stored into the pointer member of the `t3` structure.

Once values have been assigned to each structure member and correct addresses have been stored in the appropriate pointers, the addresses in the pointers are used to access each structure's name member. For example, the expression `t1.nextaddr->name` refers to the `name` member of the structure whose address is in the `nextaddr` member of the `t1` structure. The precedence of the member operator `.` and the structure pointer operator `->` are equal, and are evaluated from left to right. Thus, the expression `t1.nextaddr->name` is evaluated as `(t1.nextadd)->name`. Since `t1.nextaddr` contains the address of the `t2` structure, the proper name is accessed.

The expression `t1.nextaddr->name` can, of course, be replaced by the equivalent expression `(*t1.nextaddr).name`, which uses the more conventional indirection operator. This expression also refers to "the name member of the variable whose address is in `t1.nextaddr`."

The addresses in a linked list of structures can be used to loop through the complete list. As each structure is accessed it can be either examined to select a specific value or used to print out a complete list. For example, the `display()` function in Program 10-9 illustrates the use of a `while` loop, which uses the address in each structure's pointer member to cycle through the list and successively display data stored in each structure.

 Program 10-9

```
#include <stdio.h>
struct tele_typ
{
  char name[30];
  char phone_no[15];
  struct tele_typ *nextaddr;
};
main()
{
  static struct tele_typ t1 = {"Acme, Sam","(201) 898-2392"};
  static struct tele_typ t2 = {"Dolan, Edith","(213) 682-3104"};
  static struct tele_typ t3 = {"Lanfrank, John","(415) 718-4581"};
  struct tele_typ *first;   /* create a pointer to a structure */
```

continued

353

```
    first = &t1;           /* store t1's address in first */
    t1.nextaddr = &t2;     /* store t2's address in t1.nextaddr */
    t2.nextaddr = &t3;     /* store t3's address in t2.nextaddr */
    t3.nextaddr = NULL;    /* store the NULL address in t3.nextaddr */

    display(first);        /* send the address of the first structure */
}

display(contents)                   /* display till end of linked list */
struct tele_typ  *contents;         /* a pointer to a structure  */
{                                   /* of type tele_typ          */
    while (contents != NULL)
    {
        printf("\n%30s %20s",contents->name, contents->phone_no);
        contents = contents->nextaddr;       /* get next address */
    }
    return;
}
```

The output produced by Program 10-9 is:

```
        Acme, Sam               (201) 898-2392
        Dolan, Edith            (213) 682-3104
        Lanfrank, John          (415) 718-4581
```

The important concept illustrated by Program 10-9 is the use of the address in one structure to access members of the next structure in the list. When the display() function is called, it is passed the value stored in the variable named first. Since first is a pointer variable, the actual value passed is an address (the address of the t1 structure). display() accepts the passed value in the argument named contents. To store the passed address correctly, contents is declared as a pointer to a structure of the tele_typ type. Within display(), a while loop is used to cycle through the linked structures, starting with the structure whose address is in contents. The condition tested in the while statement compares the value in contents, which is an address, to the NULL value. For each valid address the name and phone number members of the addressed structure are displayed. The address in contents is then updated with the address in the pointer member of the current structure. The address in contents is then retested, and the process continues while the address in contents is not equal to the NULL value. display() "knows" nothing about the names of the structures declared in main() or even how many structures exist. It simply cycles through the linked list, structure by structure, until it encounters the end-of-list NULL address. Since the value of NULL is zero, the tested condition can be replaced by the equivalent expression !contents.

A disadvantage of Program 10-9 is that exactly three structures are defined in main() by name and storage for them is reserved at compile time. Should a fourth structure be required, the additional structure would have to be declared and the program recompiled. In the next section we show how to have the computer dynamically allocate and release storage for structures at run time, as storage is required. Only when a new structure is to be added to the list, and while the program is running, is storage for the new structure created. Similarly, when a structure is no longer needed and can be deleted from the list, the storage for the deleted record is relinquished and returned to the computer.

Exercises 10.4

1. Modify Program 10-9 to prompt the user for a name. Have the program search the existing list for the entered name. If the name is in the list, display the corresponding phone number; otherwise display the message, The name is not in the current phone directory.

2. Write a program containing a linked list of ten integer numbers. Have the program display the numbers in the list.

3. Using the linked list of structures illustrated in Figure 10-12, write the sequence of steps necessary to delete the record for Edith Dolan from the list.

4. Generalize the description obtained in Exercise 3 to describe the sequence of steps necessary to remove the nth structure from a list of linked structures. The nth structure is preceded by the $(n-1)$st structure and followed by the $(n+1)$st structure. Make sure to store all pointer values correctly.

5. a. A doubly linked list is a list in which each structure contains a pointer to both the following and previous structures in the list. Define an appropriate template for a doubly linked list of names and telephone numbers.
   b. Using the template defined in Exercise 5a, modify Program 10-9 to list the names and phone numbers in reverse order.

10.5   Dynamic Storage Allocation

As each variable is defined in a program, sufficient storage for it is assigned from a pool of computer memory locations made available to the compiler. Once specific memory locations have been reserved for a variable, these locations are fixed, whether they are used or not. For example, if a function requests storage for an array of 500 integers, the storage for the array is allocated and fixed while the program is running. If the application requires less than 500 integers, the unused allocated storage is not released back to the system until the program ends execution. If, on the other hand, the application requires more than 500 integers, the size of the integer array must be increased and the function defining the array recompiled.

An alternative to this fixed or static allocation of memory storage locations is the *dynamic allocation* of memory. Under a dynamic allocation scheme, storage is allocated to a program and released back to the computer while the program is running, rather than being fixed at compile time.

The dynamic allocation of memory is extremely useful when dealing with lists of structures, because it allows the list to expand as new records are added and contract as records are deleted. For example, in constructing a list of names and phone numbers, the exact number of structures ultimately needed may not be known. Rather than creating a fixed array of structures, it is extremely useful to have a mechanism whereby the list can be enlarged and shrunk as necessary. Most standard C libraries provide functions that have this dynamic allocation capability. Two of these functions, called `malloc()` and `free()`, are described in Table 10-1.

TABLE 10-1

Function Name	Description
`malloc()`	Reserves the number of bytes requested by the argument passed to the function. Returns the address of the first reserved location or `NULL` if sufficient memory is not available.
`free()`	Releases a block of bytes previously reserved. The address of the first reserved location is passed as an argument to the function.

In requesting additional storage space, the user must provide the `malloc()` function with an indication of the amount of storage needed. This may be done by either requesting a specific number of bytes or, more usually, by requesting enough space for a particular type of data. For example, the function call `malloc(10)` requests 10 bytes of storage, while the function call `malloc(sizeof(int))` requests enough storage to store an integer number. A request for enough storage for a data structure typically takes the second form. For example, using the structure declaration

```
struct tel_typ
{
  char name[25];
  char phone_no[15];
};
```

the function call `malloc( sizeof(struct tel_typ) );` reserves enough storage for one structure of the `tel_typ` type.

In allocating storage dynamically, we have no advance indication as to where the computer system will physically reserve the requested number of bytes, and we have no explicit name to access the newly created storage locations. To provide access to these locations, `malloc()` returns the address of the first location that has been reserved. This address must, of course, be assigned to a pointer. The return of a pointer by `malloc()` is especially useful for creating a linked list of data structures. As each new structure is created, the pointer returned by `malloc()` to the structure can be assigned to a member of the previous structure in the list. Before illustrating the actual dynamic allocation of such a structure in a program, we will consider one logistic problem created by `malloc()`.

The `malloc()` function always returns a pointer to the first byte of storage reserved, and considers this first byte as a character. As such, the function declaration of `malloc()` is `char *malloc()`. Any function that calls `malloc()` must include this declaration in order to be alerted that a pointer to a character will be returned. This presents a slight problem when using `malloc()` to reserve enough storage for a structure. Although `malloc()` will reserve the necessary number of bytes for a structure and return the correct address of the first reserved byte, this address will be interpreted as the address of a character. To use this address to reference subsequent structure members, it must be reinterpreted as pointing to a structure.

The mechanism for converting one data type into another is called a *cast*. In this case, then, we need to cast (or force) a pointer to a character into a pointer to a structure. The cast expression `(struct template_name *)` can be used to do this. For example, if the variable `lis_point` is a pointer to a character, the expression `(struct emp *)lis_point` redefines the address in the pointer to be an address of a structure of type `emp`. The address is not changed physically, but any subsequent reference to the address will now cause the correct number of bytes to be accessed for the appropriate structure. Casts are more fully described in Chapter 13. For now, however, we will simply use cast expressions to convert the address returned by `malloc()` into the correct pointer type for referencing a structure.

Program 10-10 illustrates using `malloc()` to create a structure dynamically in response to a user-input request.

 Program 10-10

```
#include <stdio.h>
struct tel_typ
{
  name[30];
  phone_no[15];
};
main()
{
  char key;
  char *malloc();
  struct tel_typ *rec_point;    /* rec_point is a pointer to a */
                                /* structure of type tel_typ   */
```

continued

```
  printf("Do you wish to create a new record (respond with y or n): ");
  key = getchar();
  if (key == 'y')
  {
    key = getchar()        /* get the Enter key for buffered input */
    rec_point = (struct tel_typ *)malloc(sizeof(struct tel_typ));
    populate(rec_point);
    disp_one(rec_point);
  }
  else
    printf("\nNo record has been created.");
}

populate(record)            /* get a name and phone number */
struct tel_typ *record;     /* a pointer to a structure of type tel_typ */
{
  printf("Enter a name: ");
  gets(record->name);
  printf("Enter the phone number: ");
  gets(record->phone_no);
  return;
}

disp_one(contents)          /* display the contents of one record */
struct tel_typ *contents;   /* a pointer to a structure of type tel_typ */
{
  printf("\nThe contents of the record just created is:");
  printf("\nName: %s",contents->name);
  printf("\nPhone Number: %s", contents->phone_no);
  return;
}
```

A sample session produced by Program 10-10 is:

```
Do you wish to create a new record (respond with y or n): y
Enter a name: Monroe, James
Enter the phone number: (617) 555-1817

The contents of the record just created is:
Name: Monroe, James
Phone Number: (617) 555-1817
```

In reviewing Program 10-10, notice that only three declarations are made in main(). The variable key is declared as a character variable, the malloc() function is declared as providing a pointer to a character, and the variable rec_point is declared as being a pointer to a structure of the tel_typ type. Since the declaration for the template tel_typ is global, tel_typ can be used within main() to define rec_point as a pointer to a structure of the tel_typ type.

If a user enters y in response to the first prompt in main(), a call to malloc() is made. The argument passed to malloc() is the size of the required structure. Although malloc() returns the address of the first reserved location, this address is considered as pointing to a character. To store the address in rec_point, which has been declared as a pointer to a structure, the address returned by malloc() is coerced into the proper type by use of the expression (struct tel_typ *).

Once rec_point has been loaded with the proper address, this address can be used to access the newly created structure. The function populate() is used to prompt the user for data needed in filling the structure and to store the user-entered data in the correct members of the structure. The argument passed to populate() in main() is the pointer rec_point. Like all passed arguments, the value contained in rec_point is passed to the function. Since the value in rec_point is an address, populate() actually receives the address of the newly created structure.

Within populate(), the value received by it is stored in the argument named record. Since the value to be stored in record is the address of a structure, record must be declared as a pointer to a structure. This declaration is provided by the statement struct tel_typ *record;. The statements within populate() use the address in record to locate the respective members of the structure.

The disp_one() function in Program 10-10 is used to display the contents of the newly created and populated structure. The address passed to disp_one() is the same address that was passed to populate(). Since this passed value is the address of a structure, the argument name used to store the address is declared as a pointer to the correct structure type.

One further comment is in order here. Since both populate() and disp_one() return no values to main(), they were not declared in main(). This was done in Program 10-10 to ensure that the program could be run on the computer you are using. If your compiler supports the void data type, however, the declaration

```
void populate(), disp_one();
```

should be included with main()'s other declarations.

Once you understand the mechanism of calling malloc(), you can use this function to construct a linked list of structures. As described in the previous section, the structures used in a linked list must contain one pointer member. The address in the pointer member is the starting address of the next structure in the list. Additionally, a pointer must be reserved for the address of the first structure, and the pointer member of the last structure in the list is given a NULL address to indicate that no more members are being pointed to. Program 10-11 illustrates the use of malloc() to construct a linked list of names and phone numbers. The populate() function used in Program 10-11 is the same function used in Program 10-10, while the display() function is the same function used in Program 10-9.

Program 10-11

```c
#include <stdio.h>
struct tel_typ
{
  char name[25];
  char phone_no[15];
  struct tel_typ *nextaddr;
};
main()
{
  int i;
  struct tel_typ *list, *current; /* two pointers to structures of  */
                                  /* type tel_typ                   */
  char *malloc();               /* malloc() returns a pointer to a char  */

  /* get a pointer to the first structure in the list */
  list = (struct tel_typ *) malloc(sizeof(struct tel_typ));
  current = list;

  /* populate the current structure and create two more structures */
  for(i = 0; i < 2; ++i)
  {
    populate(current);
    current->nextaddr = (struct tel_typ *) malloc(sizeof(struct tel_typ));
    current = current->nextaddr;
  }

  populate(current);            /* populate the last structure */
  current->nextaddr = NULL;   /* set the last address */
  printf("\nThe list consists of the following records:\n");
  display(list);              /* display the structures */
}

populate(record)             /* get a name and phone number */
struct tel_typ *record;    /* a pointer to a structure of type tel_typ */
{
  printf("Enter a name: ");
  gets(record->name);
  printf("Enter the phone number: ");
  gets(record->phone_no);
  return;
}

display(contents)           /* display till end of linked list */
struct tel_typ *contents; /* a pointer to a structure of type tel_typ */
{
  while (contents != NULL)
  {
    printf("\n%-30s %-20s",contents->name, contents->phone_no);
    contents = contents->nextaddr;
  }
  return;
}
```

The first time `malloc()` is called in Program 10-11, it is used to create the first structure in the linked list. As such, the address returned by `malloc()` is stored in the pointer variable named `list`. The address in `list` is then assigned to the pointer named `current`. This pointer variable is always used by the program to point to the current structure. Since the `current` structure is the first structure created, the address in the pointer named `list` is assigned to the pointer named `current`.

Within `main()`'s `for` loop, the name and phone number members of the newly created structure are populated by calling `populate()` and passing the address of the `current` structure to the function. Upon return from `populate()`, the pointer member of the `current` structure is assigned an address. This address is the address of the next structure in the list, which is obtained from `malloc()`. The call to `malloc()` creates the next structure and returns its address into the pointer member of the `current` structure. This completes the population of the `current` member. The final statement in the `for` loop resets the address in the `current` pointer to the address of the next structure in the list.

After the last structure has been created, the final statements in `main()` populate this structure, assign a NULL address to the pointer member, and call `display()` to display all the structures in the list. A sample run of Program 10-11 is provided below:

```
Enter a name: Acme, Sam
Enter the phone number: (201) 898-2392
Enter a name: Dolan, Edith
Enter the phone number: (213) 682-3104
Enter a name: Lanfrank, John
Enter the phone number: (415) 718-4581

The list consists of the following records:

Acme, Sam                    (201) 898-2392
Dolan, Edith                 (213) 682-3104
Lanfrank, John               (415) 718-4581
```

Just as `malloc()` dynamically creates storage while a program is executing, the `free()` function restores a block of storage back to the computer while the programming is executing. The only argument required by `free()` is the starting address of a block of storage that was dynamically allocated. Thus, any address returned by `malloc()` can subsequently be passed to `free()` to restore the reserved memory back to the computer. `free()` does not alter the address passed to it, but simply removes the storage that the address references.

Exercises 10.5

1. As described in Table 10-1, the `malloc()` function returns either the address of the first new storage area allocated, or NULL if insufficient storage is available. Modify

Program 10-11 to check that a valid address has been returned before a call to `populate()` is made. Display an appropriate message if sufficient storage is not available.

2. Write a C function named `delete()` that deletes an existing structure from the linked list of structures created by Program 10-11. The algorithm for deleting a linked structure should follow the sequence developed for deleting a structure developed in Exercise 4 in Section 10.4. The argument passed to `delete()` should be the address of the structure preceding the record to be deleted. In the deletion function, make sure that the value of the pointer in the deleted structure replaces the value of the pointer member of the preceding structure before the structure is deleted.

3. Write a function named `insert()` that inserts a structure into the linked list of structures created in Program 10-11. The algorithm for inserting a structure in a linked list should follow the sequence for inserting a record illustrated in Figure 10-9. The argument passed to `insert()` should be the address of the structure preceding the structure to be inserted. The inserted structure should follow this current structure. The `insert()` function should create a new structure dynamically, call the `populate` function used in Program 10-11, and adjust all pointer values appropriately.

4. We desire to insert a new structure into the linked list of structures created by Program 10-11. The function developed to do this in Exercise 3 assumed that the address of the preceding structure is known. Write a function called `find_rec()` that returns the address of the structure immediately preceding the point at which the new structure is to be inserted. (*Hint:* `find_rec()` must request the new name as input and compare the entered name to existing names to determine where the new name is to be placed.)

5. Write a function named `modify()` that can be used to modify the name and phone number members of a structure of the type created in Program 10-11. The argument passed to `modify()` should be the address of the structure to be modified. The `modify()` function should first display the existing name and phone number in the selected structure and then request new data for these members.

6. a. Write a C program that initially presents a menu of choices for the user. The menu should consist of the following choices:
- **A.** Create an initial linked list of names and phone numbers.
- **B.** Insert a new structure into the linked list.
- **C.** Modify an existing structure in the linked list.
- **D.** Delete an existing structure from the list.
- **E.** Exit from the program.

Upon the user's selection, the program should execute the appropriate functions to satisfy the request.

b. Why is the original creation of a linked list usually done by one program, and the options to add, modify, or delete a structure in the list provided by a different program?

10.6   Unions

A *union* is a data type that reserves the same area in memory for two or more variables, each of which can be a different data type. A variable that is declared as a union data type can be used to hold a character variable, an integer variable, a double precision variable, or any other valid C data type. Each of these types, but only one at a time, can actually be assigned to the union variable.

The declaration for a union is identical in form to a structure declaration, with the reserved word `union` used in place of the reserved word `struct`. For example, the declaration

```
union
{
  char key;
  int num;
  double price;
} val;
```

creates a union variable named `val`. If `val` were a structure it would consist of three individual members. As a union, however, `val` contains a single member that can be either a character variable named `key`, an integer variable named `num`, or a double precision variable named `price`. In effect, a union reserves sufficient memory locations to accommodate its largest member's data type. This same set of locations is then referenced by different variable names depending on the data type of the value currently residing in the reserved locations. Each value stored overwrites the previous value, using as many bytes of the reserved memory area as necessary.

Individual union members are referenced using the same notation as structure members. For example, if the `val` union is currently being used to store a character, the correct variable name to access the stored character is `val.key`. Similarly, if the union is used to store an integer, the value is accessed by the name `val.num`, and a double precision value is accessed by the name `val.price`. In using union members, it is the programmer's responsibility to ensure that the correct member name is used for the data type currently residing in the union.

Typically a second variable is used to keep track of the current data type stored in the union. For example, the following code could be used to select the appropriate member of `val` for display. Here the value in the variable `u_type` determines the currently stored data type in the `val` union.

```
switch(u_type)
{
  case 'c': printf("%c", val.key);
            break;
  case 'i': printf("%d", val.num);
            break;
  case 'd': printf("%f", val.price);
            break;
  default : printf("Invalid type in u_type : %c", u_type);
}
```

As they are in structures, *tag names* can be associated with a union to create templates. For example, the declaration

```
union date_time
{
    long int days;
    double time;
};
```

provides a template for a union without actually reserving any storage locations. The template can then be used to define any number of variables of the union type `date_time`. For example, the definition

```
union date_time first, second, *pt;
```

creates a union variable named `first`, a union variable named `second`, and a pointer that can be used to store the address of any union having the form of `date_time`. Once a pointer to a union has been declared, the same notation used to access structure members can be used to access union members. For example, if the assignment `pt = &first;` is made, then `pt->date` references the `date` member of the union named `first`.

Unions may themselves be members of structures and arrays, or structures, arrays, and pointers may be members of unions. In each case, the notation used to access a member must be consistent with the nesting employed. For example, in the structure defined by

```
struct
{
  char u_type;
  union
  {
     char *text;
     float rate;
  } u_tax;
}   flag;
```

the variable rate is referenced as

```
flag.u_tax.rate
```

Similarly, the first character of the string whose address is stored in the pointer `text` is referenced as

```
*flag.u_tax.text
```

Exercises 10.6

1. Assume that the following definition has been made:

```
union
{
   float rate;
   double taxes;
   int num;
} flag;
```

For this union write appropriate `printf()` function calls to display the various members of the union.

2. Define a union variable named `car` that contains an integer named `year`, an array of 10 characters named `name`, and an array of 10 characters named `model`.

3. Define a union variable named `lang` that would allow a floating point number to be referenced by both the variable names `interest` and `rate`.

4. Declare a union with the tag name `amt` that contains an integer variable named `int_amt`, a double precision variable named `dbl_amt`, and a pointer to a character named `pt_key`.

5. a. What do you think will be displayed by the following section of code?

```
union
{
   char ch;
   float btype;
} alt;
alt.ch = 'y';
printf("%f", alt.btype);
```

b. Include the code presented in Exercise 5a in a program and run the program to verify your answer to Exercise 5a.

10.7 Common Programming Errors

Three common errors are often made when using structures or unions. The first error occurs because structures and unions, as complete entities, cannot be used in relational expressions. For example, even if `tel_typ` and `phon_type` are two structures of the same type, the expression `tel_typ == phon_typ` is invalid. Individual members of a structure or union can, of course, be compared using any of C's relational operators.

The second common error is really an extension of a pointer error as it relates to structures and unions. Whenever a pointer is used to "point to" either of these data types, or whenever a pointer is itself a member of a structure or a union, care must be taken to use the address in the pointer to access the appropriate data type. Should you be confused about just what is being pointed to, remember, "If in doubt, print it out."

The final error relates specifically to unions. Since a union can store only one of its members at a time, you must be careful to keep track of the currently stored variable. Storing one data type in a union and accessing by the wrong variable name can result in an error that is particularly troublesome to locate.

10.8   Chapter Summary

1. A structure allows individual variables to be grouped under a common variable name. Each variable in a structure is referenced by its structure name, followed by a period, followed by its individual variable name. Another term for a structure is a record. The general form for declaring a structure is:

```
struct
{

    individual member declarations;

} structure_name;
```

2. A tag name can be used to create a generalized structure template describing the form and arrangement of elements in a structure. This tag name can then be used to define specific structure variables.

3. Structures are particularly useful as elements of arrays. Used in this manner, each structure becomes one record in a list of records.

4. Individual members of a structure are passed to a function in the manner appropriate to the data type of the member being passed. Some C compilers also allow complete structures to be passed, in which case the called function receives a copy of each element in the structure. The address of a structure may also be passed, which provides the called function with direct access to the structure.

5. Structure members can be any valid C data type, including structures, unions, arrays, and pointers. When a pointer is included as a structure member a linked list can be created. Such a list uses the pointer in one structure to "point to" (contain the address of) the next logical structure in the list.

6. Unions are declared in the same manner as structures. The definition of a union creates a memory overlay area, with each union member using the same memory storage locations. Thus, only one member of a union may be active at a time.

Additional Topics

Part Five

Data Files

Chapter Eleven

The data for the programs we have seen so far has either been defined internally within the programs or entered interactively during program execution. This type of data creation and retention precludes sharing data between programs and is a disadvantage in larger systems consisting of many interconnecting programs. For these larger systems, the data used by one program typically must be made available to other programs, without being recreated or redefined.

Sharing data between programs requires that the data be saved independently and separately from any single program. For example, consider the following data:

Code	Description	Price	Amount in Stock
QA134	Battery	35.89	10
QA136	Bulbs	3.22	123
CM104	Fuses	1.03	98
CM212	Degreaser	4.74	62
HT435	Cleaner	3.98	50

This data might be needed by both an inventory control program and a billing program. Therefore, the data would be stored by itself on a floppy diskette, hard disk, or magnetic tape in a data file.

A *data file* is any collection of data that is stored together under a common name on a storage medium other than the computer's main memory. This chapter describes the C statements needed to create data files and to read and write data to them.

11.1   Declaring, Opening, and Closing Files

Each data file in a computer is physically stored using a unique file name. Typically, most computers require that a *file name* consist of no more than eight characters followed by an optional period and an extension of up to three characters. Using this convention, the following are all valid computer data file names:

```
balances.dat      records        info.dat
report.bnd        prices.bnd     math.mem
```

Computer file names should be chosen to indicate both the type of data in the file and the application for which it is used. Frequently, the first eight characters are used to describe the data itself and the three characters after the decimal point are used to describe the application. For example, the file name `prices.bnd` is useful for describing a file of prices used in a bond application.

Within a C program a file is always referenced by a variable name that must be declared within the program. For files, the variable is actually a pointer to a special file structure, and as such must be declared as a pointer to a file. Examples of such variable declarations are:

```
FILE *in_file;
FILE *prices;
FILE *fp;
```

In each of these declarations, the pointer name is selected by the programmer. It is the name of the data file as it will be referenced by the program. This name need not be the same as the external name used by the computer to store the file.

The term FILE in each declaration is the tag name of a special data structure used by C for storing information about the file, including whether the file is available for reading or writing, the next available character in the file, and where this character is stored. The actual declaration of a file structure and the equivalence of the structure to the symbolic name FILE is contained in the stdio.h standard header file, which must be included at the top of each program that uses a data file.

Opening a File

Opening a file is a "cookbook" procedure that accomplishes two purposes, only one of which is directly pertinent to the programmer. First, opening a file establishes a physical communication link between the program and the data file. Since the specific details of this link are handled by the computer's operating system and are transparent to the program, the programmer normally need not consider them.

From a programming perspective, the second purpose of opening a file is relevant. Besides establishing the actual physical connection between a program and a data file, the open statement also equates the file's external computer name to the pointer name used internally by the program.

Appropriately enough, the file open function is called fopen() and is available in the standard C library supplied with each C compiler. One of the arguments passed to fopen() is the file's external name. fopen() returns the starting address of a FILE structure that is needed for reading data from the file and writing data to it. Since fopen() returns an address to a FILE, the declaration

```
FILE *fopen();
```

must be included in any program that calls fopen(). Thus, both the fopen() function that returns an address and the variable used to store this address must be declared as pointers to FILE. For example, if a data file is to be opened in main() and the pointer name out_file is used to store the address returned by fopen(), the following section of code is necessary:

```
#include <stdio.h>
main()
{
  FILE *fopen(), *out_file;         /* FILE declarations */
  any other variable declarations;
```

Here, the FILE declarations for fopen() and out_file have been combined into one declaration statement. out_file, of course, is a programmer-selected name for the file, as the file will be "known" internal to main(). If the file were to be opened in some other function, these FILE declarations would have to be included with the declarations for that function.

It now remains to actually call fopen() to connect the file's external name to its internal name. In using fopen(), two arguments are required. The first argument is the computer's name for the file; the second argument is the mode in which the file is to be used. Permissible modes are "r", "w", or "a", which represent reading, writing, or appending to a file.

A file opened for writing creates a new file and makes the file available for output by the function opening the file. If a file exists with the same name as a file opened for writing, the old file is erased. For example, the statement

```
out_file = fopen("prices.bnd","w");
```

opens a file named prices.bnd that can now be written to. Once this file has been opened, the program accesses the file using the pointer name out_file, while the computer saves the file under the name prices.bnd.

A file opened for appending makes an existing file available for data to be added to the end of the file. If the file opened for appending does not exist, a new file with the designated name is created and made available to receive output from the program. For example, the statement

```
out_file = fopen("prices.bnd","a");
```

opens a file named prices.bnd and makes it available for data to be appended to the end of the file.

The only difference between a file opened in write mode and one opened in append mode is where the data is physically placed in the file. In write mode, the data is written starting at the beginning of the file, while in append mode the data is written starting at the end of the file. For a new file, the two modes are identical.

For files opened in either write or append mode, the functions needed to write data to it are similar to the printf(), puts(), and putchar() functions used for displaying data on a terminal. These functions are described in the next section.

A file opened in read mode retrieves an existing file and makes its data available as input to the program. For example, the open statement

```
in_file = fopen("prices.bnd","r");
```

opens the file named prices.bnd and makes the data in the file available for input. Within the function opening the file, the file is read using the pointer name in_file. The functions used to read data from a file are similar to the scanf(), gets(), and getchar() functions used for inputting data from the keyboard. These functions are also described in the next section.

If a file opened for reading does not exist, the `fopen()` function returns the NULL address value. This is the same NULL address previously described in Section 10.4. It can be used to test that an existing file has, in fact, been opened.

Notice that in all the open statements, both the external file name and the mode arguments passed to `fopen()` were strings contained between double quotes. If the external file name is first stored in either an array of characters or as a string, the array or string name, without quotes, can be used as the first argument to `fopen()`.

Program 11-1 illustrates the statements required to open a file in read mode and the use of the returned value from `fopen()` to check for a successful opening of the file. The program prompts the user for the external file name and stores the name in the array `f_name[13]`.

 Program 11-1

```
#include <stdio.h>
main()
{
  FILE *in_file, *fopen();
  char f_name[13];

  printf("\nEnter a file name: ");
  gets(f_name);

  in_file = fopen(f_name,"r");          /* open the file */

  if (in_file == NULL)
  {
    printf("\nThe file cannot be opened.");
    printf("\nPlease check that the file currently exists.");
  }
  else
    printf("\nThe file has been successfully opened for reading");

}
```

Program 11-1 requests that an external data file name be entered by the user. The entered name is stored in the character array `f_name` and the array name is then passed to the `fopen()` function. A sample run using Program 11-1 produced the output:

```
Enter a file name: prices.bnd
The file has been successfully opened for reading
```

Although Program 11-1 can be used to open an existing file in read mode, it clearly lacks statements to read the data in the file and then close the file. These topics are discussed next. Before leaving Program 11-1, however, note that the opening of the file and assignment of the returned address can be included directly within the program's `if` statement. The single expression

```
if ( (in_file = fopen(name,"r")) == NULL )
```

can be used to replace the two lines

```
in_file = fopen(name,"r");
if (in_file == NULL)
```

Closing a File

A file is closed using the `fclose()` function. This function breaks the link between the file's external and internal names, releasing the internal file pointer name, which can then be used for another file. For example, the statement

```
fclose(in_file);
```

closes the `in_file` file. The argument to `fclose()` should always be the pointer name used when the file was opened. `fclose()` does not return a value.

Since all computers have a limit on the maximum number of files that can be open at one time, closing files that are no longer needed makes good sense. Any open files existing at the end of normal program execution are also automatically closed by the operating system.

Exercises 11.1

---

1. Using the reference manuals provided with your computer's operating system, determine:

  a. the maximum number of characters that can be used to name a file for storage by the computer system

  b. the maximum number of data files that can be open at the same time

2. Would it be appropriate to refer to a saved C program as a file? Why or why not?

3. Write a suitable declaration statement for each of the following file pointers: `prices`, `fp`, `coupons`, `distance`, `in_data`, `out_data`.

4. Write individual open statements to link the following external data file names to their corresponding internal pointer names:

External Name	Pointer Name	Mode
coba.mem	memo	write
book.let	letter	write
coupons.bnd	coups	append
yield.bnd	pt_yield	append
prices.dat	pri_file	read
rates.dat	rates	read

5. Write individual FILE declarations for each of the files opened in Exercise 3.

6. Write close statements for each of the files opened in Exercise 3.

7. *a.* Program 11-1 prompts the user for a file name and uses the gets() function to return a string into the character array f_name. Replace the prompt and the gets() statements with the single function call statement get_file(name);. Then write the get_file() function to prompt the user for a file name, accept a file name, and test that a valid file name has been entered. If a valid name has not been entered, print an appropriate message and have the program terminate. If a valid name has been entered, have the program open the file and check that a successful opening has occurred. Consider a valid file name as consisting of at most eight characters, the first of which is a letter.

   b. Modify the get_file() function written for Exercise 7a to request a file name continuously until a valid name has been entered. (*Hint:* Include the prompt and the gets() function call in a while or do-while loop that terminates when a valid file name is detected.)

11.2   Reading and Writing Files

Reading or writing to an open file involves almost the identical standard library functions for reading input from a terminal and writing data to a display screen. For writing to a file, these functions are:

Function	Description
fputc(c,filename)	Write a single character to the file.
fputs(string,filename)	Write a string to the file.
fprintf(filename,"format",args)	Write the values of the arguments to the file according to the format.

In each of these functions, the file name is the internal pointer name specified when the file was opened. For example, if out_file is the internal pointer name of a file opened in either the write or append modes, the following output statements are valid.

```
fputc('a',out_file);              /* write an a to the file */
fputs("Hello world!",out_file); /* write the string to the file */
fprintf(out_file,"%s %n",descrip,price);
```

Notice that the fputc(), fputs(), and fprintf() file functions are used in the same manner as the equivalent putchar(), puts(), and printf()

functions, with the addition of a file name as an argument. The file name simply directs the output to a specific file instead of to the standard display device. Program 11-2 illustrates the use of the file write function `fprintf()` to write a list of descriptions and prices to a file.

 Program 11-2

```
#include <stdio.h>
main()
{
  int i;
  FILE *fopen(), *out_file;                    /* FILE declarations */
  static float price[] = {39.95,3.22,1.03};   /* a list of prices */
  static char *descrip[] = { "Batteries",      /*     a list of      */
                             "Bulbs",          /*    descriptions    */
                             "Fuses"};

  out_file = fopen("prices.bnd","w");          /*    open the file   */

  for(i = 0; i < 3; ++i)
    fprintf(out_file,"%-9s %5.2f\n",descrip[i],price[i]);

  fclose(out_file);
}
```

When Program 11-2 is executed, a file named `prices.bnd` is created and saved by the computer. The file is a sequential file consisting of the following three lines:

```
Batteries 39.95
Bulbs      3.22
Fuses      1.02
```

The prices in the file line up one after another because the control sequence `%-9s` in the `printf()` function call forced the descriptions to be left justified in a field of nine character positions. Similarly, the prices are right justified in a field of five characters, beginning one space away from the end of the description field.

The actual storage of characters in the file depends on the character codes used by the computer. Although only 45 characters appear to be stored in the file, corresponding to the descriptions, blanks, and prices written to the file, the file actually contains 49 characters. The extra characters consist of the newline escape sequences at the end of each line and a special end-of-file marker placed as the last item in the file when the file is closed.

```
42 61 74 74 65 72 69 65 73 20 33 39 2e 39 35 0a 42 75 6c 62 73
 B  a  t  t  e  r  i  e  s     3  9  .  9  5 \n  B  u  l  b  s

20 20 20 20 20 20 33 2e 32 32 0a 46 75 73 65 73 20 20 20 20 20
                   3  .  2  2 \n  F  u  s  e  s

20 31 2e 30 33 0a 26
    1  .  0  3 \n ^Z
```

FIGURE 11–1   The `prices.bnd` File as Stored by the Computer

Assuming characters are stored using the ASCII code, the `prices.bnd` file is physically stored as illustrated in Figure 11-1.* For convenience, the character corresponding to each hexadecimal code is listed below the code. A code of 20 represents the blank character. Although the actual code used for the end-of-file marker depends on the system you are using, the hexadecimal code 26, corresponding to Control-Z, is common.

Reading data from a file is almost identical to reading data from a standard keyboard, with the addition of the file name to indicate where the data is coming from. The file functions available for reading from a file are:

Function	Description
`fgetc(filename)`	Read a character from the file.
`fgets(stringname,n,filename)`	Read n-1 characters from the file and store the characters in the given string name.
`fscanf(filename,"format",&args)`	Read values for the listed arguments from the file, according to the format.

For example, if `in_file` is the internal pointer name of a file opened in read mode, the following statements could be used to read data from the file:

```
fgetc(in_file);              /* Read the next character in the file */

fgets(message,10,in_file);   /* Read the next 9 characters from */
                             /* the file into message          */

fscanf(in_file,"%f",&price); /* Read a floating point number */
```

All the input functions correctly detect the end-of-file marker. The functions `fgetc()` and `fscanf()`, however, return the named constant EOF when the marker is detected. The function `fgets()` returns a NULL (\0) when it detects

* For systems that generate a separate line feed and carriage return for each newline character, the file will contain 52 characters.

the end of a file. Both of these named constants, EOF and NULL, are useful sentinels for detecting the end of a file being read.

Reading data from a file requires that the programmer knows how the data appears in the file. This is necessary for correct "stripping" of the data from the file into appropriate variables for storage. All files are read sequentially, so that once an item is read the next item in the file becomes available for reading.

Program 11-3 illustrates reading the prices.bnd file that was created in Program 11-2. The program also illustrates using the EOF marker, which is returned by fscanf() when the end of the file is encountered.

 Program 11-3

```c
#include <stdio.h>
main()
{
    char descrip[10];
    float price;
    FILE *fopen(), *in_file;

    in_file = fopen("prices.bnd","r");

    while (fscanf(in_file,"%s %f",descrip,&price) != EOF)
        printf("%-9s %5.2f\n",descrip,price);

    fclose(in_file);
}
```

Program 11-3 continues to read the file until the EOF marker has been detected. Each time the file is read, a string and a floating point number are input to the program. The display produced by Program 11-3 is:

```
Batteries 39.95
Bulbs      3.22
Fuses      1.02
```

In place of the fscanf() function used in Program 11-3, an fgets() function call can be used. fgets() requires three arguments: an address where the first character read will be stored, the maximum number of characters to be read, and the name of the input file. For example, the function call

```
fgets(line,81,in_file);
```

causes a maximum of 80 characters (one less than the specified number) to be read from the file named in_file and stored starting at the address contained in the pointer named line. fgets() continues reading characters until 80 characters have been read or a newline character has been encountered. If a newline character is encountered it is included with the other entered characters before the string is terminated with the end-of-string marker, \0. fgets() also detects the end-of-file marker, but returns the NULL character when the end of the file is encountered. Program 11-4 illustrates the use of fgets() in a working program.

 Program 11-4

```
#include <stdio.h>
main()
{
  char line[81],descrip[10];
  float price;
  FILE *fopen(), *in_file;

  in_file = fopen("prices.bnd","r");

  while (fgets(line,81,in_file) != NULL)
    printf("%s",line);

  fclose(in_file);
}
```

Program 11-4 is really a line-by-line text-copying program, reading a line of text from the file and then displaying it on the terminal. Thus, the output of Program 11-4 is identical to the output of Program 11-3. If it were necessary to obtain the description and price as individual variables, either Program 11-3 should be used or the string returned by fgets() in Program 11-4 must be processed further using the string scan function, sscanf(). For example, the statement

> sscanf(line,"%s %f",descrip,&price)

could be used to extract the description and price from the string stored in the line character array (see Section 9.4 for a description of in-memory string formatting).

Standard Device Files

The data file pointers we have used have all been logical file pointers. A *logical file pointer* is one that references a file of logically related data that has been saved under a common name; that is, it "points to" a data file. In addition to logical file pointers, C also supports physical file pointers. A *physical file pointer* "points to" a hardware device, such as a keyboard, screen, or printer.

The actual physical device assigned to your program for data entry is formally called the *standard input file*. Usually this is a keyboard. When a scanf() function call is encountered in a C program, the computer automatically goes to this standard input file for the expected input. Similarly, when a printf() function call is encountered, the output is automatically displayed or "written to" a device that has been assigned as the *standard output file*. For most systems this is a CRT screen, although it can be a printer.

When a program is run, the keyboard used for entering data is automatically opened and assigned to the internal file pointer name stdin. Similarly, the output device used for display is assigned to the file pointer named stdout. These file pointers are always available for programmer use.

The similarities between printf() and fprintf(), scanf() and fscanf() are not accidental. printf() is a special case of fprintf() that defaults to the standard output file, and scanf() is a special case of fscanf() that defaults to the standard input file. Thus,

```
fprintf(stdout,"Hello World!");
```

causes the same display as the statement

```
printf("Hello World!");
```

and

```
fscanf(stdin,"%d",&num);
```

is equivalent to the statement

```
scanf("%d",&num);
```

In addition to the stdin and stdout file pointers, a third pointer named stderr is assigned to the output device used for system error messages. Although stderr and stdout frequently refer to the same device, the use of stderr provides a means of redirecting any error messages away from the file being used for normal program output, as described in Appendix C.

Just as scanf() and printf() are special cases of fscanf() and fprintf(), respectively, the functions getchar(), gets(), putchar(), and puts() are also special cases of the more general file functions listed in Table 11-1.

TABLE 11-1   Correspondence Between Selected I/O Functions

Function	General Form
putchar(character)	fputc(character,stdout)
puts(string)	fputs(string,stdout)
getchar()	fgetc(stdin)
gets(stringname)	fgets(stringname,n,stdin)

The character function pairs listed in Table 11-1 can be used as direct replacements for each other. This is not true for the string-handling functions. The differences between the string-handling functions are described below.

At input, as previously noted, the `fgets()` function reads data from a file until a newline escape sequence or a specified number of characters has been read. If `fgets()` encounters a newline escape sequence, as we saw in Program 11-4, it is stored with the other characters entered. The `gets()` function, however, does not store the newline escape sequence in the final string. Both functions terminate the entered characters with an end-of-string `NULL` character.

At output, both `puts()` and `fputs()` write all the characters in the string except for the terminating end-of-string `NULL`. `puts()`, however, automatically adds a newline escape sequence at the end of the transmitted characters while `fputs()` does not.

Other Devices

The keyboard, display, and error-reporting devices are automatically opened and assigned the internal file names `stdin`, `stdout`, and `stderr`, respectively, whenever a C program begins execution. Additionally, other devices can be used for input or output if the name assigned by the system is known. For example, most IBM or IBM-compatible personal computers assign the name `prn` to the printer connected to the computer. For these computers, the statement `fprintf("prn","Hello World!");` causes the string `Hello World!` to be printed directly at the printer. As with `stdin`, `stdout`, and `stderr`, `"prn"` is the name of a physical device. Unlike `stdin`, `stdout`, and `stderr`, `prn` is not a pointer constant but the actual name of the device; as such, it must be enclosed in double quotes.

Exercises 11.2

1. a. Using the `gets()` and `fputs()` functions, write a C program that accepts lines of text from the keyboard and writes each line to a file named `text.dat` until an empty line is entered. An empty line is a line with no text—just a new line caused by pressing the ENTER (or RETURN) key.

b. Replace the `gets()` function in the program written for Exercise 1a with an equivalent call to `fgets()`.

c. Modify Program 11-4 to read and display the data stored in the `text.dat` file created in Exercise 1a.

2. Determine the operating system command provided by your computer to display the contents of a saved file. Compare its operation with the program developed for Exercise 1c. (*Hint:* Typically the operating system command is called `LIST`, `TYPE`, or `CAT`.)

3. a. Create a file named `employ.dat` containing the following data:

Anthony	A.J.	10031	7.82	12/18/62
Burrows	W.K.	10067	9.14	6/ 9/63
Fain	B.D.	10083	8.79	5/18/59
Janney	P.	10095	10.57	9/28/62
Smith	G.J.	10105	8.50	12/20/61

b. Write a program called `fcopy.c` to read the `employ.dat` file created in Exercise 3a and produce a duplicate copy of the file named `employ.bak`.

c. Modify the program written in Exercise 3b to accept the names of the original and duplicate files as user input.

d. Since `fcopy.c` always copies data from an original file to a duplicate file, can you think of a better method of accepting the original and duplicate file names than prompting the user for them each time the program is executed?

4. *a.* Write a program that opens a file and displays the contents of the file with associated line numbers. That is, the program should print 1 before displaying the first line, 2 before displaying the second line, and so on for each line in the file.

b. Modify the program written in Exercise 4a to list the contents of the file on the printer assigned to your computer.

5. *a.* Create a file containing the following data:

H.Baker	614 Freeman St.	Orange	NJ
D.Rosso	83 Chambers St.	Madison	NJ
K.Tims	891 Ridgewood Rd.	Millburn	NJ
B.Williams	24 Tremont Ave	Brooklyn	NY

b. Write a program to read and display the data file created in Exercise 5a using the following output format:

```
Name:
Address:
City, State:
```

6. *a.* Create a file containing the following names, Social Security numbers, hourly rate, and hours worked:

B. Caldwell	163-98-4182	7.32	37
D. Memcheck	189-53-2147	8.32	40
R. Potter	145-32-9826	6.54	40
W. Rosen	163-09-4263	9.80	35

b. Write a C program that reads the data file created in Exercise 6a and computes and displays a payroll schedule. The output should list the Social Security number, name, and gross pay for each individual.

7. *a.* Create a file containing the following car numbers, number of miles driven, and number of gallons of gas used by each car:

Car No.	Miles Driven	Gallons Used
54	250	19
62	525	38
71	123	6
85	1,322	86
97	235	14

b. Write a C program that reads the data in the file created in Exercise 7a and displays the car number, miles driven, gallons used, and the miles per gallon for each car. The output should additionally contain the total miles driven, total gallons used, and average miles per gallon for all the cars. These totals should be displayed at the end of the output report.

8. *a.* Create a file with the following data containing the part number, opening balance, number of items sold, and minimum stock required:

Part Number	Initial Amount	Quantity Sold	Minimum Amount
QA310	95	47	50
CM145	320	162	200
MS514	34	20	25
EN212	163	150	160

b. Write a C program to create an inventory report based on the data in the file created in Exercise 8a. The display should consist of the part number, current balance, and the amount that is necessary to bring the inventory to the minimum level.

9. *a.* Create a file containing the following data:

Name	Rate	Hours
Callaway, G.	6.00	40
Hanson, P.	5.00	48
Lasard, D.	6.50	35
Stillman, W.	8.00	50

b. Write a C program that uses the information contained in the file created in Exercise 9a to produce the following pay report for each employee:

Name   Rate   Hours   Regular Pay   Overtime Pay   Gross Pay

Any hours worked above 40 hours are paid at time and a half. At the end of the individual output for each employee, the program should display the totals of the regular, overtime, and gross pay columns.

10. *a.* Store the following data in a file:

5 96 87 78 93 21 4 92 82 85 87 6 72 69 85 75 81 73

b. Write a C program to calculate and display the average of each group of numbers in the file created in Exercise 10a. The data is arranged in the file so that each group of numbers is preceded by the number of data items in the group. Thus, the first number in the file, 5, indicates that the next five numbers should be grouped together. The number 4 indicates that the following four numbers are a group, and the 6 indicates that the last six numbers are a group. (*Hint:* Use a nested loop. The outer loop should terminate when the EOF marker is encountered.)

11.3 Random File Access

File organization refers to the way data is stored in a file. All the files we have used have *sequential organization*. This means that the characters in the file are stored in a sequential manner, one after another. Additionally, we have read the file in a sequential manner. The way data is retrieved from the file is called *file access*. The fact that the characters in the file are stored sequentially, however, does not force us to access the file sequentially.

The standard library functions `rewind()`, `fseek()`, and `ftell()` can be used to provide *random access* to a file. In random access any character in the file can be read immediately, without first having to read all the characters stored ahead of it.

The `rewind()` function resets the current position to the start of the file. `rewind()` requires the pointer name used for the file as its only argument. For example, the statement

```
rewind(in_file);
```

resets the file so that the next character accessed will be the first character in the file. A `rewind()` is done automatically when a file is opened in read mode.

The `fseek()` function allows the programmer to move to any position in the file. In order to understand this function, you must first clearly understand how data is referenced in the file.

Each character in a data file is located by its position in the file. The first character in the file is located at position 0, the next character at position 1, and so on. A character's position is also referred to as its offset from the start of the file. Thus, the first character has a 0 offset, the second character has an offset of 1, and so on for each character in the file.

The `fseek()` function requires three arguments: the pointer name of the file; the offset, as a long integer, into the file; and where the offset is to be calculated from. The general form of `fseek()` is

```
fseek(file_name, offset, origin)
```

The values of the origin argument can be either 0, 1, or 2. An origin of 0 means the offset is the true offset from the start of the file. An origin of 1 means that the offset is relative to the current position in the file, and an origin of 2 means the offset is relative to the end of the file. A positive offset means move forward in the file and a negative offset means move backward. Examples of `fseek()` are:

```
fseek(in_file,4L,0);     /* go to the fifth character in the file */
fseek(in_file,4L,1);     /* move ahead five characters */
fseek(in_file,-4L,1);    /* move back five characters */
fseek(in_file,0L,0);     /* go to start of file—same as rewind() */
fseek(in_file,0L,2);     /* go to end of file */
fseek(in_file,-10L,2);   /* go to 10 characters before the file's end */
```

In these examples, `in_file` is the name of the file pointer used when the data file was opened. Notice that the offset passed to `fseek()` must be a long integer.

The last function, `ftell()`, simply returns the offset value of the next character that will be read or written. For example, if ten characters have already been read from a file named `in_file`, the function call

```
ftell(in_file);
```

returns the long integer 10. This means that the next character to be read is offset 10 byte positions from the start of the file, and is the eleventh character in the file.

Program 11-5 illustrates the use of `fseek()` and `ftell()` to read a file in reverse order, from last character to first. As each character is read it is also displayed.

 Program 11-5

```
#include<stdio.h>
main()
{
int ch;
long int offset, last, ftell();
FILE *fopen(), *in_file;

in_file = fopen("test.dat","r");
fseek(in_file,0,2);            /* move to the end of the file */
last = ftell(in_file);        /* save the offset of the last character */
for(offset = 0; offset <= last; ++offset)
{
  fseek(in_file, -offset, 2);    /* move back to the next character */
  ch = getc(in_file);            /* get the character */
  switch(ch)
  {
    case '\n': printf("LF : ");
              break;
    case EOF : printf("EOF: ");
              break;
    default  : printf("%c : ",ch);
              break;
  }
}
fclose(in_file);
}
```

Assuming the file `test.dat` contains the following data,

Bulbs   3.12

the output of Program 11-5 is:

    EOF : 2 : 1 : . : 3 :   :   :   : s : b : l : u : B :

Program 11-5 initially goes to the last character in the file. The offset of this character, which is the end-of-file character, is saved in the variable `last`. Since `ftell()` returns a long integer, both `ftell()` and `last` have been declared as long integers.

Starting from the end of the file, `fseek()` is used to position the next character to be read, referenced from the back of the file. As each character is read, the character is displayed and the offset adjusted in order to access the next character.

Exercises 11.3

1. Determine the value of the offset returned by `ftell()` in Program 11-5. Assume that the file `test.dat` contains the data

```
Bulbs    3.12
```

2. Rewrite Program 11-5 so that the origin for the `fseek()` function used in the `for` loop is the start of the file rather than the end. The program should still print the file in reverse order.

3. The function `fseek()` returns 0 if the position specified has been reached, or 1 if the position specified was beyond the file's boundaries. Modify Program 11-5 to display an error message if `fseek()` returns 1.

4. Write a program that will read and display every second character in a file named `test.dat`.

5. Using the `fseek()` and `ftell()` functions, write a function named `f_chars()` that returns the total number of characters in a file.

6. a. Write a function named `r_bytes()` that reads and displays *n* characters starting from any position in a file. The function should accept three arguments: a file pointer, the offset of the first character to be read, and the number of characters to be read.
   b. Modify the `r_bytes()` function written in Exercise 6a to store the characters read into a string or an array. The function should accept the address of the storage area as a fourth argument.

7. Assume that a data file consisting of a group of individual lines has been created. Write a function named `print_line()` that will read and display any desired line of the file. For example, the function call `print_line(f_name,5);` should display the fifth line of the file name passed to it.

11.4 Passing and Returning File Names

Internal file names are passed to a function using the same procedures for passing all function arguments. For passing a file name this requires declaring the passed argument as a pointer to a `FILE`. For example, in Program 11-6 a file named

out_file is opened in main() and the file name passed to the function
in_out(), which is then used to write five lines of user-entered text to the file.

 Program 11-6

```
#include <stdio.h>
main()
{
  FILE *fopen(), *out_file;

  out_file = fopen("prices.dat","w");
  in_out(out_file);
  fclose(out_file);
}

in_out(fname)
FILE *fname;        /* fname is a pointer to a FILE */
{
  int count;
  char line[81];  /* enough storage for one line of text */

  printf("Please enter five lines of text:\n");
  for (count = 0; count < 5; ++count)
  {
    gets(line);
    fprintf(fname,"%s\n",line);
  }
  return;
}
```

Within main() the file is known as out_file. The value in out_file,
which is an address, is passed to the in_out() function. The function
in_out() stores the address in the argument named fname and correctly
declares fname to be a pointer to a FILE.

Returning a file name from a function also requires following the same rules
used to return any value from a function. This means including the data type of
the returned value in the function header, making sure the correct variable type
is actually returned from the function, and alerting the calling function to the
returned data type. For example, assume that the function get_open() is to
prompt a user for a file name, open the file for output, and pass the file name back
to the calling function. Since get_open() returns a file name that is actually a
pointer to a FILE, the correct function declaration for get_open() is:

FILE *get_open()

This declaration specifically declares that the function get_open() will return a pointer to a FILE. It is consistent with the pointer declarations that have been made previously.

Once a function has been declared to return a pointer to a FILE, there must be at least one variable or argument in the function consistent with this declaration that can be used for the actual returned value. Consider Program 11-7. In this program, get_open() returns a file name to main().

 Program 11-7

```c
#include <stdio.h>
main()
{
  FILE *get_open(), *out_file;

  out_file = get_open();
  in_out(out_file);
  fclose(out_file);
}

FILE *get_open()    /* get_open() returns a pointer to a FILE */
{
  FILE *fopen(), *fname;
  char name[13];

  printf("\nEnter a file name: ");
  gets(name);
  fname = fopen(name,"w");
  return(fname);
}

in_out(fname)
FILE *fname;        /* fname is a pointer to a FILE */
{
  int count;
  char line[81];  /* enough storage for one line of text */

  printf("Please enter five lines of text:\n");
  for (count = 0; count < 5; ++count)
  {
    gets(line);
    fprintf(fname,"%s\n",line);
  }
}
```

Program 11-7 is simply a modified version of Program 11-6 that now allows the user to enter a file name from the standard input device. Although the function

get_open() is in "bare bones" form, it does illustrate the correct function declaration for returning a file name. The get_open() function declaration defines the
function as returning a pointer to a FILE. Within get_open(), the returned
variable, fname, is the correct data type. Finally, since get_open() is defined in
the program after main(), main() is alerted to the returned value by the inclusion
of a declaration statement for the get_open() function.

get_open() is a "bare bones" function in that it does no checking on the
file being opened for output. If the name of an existing data file is entered, the
file will be destroyed when it is opened in write mode. A useful "trick" to
prevent this type of mishap is to open the entered file name in read mode.
Then, if the file exists, the fopen() function returns a nonzero pointer to
indicate that the file is available for input. This can be used to alert the user
that a file with the entered name currently exists in the system and to request
confirmation that the data in the file can be destroyed and the file name used
for the new output file. Before the file can be reopened in write mode, of course,
it would have to be closed. The implementation of this algorithm is left as an
exercise.

Exercises 11.4

1. A function named p_file() is to receive a file name as an argument. What declarations are required to pass a file name to p_file()?

2. a. A function name get_file() is to return a file name. What declarations are
required in the function header and internal to the file?
b. What declaration statement is required in each function that calls get_file() to
ensure correct receipt of the file name returned by get_file()? Under what conditions can this declaration be omitted?

3. Write a function named fcheck() that checks whether a file exists. The function
should be passed a file name. If the file exists, the function should return a value of 1, otherwise the function should return a value of zero.

4. Rewrite the function get_open() used in Program 11-7 to incorporate the file-
checking procedures described in the text. Specifically, if the entered file name exists, an
appropriate message should be displayed. The user should then be presented with the
option of entering a new file name or allowing the program to overwrite the existing file,
append to it, or exit.

11.5   Common Programming Errors

Four programming errors are common when using files. The most common
error is to use the file's external name in place of the internal file pointer variable
when accessing the file. The only standard library function that uses the data

file's external name is the `fopen()` function. All the other standard functions presented in this chapter require the pointer variable assigned to the file when it was initially opened.

The next error is to omit the file pointer name altogether. Programmers used to functions that access the standard input and output devices, where a specific file pointer is not required, sometimes forget to include a file pointer when accessing data files.

A third error occurs when using the EOF marker to detect the end of a file. Any variable used to accept the EOF must be declared as an integer variable, not a character variable. For example, if ch has been declared as a character variable the expression

```
while ( (c = getc(in_file)) != EOF)
```

produces an infinite loop. This occurs because a character variable can never take on an EOF code. EOF is an integer value (usually –1) that has no character representation. This ensures that the EOF code can never be confused with any legitimate character encountered as normal data in the file. To terminate the above expression, the variable ch must be declared as an integer variable.

The last error concerns the offset argument sent to the function `fseek()`. This offset must be a long integer constant or variable. Any other value passed to `fseek()` can result in an unpredictable effect.

11.6   Chapter Summary

1. A data file is any collection of data stored together in an external storage medium under a common name.

2. A text data file is opened using the `fopen()` standard library function. This function connects a file's external name with an internal pointer name. After the file is opened, all subsequent accesses to the file require the internal pointer name.

3. A file can be opened for reading, writing, or appending. A file opened for writing creates a new file and erases any existing file having the same name as the opened file. A file opened for appending makes an existing file available for data to be added to the end of the file. If the file does not exist it is created. A file opened for reading makes an existing file's data available for input.

4. The `fopen()` function and any internal file name must be declared as a pointer to a FILE. This means that a declaration similar to

```
FILE *fopen(), *f_name;
```

must be included with the declarations in which the file is opened. f_name can be replaced with any user-selected variable name.

5. In addition to any files opened within a function, the standard files `stdin`, `stdout`, and `stderr` are automatically opened when a program is run. `stdin` is the pointer name of the physical file used for data entry by `scanf()`, `stdout` is the pointer name of the physical file device used for data display by `printf()`, and `stderr` is the pointer name of the physical file device used for displaying system error messages.

6. Data files can be accessed randomly using the `rewind()`, `fseek()`, and `ftell()` functions.

7. Table 11-2 lists the standard file library functions.

TABLE 11-2   Standard File Library Functions

Function Name	Purpose
`fopen()`	Open or create a file
`fclose()`	Close a file
`getc()`	Character input
`getchar()`	Character input from stdin
`fgets()`	String input
`gets()`	String input from stdin
`fscanf()`	Formatted input
`scanf()`	Formatted input from stdin
`putc()`	Character output
`putchar()`	Character output to stdout
`fputs()`	String output
`puts()`	String output to stdout
`fprintf()`	Formatted output
`printf()`	Formatted output to stdout
`fseek()`	File positioning
`rewind()`	File positioning
`ftell()`	Position reporting

11.7   Chapter Supplement: Control Codes

In addition to responding to the codes for letters, digits, and special punctuation symbols, which are collectively referred to as *printable characters*, physical device files such as printers and CRT screens can also respond to a small set of *control codes*. These codes, which convey control information to the physical device, have no equivalent characters that can be displayed, and are called *nonprintable* characters.

Two of these codes, which are extremely useful in applications, are the *clear* and *bell control codes*. When the clear control code is sent to a printer, the printer ejects a page of paper and begins printing on the next sheet of paper. If you take care to align the printer to the top of a new page when printing begins, the clear control character can be used as an equivalent "top-of-page" command. When the equivalent clear code is sent to a CRT display, the screen is cleared of all text and the cursor is positioned at the lefthand corner of the screen.

Sending control codes to an output device is done in a manner similar to sending a printable character to a file. Recall that sending a printable character to a file requires two pieces of information: the file name and the character being written to the file. For example, the statement `putc('a',out_file);` causes the letter *a* to be written to the file named `out_file`. Instead of including the actual letter as an argument to `putc()`, we can substitute the numerical storage code for the letter. For computers that use the ASCII code, this amounts to substituting the equivalent ASCII numerical value for the appropriate letter. Referring to Appendix B, we see that in the ASCII code the value for *a* is 97 as a decimal number, 61 as a hexadecimal number, and 141 as an octal number. Any one of these numerical values can be used in place of the letter *a* in the previous `putc()` function call. Thus, the following four statements are all equivalent:

```
putc('a',out_file);
putc(97, out_file);
putc(0x61 out_file);
putc('\142',out_file);
```

Note that in each of these statements we have adhered to the notation used by C in identifying decimal and hexadecimal numbers. A number with no leading zero is considered a decimal number and a number with a leading `0x` is considered a hexadecimal value. Octal character codes must, however, be preceded by a backslash and enclosed in single apostrophes. Since the backslash identifies the number as an octal value, the normal leading zero required of octal values can be omitted. Since most control codes, by convention, are listed as octal values using three octal digits, we will retain this convention in all further examples.

The importance of substituting the numerical code for the letter is only realized when a control code rather than a character code must be sent. Since no equivalent character exists for control codes, the actual code for the command must be used. Although each computer can have its own code for clearing the CRT screen, the bell code and the code for clearing a printer are fairly universal. To activate the bell, the octal code 07 is used. The octal clear code for most printers is 014. Thus, if the file `out_file` has been opened as the printer in write mode, the statement

```
putc('\014',out_file);
```

causes the printer to eject the current page. Similarly, if scrn has been opened as the CRT screen in write mode, the statement

$$putc('\07',scrn);$$

causes the bell to be activated for a short "beep."

For personal computers, the CRT screen has its own clear code. For your computer, check the manual for the CRT screen to obtain the proper clear-screen control code. You must also check the name by which your computer "knows" the printer and CRT screen. For IBM personal computers the printer has the name prn and the CRT screen the name con (short for console). Program 11-8 illustrates the use of control codes to eject a page of paper from the printer and alert the user with a "beep" if the printer is not turned on. Using #define commands, the appropriate codes have been equated to more readable symbolic names.

 Program 11-8

```c
#include <stdio.h>
#define BELL '\07'
#define TOP_OF_PAGE '\014' /* page eject code */
main()
{
  FILE *printer, *fopen;

  printer = fopen("prn", "w");
  check(printer);
}

check(printer)    /* make sure printer is ready and eject a page */
FILE *printer;
{

  if(printer == 0)          /* check that the file has been opened */
  {
    putc(BELL,stdout);
    printf("The printer cannot be opened for output.");
    printf("\nPlease check the printer is on and ready for use.");
  }
  else
    putc(TOP_OF_PAGE,printer);
  return;
}
```

The statements in the function check() are used to ensure that the printer has been opened and is ready for output. The symbolic constants BELL and TOP_OF_PAGE can be used freely within the check() function because they have been defined globally at the top of the program. Each of these constants is sent using a putc() function call. Since the CRT screen is the standard output device for the computer used to run Program 11-8, the CRT did not have to be opened as a new file. Instead, the file name stdout was used to send the BELL constant to the screen.

In addition to the BELL code, all CRT screens have control codes to position the cursor directly at different screen locations. This enables the programmer to place messages anywhere on the screen. Since these codes differ for various CRT models, you should check the manual for your computer to determine the proper codes. Additionally, many C compilers for personal computers include standard library functions that provide the same cursor-positioning capabilities.

Bit Operations

Chapter Twelve

C operates with complete data entities that are stored as one or more bytes, such as character, integer, and double precision constants and variables. In addition, C provides for the manipulation of individual bits of character and integer constants and variables. Generally these bit manipulations are used in engineering and computer science programs and are not required in commercial applications.*

The operators that are used to perform bit manipulations are called *bit operators.* They are listed in Table 12-1.

TABLE 12-1 Bit Operators

Operator	Description
&	Bitwise AND
|	Bitwise Inclusive OR
^	Bitwise Exclusive OR
~	Bitwise one's complement
<<	Left shift
>>	Right shift

All the operators except ~ listed in Table 12-1 are *binary operators,* requiring two operands. In using the bit operators each operand is treated as a binary number consisting of a series of individual 1s and 0s. The respective bits in each operand are then compared on a bit-by-bit basis and the result is determined based on the selected operation.

12.1 The AND Operator

The AND operator causes a bit-by-bit AND comparison between its two operands. The result of each bit-by-bit comparison is a 1 only when both bits being compared are 1s, otherwise the result of the AND operation is a 0. For example, assume that the following two eight-bit numbers are to be ANDed:

```
1 0 1 1 0 0 1 1
1 1 0 1 0 1 0 1
```

To perform an AND operation, each bit in one operand is compared to the bit occupying the same position in the other operand. Figure 12-1 illustrates the correspondence between bits for these two operands. As shown in the figure,

* This chapter may be omitted with no loss of subject continuity.

```
  1 0 1 1 0 0 1 1
& 1 1 0 1 0 1 0 1
  ───────────────
  1 0 0 1 0 0 0 1
```

FIGURE 12–1 A Sample AND Operation

when both bits being compared are 1s, the result is a 1, otherwise the result is a 0. The result of each comparison is, of course, independent of any other bit comparison.

Program 12-1 illustrates the use of an AND operation. In this program, the variable op1 is initialized to the octal value 325, which is the octal equivalent of the binary number 1 1 0 1 0 1 0 1, and the variable op2 is initialized to the octal value 263, which is the octal representation of the binary number 1 0 1 1 0 0 1 1. These are the same two binary numbers illustrated in Figure 12-1.

 Program 12-1

```
main()
{
   int op1 = 0325, op2 = 0263;

   printf("%o ANDed with %o is %o", op1, op2, op1 & op2);
}
```

Program 12-1 produces the following output:

```
325 ANDed with 263 is 221
```

The result of ANDing the octal numbers 325 and 263 is the octal number 221. The binary equivalent of 221 is the binary number 1 0 0 1 0 0 0 1, which is the result of the AND operation illustrated in Figure 12-1.

AND operations are extremely useful in masking, or eliminating, selected bits from an operand. This is a direct result of the fact that ANDing any bit (1 or 0) with a 0 forces the resulting bit to be a 0, while ANDing any bit (1 or 0) with a 1 leaves the original bit unchanged. For example, assume that the variable op1 has the arbitrary bit pattern x x x x x x x x, where each x can be either 1 or 0, independent of any other x in the number. The result of ANDing this binary number with the binary number 0 0 0 0 1 1 1 1 is:

```
op1  =     x x x x x x x x
op2  =     0 0 0 0 1 1 1 1
         ──────────────────
Result =   0 0 0 0 x x x x
```

397

As can be seen from this example, the zeros in op2 effectively mask, or eliminate, the respective bits in op1, while the ones in op2 filter, or pass, the respective bits in op1 through with no change in their values. In this example, the variable op2 is called a *mask*. By choosing the mask appropriately, any individual bit in an operand can be selected, or filtered, out of an operand for inspection. For example, ANDing the variable op1 with the mask 0 0 0 0 0 1 0 0 forces all the bits of the result to be zero, except for the third bit. The third bit of the result will be a copy of the third bit of op1. Thus, if the result of the AND is zero, the third bit of op1 must have been zero, and if the result of the AND is a nonzero number, the third bit must have been a 1.

Program 12-2 uses this masking property to convert lowercase letters in a word into their uppercase form, assuming the letters are stored using the ASCII code. The algorithm for converting letters is based on the fact that the binary code for lowercase and uppercase letters in ASCII are the same except for bit six, which is a 1 for lowercase letters and 0 for uppercase letters. For example, the binary code for the letter a is 01100001 (hex 61), while the binary code for the letter A is 01000001 (hex 41). Similarly, the binary code for the letter z is 01111010 (hex 7A), while the binary code for the letter Z is 01011010 (hex 5A). (See Appendix B for the hexadecimal values of the upper and lowercase letters.) Thus, given a lowercase letter, it can be converted into its uppercase form by forcing the sixth bit to zero. This is accomplished in Program 12-2 by masking the letter's code with the binary value 11011111, which has the hexadecimal value DF.

 Program 12-2

```c
#include <stdio.h>
main()
{
  char word[81];       /* enough storage for a complete line */

  printf("Enter a string of both upper and lowercase letters:\n");
  gets(word);
  printf("\nThe string of letters just entered is:\n");
  puts(word);
  upper(word);
  printf("\nThis string, in uppercase letters, is:\n");
  puts(word);
}
upper(word)
char *word;
{
  while (*word != '\0')
    *word++ &= 0XDF;
}
```

A sample run using Program 12-2 follows:

```
Enter a string of both upper and lowercase letters:
abcdefgHIJKLMNMOPqrstuvwxyz

The string of letters just entered is:
abcdefgHIJKLMNOPqrstuvwxyz

This string, in uppercase letters, is:
ABCDEFGHIJKLMNOPQRSTUVWXYZ
```

Notice that the lowercase letters are converted to uppercase form, while uppercase letters are unaltered. This is because bit six of all uppercase letters is zero to begin with, so that forcing this bit to zero using the mask has no effect. Only when bit six is a 1, as it is for lowercase letters, is the input character altered.

12.2 The Inclusive OR Operator

The inclusive OR operator, |, performs a bit-by-bit comparison of its two operands in a similar fashion to the bit-by-bit AND. The result of the OR comparison, however, is determined by the following rule:

The result of the comparison is 1 if either bit being compared is a 1, otherwise the result is a 0.

Figure 12-2 illustrates an OR operation. As shown in the figure, when either of the two bits being compared is a 1, the result is a 1, otherwise the result is a 0. As with all bit operations, the result of each comparison is, of course, independent of any other comparison.

Program 12-3 illustrates an OR operation, using the octal values of the operands illustrated in Figure 12-2.

FIGURE 12–2 A Sample OR Operation

```
  1 0 1 1 0 0 1 1
| 1 1 0 1 0 1 0 1
  ───────────────
  1 1 1 1 0 1 1 1
```

Program 12-3

```
main()
{
   int op1 = 0325, op2 = 0263;

   printf("%o ORed with %o is %o", op1, op2, op1 | op2);
}
```

Program 12-3 produces the following output:

```
325 ORed with 263 is 367
```

The result of ORing the octal numbers 325 and 263 is the octal number 367. The binary equivalent of 367 is 1 1 1 1 0 1 1 1, which is the result of the OR operation illustrated in Figure 12-2.

Inclusive OR operations are extremely useful in forcing selected bits to take on a 1 value or for passing through other bit values unchanged. This is a direct result of the fact that ORing any bit (1 or 0) with a 1 forces the resulting bit to be a 1, while ORing any bit (1 or 0) with a 0 leaves the original bit unchanged. For example, assume that the variable op1 has the arbitrary bit pattern x x x x x x x x, where each x can be either 1 or 0, independent of any other x in the number. The result of ORing this binary number with the binary number 1 1 1 1 0 0 0 0 is:

$$
\begin{array}{ll}
\text{op1} = & \text{x x x x x x x x} \\
\text{op2} = & \text{1 1 1 1 0 0 0 0} \\
\hline
\text{Result} = & \text{1 1 1 1 x x x x}
\end{array}
$$

As can be seen from this example, the ones in op2 force the resulting bits to 1, while the zeros in op2 filter, or pass, the respective bits in op1 through with no change in their values. Thus, using an OR operation a similar masking operation can be produced as with an AND operation, except the masked bits are set to ones rather than cleared to zeros. Another way of looking at this is to say that ORing with a zero has the same effect as ANDing with a one.

Program 12-4 uses this masking property to convert uppercase letters in a word into their respective lowercase form, assuming the letters are stored using the ASCII code. The algorithm for converting letters is similar to that used in Program 12-2, and converts uppercase letters into their lowercase form by forcing the sixth bit in each letter to a one. This is accomplished in Program 12-4 by masking the letter's code with the binary value 00100000, which has the hexadecimal value 20.

Program 12-4

```
#include <stdio.h>
main()
{
  char word[81];       /* enough storage for a complete line */

  printf("Enter a string of both upper and lowercase letters:\n");
  gets(word);
  printf("\nThe string of letters just entered is:\n");
  puts(word);
  lower(word);
  printf("\nThis string, in lowercase letters, is:\n");
  puts(word);
}
lower(word)
char *word;
{
  while (*word != '\0')
    *word++ |= 0X20;
}
```

A sample run using Program 12-4 follows:

```
Enter a string of both upper and lowercase letters:
abcdefgHIJKLMNOPqrstuvwxyz

The string of letters just entered is:
abcdefgHIJKLMNOPqrstuvwxyz

This string, in lowercase letters, is:
abcdefghijklmnopqrstuvwxyz
```

Notice that the uppercase letters are converted to lowercase form, while lower-case letters are unaltered. This is because bit six of all lowercase letters is one to begin with, so that forcing this bit to one using the mask has no effect. Only when bit six is a zero, as it is for uppercase letters, is the input character altered.

12.3   The Exclusive OR Operator

The exclusive OR operator, ^, performs a bit-by-bit comparison of its two operands. The result of the comparison is determined by the following rule:

The result of the comparison is 1 if one and only one of the bits being compared is a 1, otherwise the result is 0.

Figure 12-3 illustrates an exclusive OR operation. As shown in the figure, when both bits being compared are the same value (both 1 or both 0), the result is a zero. Only when both bits have different values (one bit a 1 and the other a 0) is the result a 1. Again, each pair or bit comparison is independent of any other bit comparison.

An exclusive OR operation can be used to create the opposite value, or complement, of any individual bit in a variable. This is a direct result of the fact that exclusive ORing any bit (1 or 0) with a 1 forces the resulting bit to be of the opposite value of its original state, while exclusive ORing any bit (1 or 0) with a 0 leaves the original bit unchanged. For example, assume that the variable op1 has the arbitrary bit pattern x x x x x x x x, where each x can be either 1 or 0, independent of any other x in the number. Using the notation that $\bar{x}$ is the complement (opposite) value of x, the result of exclusive ORing this binary number with the binary number 0 1 0 1 0 1 0 1 is:

$$
\begin{array}{rl}
\text{op1 =} & \text{x x x x x x x x} \\
\text{op2 =} & \text{0 1 0 1 0 1 0 1} \\
\hline
\text{Result =} & \text{x } \bar{x} \text{ x } \bar{x} \text{ x } \bar{x} \text{ x } \bar{x}
\end{array}
$$

As can be seen from this example, the ones in op2 force the resulting bits to be the complement of their original bit values, while the zeros in op2 filter, or pass, the respective bits in op1 through with no change in their values.

Many encryption methods use the exclusive OR operation to code data. For example, the string Hello there world! initially used in Program 1-1 can be encrypted by exclusive ORing each character in the string with a mask value of 52. The choice of the mask value, which is referred to as the encryption key, is arbitrary, and any key value can be used.

Program 12-5 uses an encryption key of 52 to code a user-entered message.

FIGURE 12–3 A Sample Exclusive OR Operation

```
  1 0 1 1 0 0 1 1
^ 1 1 0 1 0 1 0 1
  ───────────────
  0 1 1 0 0 1 1 0
```

Program 12-5

```c
#include <stdio.h>
main()
{
  char message[81];        /* enough storage for a complete line */

  printf("Enter a sentence:\n");
  gets(message);
  printf("\nThe sentence just entered is:\n");
  puts(message);
  encrypt(message);
  printf("\nThe encrypted version of this sentence is:\n");
  puts(message);
}
encrypt(message)
char *message;
{
  while (*message != '\0')
    *message++ ^= 52;
}
```

Following is a sample run using Program 12-5.

```
Enter a sentence:
Hello there world!

The sentence just entered is:
Hello there world!

The encrypted version of this sentence is:
|QXX[@\QFQC[FXP
```

Decoding an encrypted message requires exclusive ORing the coded message using the original encryption key, which is left as a homework exercise.

12.4 The Complement Operator

The complement operator, ~, is a unary operator that changes each 1 bit in its operand to 0 and each 0 bit to 1. For example, if the variable op1 contains the binary number 11001010, ~op1 replaces this binary number with the number 00110101. The complement operator in conjunction with the AND operator can be used to force any bit in an operand to zero, independent of the actual number of bits used to store the number. For example, the statement

```
op1 = op1 & ~07;
```

or its shorter form,

```
op1 &= ~07;
```

both set the last three bits of op1 to zero, regardless of how op1 is stored within the computer. Either of these two statements can, of course, be replaced by ANDing the last three bits of op1 with zeros, if the number of bits used to store op1 is known. In a computer that uses 16 bits to store integers, the appropriate AND operation is

```
op1 = op1 & 0177770;
```

For a computer that uses 32 bits to store integers, the above AND sets the leftmost or higher order 16 bits to zero also, which is an unintended result. The correct statement for 32 bits is:

```
op1 = op1 & 037777777770;
```

Using the complement operator in this situation frees the programmer from having to determine the storage size of the operand and, more importantly, makes the program portable between machines using different integer storage sizes.

12.5 Different-Size Data Items

When the bit operators &, |, and ^ are used with operands of different sizes, the shorter operand is always increased in bit size to match the size of the larger operand. Figure 12-4 illustrates the extension of a 16-bit unsigned integer into a 32-bit number.

As the figure shows, the additional bits are added to the left of the original number and filled with zeros. This is the equivalent of adding leading zeros to the number, which has no effect on the number's value.

When extending signed numbers, the original leftmost bit is reproduced in the additional bits that are added to the number. As illustrated in Figure 12-5,

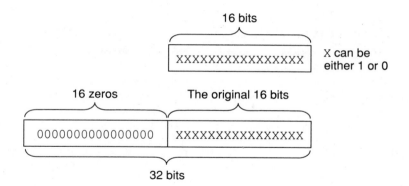

FIGURE 12–4 Extending 16-Bit Unsigned Data to 32 Bits

if the original leftmost bit is 0, corresponding to a positive number, 0 is placed in each of the additional bit positions. If the leftmost bit is 1, which corresponds to a negative number, 1 is placed in the additional bit positions. In either case, the resulting binary number has the same sign and magnitude of the original number.

FIGURE 12–5 Extending 16-Bit Signed Data to 32 Bits

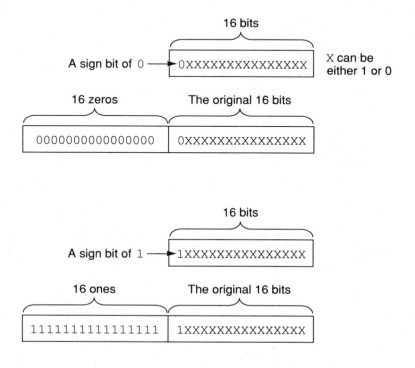

12.6 The Shift Operators

The left shift operator, <<, causes the bits in an operand to be shifted to the left by a given amount. For example, the statement

$$op1 = op1 << 4;$$

causes the bits in op1 to be shifted four bits to the left, filling any vacated bits with a zero. Figure 12-6 illustrates the effect of shifting the binary number 1111100010101011 to the left by four bit positions.

For unsigned integers, each left shift corresponds to multiplication by two. This is also true for signed numbers using two's complement representation, as long as the leftmost bit does not switch values. Since a change in the leftmost bit of a two's complement number represents a change in both the sign and magnitude represented by the bit, such a shift does not represent a simple multiplication by two.

The right shift operator, >>, causes the bits in an operand to be shifted to the right by a given amount. For example, the statement

$$op1 = op1 >> 3;$$

causes the bits in op1 to be shifted to the right by three bit positions. Figure 12-7a illustrates the right shift of the unsigned binary number 1111100010101011 by three bit positions. As illustrated, the three rightmost bits are shifted "off the end" and are lost.

For unsigned numbers, the leftmost bit is not used as a sign bit. For this type of number, the vacated leftmost bits are always filled with zeros. This is the case that is illustrated in Figure 12-7a.

For signed numbers, what is filled in the vacated bits depends on the computer. Most computers reproduce the original sign bit of the number.

FIGURE 12-6 An Example of a Left Shift

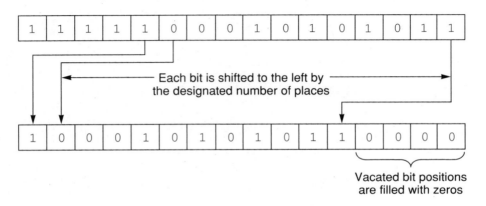

Each bit is shifted to the left by the designated number of places

Vacated bit positions are filled with zeros

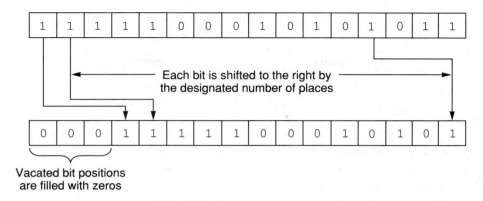

FIGURE 12-7a An Unsigned Arithmetic Right Shift

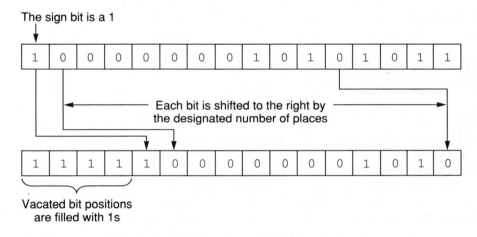

FIGURE 12-7b The Right Shift of a Negative Binary Number

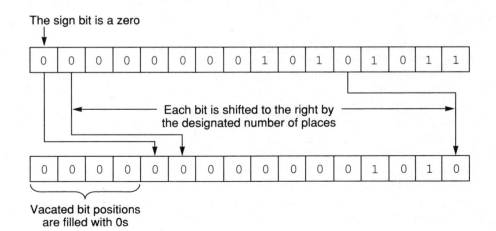

FIGURE 12-7c The Right Shift of a Positive Binary Number

Figure 12-7b illustrates the right shift of a negative binary number by four bit positions, where the sign bit is reproduced in the vacated bits. Figure 12-7c illustrates the equivalent right shift of a positive signed binary number.

The type of fill illustrated in Figures 12-7b and c, where the sign bit is reproduced in vacated bit positions, is called an *arithmetic right shift*. In an arithmetic right shift, each single shift to the right corresponds to a division by two.

Instead of reproducing the sign bit in right-shifted signed numbers, some computers automatically fill the vacated bits with zeros. This type of shift is called a *logical shift*. For positive signed numbers, where the leftmost bit is zero, both arithmetic and logical right shifts produce the same result. The results of these two shifts are only different when negative numbers are involved.

Exercises

1. Determine the results of the following operations:

a.	11001010	*b.*	11001010	*c.*	11001010
	& 10100101		| 10100101		^ 10100101

2. Write the octal representations of the binary numbers given in Exercise 1.

3. Determine the octal results of the following operations, assuming unsigned numbers:
  a. the octal number 0157 shifted left by one bit position
  b. the octal number 0701 shifted left by two bit positions
  c. the octal number 0673 shifted right by two bit positions
  d. the octal number 067 shifted right by three bit positions

4. Repeat Exercise 3 assuming that the numbers are treated as signed values.

5. a. Assume that the arbitrary bit pattern xxxxxxxx, where each x can represent either 1 or 0, is stored in the integer variable flag. Determine the octal value of a mask that can be ANDed with the bit pattern to reproduce the third and fourth bits of flag and set all other bits to zero. The rightmost bit in flag is considered bit 1.
  b. Determine the octal value of a mask that can be inclusively ORed with the bit pattern in flag to reproduce the third and fourth bits of flag and set all other bits to one. Again, consider the rightmost bit in flag to be bit 1.
  c. Determine the octal value of a mask that can be used to complement the values of the third and fourth bits of flag and leave all other bits unchanged. Determine the bit operation that should be used with the mask value to produce the desired result.

6. a. Write the two's complement form of the decimal number −1, using eight bits. (*Hint:* Refer to Section 2.8 for a review of two's complement numbers.)
  b. Repeat Exercise 6a using 16 bits to represent the decimal number −1 and compare your answer to your previous answer. Could the 16-bit version have been obtained by sign-extending the 8-bit version?

7. As was noted in the text, Program 12-2 has no effect on uppercase letters. Using the ASCII codes listed in Appendix B, determine what other characters would be unaffected by Program 12-2.

8. Modify Program 12-2 so that a complete sentence can be read in and converted to low-ercase values. (*Hint:* When a space is masked by Program 12-2, the resulting character is \0, which terminates the output.)

9. Modify Program 12-4 to allow a complete sentence to be input and converted to upper-case letters. Make sure that your program does not alter any other characters or symbols entered.

10. Modify Program 12-5 to permit the encryption key to be a user-entered input value.

11. Modify Program 12-5 to have its output written to a file named `coded.dat`.

12. Write a C program that reads the encrypted file produced by the program written for Exercise 10, decodes the file, and prints the decoded values on your system's standard output device.

13. Write a C program that displays the first eight bits of each character value input into a variable named `ch`. (*Hint:* Assuming each character is stored using eight bits, start by using the hexadecimal mask 80, which corresponds to the binary number `10000000`. If the result of the masking operation is a zero, display a zero; else display a one. Then shift the mask one place to the right to examine the next bit, and so on until all bits in the variable `ch` have been processed.)

14. Write a C program that reverses the bits in an integer variable named `okay` and stores the reversed bits in the variable named `rev_okay`. For example, if the bit pattern `11100101`, corresponding to the octal number 0345, is assigned to `okay`, the bit pattern `10100111`, corresponding to the octal number 0247, should be produced and stored in `rev_okay`.

12.7 Chapter Summary

1. Individual bits of character and integer variables and constants can be manipulated using C's bit operators. These are the AND, inclusive OR, exclusive OR, one's complement, left shift, and right shift operators.

2. The AND and inclusive OR operators are useful in creating masks. These masks can be used to pass or eliminate individual bits from the selected operand. The exclusive OR operator is useful in complementing an operand's bits.

3. When the AND and OR operators are used with operands of different sizes, the shorter operand is always increased in bit size to match the size of the larger operand.

4. The shift operators produce different results depending on whether the operand is a signed or an unsigned value.

Additional
Capabilities

Chapter Thirteen

Previous chapters have presented C's basic capabilities and structure. Variations on these capabilities, which are almost endless, are a source of delight to many programmers who continuously find new possibilities of expression using variations of the basic language building blocks. This chapter presents some of these additional capabilities.

13.1 Expressions Revisited

One of the most common pitfalls in C results from misunderstanding the full implications of an expression. Recall that an expression is any combination of operands and operators that yields a result. This definition is extremely broad and more encompassing than is initially apparent. For example, all of the following are valid C expressions:

```
a + 5
a = b
a == b
a = b = c = 6
flag = a == b
```

Assuming that the variables are suitably declared, each of the above expressions yields a result. Program 13-1 uses the `printf()` function to display the value of the first three expressions for specific initial values of the variables a and b.

 Program 13-1

```
main()
{
   int a = 7, b = 10;

   printf("\nThe value of the first expression is %d", a + 5);
   printf("\nThe value of the second expression is %d", a = b);
   printf("\nThe value of the third expression is %d", a == b );
}
```

The display produced by Program 13-1 is:

```
The value of the first expression is 12
The value of the second expression is 10
The value of the third expression is 1
```

As the output of Program 13-1 illustrates, each expression, by itself, has a value associated with it. The value of the first expression is the sum of the variable a plus 5, which is 12. The value of the second expression is 10, which is also assigned to the variable a. The value of the third expression is one, since a is now equal to b, and a true condition is represented in C with a value of one. If the values in a and b had not been the same, the relational expression a == b would be false and would have a value of 0.

In this section we will review the rules for evaluating expressions with multiple operators and "mixed" operands of different data types. We will also introduce a new expression type and C operator.

Expressions containing multiple operators are always evaluated by the priority, or precedence, of each operator. Table A-1 in Appendix A lists the relative priority of each C operator and its associativity.

Even when the order of evaluation is known, expressions with multiple operators can still produce unusual and undesired results, remaining a potential trap for the unwary. For example, consider the statement

```
flag = a == b;
```

Consulting Table A-1 we see that the == operator has a higher precedence than the = operator. Therefore, a is first compared to b. If a is equal to b, the result of the expression a == b is 1, otherwise it is 0. The value of this expression is then assigned to flag. Thus, the variable flag will have either a value of 1 or a value of 0 after the statement is executed. A problem arises if the expression is inadvertently typed as flag = a = b. Here, the value of b is first assigned to a, which is then assigned to flag. Because of the mistake of typing an equal operator instead of the comparison operator, flag is assigned the value of b, rather than the 1 or 0 that was intended.

The real problem with the statement flag = a == b; is that it has been used in place of the more obvious and complete statement

```
if (a == b)
    flag = 1;
else
    flag = 0;
```

Although the same error can be made in substituting an equal operator for the comparison operator in this statement, the error can be detected more easily than in the more obscure expression flag = a == b.

Because of the generality of C expressions and the fact that most sequences of operands connected by operators can be evaluated to produce a result (including an unintended one), it is extremely important to be careful in creating expressions. To avoid undesired results and to make program checking, testing, and debugging easier, keep expressions as simple and as uncomplicated as possible. Generally, expressions using arithmetic operators (+, −, *, /, %, etc.)

should not be mixed with expressions using relational and logical operators (==, <, >, &&, | |, etc.), which, in turn, should not be mixed with expressions using bit operators (&, |, etc.).

One further point must be mentioned. Although Table A-1 appears to be all-inclusive, it is not. In particular, the order of evaluations for operands is not specified, as it is not specified in most computer languages. For example, in the expression a + b it is not known which operand is accessed first. Generally this is not a problem because the order of operand access doesn't affect the result of the expression. However, in expressions such as

```
(val[i]) + (i++)
```

the order of access is important. Here the subscript may be either the old or the new value of i, depending on which operand is accessed first.

Similarly, the order of evaluation of function arguments is not specified in C. Thus, the function call

```
printf("%d %d", i, i++);
```

may result in the same number being printed twice if the second argument is evaluated before the first argument.

Expressions that depend on the order of operand access should always be avoided, because they can produce different results on different computers. Such expressions can always be replaced with temporary variables that explicitly define the desired evaluation order. For example, the statements

```
n = i++;
printf("%d %d", i, n);
```

clearly indicate the values that are passed to the printf() function.

Casts

We have already seen the forced conversion of an operand's data type in mixed binary arithmetic expressions. Such expressions consist of a binary arithmetic operator (+, −, *, /, or %) connecting two operands of different data types. For example, if val is a double precision variable and num is an integer variable, num's value is converted to double precision in the expression val + num.

The general rules for converting operands in mixed arithmetic expressions were presented in Chapter 2. A more complete set of conversion rules for arithmetic operators is listed in Table 13-1.

Forced conversions also take place across assignment operators. Here the value of the expression on the right side of the equal sign is converted to the data type of the variable to the left of the equal sign, which also becomes the value of the complete expression. For example, consider the evaluation of the expression

```
a = b * d - e % f
```

TABLE 13-1   Conversion Rules for Arithmetic Operators*

Rule 1. All character and short integer operands are always converted to integer values. All floating point operands are converted to double precision values.

Rule 2 If one operand is a double precision value, then the other operand is converted to a double precision value and the result of the expression is a double precision value.

Rule 3. If one operand is a long integer value, then the other operand is converted to a long integer value and the resulting value of the expression is a long integer value.

Rule 4. If one operand is an unsigned integer value, then the other operand is converted to an unsigned integer value and the resulting value of the expression is an unsigned value.

Rule 5. If both operands are of type int, no conversions occur and the resulting value of the expression is an integer value.

*These rules are applied in sequence.

where a and d are integer variables, e is a short integer variable, f is a long integer variable, and b is a floating point variable. According to the order of operator precedence, the * and % operators will be evaluated first, followed by the subtraction and assignment operators. Thus, the priority of evaluation is

$$a = ((b * d) - (e \% f))$$

Internally, the expression b * d consists of a floating point and integer operand. Referring to Rule 1 in Table 13-1, the value of b is converted to a double precision number. Since one of the operands is a double precision variable, Rule 2 provides that the second operand's value is converted to a double precision number and the resulting value of the expression b * d is a double precision number.

In the expression e % f, since f is a long integer variable, the value of e is converted to a long integer (Rule 3) and the value of the expression is itself a long integer value.

The subtraction of (e % f) from (b * d) forces the conversion of (e % f) to a double precision number. This occurs because the operand (b * d) is a double precision value. Finally, since the left side of the assignment operator is an integer value, the double precision value of the expression (b * d) – (e % f) is forced to become an integer value.

In addition to the forced conversions that are made automatically to operands in mixed arithmetic expressions, C also provides for user-specified type conversions. The operator used to force the conversion of a value to another type is the *cast operator*. This is a unary operator having the symbol (data type), where *data type* is the desired data type of the operand following the cast. For example, the expression

$$(int) (a * b)$$

assures that the value of the expression a * b is converted to an integer value. The parentheses around the expression (a * b) are required because the cast operator has a higher precedence than the multiplication operator.

As a last example, consider the expression (int) a * b, where both a and b are double precision variables. Here, only a's value is cast into an integer before multiplication by b. The cast into an integer value causes the fractional part of a's value to be truncated for the computation (a's stored value is unchanged). Since b is a double precision operand, the value of the operand (int) a is converted back to a double precision number (Rule 2 in Table 13-1). The forced conversion back to a double precision number, however, does not restore the fractional part of a.

Conditional Expressions

In addition to expressions formed with the arithmetic, relational, logical, and bit operators, C provides a *conditional expression*. A conditional expression uses the conditional operator, ?:, and provides an alternate way of expressing a simple if-else statement.

The general form of a conditional expression is:

```
expression1 ? expression2 : expression3
```

If the value of *expression1* is nonzero (true), *expression2* is evaluated, otherwise *expression3* is evaluated. The value for the complete conditional expression is the value of either *expression2* or *expression3*, depending on which expression was evaluated. As always, the value of the expression may be assigned to a variable.

Conditional expressions are most useful in replacing simple if-else statements. For example, the if-else statement

```
if ( hours > 40)
    rate =  .045;
else
    rate =  .02;
```

can be replaced with the one-line statement

```
rate = (hours > 40) ? .045 : .02;
```

Here, the complete conditional expression

```
(hours > 40) ? .045 : .02
```

is evaluated before any assignment is made to rate, because the conditional operator, ?:, has a higher precedence than the assignment operator. Within the conditional expression, the expression hours > 40 is evaluated first. If this expression has a nonzero value, which is equivalent to a logical true value, the value of the complete conditional expression is set to .045; otherwise the conditional expression has a value of .02. Finally, the value of the conditional expression, either .045 or .02, is assigned to the variable `rate`.

The conditional operator, `?:`, is unique in C in that it is a *ternary operator*. This means that the operator connects three operands. The first operand is always evaluated first. It is usually a conditional expression that uses the logical operators.

The next two operands are any other valid expressions, which can be single constants, variables, or more general expressions. The complete conditional expression consists of all three operands connected by the condition operator symbols, `?` and `:`.

Conditional expressions are only useful in replacing `if-else` statements when the expressions in the equivalent `if-else` statement are not long or complicated. For example, the statement

```
max_val = a > b ? a : b;
```

is a one-line statement that assigns the maximum value of the variables `a` and `b` to `max_val`. A longer, equivalent form of this statement is:

```
if (a > b)
    max_val = a;
else
    max_val = b;
```

Because of the length of the expressions involved, a conditional expression would not be useful in replacing the following `if-else` statement:

```
if (amount > 20000)
    taxes = .025 * (amount - 20000) + 400;
else
    taxes = .02 * amount;
```

Exercises 13.1

1. Evaluate the following expressions. Assume that all variables are integers and that a has a value of 2, b has a value of 3, c has a value of 4, and d has a value of 5 before each expression is evaluated.

a. b + 3

b. a = b + 3

c. a = b = c = d + 4 * a

d. flag = a = b

e. flag = a == b || c == d

f. d == a = b

g. a + b > 20

h. num = a + b > 20

i. a || b

j. num = a || b

2. Which of the expressions in Exercise 1 should not be included in a program? Why?

3. Rewrite the statement `a = b = c = amount * rate;` as a series of three individual assignment statements.

4. Rewrite the following statements as `if-else` statements:
   a. `flag = a >= b;`
   b. `flag = a == b || c == d;`

5. Rewrite the statements in Exercise 4 using conditional expressions.

6. Rewrite each of the following `if-else` statements using a conditional expression:

a. `if (a < b);`
   `min_val = a;`
   `else`
   `min_val = b;`

b. `if (num < 0)`
   `sign = -1;`
   `else`
   `sign = 1;`

c. `if (flag == 1)`
   `val = num;`
   `else`
   `val = num * num;`

d. `if (credit == plus)`
   `rate = prime;`
   `else`
   `rate = prime + delta;`

e. `if (!bond)`
   `cou = .075;`
   `else`
   `cou = 1.1;`

13.2   User-Specified Data Types

In this section we present two user-specified data types. The first permits a user to create new data types. Since the creation of a data type requires the programmer to specifically list or enumerate the values appropriate to the data type, these data types are referred to as enumerated data types. The second capability allows the programmer to create new names for existing data types.

Enumerated Data Types

An *enumerated data type* is a user-created data type in which the values appropriate to the data type are specified in a user-defined list. Such data types are identified by the reserved word `enum` followed by an optional, user-selected name for the data type and a listing of acceptable values for the data type. Consider the following user-specified data types:

```
enum flag {true, false};
enum time {am, pm};
enum day {mon, tue, wed, thr, fri, sat, sun};
enum color {red, green, yellow};
```

The first user-specified data type is the type `flag`. Any variable subsequently declared to be of this type can take on only a value of true or false. The second statement creates a data type named time. Any variable subsequently declared to be of type time can take on only a value of am or pm. Similarly, the third and fourth statements create the data types day and color, respectively, and list the valid values for variables of these two types. For example, the statement

```
enum color a,b,c;
```

declares the variables a, b, and c to be of type color, and is consistent with the declaration of variables using standard C data types such as char, int, float, or double. Once variables have been declared as enumerated types, they may be assigned values or compared to variables or values appropriate to their type. This again is consistent with standard variable operations. For example, for the variables a, b, and c declared above, the following statements are valid:

```
a = red;
b = a;
if (c == yellow) printf("\nThe color is yellow");
```

Internally, the acceptable values for each enumerated data type are ordered and assigned sequential integer values beginning with 0. For example, for the values of the user-defined type color, the correspondences created by the C compiler are that red is equivalent to 0, green is equivalent to 1, and yellow is equivalent to 2. The equivalent numbers are required when inputting values using scanf() or printing values using printf().

Program 13-2 illustrates a user-defined data type.

 Program 13-2

```
main()
{
  enum color {red,green,yellow};
  enum color crayon = red;   /* crayon is declared to be of type */
                             /* color and initialized to red     */
  printf("\nThe color is %d", crayon);
  printf("\nEnter in a value: ");
  scanf("%d", &crayon);
  if (crayon == red)
    printf("The crayon is red.");
  else if (crayon == green)
    printf("The crayon is green.");
  else if (crayon == yellow)
    printf("The crayon is yellow.");
  else
    printf("The color is not defined.");
}
```

A sample run of Program 13-2 produced the following output:

```
The color is 0
Enter a value: 2
The crayon is yellow.
```

As illustrated in Program 13-2, expressions containing variables declared as user-defined data types must be consistent with the values specifically listed for the type. Although a `switch` statement would be more appropriate in Program 13-2, the expressions in the `if-else` statement better highlight the use of enumerated values. Program 13-2 also shows that the initialization of a user-specified data type variable is identical to the initialization of standard data type variables. For input and output purposes, however, the equivalent integer value assigned by the C compiler to each enumerated value must be used in place of the actual data type value. This is also seen in the program.

In order to assign equivalent integers to each user-specified value, the C compiler retains the order of the values as they are listed in the enumeration. A side effect of this ordering is that expressions can be constructed using relational and logical operators. For example, for the data type `color` created in Program 13-2, expressions such as `crayon < yellow` and `red < green` are both valid.

The numerical value assigned by the compiler to enumerated values can be altered by direct assignment when a data type is created. For example, the definition

```
enum color (red, green = 7, yellow);
```

causes the compiler to associate the value `red` with the integer 0 and the value `green` with the integer 7. Altering the integer associated with the value `green` causes all subsequent integer assignments to be altered too; thus, the value `yellow` is associated with the integer 8. If any other values were listed after `yellow`, they would be associated with the integers 9, 10, 11, etc., unless another alteration was made.

Naming a user-defined data type is similar to naming a template for structures. Just as a template name can be omitted when defining a structure by declaring the structure directly, the same can be done with user-defined data types. For example, the declaration `enum {red, green, yellow} crayon;` defines `crayon` to be an enumerated variable with the valid values of `red`, `green`, and `yellow`.

Scope rules applicable to the standard C data types also apply to enumerated data types. For example, placing the statement `enum color {red, green, yellow};` before the `main()` function in Program 13-2 would make the data type named `color` global and available for any other function in the file.

Finally, since there is a one-to-one correspondence between integers and user-defined data types, the cast operator can either coerce integers into a user-specified data value or coerce a user-specified value into its equivalent integer.

Assuming that `val` is an integer variable with a value of 1, and `color` has been declared as in Program 13-2, the expression `(enum color) val` has a value of `green` and the expression `(int) yellow` has a value of 2. The compiler will not warn you, however, if a cast to a nonexistent value is attempted.

The `typedef` Statement

In addition to creating new data types, C allows both standard and user-defined data types to be renamed using `typedef` statements. The statement

```
typedef float REAL;
```

makes the name `REAL` a synonym for `float`. The name `REAL` can now be used in place of the term `float` anywhere in the program after the synonym has been declared. For example, the definition

```
REAL val;
```

is equivalent to the definition

```
float val;
```

The `typedef` statement does not create a new data type; it creates a new name for an existing data type. Using uppercase names in `typedef` statements is not mandatory. It is done simply to alert the programmer to a user-specified name, similar to uppercase names in `#define` statements. In fact, the equivalence produced by a `typedef` statement can frequently be produced equally well by a `#define` statement. The difference between the two, however, is that `typedef` statements are processed directly by the compiler while `#define` statements are processed by the preprocessor. Compiler processing of `typedef` statements allows for text replacements that are not possible with the preprocessor. For example, the statement

```
typedef float REAL;
```

actually specifies that `REAL` is a placeholder that will be replaced with another variable name. A subsequent declaration such as

```
REAL val;
```

has the effect of substituting the variable named `val` for the placeholder named `REAL` in the terms following the word `typedef`. Substituting `val` for `REAL` in the `typedef` statement and retaining all terms after the reserved word `typedef` results in the equivalent declaration `float val;`.

Once the mechanics of the replacement are understood, more useful equivalences can be constructed. Consider the statement

```
typedef int ARRAY[100];
```

Here the name ARRAY is actually a placeholder for any subsequently defined variables. Thus, a statement such as ARRAY first, second; is equivalent to the two definitions

```
int first[100];
int second[100];
```

Each of these definitions is obtained by replacing the name ARRAY with the variable names first and second in the terms following the reserved word typedef.

As another example, consider the following statement:

```
typedef struct
        {
            char name[20];
            int id_num;
        } EMP_REC;
```

Here EMP_REC is a convenient placeholder for any subsequent variable. For example, the declaration EMP_REC employee[75]; is equivalent to the declaration

```
struct
{
    char name[20];
    int id_num;
} employee[75];
```

This last declaration is obtained by directly substituting the term employee[75] in place of the word EMP_REC in the terms following the word typedef in the original typedef statement.

13.3 Defining Macros

In its simplest form, the #define preprocessor command is used to equate constants and operators to symbolic names. For example, the statement

```
#define SALESTAX .05
```

equates the symbolic name SALESTAX to the number .05. When SALESTAX is used in any subsequent statement or expression the equivalent value of .05 is substituted for the symbolic name. The substitutions are made by the C preprocessor just prior to program compilation.

C places no restrictions on the equivalences that can be established with the #define statement. The symbolic name following the #define designation can be equated to any text and can even include arguments. For example, all of the following are valid equivalences:

```
#define  PI       3.1416
#define  TIMES    *
#define  EQUALS   =
#define  FORMAT   "Answer is %f"
```

The use of these equivalence statements is illustrated in Program 13-3.

 Program 13-3

```
#define  PI       3.1416
#define  TIMES    *
#define  EQUALS   =
#define  FORMAT   "Answer is %f"
main()
{
  float circum, radius = 6.3;

  circum EQUALS 2.0 TIMES PI TIMES radius;
  printf(FORMAT,circum);
}
```

Before Program 13-3 is compiled, the preprocessor directly substitutes the equivalent operator, constant, variable, or text in place of each subsequent occurrence of the symbolic name.

In addition to using #define preprocessor commands for simple equivalences, as in Program 13-3, these statements can also be used to equate symbolic names to either partial or complete expressions. When the equivalent text consists of more than a single value, operator, or variable, the symbolic name is referred to as a *macro*, and the substitution of the text in place of the symbolic name is called a *macro expansion* or *macro substitution*. The word macro refers to the direct, in-line expansion of one word into many words. For example, the equivalence established by the statement

```
#define CONVERT   2.0 * 3.1416
```

enables us to write the statement

```
circum = CONVERT * radius;
```

When this statement is encountered by the preprocessor, the symbolic name CONVERT is replaced by the equivalent text 2.0 * 3.1416. The compiler always receives the expanded version after the text has been inserted in place of the symbolic name by the preprocessor. This direct substitution of the text for CONVERT occurs in every place that CONVERT is encountered after it has been defined. This allows a previously defined symbolic name to be used in subsequent symbolic definitions. For example, the definition for CONVERT could have been established using the following set of #define commands:

```
#define PI          3.1416
#define CONVERT   2.0 * PI
```

Since PI is made equivalent to the constant 3.1416 in the first #define command, it can be used legitimately in any following #define command.

In addition to using #define commands for straight text substitutions, these commands can also be used to define equivalences that use arguments. For example, in the preprocessor command

```
#define SQUARE(x)     x * x
```

x is an argument. Here, SQUARE(x) is a true macro that is expanded into the expression x * x, where x is itself replaced by the variable or constant used when the macro is utilized. For example, the statement

```
y = SQUARE(num);
```

is expanded into the statement

```
y = num * num;
```

The advantage of using a macro such as SQUARE(x) is that since the data type of the argument is not specified, the macro can be used with any data type argument. If num, for example, is an integer variable, the expression num * num produces an integer value. Similarly, if num is a double precision variable, the SQUARE(x) macro produces a double precision value. This is a direct result of the text substitution procedure used in expanding the macro and is an advantage of making SQUARE(x) a macro rather than a function.

Care must be taken when defining macros with arguments. For example, in the definition of SQUARE(x), there must be no space between the symbolic name SQUARE and the left parenthesis used to enclose the argument. There can, however, be spaces within the parentheses if more than one argument is used.

Additionally, since the expansion of a macro involves direct text substitution, unintended results may occur if you do not use macros carefully. For example, the assignment statement

```
val = SQUARE(num1 + num2);
```

does not assign the value of $(num1 + num2)^2$ to val. Rather, the expansion of SQUARE(num1 + num2) results in the equivalent statement

```
val = num1 + num2 * num1 + num2;
```

This statement results from the direct text substitution of the term `num1 + num2` for the argument `x` in the expression `x * x` that is produced by the preprocessor.

To avoid unintended results, always place parentheses around all macro arguments wherever they appear in the macro. For example, the macro

```
#define SQUARE(x)   ((x) * (x))
```

ensures that a correct result is produced whenever the macro is invoked. Now the statement

```
val = SQUARE(num1 + num2);
```

is expanded to produce the desired assignment

```
val = ((num1 + num2) * (num1 + num2));
```

Macros are extremely useful when the calculations or expressions they contain are relatively simple and can be kept to one or at most two lines. Larger macro definitions tend to become cumbersome and confusing and are better written as functions. If necessary, a macro definition can be continued on a new line by typing a backslash character, \, before the RETURN or ENTER key is pressed. The backslash acts as an escape character that causes the preprocessor to treat the RETURN literally and not include it in any subsequent text substitutions.

The advantage of using a macro instead of a function is an increase in execution speed. Since the macro is directly expanded and included in every expression or statement using it, there is no execution time loss due to the call and return procedures required by a function. The disadvantage is the increase in required program memory space when a macro is used repeatedly. Each time a macro is used the complete macro text is reproduced and stored as an integral part of the program. Thus, if the same macro is used in ten places, the final code includes ten copies of the expanded text version of the macro. A function, however, is stored in memory only once. No matter how many times the function is called, the same code is used. The memory space required for one copy of a function used extensively throughout a program can be considerably less than the memory required for storing multiple copies of the same code defined as a macro.

Exercises 13.3

1. a. Define a macro named `NEGATE(x)` that produces the negative of its argument.
  b. Include the `NEGATE(x)` macro defined in Exercise 1a in a complete C program and run the program to confirm proper operation of the macro for various cases.

2. *a.* Define a macro named ABS_VAL(x) that produces the absolute value of its argument.
   b. Include the ABS_VAL(x) macro defined in Exercise 2a in a complete C program and run the program to confirm proper operation of the macro for various cases.

3. *a.* Define a macro named CIRCUM(r) that determines the circumference of a circle of radius *r*. The circumference is determined from the relationship circumference = 2.0 * PI * radius, where PI equals 3.1416.
   b. Include the CIRCUM(r) macro defined in Exercise 3a in a complete C program and run the program to confirm proper operation of the macro for various cases.

4. *a.* Define a macro named MIN(x, y) that determines the minimum value of its two arguments.
   b. Include the MIN(x, y) macro defined in Exercise 4a in a complete C program and run the program to confirm proper operation of the macro for various cases.

5. *a.* Define a macro named MAX(x, y) that determines the maximum value of its two arguments.
   b. Include the MAX(x, y) macro defined in Exercise 5a in a complete C program and run the program to confirm proper operation of the macro for various cases.

13.4   Command Line Arguments

Arguments can be passed to any function in a program, including the main() function. In this section we describe the procedures for passing arguments to main() when a program is initially invoked and having main() correctly receive and store the arguments passed to it. Both the sending and receiving sides of the transaction must be considered. Fortunately, the interface for transmitting arguments to a main() function has been standardized in C, so both sending and receiving arguments can be done almost mechanically.

All the programs that have been run so far have been invoked by typing the name of the executable version of the program after the operating system prompt is displayed. The command line for these programs consists of a single word, which is the name of the program. For computers that use the UNIX® Operating System the prompt is usually the $ symbol and the executable name of the program is a.out. For these systems, the simple command line $a.out begins program execution of the last compiled source program currently residing in a.out.

If you are using a C compiler on an IBM PC, the equivalent operating system prompt is either A> or C>, and the name of the executable program is typically the same name as the source program with an .exe extension rather than a .c extension. Assuming that you are using an IBM PC with the A> operating system prompt, the complete command line for running an executable program named showad.exe is A> showad. As illustrated in Figure 13-1, this command line causes the showad program to begin execution with its main() function, but no arguments are passed to main().

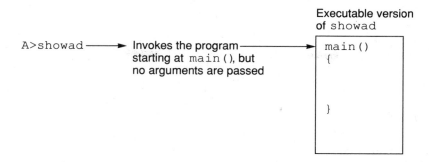

FIGURE 13-1 Invoking the showad Program

Now assume that we want to pass the three separate string arguments three blind mice directly into showad's main function. Sending arguments into a main() function is extremely easy. It is accomplished by including the arguments on the command line used to begin program execution. Because the arguments are typed on the command line, they are, naturally, called *command line arguments*. To pass the arguments three blind mice directly into the main() function of the showad program, we only need to add the desired words after the program name on the command line:

        A> showad three blind mice

Upon encountering the command line showad three blind mice, the operating system stores it as a sequence of four strings. Figure 13-2 illustrates the storage of this command line, assuming that each character uses one byte of storage. As shown in the figure, each string terminates with the standard C null character \0.

Sending command line arguments to main() is always this simple. The arguments are typed on the command line and the operating system nicely stores them as a sequence of separate strings. We must now handle the receiving side of the transaction and let main() know that arguments are being passed to it.

Arguments passed to main(), like all function arguments, must be declared as part of the function's definition. To standardize argument passing to a main() function, only two items are allowed: a number and an array. The number is an integer variable, which must be named argc (short for argument counter), and the array is a one-dimensional list, which must be named argv (short for argument values). Figure 13-3 illustrates these two arguments.

The integer passed to main() is the total number of items on the command line. In our example, the value of argc passed to main() is four, which includes

FIGURE 13-2 The Command Line Stored in Memory

| s | h | o | w | a | d | \0 | t | h | r | e | e | \0 | b | l | i | n | d | \0 | m | i | c | e | \0 |

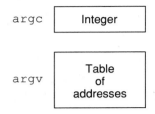

FIGURE 13–3 An Integer and an Array Are Passed to main()

the name of the program plus the three command line arguments. The one-dimensional list passed to main() is a list of pointers containing the starting storage address of each string typed on the command line, as illustrated in Figure 13-4.

We can now write the complete function definition for main() to receive arguments. Since an integer and an array are passed to main() and C requires that these two items be named argc and argv, respectively, the first line in main()'s definition must be main(argc,argv).

To complete main()'s definition, we must declare the data types of these two arguments. Because argc is an integer, its declaration is int argc;. Because argv is the name of an array whose elements are addresses that point to where the actual command line arguments are stored, its proper declaration is char *argv[];. This is nothing more than the declaration of an array of pointers. It is read "argv is an array whose elements are pointers to characters." Putting all this together, the full function header for a main() function that will receive command line arguments is:

```
main(argc,argv)        /* standard main() function */

int argc;              /* header for receiving      */
char *argv[];          /* command line arguments    */
```

FIGURE 13–4 Addresses Are Stored in the argv Array

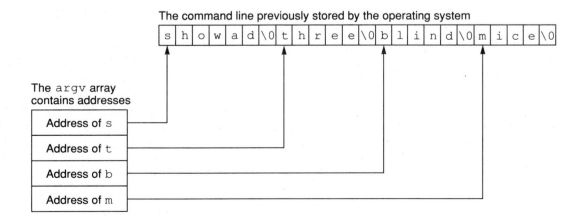

No matter how many arguments are typed on the command line, main() only needs the two standard pieces of information provided by argc and argv: the number of items on the command line and the list of starting addresses indicating where each argument is actually stored.

Program 13-4 verifies our description by printing the data actually passed to main(). The variable argv[i] used in Program 13-4 contains an address. The notation *argv[i] refers to "the character pointed to" by the address in argv[i].

 Program 13-4

```
#include <stdio.h>
main(argc,argv)
int argc;       /* number of items on the command line */
char *argv[];   /* an array of addresses */
{
  int i;

  printf("\nThe number of items on the command line is %d\n\n",argc);
  for (i = 0; i < argc; ++i)
  {
    printf("The address stored in argv[%d] is %u\n", i, argv[i]);
    printf("The character pointed to is %c\n\n", *argv[i]);
  }
}
```

Assuming that the executable version of Program 13-4 is named showad.exe, a sample output for the command line showad three blind mice is:

```
The number of items on the command line is 4

The address stored in argv[0] is 786435
The character pointed to is s

The address stored in argv[1] is 786442
The character pointed to is t

The address stored in argv[2] is 786448
The character pointed to is b

The address stored in argv[3] is 786454
The character pointed to is m
```

The addresses displayed by Program 13-4 clearly depend on the machine used to run the program. Figure 13-5 illustrates the storage of the command

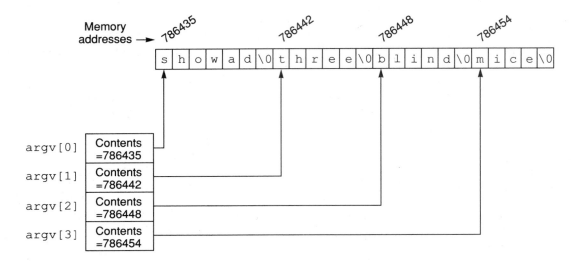

FIGURE 13-5 The Command Line Stored in Memory

line as displayed by the sample output. As anticipated, the addresses in the argv array "point" to the starting characters of each string typed on the command line.

Once command line arguments are passed to a C program, they can be used like any other C strings. Program 13-5 causes its command line arguments to be displayed from within main().

 Program 13-5

```
/* A program that displays command line arguments */
#include <stdio.h>
main(argc,argv)
int argc;        /* standard argument declarations         */
char *argv[];    /* for receiving command line arguments */
{
  int i;

  printf("\nThe following arguments were passed to main(): ");
  for (i = 1; i < argc; ++i)
    printf("%s ", argv[i]);
}
```

Assuming that the name of the executable version of Program 13-5 is a.out, the output of this program for the command line a.out three blind mice is:

The following arguments were passed to main(): three blind mice

Notice that when the addresses in `argv[]` are passed to the `printf()` function in Program 13-5, the strings pointed to by these addresses are displayed. When these same addresses were passed to the `printf()` function in Program 13-4, the actual values of the addresses were printed. The difference in displays is caused by the `printf()` function. When a `%s` control sequence is used in `printf()`, as it is in Program 13-5, it alerts the function that a string will be accessed. `printf()` then expects the address of the first character in the string; this is exactly what each element in `argv[]` supplies. Once `printf()` receives the address, the function performs the required indirection to locate the actual string that is displayed. The `%u` control sequence used in Program 13-4 treats its argument as an unsigned integer and thus displays the value in `argv[i]`. As we have noted before, the use of the `%u` control sequence to display addresses is actually incorrect. Pointers are not unsigned integers—they are a unique data type that may or may not require the same amount of storage as an integer. The use of the `%u` control sequence simply provides us with a convenient way of displaying an address, since no specific control sequence exists for the output of addresses. Converting a pointer using the `%u` control sequence may actually display a meaningless number. The display, however, has no impact on how addresses are used within the program; it simply provides us with a useful output representation.

One final comment about command line arguments is in order. Any argument typed on a command line is considered to be a string. If you want numerical data passed to `main()`, it is up to you to convert the passed string into its numerical counterpart. This is seldom an issue, however, since most command line arguments are used as flags to pass appropriate processing control signals to an invoked program.

Exercises 13.4

1. a. Write a program that accepts the name of a data file as a command line argument. Have your program open the data file and display its contents, line by line, on the CRT screen.

   b. Would the program written for Exercise 1a work correctly for a program file?

2. a. Modify the program written for Exercise 1a so that each line displayed is preceded by a line number.

   b. Modify the program written for Exercise 2a so that the command line argument -p will cause the program to list the contents of the file on the printer attached to your system.

3. Write a program that accepts a command line argument as the name of a data file. Given the name, your program should display the number of characters in the file. (*Hint:* Use the `fseek()` and `ftell()` library functions discussed in Section 12.3.)

4. Write a program that accepts two integer values as command line arguments. The program should multiply the two values entered and display the result. (*Hint:* The command line must be accepted as string data and converted to numerical values before multiplication.)

13.5 The goto Statement

The goto statement provides an unconditional transfer of control to some other statement in a program. The general form of a goto statement is

```
goto label;
```

where *label* is any unique name chosen according to the rules for creating variable names. The label name must appear, followed by a colon, in front of any other statement in the function that contains the goto statement. For example, the following section of code transfers control to the label named err if division by zero is attempted:

```
if (denom == 0.0)
   goto err;
else
   result = num / denom;
         .
         .
err: printf("Error - Attempted Division by Zero";
```

The astute reader will realize that in this case goto provides a cumbersome solution to the problem. It would require a second goto above the printf() statement to stop this statement from always being executed. Generally it is much easier either to call an error routine for unusual conditions or to use a break statement if this is necessary.

Theoretically, a goto statement is never required because C's normal structures provide sufficient flexibility to handle all possible flow control requirements. Also, gotos tend to complicate programs. For example, consider the following code:

```
if (a == 100)
   goto first;
else
   x = 20;
goto sec;
first: x = 50;
  sec: y = 10;
```

Written without a goto this code is:

```
if (a == 100)
   x = 50;
else
   x = 20;
y = 10;
```

Both sections of code produce the same result; however, the second version is clearly easier to read. It is worthwhile to convince yourself that the two sections of code do, in fact, produce the same result by running the code on your computer. This will let you experience the sense of frustration when working with goto-invaded code.

In C, the goto statement should be used in a limited manner, if at all. The presence of goto statements can rapidly make a program extremely difficult to understand and almost impossible to modify.

13.6 Chapter Summary

1. A cast can be used to explicitly change the data type of a value. The general form of a cast is

```
(desired data type) expression
```

The cast changes the value of the expression to the indicated data type. For example, (int) 2.6789 converts 2.6789 to the integer value of 2. When casts are used with variables, the data type of the variable and the variable's contents are not changed—only the value of the variable in the expression using the cast is altered.

2. A conditional expression provides an alternate way of expressing a simple if-else statement. The general form of a conditional expression is:

```
expression1 ? expression2 : expression3
```

The equivalent if-else statement for this is:

```
if (expression1)
   expression2;
else
   expression3;
```

3. An enumerated data type is a user-defined scalar data type. The user must select a name and list the acceptable values for the data type. For example, the enumeration

```
enum color {red, green, yellow}
```

creates a color data type. Any variable may be subsequently declared with this data type and may store one of the acceptable values listed.

4. A `typedef` statement creates synonyms for both standard and enumerated data types. For example, the statement

```
typedef int WHOLE_NUM;
```

makes `WHOLE_NUM` a synonym for `int`.

5. Using the `#define` command, complete expressions can be equated to symbolic names. These expressions can include arguments.

6. Arguments passed to `main()` are termed command line arguments. C provides a standard argument-passing procedure in which `main()` can accept any number of arguments passed to it. Each argument passed to `main()` is considered a string and is stored using a pointer array named `argv`. The total number of arguments on the command line is stored in an integer variable named `argc`.

7. C also provides a `goto` statement. In theory this statement need never be used. In practice it produces confusing and unstructured code, and should be used only in a very limited and controlled manner, if at all.

The ANSI
C Standard

Chapter Fourteen

Since its introduction in 1972, C has emerged as one of the most versatile and powerful computer languages developed. In 1983, in recognition of the importance and widespread academic and commercial acceptance of C, the American National Standards Institute (ANSI) began establishing a standard for the language, similar to standards that had been established for FORTRAN and COBOL. A standard is very important to the computing community because it provides the basis by which programs developed under one compiler for execution on one computer will be compatible and executable on other computers. As noted in the foreword to the 1989 draft of the ANSI C Standard, "The need for a single, clearly-defined standard had arisen in the C community due to a rapidly expanding use of the C programming language and the variety of differing translator implementations that had been and were being developed." The standard was adopted in 1990.

Although the de facto C programming language standard has been the definition of the language contained in *The C Programming Language* by Brian W. Kernighan and Dennis M. Ritchie (1978, Prentice Hall, Englewood Cliffs, NJ), various extensions had been incorporated into the language by different compiler manufacturers. The new ANSI standard's purpose is to present a clear, consistent standard for C that codifies the common exiting definition of C provided by Kernighan and Ritchie while including valuable enhancements that have become part of the various dialects of C in common use.[1] The C language that has been presented in this text has been based on the Kernighan and Ritchie definition, which is commonly referred to as traditional C. Since all aspects of traditional C presented in this text have been incorporated in the ANSI standard, all the C programs in the text will compile under the new standard.[2] Nevertheless, the ANSI standard defines several new features that extend traditional C, and has made an important extension to the definition and declaration of functions. These new features are described in this chapter's remaining sections.

14.1 New Names and Additional Features

The central philosophy of the ANSI Standards Committee in developing a new C standard was to codify common existing practice and establish a set of clear, unambiguous rules that included consideration of extensions made in various C implementations. Additionally, the committee sought to preserve C's tradi-

---

[1] A copy of the ANSI C Standard may be obtained from Global Engineering Documents, 2805 McGraw Avenue, Irvine, California, 92714 (800) 854-7179. The cost of the standard in July 1990 was $68.

[2] The one exception being that the header file `stdio.h`, which contains declarations for `printf()` and `scanf()`, should be included in all programs using these functions. Since both of these functions return an integer, which is the default return type, their declarations in traditional C are often omitted.

tional versatile and flexible nature, which is reflected in the statement that "C trusts the experienced programmer and provides the tools to get the job done." Following is a list of the major additions to traditional C made in the adopted standard:

1. The length of all symbolic names has been increased from 8 to 31 characters. Thus, under ANSI C the following are all valid symbolic names:

```
a1
experiment
finalgrade
name_length
s_p_r_e_a_d_o_u_t
one_long_variable_name
z2345678901234567890123456789012
```

As in traditional C, the distinction between upper and lowercase letters is retained in ANSI C. Thus, C remains a case sensitive language.

2. Three new keywords have been added to the list of keywords presented in Table 1-1 (see Chapter 1). The additional keywords are `const`, `signed`, and `volatile`. All of these keywords are type qualifiers.

3. Several new data types, including `signed char`, `unsigned char`, `unsigned short`, `unsigned long`, and `long double`, have been added to the language. Additionally, the existing data types `short`, `int`, and `long` have been given the new designations `signed short`, `signed int`, and `signed long`, respectively.

4. A new constant `'\a'`, which denotes activation of the bell, has been added.

5. The use of a header file, such as `stdio.h`, is required for each system function used in a program. (In traditional C header files are frequently optional as noted in the footnote to the previous page.)

6. The pound sign (#) used to define a preprocessor command need not be written in column one, as it is in traditional C.

7. Implementation of a new function header line that includes function arguments and their data types. (This feature, which constitutes the most important change from traditional C, is described in detail in the next section.)

8. Implementation of a new declaration for a called function, referred to as a *function prototype*, which includes the data types of all arguments expected by the called function. (This feature is also described in the next section.)

9. The addition of a `void` type (see Section 6.2).

10. The ability to initialize automatic arrays as well as static and extern arrays.

11. Binary files are included in the standard. File access to binary files is provided using the modes `rb` (read an existing binary file), `wb` (write to a new binary), and `ab` (append to a binary file). Also, in addition to traditional C's file access modes of `r`, `w`, and `a`, the file access modes `r+` (open existing

text file for reading and writing), w+ (open a new text file for reading and writing), a+ (open an existing or new text file for appending), r+b (open an existing binary file for reading and writing), w+b (open a new binary file for reading and writing), and a+b (open an existing or new binary file for appending) are included as part of the ANSI standard.

12. Structures are allowed as arguments to functions and may be returned by functions.

13. The ability to initialize automatic structures as well as static and extern structures has been added.

14. The return of a pointer to a void type in all dynamic memory allocation functions, such as malloc(), rather than a pointer to a char data type has been defined. The returned pointer must be cast into the desired pointer type to reflect the actual data type being accessed.

14.2   Function Definitions and Declarations

The most important change made to traditional C in the ANSI standard is the way functions are defined and declared. Formally, the definition of a function, in both traditional and ANSI C, begins with the first line of the function's header and ends with the last line of the function's body. Each function is defined once (that is, written once) in a program and can be called by any function within the program that suitably declares it.

In ANSI C, a function header consists of a single line that contains the function's name, its argument names and data types, and optionally the function's returned value type. If the latter is omitted, the function, by default, is defined to return an integer value. For example, the function header

```
float find_max(float x, float y)
```

declares the returned data type and name of the function as well as declaring the data types and names of all arguments.[3] The portion of the function header that contains the function name and arguments is formally referred to as a *function declarator*. It should also be noted that in the ANSI C Standard the term *parameter* is used instead of the terms argument or formal argument for the list of names included within a function declarator. The term *argument* is retained in ANSI C to refer to the list of names or values used in a function call; that is, the actual arguments.

---

[3] In traditional C this single function header would be written using the two lines:

```
float find_max(x,y)
float x, y;
```

All parameters listed in the function declarator must be separated by commas and must have their individual data types specified separately. If a data type is omitted, the parameter, by default, is of type integer. Thus, the declarator `find_max(float x, y)` *does not* declare both parameters x and y to be of type `float`; rather, it declares the parameter x to be of type `float` and the parameter y to be of type `int`. Similarly, omitting the data type of the function immediately preceding the function's declarator, by default, defines the function's return value to be of type `integer`. Thus both function headers

`int max_it(float x, float y)`

and

`max_it(float x, float y)`

declare that the function `max_it()` returns an integer value.

Within a function header the keyword `void` is used to declare that either the function returns no value or has no parameters. For example, the function header

`void display(int x, double y)`

declares that the function `display()` returns no value, while the function header

`double print_message(void)`

declares that the function `print_message()` has no parameters but returns a value of type `double`. As always, a function header line is never terminated with a semicolon. Using the new function header line a complete C function has the form:[4]

```
return-type function-name(parameter list)
{
  declarations;
  statements;
}
```

As in traditional C, functions can never be nested. A calling function must, as in traditional C, be alerted to the data type of the value being returned. Additionally, in ANSI C, a calling function must be alerted to the data types of the parameters required by the called function. In ANSI C, this information is contained in declarations referred to as function prototypes. A *function prototype* is a declaration of a function that includes parameter types; the function

---

[4] Additionally, a storage class of either static or extern may be specified. The default storage class is extern, as in traditional C.

prototype must agree with the returned data type and parameter types contained in the function's header line. For example, consider Program 14-1.

 Program 14-1

```
#include <stdio.h>
main ( )
{
 void find_max(int, int);        /* this is a function prototype   */
 int firstnum, secnum;

  printf("Enter a number: ");
  scanf("%d", &firstnum);
  printf("Great! Please enter a second number: ");
  scanf("%d", &secnum);

  find_max(firstnum, secnum);         /* call the function */
}

/* following is the function find_max */

void find_max(int x, int y)        /* function header      */
{                                  /* start of function body    */
  int max;                         /* variable declaration       */

  if (x >= y)                      /* find the maximum number */
     max = x;
  else
     max = y;

  printf("\nThe maximum of the two numbers is %d.", max);
}                /* end of function body and function definition */
```

In Program 14-1 the declaration statement, which is formally referred to as a function prototype, contained within main,

```
void find_max(int, int);
```

declares both the return type and the data types of the parameters that must be transmitted to the function find_max(). It should be noted that if this function prototype were placed above the function header line for main(), it would become a global function prototype. Also notice that the file header stdio.h, which contains the function prototypes for the printf() and scanf() functions called in main() has been included as a global header in the program. The general form of the function prototype used in Program 14-1 is:

```
data-type function-name(list of parameter data types);
```

The use of function prototypes permits error checking of parameter types by the compiler. Thus, the compiler will produce an error message (typically, TYPE MISMATCH) if the function prototype does not agree with the return and parameter data types contained in the function's header line. The prototype also serves another task; it ensures conversion of all actual arguments into the expected data type when the function is called. Thus, for example, if the function call

```
find_max(25, 78.795);
```

were made within main(), the 78.795 would be converted to the integer value 78 before transmittal to find_max(). Similarly, if the function call

```
find_max(n, p);
```

is made, where n is an integer argument and p a floating point argument, a truncated value of p would be received by find_max() (the value stored in p, within main(), is not altered). In traditional C, where function prototypes are not used, this cast into the required argument types is not made and no argument checking is provided.

In addition to providing the data types of all arguments, the function prototype may optionally contain parameter names. For example, the function prototype

```
void find_max(int q, int p);
```

includes the names of two parameters. Since the scope of the parameter names contained within a function prototype extends only to the closing parentheses of the prototype, these names present no constraint on the names of either actual arguments when the function is called or parameter names used when the function is defined.

Exercises 14.1

1. For the following function headers, determine the number, type, and order (sequence) of values that should be passed to the function when it is called and the data type of the value returned by the function. Additionally, write a function prototype for each function:

a. `int factorial(int n)`

b. `double price(int type, double yield, double maturity)`

c. `double yield(int type, double price, maturity)`

d. `char interest(char flag, float price, float time)`

e. `total(amount, rate)`

f. `float roi(int a, int b, char c, char d, float e, float f)`

g. `void get_val(int item, int iter, char decflag)`

2. Write function headers for the following:

a. A function named `check()`, which has three arguments. The first argument should accept an integer number, the second argument a floating point number, and the third argument a double-precision number. The function returns no value.

b. A function named `find_abs()` that accepts a double-precision number passed to it and displays its absolute value.

c. A function named `mult()` that accepts two floating point numbers as arguments, multiplies these two numbers, and returns the result.

d. A function named `sqr_it()` that computes and returns the square of the integer value passed to it. Use a function prototype and a single line header for the function's definition.

e. A function named `powfun()` that raises an integer number passed to it to a positive integer power and returns the result.

f. A function that produces a table of the numbers from 1 to 10, their squares, and cubes. No arguments are to be passed to the function and the function returns no value.

3. Modify Program 6-4 to use both a function prototype and a function declarator for the function `tempvert()` that are in conformance with the ANSI C Standard.

4. *a.* Write a function named `find_abs()`, with a single function header line, that accepts a double-precision number passed to it, computes its absolute value, and returns the absolute value to the calling function.

b. Include the function written in Exercise 4a in a working program. Make sure your function is called from `main()` and correctly returns a value to `main()`. Have `main()` use a function prototype to declare the `find_abs()` function and use `printf()` to display the value returned. Test the function by passing various data to it.

5. *a.* Write a function called `mult()` that accepts two double-precision numbers as parameters, multiplies these two numbers, and returns the result to the calling function.

b. Include the function written in Exercise 5a in a working program. Make sure your function is called from `main()` and correctly returns a value to `main()`. Have `main()` use a function prototype to declare the `mult()` function and use `printf()` to display the value returned. Test the function by passing various data to it.

6. *a.* Write a function named `powfun()` that raises an integer number passed to it to a positive integer power and returns the result to the calling function. Declare the variable used to return the result as a long integer data type to ensure sufficient storage for the result.

b. Include the function written in Exercise 6a in a working program. Make sure your function is called from `main()` and correctly returns a value to `main()`. Have `main()` use a function prototype to declare the `powfun()` function and use `printf()` to display the value returned. Test the function by passing various data to it.

7. *a.* A second-degree polynomial in x is given by the expression $ax^2 + bx + c$, where a, b, and c are known numbers and a is not equal to zero. Write a function named `poly_two(a,b,c,x)` that computes and returns the value of a second-degree polynomial for any passed values of a, b, c, and x.

b. Include the function written in Exercise 7a in a working program. Make sure your function is called from `main()` and correctly returns a value to `main()`. Have `main()` use a function prototype to declare the `poly_two()` function and use `printf()` to display the value returned. Test the function by passing various data to it.

14.3   Chapter Summary

The ANSI C Standard codified the majority of C features described in the original Kernighan and Ritchie definition of the language and standardized a number of enhancements that have proven to be of value since the language was introduced in 1972. The most significant changes, from an introductory viewpoint, have been:

1. The length of all symbolic names has been increased from 8 to 31 characters.
2. The addition of several new data types including `signed char`, `unsigned char`, `unsigned short`, `unsigned long`, and `long double`. Additionally, the existing data types `short`, `int`, and `long` have been given the new designations `signed short`, `signed int`, and `signed long`, respectively.
3. The addition of a new `void` function type.
4. A new function definition form. In ANSI C a function definition has the form:

```
storage-class return-type function-declarator
{
  declarations;
  statements;
}
```

The first line of a function definition is called the *function header*. The storage class of the function specified in the header is optional and can be either `static` or `extern`. If no storage class is specified it defaults to `extern`. The returned data type is, by default, an integer when no returned data type is specified. The function declarator must be included for each function and is of the form:

```
function-name(parameter list)
```

The parameter list must include the names of all parameters, which were formerly referred to as formal arguments, and their data types.

5. A new means of declaring a function called a *function prototype* has been specified. The prototype provides a declaration for a function that specifies the data type returned by the function, its name, and the data types of the

parameters expected by the function. As with all declarations, a function prototype is terminated with a semicolon and may be included within local variable declarations, or as a global declaration. The most common form of a function prototype is:

```
data-type function-name(list of parameter data types);
```

Appendixes

Appendix A   Operator Precedence Table

Table A-1 presents the symbols, precedence, descriptions, and associativity of C's operators. Operators toward the top of the table have a higher precedence than those toward the bottom. Operators within each box have the same precedence and associativity.

TABLE A-1   Summary of C Operators

Operator	Description	Associativity
() [ ] -> .	Function call Array element Structure member pointer reference Structure member reference	Left to right
++ -- - ! ~ (type) sizeof & *	Increment Decrement Unary minus Logical negation One's complement Type conversion (cast) Storage size Address of Indirection	Right to left
* / %	Multiplication Division Modulus (remainder)	Left to right
+ -	Addition Subtraction	Left to right
<< >>	Left shift Right shift	Left to right
< <= > >=	Less than Less than or equal to Greater than Greater than or equal to	Left to right
== !=	Equal to Not equal to	Left to right
&	Bitwise AND	Left to right
^	Bitwise exclusive OR	Left to right
|	Bitwise inclusive OR	Left to right
&&	Logical AND	Left to right
||	Logical OR	Left to right
?:	Conditional expression	Right to left
= += -= *= /= %= &= ^= |= <<= >>=	Assignment Assignment Assignment Assignment Assignment	Right to left
	Comma	Left to right

Appendix B   ASCII Character Codes

Key(s)	Dec	Oct	Hex	Key	Dec	Oct	Hex	Key	Dec	Oct	Hex
Ctrl 1	0	0	0	+	43	53	2B	V	86	126	56
Ctrl A	1	1	1	,	44	54	2C	W	87	127	57
Ctrl B	2	2	2	-	45	55	2D	X	88	130	58
Ctrl C	3	3	3	.	46	56	2E	Y	89	131	59
Ctrl D	4	4	4	/	47	57	2F	Z	90	132	5A
Ctrl E	5	5	5	0	48	60	30	[	91	133	5B
Ctrl F	6	6	6	1	49	61	31	\	92	134	5C
Ctrl G	7	7	7	2	50	62	32	]	93	135	5D
Ctrl H	8	10	8	3	51	63	33	^	94	136	5E
Ctrl I	9	11	9	4	52	64	34	_	95	137	5F
\n	10	12	A	5	53	65	35	`	96	140	60
Ctrl K	11	13	B	6	54	66	36	a	97	141	61
Ctrl L	12	14	C	7	55	67	37	b	98	142	62
RETURN	13	15	D	8	56	70	38	c	99	143	63
Ctrl N	14	16	E	9	57	71	39	d	100	144	64
Ctrl O	15	17	F	:	58	72	3A	e	101	145	65
Ctrl P	16	20	10	;	59	73	3B	f	102	146	66
Ctrl Q	17	21	11	<	60	74	3C	g	103	147	67
Ctrl R	18	22	12	=	61	75	3D	h	104	150	68
Ctrl S	19	23	13	>	62	76	3E	i	105	151	69
Ctrl T	20	24	14	?	63	77	3F	j	106	152	6A
Ctrl U	21	25	15	@	64	100	40	k	107	153	6B
Ctrl V	22	26	16	A	65	101	41	l	108	154	6C
Ctrl W	23	27	17	B	66	102	42	m	109	155	6D
Ctrl X	24	30	18	C	67	103	43	n	110	156	6E
Ctrl Y	25	31	19	D	68	104	44	o	111	157	6F
Ctrl Z	26	32	1A	E	69	105	45	p	112	160	70
Esc	27	33	1B	F	70	106	46	q	113	161	71
Ctrl <	28	34	1C	G	71	107	47	r	114	162	72
Ctrl /	29	35	1D	H	72	110	48	s	115	163	73
Ctrl =	30	36	1E	I	73	111	49	t	116	164	74
Ctrl -	31	37	1F	J	74	112	4A	u	117	165	75
Space	32	40	20	K	75	113	4B	v	118	166	76
!	33	41	21	L	76	114	4C	w	119	167	77
"	34	42	22	M	77	115	4D	x	120	170	78
#	35	43	23	N	78	116	4E	y	121	171	79
$	36	44	24	O	79	117	4F	z	122	172	7A
%	37	45	25	P	80	120	50	{	123	173	7B
&	38	46	26	Q	81	121	51	|	124	174	7C
'	39	47	27	R	82	122	52	}	125	175	7D
(	40	50	28	S	83	123	53	~	126	176	7E
)	41	51	29	T	84	124	54	del	127	177	7F
*	42	52	2A	U	85	125	55				

Appendix C   Input, Output, and Standard Error Redirection

The display produced by the printf() function is normally sent to the terminal where you are working. This terminal is called the standard output device because it is where the display is automatically directed, in a standard fashion, by the interface between your C program and your computer's operating system.

On most systems it is possible to redirect the output produced by printf() to some other device, or to a file, using the output redirection symbol, >, at the time the program is invoked. In addition to the symbol, you must specify where you want the displayed results to be sent.

For purposes of illustration, assume that the command to execute a compiled program named salestax, without redirection, is

```
salestax
```

This command is entered after your computer's system prompt is displayed on your terminal. When the salestax program is run, any printf() function calls within it automatically cause the appropriate display to be sent to your terminal. Suppose we would like to have the display produced by the program sent to a file named results. To do this requires the command

```
salestax > results
```

The redirection symbol, >, tells the operating system to send any display produced by printf() directly to a file named results rather than to the standard output device used by the system. The display sent to results can then be examined by using either an editor program or issuing another operating system command. For example, under the UNIX® Operating System the command

```
cat results
```

causes the contents of the file results to be displayed on your terminal. The equivalent command under the IBM PC disk operating system (DOS) is

```
type results
```

In redirecting an output display to a file, the following rules apply:

1. If the file does not exist, it will be created.
2. If the file exists, it will be overwritten with the new display.

In addition to the output redirection symbol, the output append symbol, >>, can also be used. The append symbol is used in the same manner as the redirection symbol, but causes any new output to be added to the end of a file. For example, the command

```
salestax >> results
```

causes any output produced by `salestax` to be added to the end of the `results` file. If the `results` file does not exist, it will be created.

Besides having the display produced by `printf()` redirected to a file, using either the > or >> symbols, the display can also be sent to a physical device connected to your computer, such as a printer. You must, however, know the name used by your computer for accessing the desired device. For example, on an IBM PC or compatible computer, the name of the printer connected to the terminal is designated as `prn`. Thus, if you are working on an IBM or compatible machine, the command

```
salestax > prn
```

causes the display produced in the salestax program to be sent directly to the printer connected to the terminal. In addition to `printf()`, output redirection also affects the placement of displays produced by the `puts()` and `putchar()` functions, and any other function that uses the standard output device for display.

Corresponding to output redirection, it is also possible to redesignate the standard input device for an individual program run using the input redirection symbol, <. Again, the new source for input must be specified immediately after the input redirection symbol.

Input redirection works in a similar fashion to output redirection but affects the source of input for the `scanf()`, `gets()`, and `getchar()` functions. For example, the command

```
salestax < dat_in
```

causes any input functions within `salestax` that normally receive their input from the keyboard to receive it from the `dat_in` file instead. This input redirection, like its output counterpart, is only in effect for the current execution of the program. As you might expect, the same run can have both an input and output redirection. For example, the command

```
salestax < dat_in > results
```

causes an input redirection from the file `dat_in` and an output redirection to the file `results`.

In addition to standard input and output redirection, the device to which all error messages are sent can also be redirected. On many systems this file is given an operating system designation as device file 2. Thus, the redirection

```
2> err
```

causes any error messages that would normally be displayed on the standard error device, which is usually your terminal, to be redirected to a file named err. As with standard input and output redirection, standard error redirection can be included on the same command line used to invoke a program. For example, the command

```
salestax < dat_in > show 2> err
```

causes the compiled program named salestax to receive its standard input from a file named dat_in, write its results to a file named show, and send any error messages to a file named err.

As the redirection of input, output, and error messages is generally a feature of the operating system used by your computer and not typically part of your C compiler, you must check the manuals for your particular operating system to ensure these features are available.

Appendix D   Program Life Cycle

Just as people and products have a life cycle, so do programs. A program's life cycle is divided into three main stages as illustrated in Figure D-1. These stages consist of program development, program documentation, and program maintenance.

The development stage is where a program is initially developed. At this stage, requirements must be understood and the structure of the program planned using the top-down development procedure presented in Section 1.5. The documentation stage, as its name implies, consists of creating, both within the program and in separate documents, sufficient user and programmer support references and explanations. At the maintenance stage the program is modified or enhanced as new demands and requirements are obtained or program errors are detected.

The writing of a program in a computer language is formally called coding (informally, of course, it is called programming). And that, after all, is what we have been doing—writing programs in a language, or code, that can be decoded and used by the computer. As we saw in Section 1.5, the coding of a program is but one component in the program's development stage. The total development effort is composed of four distinct phases, as illustrated in Figure D-2.

FIGURE D–1 A Program's Life Cycle

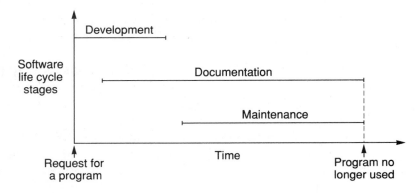

FIGURE D–2 The Phases of Program Development

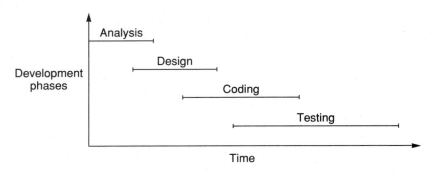

451

Listed below are both the steps in the top-down development procedure corresponding to each development phase and the relative amount of effort that is typically expended on each phase in large engineering and scientific programming projects. As can be seen from this listing, coding is not the major element in overall program development.

Phase	Top-Down Development Step	Effort
Analysis	Steps 1 and 2	10%
Design	Step 3	20%
Coding	Step 4	20%
Testing	Step 5	50%

Many new programmers have trouble because they spend the majority of their time coding the program, without spending sufficient time understanding and designing the program. In this regard, it is worthwhile to remember the programming proverb, "It is impossible to write a successful program for a problem or application that is not fully understood."

It is for this reason that the analysis phase is one of the most important, because if the requirements are not fully and completely understood before programming begins, the results are almost always disastrous. Once a program structure is created and the program is written, new or reinterpreted requirements often cause havoc. An analogy with house construction is useful to illustrate this point.

Imagine designing and building a house without fully understanding the architect's specifications. After the house is completed, the architect tells you that a bathroom is required on the first floor, where you have built a wall between the kitchen and the dining room. In addition, that particular wall is one of the main support walls for the house and contains numerous pipes and electrical cables. In this case, adding one bathroom requires a rather major modification to the basic structure of the house.

Experienced programmers understand the importance of analyzing and understanding a program's requirements before coding, if for no other reason than that they too have constructed programs that later had to be entirely dismantled and redone. The following exercise should give you a sense of this experience.

Figure D-3 illustrates the outlines of six individual shapes from a classic children's puzzle. Assume that as one or more shapes are given, starting with shapes A and B, an easy-to-describe figure must be constructed.

FIGURE D-3 Six Individual Shapes

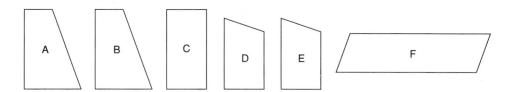

Typically, shapes A and B are initially arranged to obtain a square, as illustrated in Figure D-4. Next, when shape C is considered, it is usually combined with the existing square to form a rectangle, as illustrated in Figure D-5. Then when pieces D and E are added, they are usually arranged to form another rectangle, which is placed alongside the existing rectangle to form a square, as shown in Figure D-6.

The process of adding new pieces onto the existing structure is identical to constructing a program and then adding to it as each subsequent requirement is understood. The problem arises when the program is almost finished and a requirement is added that does not fit easily into the established pattern. For example, assume that the last shape (shape F) is now to be added. This last piece does not fit into the existing pattern that has been constructed. In order to include this piece with the others, the pattern must be completely dismantled and restructured.

Unfortunately, many programmers structure their programs in the same manner used to construct Figure D-6. Rather than taking the time to understand the complete set of requirements, new programmers frequently start coding based on the understanding of only a small subset of the total requirements. Then, when a subsequent requirement does not fit the existing program structure, the programmer is forced to dismantle and restructure either parts or all of the program.

Now, let's approach the problem of creating a figure from another view. If we started by arranging the first set of pieces as a parallelogram, all the pieces could be included in the final figure, as illustrated in Figure D-7.

FIGURE D–4 Typical First Figure

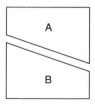

FIGURE D–5 Typical Second Figure

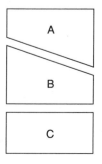

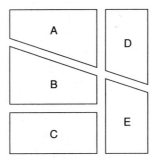

FIGURE D–6 Typical Third Figure

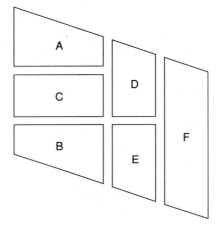

FIGURE D–7 Including All the Pieces

It is worthwhile observing that the piece that caused us to dismantle the first figure (Figure D-6) actually sets the pattern for the final figure illustrated in Figure D-7. This is often the case with programming requirements. The requirement that seems to be the least clear is frequently the one that determines the main interrelationships of the program. Thus, it is essential to include and understand all the known requirements before coding is begun. In practical terms, this means doing the analysis and design before any coding is attempted.

Appendix E   Program Entry, Compilation, and Execution under the DOS, UNIX, VAX-VMS, and PRIME Operating Systems

In this appendix, we first examine the steps to take to enter, compile, and execute a C program. The specific instructions required by the DOS, UNIX, VAX-VMS, and PRIME operating systems are then provided.

General Introduction

As illustrated in Figure E-1, a computer can be thought of as a self-contained world that is entered by a special set of steps called a login procedure. For some computers such as IBM, Apple, and other desk-top computers, the login procedure is usually as simple as turning the computer's power switch on. Larger multiuser systems, such as DEC, VAX, and PRIME computers, typically require a login procedure consisting of turning a terminal on and supplying an account number and password.

FIGURE E–1   Viewing a Computer as a Self-Contained World

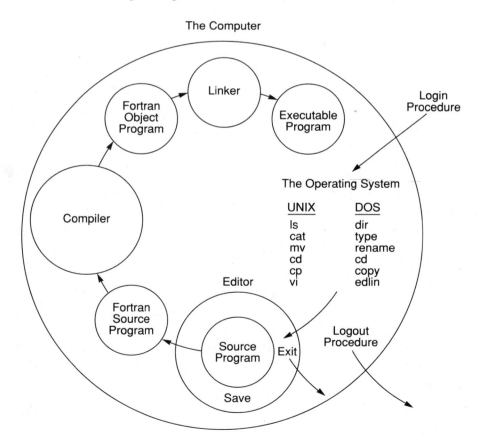

Once you have successfully logged in to your computer system, you are automatically placed under the control of .a computer program called the operating system (unless the computer is programmed to switch into a specific application program). The operating system is the program that controls the computer. It is used to access the services provided by the computer, which include the programs needed to enter, compile, and execute a C program.

Communicating with the operating system is always accomplished using a specific set of commands that the operating system recognizes. Although each computer system (IBM, Apple, DEC, PRIME, etc.) has its own set of operating system commands, all operating systems provide commands that allow you to log in to the system, exit from the system, create your own programs, and to quickly list, delete, copy, or rename your programs.

The specific operating system commands and any additional steps used for exiting from a computer, such as turning the power off, are collectively referred to as the logout procedure. Make sure you know the logout procedure for your computer at the time you log in to ensure that you can effectively "escape" when you are ready to leave the system. Since the login and logout procedures for each computer are system dependent, determine these procedures for the system you will be using and list them below:

Login Procedure:_____

_____

Logout Procedure:_____

_____

Specific Operating Systems

Each operating system provides a basic set of commands that allow you to list the names of the programs in the system, type the contents of a program, copy programs, rename programs, and delete programs. Table E-1 lists the operating system commands provided by the IBM DOS, UNIX, VAX-VMS, and PRIME operating systems to perform these and other functions. Space has also been left in the table to list the specific operating system command names used by your system to perform these tasks.

The commands listed in Table E-1 to list, copy, delete, or rename programs are all concerned with manipulating existing programs. Let us now turn our attention to creating, compiling, and executing a new C program. The procedures for doing these tasks are illustrated in Figure E-2. As shown in this figure, the procedure for creating an executable C program consists of three distinct operations: editing (creating or modifying the source code), compiling, and linking. Although every operating system provides an editor program that can be used to create C programs, not all operating systems provide a C compiler.

Fortunately, UNIX, VAX, and PRIME operating systems all have a C compiler that is typically installed along with the operating system. For IBM and IBM-compatible PC computers, a separate compiler, such as Borland's Turbo C, Microsoft's Quick C, or Microsoft's standard C compiler must be purchased and installed to provide the capability of compiling C programs.

TABLE E-1 Operating System Commands

Task	DOS	UNIX	VAX	PRIME	Your System
Obtain a directory of programs	dir	ls	dir	LS	
Change to a new directory	cd	cd	cd	DOWN and BACK	
List current directory name	cd	pwd	cd	WHERE	
List a program	type	cat	cat	SLIST	
Copy a program	copy	cp	cp	COPY	
Delete a program	erase	rm	rm	DELETE	
Rename a program	rename	mv	rn	CN	

Editing

Both the creation of a new C program and the modification of an existing C program require the use of an editor program. The function of the editor is to allow a user to type statements at a keyboard and save the typed statements together under a common name, called a source program file name.

As previously illustrated in Figure E-1, an editor program is contained within the environment controlled by the operating system. Like all services provided by the operating system, this means that the editor program can only be accessed using an operating system command. Table E-2 lists operating system commands required by the UNIX, DOS, VAX-VMS, and PRIME operating systems to enter their respective editors. As the UNIX operating system supplies two editor programs, a screen editor named `vi` and a line editor named `ed`, two separate commands are provided in UNIX for accessing the desired editor.

TABLE E-2

Operating System	Command to Enter the Editor	Command to Save and Exit	Command to Exit without Saving
DOS	EDLIN	E	q
UNIX (screen editor)	vi	:wq or ZZ	:q!
UNIX (line editor)	e	w and then q or ctrl Z	q
VAX-VMS	E	ctrl E	pfi Q
PRIME	PED	.FILE	.QUIT

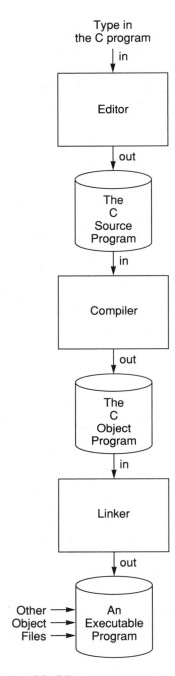

FIGURE E–2 Creating an Executable C Program

Once the editor program has been requested, the operating system relinquishes control to this program. Again, as illustrated in Figure E-1, this means that you temporarily leave the world controlled by the operating system and its commands and enter the world controlled by the editor. The editor, like the operating system, has its own set of services and commands. The services provided by the editor include entering C statements, modifying and deleting existing statements in a program, listing a program, naming a program, saving a program, and exiting from the editor back into the operating system with or without saving the program.

In using an editor you must carefully distinguish between entering a C statement and entering an editor command. Some editors make this distinction by using special keys to alert the editor that what is being typed is a command to the editor rather than the line of a program (for example, in BASIC, the line number informs the editor that the entered line is a program statement and the absence of a line number informs the editor that the entered line is an editor command). Other editors, including those listed in Table E-2, contain two modes: a *text mode* for entering and modifying program statements, and a *command mode* for entering editor commands. Table E-3 lists the commands provided by the UNIX, DOS, VAX-VMS, and PRIME editors for alerting the editor as to whether the text being typed is a command or a program statement.

TABLE E-3 Switching between Command and Text Modes

Editor	Commands to Enter Text Mode from Command Mode	Commands to Enter Command Mode from Text Mode
DOS - EDLIN	i or type at line no.	ctrl and C keys
UNIX - vi	a, i, o, c, s	Esc key
UNIX - ed	a, i, o, c, s	. (period)
VAX - EDT	c	ctrl Z
PRIME - PED	always in text mode	. followed by command

In command mode, each editor permits you to perform the tasks listed in Table E-4. Once you have determined the editor you will be using, fill in Table E-4 (for some of these tasks, the required commands can be found in Tables E-2 and E-3).

Compiling and Linking

Translating a C source program into a form that can be executed by the computer is accomplished using a *compiler* program. The output produced by the compiler is called an *object* program. An object program is simply a translated version of the source program that can be executed by the computer system with one more processing step. Let us see why this is so.

Most C programs contain statements that use preprogrammed routines, called intrinsic functions, for finding such quantities as square roots, logarithms, trigonometric values, absolute values, or other commonly encountered mathematical calculations. Additionally, a large C program may be stored in two or more separate program files. However, multiple files must ultimately be combined to form a single program before the program can be executed. In both of these cases it is the task of the *linker* to combine all of the intrinsic functions and individual object files into a single program ready for execution. This final program is called an executable program.

TABLE E-4 Editor Commands

Task	Command	Example
Save the program and exit from the editor		
Save the program without exiting from the editor		
Exit from the editor without saving the program		
Switch to text mode (if applicable)		
Switch to command mode (if applicable)		
List the complete program from within the editor		
List a set of lines from within the editor		
List a single line from within the editor		
Delete the complete program from within the editor		
Delete a set of lines from within the editor		
Delete a single line from within the editor		
Name a program from within the editor		

Both the compiler and the linker programs can be accessed using individual operating system commands. For ease of operation, however, all operating systems that provide a C compiler also provide a single command that both compiles a C program and links it correctly with any required other object programs using one command. Table E-5 lists the commands required by the UNIX, VAX-VMS, and PRIME operating systems to either compile only, link only, or compile and link a C program to produce an executable program. (Since DOS does not provide a C compiler, no entry is included in Table E-5 for this operating system.) Space has been left in the table to enter the command used by your computer for performing these operations.

Finally, once the C source program has been compiled and linked, it must be run. In both the VAX-VMS and PRIME operating systems execution of the executable program is begun by simply typing the name of the program in response to the operating system prompt. In the UNIX operating system the executable program produced by the linker is named a.out. Thus, for the UNIX operating system the execution of the last compiled and linked C program is initiated by typing a.out in response to the operating system prompt. Deter-

TABLE E-5 Specific Operating System Compile and Link Commands

Operating System	Compile and Link Command	Compile Only Command	Link Command
UNIX	cc filename(s)	cc filename(s) -c	ld objectname(s) -lc
VAX-VMS	—	cc filename	lin filename
PRIME	clg c -br l	cc filename	bind :li ccmain :lo filename :li g_lib :li
Your System			

Note: For each operating system listed in Table E-5, every source filename being compiled must end in a .c, and every object filename being linked must end in a .o. The output of a compile only command automatically produces an equivalent .o object file if the compilation is successful.

mine and then list the command used by your computer for performing this operation:

Operating system command to
execute a compiled and linked program:_____

Appendix F   Using Borland's Turbo C Compiler

Borland's *Turbo C* compiler provides a complete integrated programming development system that permits the user to enter, edit, compile, link, and execute C programs. Additionally, it provides a conventional command-line version. In this appendix both versions of the compiler are described. Before reading this appendix, however, you should understand the introductory material on program entry, compilation, and execution presented in the general introduction to Appendix E.

The integrated development environment of the Turbo C compiler is a menu-driven program, which is invoked by typing TC in response to the system prompt. Assuming the system prompt is C>, the command

```
C>  TC
```

invokes the integrated development version of the Turbo C compiler. This version permits the programmer to create, edit, compile, link, and run a program using a choice of menu options provided by Turbo C. In response to the TC command, the Turbo C start-up window illustrated in Figure F-1 is displayed.

The choices available to the user are listed in the menu-bar at the top of the window. Once this start-up window is displayed, you can select File, Edit,

FIGURE F-1 The Turbo C Start-Up Window

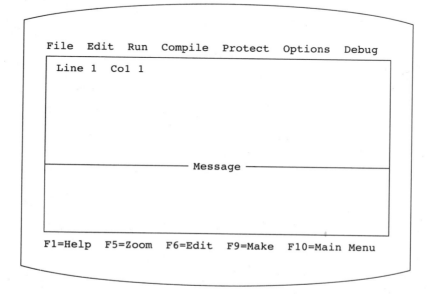

Run, Compile, Project, Options, or Debug. The selection is made by either pressing the Alt key and the first letter of the desired choice (for example, pressing the Alt key and F key simultaneously selects the File choice), or by moving to the desired choice using the cursor keys and then pressing the Enter key.

To initially enter a C program, you must select the File option. Once this option is selected, the File window illustrated in Figure F-2 is displayed. From this File window select the Load option by typing the letter L. A box is then presented that allows you to type in the name of your C program. In this box enter the name you wish to give your program, such as hello.c, and push the Enter key. (Although Turbo C does not require that your C program's name end in a period followed by the c, this is a convention that is required by most other compilers and used by most Turbo C programmers.)

After you have named your program and pushed the Enter key, Turbo C transfers control to its editor. In editor mode, you can type your program and move to any desired area by using the cursor arrow keys. Most of the editor commands are the same as those used in the WordStar word processing program. Of these commands, the ones that are used most often are listed in Table F-1.

TABLE F-1 Commonly Used Editing Commands

Command	Description
Ctrl and Y keys pushed simultaneously	Delete the line of text containing the cursor
Ctrl and T keys pushed simultaneously	Delete the word containing the cursor
Ctrl and K keys pushed simultaneously, followed by pushing the B key	Mark the start of a block starting at the cursor
Ctrl and K keys pushed simultaneously, followed by pushing the K key	Mark the end of a block immediately to the left of the cursor
Ctrl and K keys pushed simultaneously, followed by pushing the C key	Put a copy of the marked block immediately to the right of the current cursor position
Ctrl and K keys pushed simultaneously, followed by pushing the V key	Move the marked block immediately to the right of the current cursor position

FIGURE F–2 The Turbo C File Window

```
Load           F3
Pick       Alt-F3
New
Save           F2
Write to
Directory
Change dir
OS shell
Quit       Alt-X
```

After you have completed typing and editing your program, it can be compiled, linked, and run by pushing the `Alt` and `R` keys at the same time. This combination selects the `Run` option from the start-up window. At this point, Turbo C attempts to compile, link, and begin execution of your program. If your program has no errors an executable version of your program is created and automatically run. For example, if our `hello.c` program successfully compiles and links, the executable program `hello.exe` is created and automatically saved before it is run by Turbo C.

Should an error occur in either the compilation or linking stages, the program returns control to the editor, an error message is displayed in a message window at the bottom of the screen, and the cursor is automatically placed on the line in the program at which the error is detected. Unfortunately, this sometimes can be misleading as the error may actually be on the previous line. For example, the C code

```
int a
b = 22;
```

will indicate an error on the line `b = 22;`. The actual error occurs, however, because the line immediately preceding this is not terminated by a semicolon. Since white space is ignored by all C compilers (see Section 1.4), these two lines are read as

```
int a b = 22;
```

Once the semicolon is detected, the C compiler realizes an error has occurred and locates the cursor on what it detects as the offending line, namely, `b = 22;`.

To correct the error, you must push the `F6` key to move control from the message window into the program and then make your corrections. If multiple errors are indicated, pushing the `F6` key once more places you back in the message window at the next error message. This process of moving from the message window into the program to make the corrections is continued until all of your corrections have been made. At that point another run can be attempted by pushing the `Alt` and `R` keys simultaneously.

At any time during the editing process you can save a copy of your program by pushing the `Alt` and `F` keys simultaneously and then pushing the `S` (for `Save`) key. To quit the Turbo C program and return to the operating system, you may either push the `Alt` and `X` keys simultaneously, or push the `Alt` and `F` keys to get back into the `File` option and then push the `Q` key (for quit).

Once you are back at the system prompt you may run any C program that was successfully compiled and linked by Turbo C. For example, and again assuming that the system prompt is `C>`, typing

```
C> hello
```

would cause the `hello` program to begin execution.

In addition to the integrated environment provided by Turbo C, a command-line version is also available. In the command line version an editor must first be used to create a C program. Once the C program has been created, it can be compiled and linked using the command TCC. For example, issuing the command

```
C> TCC hello.c
```

would cause the compiler to compile and link the hello.c program. If the compilation and linkage is successful, the executable version of this program, named hello.exe, is created. The executable version can be run by issuing the command

```
C> hello
```

If the compilation is unsuccessful, the editor must be invoked and the errors corrected before recompilation.

Appendix G   Using Microsoft's Quick C Compiler

Microsoft's *Quick C* compiler provides a complete integrated programming development system that lets the user enter, edit, compile, link, and execute C programs. Additionally, it provides a conventional command-line version. In this appendix, both versions of the compiler are described. Before reading this appendix, however, you should understand of the introductory material on program entry, compilation, and execution presented in the general introduction to Appendix E.

The Microsoft Quick C compiler is a menu-driven program, which is invoked by typing QC in response to the system prompt. Assuming the system prompt is C>, the command

```
C>  QC
```

invokes the integrated development version of the Quick C compiler. This version permits the programmer to create, edit, compile, link, and run a program using a choice of menu options provided by Quick C. In response to the QC command the Quick C start-up window illustrated in Figure G-1 is displayed.

The choices available to the user are listed in the menu-bar at the top of the window. Once this start-up window is displayed, you have a choice of selecting

FIGURE G–1 The Quick C Start-Up Window

466

File, Edit, View, Search, Run, Debug, or Calls. The selection is made by either pressing the Alt key and the first letter of the desired choice (for example, pressing the Alt key and F key at the same time selects the File choice), or by moving to the desired choice using the cursor keys and then pressing the Enter key. Table G-1 lists the options provided by each menu choice.

TABLE G-1   Quick C Menu Options

Menu	Options Provided
File	Create, load, merge, print, and save source files. Also provides access to the operating system and exit from Quick C.
Edit	Add, modify, copy, and delete source text.
View	Customize the display of programs and alter the programming environment.
Search	Find, replace, and display source file text.
Run	Compile and run C programs.
Debug	Select and control debugging features.
Calls	Display the hierarchy of function calls specified by a C program.

To initially enter a C program, you must select the File option. Once this option is selected, the File menu illustrated in Figure G-2 is displayed. From this File menu select the New option by typing the letter N if you will be creating a new program or select the Open option by typing the letter O if you want to load an existing file. When you select the O option a box is presented that allows you to select the name of your existing C program.

After you have selected either a new or existing program, Quick C transfers control to its editor. In editor mode you can type in your program and move to any desired point in the program using the cursor arrow keys. Table G-2 lists the most commonly used editor commands, many of which are the same as those used in the WordStar word processing program.

FIGURE G–2 The Quick C File Menu

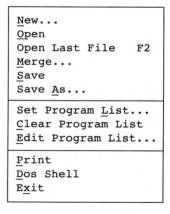

```
New...
Open
Open Last File    F2
Merge...
Save
Save As...

Set Program List...
Clear Program List
Edit Program List...

Print
Dos Shell
Exit
```

TABLE G-2 Commonly Used Editor Commands

Command	Description
Ctrl and Y keys pushed simultaneously	Delete the line of text containing the cursor
Ctrl and T keys pushed simultaneously	Delete the word containing the cursor
Shift and cursor key	Mark a block of characters
Ctrl and Ins keys pushed simultaneously	Put a copy of the marked block immediately to the left of the current cursor position

After you have completed typing and editing your program, it can be compiled, linked, and run by pushing the `Alt` and `R` keys at the same time. This combination selects the `Run` menu, from which the `Start` option must be selected. Alternatively, by holding the `Shift` and `F5` keys down together while in the editing mode also initiates the compilation and execution of the program being edited. If your program has no errors, an executable version of your program is created and automatically run. For example, if our `hello.c` program successfully compiles and links, the executable program `hello.exe` would be created and automatically saved before it is run by Quick C.

Should an error occur in either the compilation or linking stages, the program returns control to the editor, an error message is displayed in a message window at the bottom of the screen, and the cursor is automatically placed on the line in the program at which the error is detected. Unfortunately, this sometimes can be misleading as the error may actually be on the previous line. For example, the C code

```
int a
b = 22;
```

will indicate an error on the line `b = 22;`. The actual error occurs, however, because the line immediately preceding this is not terminated by a semicolon. Since white space is ignored by all C compilers (see Section 1.4), these two lines are read as

```
int a b = 22;
```

Once the semicolon is detected, the compiler realizes an error has occurred, and locates the cursor on what it detects as the offending line, namely, `b = 22;`.

If multiple errors are indicated, pressing the `Shift` and `F3` keys simultaneously moves the cursor to the line in the program that caused the next error and displays the error message in the error window. Similarly, pressing the `Shift` and `F4` keys simultaneously moves the cursor to the line in the program that caused the previous error and displays the previous error message in the error window. When all errors have been corrected another run can be attempted by pushing the `Shift` and `F5` keys simultaneously.

At any time during the editing process, you can save a copy of your program by pushing the Alt and F keys simultaneously and then pushing the S (for save) key. To quit the program and return to the operating system, you may either push the Alt and X keys simultaneously, or push the Alt and F keys to get back into the File option and then push the X key.

Once you are back at the system prompt, you may rerun any C program that was successfully compiled and linked by Quick C. For example, and again assuming that the system prompt is C>, typing

```
C> hello
```

would cause the hello program to begin execution.

In addition to the integrated environment provided by Quick C, a command-line version is also available. In the command-line version an editor must first be used to create a C program. Once the C program has been created, it can be compiled and linked using the command QCL. For example, issuing the command

```
C> QCL hello.c
```

would cause the compiler to compile and link the hello.c program. If the compilation and linkage is successful, the executable version of this program, named hello.exe, is created. The executable version can then be run by issuing the command

```
C> hello
```

If the compilation were unsuccessful, the editor must be invoked and the errors corrected before recompilation.

Appendix H   Solutions

Section 1.1

3. Step 1: Pour the contents of the first cup into the third cup
Step 2: Rinse out the first cup
Step 3: Pour the contents of the second cup into the first cup
Step 4: Rinse out the second cup
Step 5: Pour the contents of the third cup into the second cup

5. Step 1: Compare the first number with the second number and use the smallest of these numbers for the next step
Step 2: Compare the smallest number found in step 1 with the third number. The smallest of these two numbers is the smallest of all three numbers.

7. a. Step 1: Compare the first name in the list with the name JONES. If the names match, stop the search; else go to step 2.
Step 2: Compare the next name in the list with the name JONES. If the names match, stop the search; else repeat this step.

Section 1.2

1.

m1234()	Valid. Not a mnemonic.
new_bal()	Valid. A mnemonic.
abcd()	Valid. Not a mnemonic.
A12345()	Valid. Not a mnemonic.
1A2345()	Invalid. Violates Rule 1; starts with a number.
power()	Valid. A mnemonic.
abs_val()	Valid. A mnemonic.
invoices()	Valid. A mnemonic.
do()	Invalid. Violates Rule 3; is a reserved word.
while()	Invalid. Violates Rule 3; is a reserved word.
add_5()	Valid. Could be a mnemonic.
taxes()	Valid. A mnemonic.
net_pay()	Valid. A mnemonic.
12345()	Invalid. Violates Rule 1; starts with a number.
int()	Invalid. Violates Rule 3; is a reserved word.
new_balance()	Valid. A mnemonic.
a2b3c4d5()	Valid. Not a mnemonic.
salestax()	Valid. A mnemonic.
amount()	Valid. A mnemonic.
$taxes()	Invalid. Violates Rule 1; starts with a special character.

3. a.
```
main()
{
    input();      /* input the items purchased */
    salestax();   /* compute required salestax */
    balance();    /* determine balance owed */
    calcbill();   /* determine and output bill */
}
```

b. These functions might be used to determine the billing for an order for goods purchased. The purpose of each function, as indicated by its name, is given in the comment statements (/* ... */) for each function call.

Note for Exercises 5 through 9

Many solutions are possible for these exercises. The following are possible answers.

7. Determine which vegetables to grow
Determine how much land each vegetable will require
Buy the seeds and plants
Prepare the soil for each vegetable
Find out when last major frost is expected to determine the right time to plant each seed
   or plant
Properly plant each type of seed or plant

Section 1.3

1. a. `main()`
```
{
    printf("Joe Smith");
    printf("\n99 Somewhere Street");
    printf("\nNonesuch, N.J., 07030");
}
```
3. a. Six `printf()` statements would be used.
   b. One would work by including newline escape sequences between each two items displayed. Using one line is undesirable since it would make column alignment difficult and the program code hard to debug.
   c. `main()`
```
{
    printf("PART NO.        PRICE\n\n");
    printf("T1267          $6.34\n");
    printf("T1300          $8.92\n");
    printf("T2401          $65.40\n");
    printf("T4482          $36.99\n");
}
```

Section 1.4

1. a. Yes.
   b. It is not in standard form. To make programs more readable and easier to debug, the standard form presented in Section 1.4 of the textbook should be used.
3. a. Two backslashes in a row results in one backslash being displayed.
   b. `printf("\\ is a backslash.\n");`

Section 2.1

1. a. float or double
  b. integer
  c. float or double
  d. integer
  e. float or double

3. $1.26e^2$ $6.5623e^2$ $3.42695e^3$ $4.8932e^3$ $3.21e^{-1}$ $1.23e^{-2}$ $6.789e^{-3}$

9. a. $64 * 1024 = 65{,}536$ bytes
  b. $128 * 1024 = 131{,}072$ bytes
  c. $192 * 1024 = 196{,}608$ bytes
  d. $256 * 1024 = 262{,}144$ bytes
  e. $64 * 1024 = 65{,}536$ words $* 2$ bytes/word $= 131{,}072$ bytes
  f. $64 * 1024 = 65{,}536$ words $* 4$ bytes/word $= 262{,}144$ bytes
  g. $360 * 1024 = 368{,}640$ bytes

Section 2.2

1. a. $2 * 3 + 4 * 5$
  b. $(6 + 18) / 2$
  c. $4.5 / (12.2 - 3.1)$
  d. $4.6 * (3.0 + 14.9)$
  e. $(12.1 + 18.9) * (15.3 - 3.8)$

3. As all operands are floating point numbers, the result of each valid expression is a floating point number.

  a. 5.   *g.* −50.
  b. 10.   *h.* −2.5
  c. 24.0   *i.* invalid expression
  d. 0.2   *j.* 10.
  e. 3.6   *k.* 53.
  f. invalid expression

7. a. $'m' - 5 = 'h'$ *e.* $'b' - 'a' = 1$
  b. $'m' + 5 = 'r'$ *f.* $'g' - 'a' + 1 = 6 + 1 = 7$
  c. $'G' + 6 = 'M'$ *g.* $'G' - 'A' + 1 = 6 + 1 = 7$
  d. $'G' - 6 = 'A'$

Section 2.3

1. answer1 is the integer 2
answer2 is the integer 5

5. a. The comma is within the control string and the statement is not terminated with a semicolon. This statement will generate a compiler error, even if the semicolon is appended to the statement.
  b. The statement uses a floating point control sequence with an integer argument. The statement will compile and print an unpredictable result.
  c. The statement uses an integer control sequence with a floating point constant. The statement will compile and print an unpredictable result.
  d. The statement has no control sequences for the numerical arguments. The statement will compile and print the letters a b c. The constants are ignored.

e. The statement uses a floating point control sequence with an integer argument. The statement will compile and print an unpredictable result.

f. The f conversion character has been omitted from the control string. The statement will compile and print %3.6. The constants have no effect.

g. The formatting string must come before the arguments. The statement will compile and produce no output.

9. The value of 14 in octal is 16
The value of 14 in hexadecimal is E.
The value of 0xA in decimal is 10.
The value of 0xA in octal is 12.

Section 2.4

1. The following are not valid:

`12345`	does not begin with either a letter or underscore
`while`	reserved word
`$total`	does not begin with either a letter or underscore
`new bal`	cannot contain a space
`9ab6`	does not begin with either a letter or underscore
`sum.of`	contains a special character

3. a. `int count;`
 b. `float grade;`
 c. `double yield;`
 d. `char initial;`

7. a.
```
main ()
   {
      int num1;        /* declare the integer variable num1  */
      int num2;        /* declare the integer variable num2  */
      int total;       /* declare the integer variable total */

      num1 = 25;                /* assign the integer 25 to num1        */
      num2 = 30;                /* assign the integer 30 to num2        */
      total = num1 + num2;     /* assign the sum of num1 and num2 to total */
      printf("The total of %d and %d is %d.\n",num1,num2,total");
       /*          prints:                                        */
       /*          The total of 25 and 30 is 55.                  */
   }
```

9.
```
main ()
 {
   int length, width, perim;

   length = 16;
   width = 18;
   perim = length + length + width + width;
   printf("The perimeter is %d.",perim);
 }
```

473

13. Every variable has a type (e.g., `int`, `float`, etc.), a value, and an address in memory where it is stored.

15. a.

Address:	159	160	161	162	163	164	165	166
					W	O	W	!

rate   Ch1   Ch2   Ch3   Ch4

Address:	167	168	169	170	171	172	173	174

taxes

Address:	175	176	177	178	179	180	181	182
			0	0				

num   count

The empty addresses above are usually filled with "garbage" values, meaning their contents are whatever happened to be placed there by the computer or by the previously run program.

Section 2.5

1. a. For an IBM PC or compatible computer, the storage size of a character is one byte and an integer is two bytes.

b. On an IBM PC or compatible computer, two bytes are reserved for short integers, two bytes for unsigned integers, and four bytes for long integers.

3. Only a definition statement is necessary to set aside the right amount of storage space for a variable.

Section 3.1

1.
```
main()
{
              ◄─────────────── missing declaration for all variables

    width = 15◄────── missing semicolon
    area = length * width;◄────── no value assigned to length
    printf("The area is %d",area◄────── missing ");
}
```

The corrected program is:

```
main ()
{
  int length, width, area;

  width = 15;
  length = 20;    /* must be assigned some value */
  area = length * width;
  printf("The area is %d", area);
}
```

b.
```
main ()
{
   int length, width, area;

   area = length * width;  ⟵——————  this should come after the assignment of
   length = 20;                        values to length and width
   width = 15;
   printf("The area is %d", area);
}
```

The corrected program is:

```
main ()
{
   int length, width, area;

   length = 20;
   width = 15;
   area = length * width;
   printf("The area is %d", area);
}
```

c.
```
main ()
{
   int length, width, area;

   length = 20;
   width = 15;
   length * width = area;  ⟵————incorrect  assignment  statement
   printf("The area is %d", area);
}
```

The corrected program is:

```
main ()
{
   int length, width, area;

   length = 20;
   width = 15;
   area = length * width;
   printf("The area is %d", area);
}
```

3. *a.*
```
main ()
{
   float radius, circum;

   radius = 3.3;    /* could have been done in the declaration */
   circum = 2 * 3.1416 * radius;
   printf("The circumference is %f inches",circum);
}
```

5. *a.*
```
main ()
{
   float length, width, depth, volume;

   length = 25.0;
   width = 10.0;
   depth = 6.0;
   volume = length * width * depth;
   printf("The volume of the pool is %f",volume);
}
```

7. *a.*
```
main ()
{
   float  total;

   total = 12*.50 + 20*.25 + 32*.10 + 45*.05 + 27*.01;
   printf("The total amount is $%5.2f\n", total);
}
```

9. *c.*
```
main ()
{
   float speed = 58.0, dist = 183.67, time;

   time = dist/speed;
   printf("The elapsed time for the trip is %f hours",time);
}
```

11. The second expression is correct because the assignment of 25 to b is done before the subtraction. Without the parentheses the subtraction has the higher precedence, and the expression a − b is calculated, yielding a value, say 10. The subsequent attempt to assign the value of 25 to this value is incorrect, and is equivalent to the expression 10 = 25. Values can only be assigned to variables.

Section 3.2

1. &average means "the address of the variable named average."

3. *a.*
```
main ()
{
    char key, choice;
    int num, count;
    long date;
    float yield;
    double price;

    printf("The address of the variable key is %u\n",&key);
    printf("The address of the variable choice is %u\n",&choice);
    printf("The address of the variable num is %u\n",&num);
    printf("The address of the variable count is %u\n",&count);
    printf("The address of the variable date is %u\n",&date);
    printf("The address of the variable yield is %u\n",&yield);
    printf("The address of the variable price is %u\n",&price);
}
```

5. *a.* `*x_addr`
   b. `*y_addr`
   c. `*pt_yld`
   d. `*pt_miles`
   e. `*mptr`
   f. `*pdate`
   g. `*dist_ptr`
   h. `*tab_pt`
   i. `*hours_pt`

7. *a.* Each of these variables is a pointer. This means that addresses will be stored in each of these variables.
   b. They are not very descriptive names and do not give an indication that they are pointers.

9. All pointer variable declarations must have an asterisk. Therefore, c, e, g, and i are pointer declarations.

11.

Variable: `pt_num` Address: `500`	Variable: `amt_addr` Address: `564`
8096	16256
Variable: `z_addr` Address: `8024`	Variable: `num_addr` Address: `10132`
20492	18938
Variable: `pt_day` Address: `14862`	Variable: `pt_yr` Address: `15010`
20492	694
Variable: `years` Address: `694`	Variable: `m` Address: `8096`
1987	
Variable: `amt` Address: `16256`	Variable: `firstnum` Address: `18938`
154	154
Variable: `balz` Address: `20492`	Variable: `k` Address: `24608`
25	154

Section 3.3

1. a. `scanf("%d", &firstnum);`

  b. `scanf("%f", &grade);`

  c. `scanf("%lf", &secnum); /* note - the lf is required */`

  d. `scanf("%c", &keyval);`

  e. `scanf("%d %d %f", &month, &years, &average);`

f. `scanf("%c %d %d %lf %lf",&ch, &num1, &num2, &grade1, &grade2);`

g. `scanf("%f %f %f %lf %lf",&interest, &principal, &capital,`
                                 `&price, &yield);`

h. `scanf("%c %c %c %d %d %d",&ch, &letter1, &letter2, &num1,`
                                 `&num2, &num3);`

i. `scanf("%f %f %f %lf %lf %lf",&temp1, &temp2, &temp3,`
                                 `&volts1, &volts2);`

3. *a.* Missing `&` operator in front of `num1`. The correct form is

    scanf("%d", &num1);

b. Missing `&` operator in front of `firstnum` and wrong control sequence for `price`.
The correct form is

    scanf("%d %f %lf", &num1, &firstnum, &price);

c. The wrong control sequence for `num1` and `secnum`. The correct form is

    scanf("%d %f %lf", &num1, &secnum, &price);

d. Missing `&` operators in front of all the variables. The correct form is

    scanf("%d %d %lf", &num1, &num2, &yield);

e. Missing control string entirely. The correct form is

    scanf("%d %d", &num1, &num2);

f. Reversed address and control string. The correct form is

    scanf("%d", &num1);

5. *a.*
```
main ()
{
   float fahr, cel;

   printf("Enter the temperature in degrees Fahrenheit: ");
   scanf("%f", &fahr);
   cel = (5.0/9.0)*(fahr - 32.0);
   printf("\n%f degrees Fahrenheit is %f degrees Celsius", fahr, cel);
}
```

7. *a.*
```
main()
{
   float miles, gallons;

   printf("Enter the miles driven: ");
   scanf("%f",&miles);
   printf("Enter the gallons of gas used: ");
   scanf("%f",&gallons);
   printf("The miles/gallon is %5.2f",miles/gallons);
}
```

9. a.
```
main ()
{
    float num1, num2, num3, num4, avg;

    printf("Enter a number: ");
    scanf("%f", &num1);
    printf("\nEnter a second number: ");
    scanf("%f", &num2);
    printf("\nEnter a third number: ");
    scanf("%f", &num3);
    printf("\nEnter a fourth number: ");
    scanf("%f", &num4);
    avg = (num1 + num2 + num3 + num4) / 4.0;
    printf("\nThe average of the four numbers is %f", avg);
}
```

13. a. It is easy for a user to enter incorrect data. If wrong or unexpected data is given by the user, either incorrect results will be obtained or the program will "crash." A "crash" is an unexpected and premature program termination.
b. In a data type check, the input is checked to ensure that the values entered are of the correct type for the declared variables. This includes checking that integer values are entered for integer variables, and so on. A data reasonableness check, on the other hand, determines that the value entered is reasonable for the particular program. Such a check would determine that a large number was entered when a very small number was expected, or a small number was entered when a large number was expected, or that a zero or a negative number was entered when a positive number was expected (which, for example, could cause problems if the number was the denominator in a division), and so on.
c. Data type checks would ensure that the month, day, and year were all entered as integers. Some simple reasonableness checks would ensure that a month was between 1 and 12, a day between 1 and 31, and a year between reasonable limits for the application. More complex reasonableness checks might check that a day in months 1, 3, 5, 7, 8, 10, and 12 were between 1 and 31, those in months 4, 6, 9, and 11 were between 1 and 30, and those in month 2 were between 1 and 28, except if the year is a leap year in which case the day must be between 1 and 29 in month 2.

15.
```
main ()
{
    float num1, num2, temp;

    printf("Please type in a number: ");
    scanf("%f", &num1);
    printf("Please type in another number: ");
    scanf("%f", &num2);
    printf("\nBefore the swap num1 is %f and num2 is %f", num1, num2);
    temp = num1;    /* store num1 in temp */
    num1 = num2;    /* copy num2 to num1   */
    num2 = temp;    /* copy temp to num2   */
    printf("\nAfter the swap num1 is %f and num2 is %f", num1, num2);
}
```

Section 3.5

1.
```
#define PI 3.1416
main ()
{
   float radius,circum;

   printf("\nEnter a radius: ");
   scanf("%f", &radius);
   circum = 2.0 * PI * radius;
   printf("\nThe circumference of the circle is %f", circum);
}
```

3.
```
#define CONVERT (5.0/9.0)
#define FREEZING 32.0
main()
{
   float fahren,celsius;

   printf("\nEnter a temperature in degrees Fahrenheit: ");
   scanf("%f", &fahren);
   celsius = CONVERT * (fahren - FREEZING);
   printf("\nThe equivalent Celsius temperature is %f", celsius);
}
```

Section 4.1

1. a. The relational expression is true. Therefore, its value is 1.
   b. The relational expression is true. Therefore, its value is 1.
   c. The final relational expression is true. Therefore, its value is 1.
   d. The final relational expression is true. Therefore, its value is 1.
   e. The final relational expression is true. Therefore, its value is 1.
   f. The arithmetic expression has a value of 10.
   g. The arithmetic expression has a value of 4.
   h. The arithmetic expression has a value of 0.
   i. The arithmetic expression has a value of 10.

3. a. `age == 30`
   b. `temp > 98.6`
   c. `ht < 6.00`
   d. `month == 12`
   e. `let_in == 'm'`
   f. `age == 30 && ht > 6.00`
   g. `day == 15 && month == 1`
   h. `age > 50 || employ >= 5`
   i. `id < 500 && age > 55`
   j. `len > 2.00 && len < 3.00`

Section 4.2

```
1. #define LIMIT 20000
   #define REGRATE .02
   #define HIGHRATE .025
   #define FIXED 400
   main ()
   {
     float taxable, taxes;

     printf("Please type in the taxable income: ");
     scanf("%f", &taxable);
     if (taxable <= LIMIT)
       taxes = REGRATE * taxable;
     else
       taxes = HIGHRATE * (taxable - LIMIT) + FIXED;
     printf("\n\nTaxes are $%7.2f", taxes);
   }
```

```
7. a. main ()
      {
        int month, day;

        printf("Enter a month (use a 1 for Jan, 2 for Feb, etc.): ");
        scanf("%d", &month);
        printf("Enter a day of the month: ");
        scanf("%d", &day);

        if (month > 12 || month < 1)
          printf("\nAn incorrect month was entered.");

        if (day < 1 || day > 31)
        printf("\nAn incorrect day was entered.");
      }
```

b. If the user enters a floating point number, the `scanf` format string will assign the integer part of the number to the integer month variable, so that the month will be correct. It will then attempt to use the remaining fractional value for the day input, resulting in an incorrect value assigned to the day variable.

A possible solution is to accept the month variable as a floating point number, and then reassign it to an integer variable to correctly truncate it. No harm is done then if an integer is entered for the month (`scanf ()` will first convert it to a floating point number) or if a floating point number is entered. More correctly, a cast should be used, as described in Chapter 14.

9.
```
main ()
{
    char in_key;
    int position;

    printf("Enter a lowercase letter: ");
    scanf("%c", &in_key);
    if (in_key >= 'a' && in_key <= 'z')
    {
        position = in_key - 'a' + 1;
        printf("The character's position is %d", position);
    }
    else
        printf("The character just entered is not a lowercase letter");
}
```

13. The error is that the intended relational expression `letter == 'm'` has been written as the assignment expression `letter = 'm'`. When the expression is evaluated the character m is assigned to the variable letter and the value of the expression itself is the value of `'m'`. Since this is a nonzero value it is taken as True and the message is displayed.

   Another way of looking at this is to realize that the `if` statement, as written in the program, is equivalent to the following two statements:
```
        letter = 'm';
        if(letter) printf("Hello there!");
```

A correct version of the program is:
```
main ()
{
    char letter;

    printf("Enter a letter: ");
    scanf("%c", &letter);
    if (letter == 'm') printf("Hello there!");
}
```

Section 4.3

1.
```
main ()
{
    float grade;
    char letter;

    printf("Enter the student's numerical grade: ");
    scanf("%f", &grade);
    if (grade >= 90.0) letter = 'A';
    else if (grade >= 80.0) letter = 'B';
    else if (grade >= 70.0) letter = 'C';
    else if (grade >= 60.0) letter = 'D';
    else letter = 'F';
    printf("\nThe student receives a grade of %c", letter);
}
```

Notice that an `else-if` chain is used. If simple `if` statements were used, a grade entered as `75.5`, for example, would be assigned a `"C"` because it was greater than `60.0`. But, the grade would then be reassigned to `"D"` because it is also greater than `60.0`.

3.
```
main ()
{
   float fahr,cels,in_temp;
   char letter;

   printf("Enter a temperature followed by");
   printf(" one space and the temperature's type\n");
   printf(" (an f designates a fahrenheit temperature\n");
   printf("  and a c designates a celsius temperature): ");
   scanf("%f %c", &in_temp, &letter);
   if (letter == 'f' || letter == 'F')
   {
      cels = (5.0/9.0)*(in_temp - 32.0);
      printf("\n%6.2f deg Fahrenheit = %6.2f deg Celsius", in_temp, cels);
   }
   else if (letter == 'c' || letter == 'C')
   {
      fahr = (9.0/5.0)*in_temp + 32.0;
      printf("\n%6.2f deg Celsius = %6.2f deg Fahrenheit", in_temp, fahr);
   }
   else printf("\nThe data entered is invalid.");
}
```

5. a. This program will run. It will not, however, produce the correct result.

b. and c. This program evaluates correct incomes for `mon_sales` less than `20000.00` only. If `20000.00` or more were entered, the first `else if` statement would be executed and all others would be ignored. That is, for `20000.00` or more, the income for `>= 10000.00` would be calculated and displayed.

Had `if` statements been used in place of the `else if` statements, the program would have worked correctly, but inefficiently (see comments for Exercise 4.b.).

Section 4.4

1.
```
switch (let_grad)
{
   case 'A':
      printf("The numerical grade is between 90 and 100");
      break;
   case 'B':
      printf("The numerical grade is between 80 and 89.9");
      break;
   case 'C':
      printf("The numerical grade is between 70 and 79.9");
      break;
```

```
  case 'D':
    printf("How are you going to explain this one");
    break;
  default:
    printf("Of course I had nothing to do with the grade.");
    printf("\nThe professor was really off the wall.");
}
```

Section 5.1

1.
```
main ()
{
  int count = 2;

  while (count <= 10)
  {
    printf("%d  ",count);
    count +=2;

  }
}
```

3. a. 21 items are displayed, which are the integers from 1 to 21.

 c. 21 items are still displayed, but they would be the integers from 0 to 20 because the printf now occurs before the increment.

Section 5.2

3. a.
```
main ()
{
  float cels, fahr, incr;
  int num;

  printf("Enter the starting temperature ");
  printf("in degrees Celsius: ");
  scanf("%f", &cels);
  printf("\n\nEnter the number of conversions to be made: ");
  scanf("%d", &num);
  printf("\n\nNow enter the increment between conversions ");
  printf("in degrees Celsius: ");
  scanf("%f", &incr);
  printf("\n\n\nCelsius      Fahrenheit\n");
  printf("---------------------\n");
  while (count <= num)
  {
    fahr = (9.0/5.0)*cels + 32.0;
    printf("%7.2f%15.2f\n", cels, fahr);
    cels = cels + incr;
  }
}
```

7. This program will still calculate the correct values, but the average is now calculated four times. Since it is only the final average that is desired, it is better to calculate the average once, outside of the `while` loop.

9. a.
```
main ()
    {
        int id, inven, income, outgo, bal, count;

        count = 1;
        while (count <= 3)
        {
          printf("\nEnter book ID: ");
          scanf("%d", &id);
          printf("\nEnter inventory at the beginning of the month: ");
          scanf("%d", &inven);
          printf("\nEnter the number of copies received during the month: ");
          scanf("%d", &income);
          printf("\nNow enter the number of copies sold during the month: ");
          scanf("%d", &outgo);
          bal = inven + income - outgo;
          printf("\n\nBook #%d new balance is %d", id, bal);
          ++count;
        }
    }
```

Section 5.3

1. 20   16   12   8   4   0

5.
```
main ()
  {

    int conv, count;
    float f, c;

    printf("Enter the number of temperature conversions");
    printf("\nfrom Fahrenheit to Celsius to be performed: ");
    scanf("%f", &conv);
    printf("\nFahrenheit       Celsius\n");
    printf("----------       -------\n");
    for (f = 20.0, count = 1; count <= conv; ++count)
    {
      c = (f - 32.0)*(5.0/9.0);
      printf("%4.1f       %5.2f\n", f, c);
      f += 4.0;
    }
  }
```

7.
```
main()
{
   int count;
   float fahren, celsius;

   for(count = 1; count <= 6; ++count)
   {
     printf("\nEnter a fahrenheit temperature: ");
     scanf("%f", &fahren);
     celsius = (5.0/9.0)*(fahren - 32.0);
     printf(" The corresponding celsius temperature is %5.2f\n",celsius);
   }
}
```

13.
```
main ()
{
   int yr;
   double sales, profit, tot_sales=0.0, tot_profit=0.0;

   printf("SALES AND PROFIT PROJECTION\n");
   printf("--------------------------\n\n");
   printf("YEAR             EXPECTED SALES        PROJECTED PROFIT\n");
   printf("----             --------------        ----------------\n");
   for (yr = 1, sales = 10000000.00; yr <= 10; ++yr)
   {
     profit = 0.10*sales;
     printf("%3d               $%11.2f              $%10.2f\n",
            yr, sales, profit);
     tot_sales = tot_sales + sales;
     tot_profit = tot_profit + profit;
     sales = 0.96*sales;
   }
   printf("-----------------------------------------------------------");
   printf("\nTotals:            $%10.2f                $%9.2f\n",
          tot_sales, tot_profit);
}
```

15.
```
main ()
{
   int i, j, results;
   float total, avg, data;

   for (i = 1; i <= 4; ++i)
   {
     printf("Enter the number of results for experiment #%d: ",i);
     scanf("%d",&results);
     printf("Enter %d results for experiment #%d: ",results,i);
     for (j = 1, total = 0.0; j <= results; ++j)
     {
       scanf("%f", &data);
       total += data;
     }
     avg = total/results;
     printf("   The average for experiment #%d is %.2f\n\n", i, avg);
   }
}
```

Section 5.4

3. a.
```
main ()
{
    int num, digit;

    printf("Enter an integer: ");
    scanf("%d", &num);
    printf("\nThe number reversed is: ");
    do
    {
        digit = num % 10;
        num /= 10;
        printf("%d", digit);
    } while (num > 0);
}
```

Section 6.1

1. a. `factorial()` expects to receive one integer value.

b. `price()` expects to receive one integer and two double precision values, in that order.

c. An `int` and two double precision values, in that order, must be passed to `yield()`.

d. A character and two floating point values, in that order, must be passed to `interest()`.

e. Two floating point values, in that order, must be passed to `total()`.

f. An integer, character, double precision, integer, double precision, integer, and character value, in that order, are expected by `roi()`. Notice that even though the `roi()`'s arguments are grouped together and declared by data type, the order is determined by their placement within the parentheses of the function's declaration line.

g. Two integers and two character values, in that order, are expected by `get_val()`.

h. The `tolower()` function expects to receive one character.

g. `sin()` expects to receive one double precision value.

3. a. The `find_abs()` function is included within the larger program written for Exercise 3.b.

b.
```
main()
{
    double dnum;
    printf("\nEnter a number: ");
    scanf("%lf", &dnum);        /* the %lf is required for doubles */
    find_abs(dnum);
}

find_abs(num)
double(num);        /* declare the argument's data type */
{
    double abs_val;  /* a double precision variable */

    if (num < 0) abs_val = -num
        else abs_val = num;
    printf("The absolute value of %f is %f",num, abs_val);
}
```

5. a. The `sqr_it()` function is included within the larger program written for Exercise 5b.

b.
```c
main()
{
  double first;

  printf("Please enter a number: ");
  scanf("%lf",&first);     /* the %lf must be used for a double */
  sqr_it(first);
}

sqr_it(num)
double num;  /* argument declaration */
{
  printf("The square of %f is %f", num, num*num);
}
```

7. a. The function for producing the required table is included within the larger program written for Exercise 7b.

b.
```c
main()
{
  table();     /* call the table() function */
}

table()
{
  int num;

  printf("NUMBER     SQUARE     CUBE\n");
  printf("------     ------     ----\n");

  for (num = 1; num <= 10; ++num)
    printf("%3d      %3d      %4d\n", num, num*num, num*num*num);
}
```

Section 6.2

1.
```c
main()
{
  float find_max();
  float firstnum, secnum, maxnum;

  printf("Enter a number: ");
  scanf("%f", &firstnum);
  printf("\nGreat! Please enter a second number: ");
  scanf("%f", &secnum);
  maxnum = find_max(firstnum,secnum);
  printf("\n\nThe maximum of the two numbers is %f",maxnum);
}
```

```
float find_max(x,y)      /* the function returns a float */
float x,y;               /* two floating point arguments */
{
   float max;            /* variable declaration */

   if (x >= y)
      max = x;
   else
      max = y;
   return(max);
}
```

3. The following sections of code would be included within the calling function. Since a complete function definition is not given in Exercise 2, we do not know the data types of the values expected by the functions.

a.
```
float abs();
float ret_num;
        .
        .
   ret_num = abs(first, sec, third, fourth);
```
b.
```
double square_it();
double ret_val;
        .
        .
   ret_val = square_it(val);
```
c.
```
char key_char();
char ret_char;
        .
        .
   ret_char = key_char();
```
d.
```
int factorial();
int fact;
        .
        .
   fact = factorial(n);
```

5. *a.* The `mult()` function is included in the program written for Exercise 5b.

b.
```
main()
{
   double mult();    /* mult() returns a double precision value */
   double first,second;

   printf("Please enter a number: ");
   scanf("%lf",&first);
   printf("Please enter another number: ");
   scanf("%lf", &second);
   printf("The product of these numbers is %f",mult(first,second));
}

double mult(num1,num2)
double num1,num2;   /* argument declaration */
{
   return (num1*num2);
}
```

7. The polynomial function is included within the following working program.

```
main ()
{
   float a, b, c, x;
   float result;
   float poly_two();

   printf("Enter the coefficient for x^2 : ");
   scanf("%f", &a);
   printf("\nEnter the coefficient for x : ");
   scanf("%f", &b);
   printf("\nEnter the constant: ");
   scanf("%f", &c);
   printf("\nEnter the value for x: ");
   scanf("%f", &x);
   result = poly_two(a, b, c, x);
   printf("\n\n\nThe result is  %f", result);
}

float poly_two(c1, c2, c3, x)
float c1, c2, c3, x;
{
   return (c1*x*x + c2*x + c3);
}
```

9. a. The whole () function is included within the complete program written for Exercise 9b.

b.
```
main ()
   {
      int whole();
      double num;

      printf("Enter a number: ");
      scanf("%lf", &num);
      printf("\n\nThe whole part of %f is %d\n", num, whole(num));
   }

   int whole(n)
   double n;
   {
      int a;

      a = n;   /* a = (int) n is preferred - see Section 14.1 */
      return(a);
   }
```

Section 6.3

1.
```c
#include <math.h>
main ()
{
    double x = 0.0, sqrt ();

    while(x != 999)
    {
        printf("Enter a number to take the square root of ");
        printf("\n or 999 to quit: ");
        scanf("%lf", &x);
        printf("\nThe square root of %lf is %lf\n\n", x, sqrt(x));
    }
}
```

3.
```c
#include <math.h>
main ()
{
    double pow(), base, expon;
    int i;

    for(i = 1; i <= 4; ++i)
    {
        printf("\nEnter the number to be raised, a space, and the exponent: ");
        scanf("%lf %lf", &base, &expon);
        printf("\n\n%lf raised to %lf is %lf\n", base, expon, pow(base, expon));
    }
}
```

5.
```c
#include <stdio.h>
#include <ctype.h>
main ()
{
    char ch;

    ch = toupper(getchar());
    while(ch != 'F')
    {
        putchar(ch);
        ch = toupper(getchar());
    }
}
```

Section 6.4

1. a.

Variable name	Data type	Scope
price	integer	global to `main()`, `roi()`, and `step()`
years	long integer	global to `main()`, `roi()`, and `step()`
yield	double precision	global to `main()`, `roi()`, and `step()`
bondtype	integer	local to `main()` only
interest	double precision	local to `main()` only
coupon	double precision	local to `main()` only
count	integer	local to `roi()` only
eff_int	double precision	local to `roi()` only
numofyrs	integer	local to `step()` only
fracpart	float	local to `step()` only

Note that although arguments of each function assume a value which is dependent on the calling function, these arguments can change values within their respective functions. This makes them behave as if they were local variables within the called function.

Section 6.5

1. a. Local variables may be automatic, static, or register. It is important to realize, however, that not all variables declared inside of functions are necessarily local. An example of this is an external variable.

b. Global variables may be static or external.

3. The first function declares `yrs` to be a static variable and assigns a value of 1 to it only once, when the function is compiled. Thereafter, each time the function is called the value in `yrs` is increased by 2. The second function also declares `yrs` to be static, but assigns it the value 1 every time it is called, and the value of `yrs` after the function is finished will always be 3. By resetting the value of `yrs` to 1 each time it is called, the second function defeats the purpose of declaring the variable to be static.

5. The scope of a variable means where in the program the variable is recognized and can be used within an expression. If, for example, the variable `years` is declared inside a function, it is local and its scope is inside that function only. If the variable is declared outside of any function, it is global and its scope is anywhere below the declaration but within that file, unless another file of the same program declares that same variable to be external.

Section 6.6

1. a. `double *price;`
  b. `int *minutes;`
  c. `char *key;`
  d. `double *yield;`

3.
```
main ()
{
   int firstnum, secnum, max;


   printf("Enter a number: ");
   scanf("%d", &firstnum);
   printf("\nGreat! Please enter a second number: ");
   scanf("%d", &secnum);
   find_max(firstnum, secnum, &max);
   printf("\n\nThe maximum of the two numbers is %d.", max);
}

find_max(x, y, max_addr)
int x, y, *max_addr;
{
   if (x >= y)
     *max_addr = x;
   else
     *max_addr = y;
   return;
}
```

Notice that `find_max` was not declared in the function `main()` because we're not returning any value; rather there is a "return by reference." In other words, no value is being passed back to `main()`; instead a memory location's content known to both `main()` and `find_max()` is being altered.

9. In `main()` the variables `min` and `hour` refer to integer quantities, while in `time()` the variables `min` and `hours` are pointers to integers. Thus, there are four distinct variables in all, two of which are known in `main()` and two of which are known in `time()`. The computer (actually, the compiler) keeps track of each variable with no confusion. The effect on a programmer, however, may be quite different.

When used in `main()` the programmer must remember to use the names `min` and `hour` as integer variables. When in `time()` the programmer must "switch" viewpoints and use the same names as pointer variables. Debugging such a program can be quite frustrating because the same names are used in two different contexts. It is, therefore, more advisable to avoid this type of situation by adopting different names for pointers than those used for other variables. A useful "trick" is to either prepend each pointer name with a `pt_` notation or append each pointer name with `_addr`.

Section 7.1

1. a. `double interest[60];`
   b. `float temp[30];`
   c. `char code[25];`
   d. `int year[100];`

   e. `double coupon[26];`
   f. `float dist[1000];`
   g. `int code[20];`

3. a.
```
main()
{
   int temp[15], total = 0, count;
   float avg;

   for(count = 0; count <= 14; ++count)
   {
      printf("Enter element #%d: ", count + 1);
      scanf("%d", &temp[count]);
      total += temp[count];
   }
            avg = total/15.0;
   for(count = 0; count <= 14; ++count)
      printf("\nElement #%d = %d", count, temp[count]);
   printf("\n   The average is %f\n\n", avg);
}
```

c.
```
main()
{
   int temp[15], total = 0, count, index, max = 0;
   float avg;

   for(count = 0; count <= 14; ++count)
   {
      printf("\nEnter element #%d: ", count + 1);
      scanf("%d", &temp[count]);
      if(temp[count]  max)
      {
         max = temp[count];
         index = count;
      }
   }
   for(count = 0; count <= 14; ++count)
      printf("\nElement #%d = %d", count, temp[count]);
   printf("\n\nThe maximum value is: %d", max);
   printf("\nThis is element %d in the list of numbers\n\n", index);
}
```

5.
```
main()
{
   int i,quantity[10];
   float price[10], amount[10];

   for(i = 0; i <= 9; ++i)
   {
      printf("Enter price for item #%d: ", i + 1);
      scanf("%f", &price[i]);
      printf("Enter the quantity for item #%d: ", i + 1);
      scanf("%d", &quantity[i]);
      amount[i] = price[i]*quantity[i];
   }
   printf("\n\nQuantity          Price          Amount");
   printf("\n--------          -----          ------");
   for(i = 0; i <= 9; ++i)
      printf("\n%5d %17.2f %15.2f", quantity[i], price[i], amount[i]);
}
```

Section 7.2

1. a. `static int grades[10] = {89, 75, 82, 93, 78, 95, 81, 88, 77, 82};`
  b. `static double amount[5] = {10.62, 13.98, 18.45, 12.68, 14.76};`
  c. `static double rates[100] = {6.29, 6.95, 7.25, 7.35, 7.40, 7.42};`
  d. `static float temp[64] = {78.2, 69.6, 68.5, 83.9, 55.4, 67.0, 49.8,`
                          `58.3, 62.5, 71.6};`
  e. `static char code[15] = {'f', 'j', 'm', 'q', 't', 'w', 'z'};`

Note: This last declaration creates an array having one more character than the first two. The extra character is the null character.

3. a. The four declarations are contained within the program written for Exercise 3b.
  b.
```
main()
{
   static char messag1[] = "Input the following data";
   static char messag2[] = "------------------------";
   static char messag3[] = "Enter the date:";
   static char messag4[] = "Enter the Account Number:";

   printf("\n%s",messag1);
   printf("\n%s",messag2);
   printf("\n%s",messag3);
   printf("\n%s",messag4);
}
```

5. a.
```
main()
{
   int i;
   static float prices[8] = {16.24, 18.98, 23.75, 16.29,
                             19.54, 14.22, 11.13, 15.39};

   printf("\nThe values stored in the array are:");
   for(i = 0; i < 7; ++i)
      printf("\n  %5.2f", prices[i]);
}
```
  b.
```
float prices[8] = {16.24, 18.98, 23.75, 16.29,
                   19.54, 14.22, 11.13, 15.39};
main()
{
   int i;

   printf("\nThe values stored in the global array are:");
   for(i = 0; i < 7; ++i)
      printf("\n  %5.2f", prices[i]);
}
```

7.
```
static double prices[5] = {9.92, 6.32, 12.63, 5.95, 10.29};
main()
{
   int i;
   double units[5], amounts[5], total= 0;

   for(i = 0; i <= 4; ++i)
   {
      printf("\nEnter units[%d]: ", i);
      scanf("%lf", &units[i]);
      amounts[i] = units[i]*prices[i];
      total += amounts[i];
   }
   printf("\n\nPrice          Units          Amount");
   printf("\n-----          -----          ------");
   for(i = 0; i <= 4; ++i)
      printf("\n%5.2lf%15.2lf%16.2lf", prices[i], units[i], amounts[i]);
   printf("\n                              ------");
   printf("\nTotal: %29.2f", total);
}
```

Section 7.3

1.
```
sort_arr(in_array)              or            sort_arr(in_array)
   double in_array[500];                         double in_array[];
```

5.
```
main()
{
   static float rates[9] = {6.5, 7.2, 7.5, 8.3, 8.6,
                            9.4, 9.6, 9.8, 10.0};

   show(rates);
}

show(rates)
float rates[];
{
   int i;

   printf("The elements stored in the array are:");
   for(i = 0; i <= 8; ++i)
      printf("\n %4.1f", rates[i]);
}
```

```
7. main()
   {
      static double price[10] = {10.62, 14.89, 13.21, 16.55, 18.62,
                                  9.47, 6.58, 18.32, 12.15, 3.98};
      static double quantity[10] = {4.0, 8.5, 6.0, 7.35, 9.0,
                                     15.3, 3.0, 5.4, 2.9, 4.8};
      static double amount[10];   /* Automatically assigns zeros */
                                  /* to each element */
      int i;

      extend(price, quantity, amount);
      printf("The elements in the amount array are:");
      for(i = 0; i <= 9; ++i)
        printf("\n %7.3lf", amount[i]);
   }

   extend(prc, qnty, amt)
   double prc[], qnty[], amt[];
   {
      int i;

      for(i = 0; i <= 9; ++i)
        amt[i] = prc[i]*qnty[i];
   }
```

Section 7.4

1. a. `int array[6][10];`   d. `char letter[15][7];`
   b. `int codes[2][5];`   e. `double vals[10][25];`
   c. `char keys[7][12];`   f. `double test[16][8];`

3.
```
double add_ele(array)
double array[][5];
{
   int i, j;
   double total = 0;

   for(i = 0; i <= 3; ++i)
    for(j = 0; j <= 4; ++j)
     total += array[i][j];
   return(total);
}
```

5. c. Yes, any function receiving a multidimensional array can be generalized to handle any number of elements by passing either the number of elements in each dimension or the total number of elements.

Section 8.1

1. a. `*(prices + 5)`   **f.** `*(temp + 20)`
   b. `*(grades + 2)`   **g.** `*(celsius + 16)`
   c. `*(yield + 10)`   **h.** `*(num + 50)`
   d. `*(dist + 9)`   **i.** `*(time + 12)`
   e. `*mile`

3. a. The declaration `double prices [5];` causes storage space for five double
   precision numbers, creates a pointer constant named `prices`, and equates the pointer
   constant to the address of the first element (`&prices[0]`)
   b. Each element in prices contains four bytes and there are five elements for a total of
   20 bytes.
   c.

```
prices
```

```
&prices[0]
```

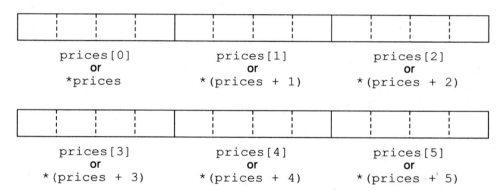

```
    prices[0]            prices[1]            prices[2]
       or                  or                   or
    *prices           *(prices + 1)        *(prices + 2)
```

```
    prices[3]            prices[4]            prices[5]
       or                  or                   or
 *(prices + 3)        *(prices + 4)        *(prices + 5)
```

   d. The byte offset for this element, from the beginning of the array, is 3 * 4 = 12 bytes.

5.
```
main()
{
    static float rates[] = {12.9, 18.6, 11.4, 13.7, 9.5, 15.2, 17.6};
    int i;

    printf("The elements of the array are:\n");
    for(i = 0; i <= 6; ++i)
       printf("\n%5.2f", *(rates + i)); /* The variable pointed to by */
}                                       /* rates offset by i          */
```

Section 8.2

3. a.
```
main()
{
    static char strng[] = "Hooray for all of us";
    char *mess_pt;

    mess_pt = &strng[0];    /* mess_pt = strng; is equivalent */
    printf("The elements in the array are: ");
    for(  ; *mess_pt != '\0'; ++mess_pt)
        printf("%c", *mess_pt);
}
```
b.
```
main()
{
    static char strng[] = "Hooray for all of us";
    char *mess_pt;

    mess_pt = &strng[0];    /* mess_pt = strng; is equivalent */
    printf("The elements in the array are: ");
    while (*mess_pt != '\0')    /* search for the null character */
        printf("%c", *mess_pt++);
}
```

Section 8.3

1.
```
sort_arr(in_array)
double in_array[500];

sort_arr(in_array)
double in_array[];

sort_arr(in_array)
double *in_array;
```

5. The problem to this method of finding the maximum value lies in the line

```
if(max < *vals++)    max = *vals;
```

This statement compares the correct value to max, but then increments the address in the pointer before any assignment is made. Thus, the element assigned to max by the expression max = *vals is one element beyond the element pointed to within the parentheses.

9. a. The following output is obtained:

33

16

99

34

This is why:

```
*(*val)  =  *(val[0])  =  val[0][0]  =  33;
*(*val + 1)  =  *(val[1])  =  val[1][0]  =  16;
*(*(val + 1) + 2)  =  *(*(val[1]) + 2)  =  *(val[1][2])  =  99;
*(*val) + 1  =  *(val[0]) + 1  =  val[0][0] + 1  =  33 + 1  =  34.
```

In other words, for any two-dimensional array, arr[x][y], what we really have is two levels of pointers. What's meant by *(arr + x) is that there are x number of pointers, each successively pointing to arr[1][0], arr[2][0], arr[3][0], ..., arr[x][0]. So an expression such as *(*(arr + x) + y) translates to arr[x][y].

Section 9.1

1. b.
```
#include <stdio.h>
main()
{
  char line[81];

  printf("Enter a string.\n");
  gets(line);
  vowels(line);
}
vowels(strng)
char strng[];
{
  int i = 0, v = 0;   /* Array element number = i; vowel counter = v  */
  char c;
  while((c = strng[i++]) != '\0')
  switch(c)
  {
    case 'a':
    case 'e':
    case 'i':
    case 'o':
    case 'u':
      putchar(c);
      ++v;
  }
  putchar('\n');
  printf("There were %d vowels.", v);
}
```

3. a. The function is included in the program written for Exercise 3b.

b. `main()`

```
main()
{
   char strng[81];

   printf("Enter a line of text\n");
   gets(strng);
   count_str(strng);
}

count_str(message)
char message[];
{
   int i;

   for(i = 0; message[i] != '\0'; ++i);    /* The semicolon at the end   */
                                           /* of this statement is the   */
                                           /* null statement             */
   printf("\nThe number of total characters, including blanks, in");
   printf(" the line just entered is %d.", i);
}
```

7.
```
#include <stdio.h>
main()
{
   char word[81];

   printf("Enter a string\n");
   gets(word);
   printf("\n%s\n",word);
   del_char(word, 13, 5); /* string, how many to delete, starting position */
   puts(word);                 /* display the edited string */
}

del_char(strng, x, pos)
char strng[];
int x, pos;
{
   int i, j;
   i = pos-1;    /* first element to be deleted (actually, overwritten) */
   j = i + x;    /* first element beyond delete range */
   while (strng[j] != '\0')
      strng[i++] = strng[j++];  /* copy over an element */
   strng[i] = '\0';   /* close off the edited string */
   return;
}
```

This program assumes the number of characters to be deleted actually exists. Otherwise the `while` loop would not terminate (unless it just happened to encounter another null character somewhere in memory beyond the original string).

9. a. The to_upper() function is included in the program written for Exercise 9c.

  c.
```
main()
{
   char strng[81];
   int i = 0;

   printf("Enter a line of text\n");
   gets(strng);
   while (strng[i] != '\0')   /* get the character */
   {
     strng[i] = to_upper(strng[i]); /* send it to the function */
     ++i;                      /* move to next character */
   }
   printf("The string, with all lower case letters converted, is:\n");
   puts(strng);
}

to_upper(ch)
char ch;
{

   if ( ch >= 'a' && ch <= 'z')    /* test it */
      return(ch - 'a' + 'A');      /* change it, if necessary */
   else
      return(ch);

}
```

11.
```
main()
{
   char strng[81];
   int i = 0, count = 1;

   printf("Enter a line of text\n");
   gets(strng);
   if(strng[i] == ' ' || strng[i] == '\0')
      --count;
   while(strng[i] != '\0')
   {
      if(strng[i] == ' ' && (strng[i + 1] != ' ' && strng[i + 1] != '\0'))
          ++count;       /* encountered a new word */
      ++i;               /* move to the next character */
   }
   printf("\nThe number of words in the line just entered is %d", count);
}
```

The program increases the word count whenever a transition from a blank to a non-blank character occurs. Thus, even if words are separated by more than one space the word count will be incremented correctly. Initially the program assumes the text starts with a word (count = 1). If the first character is either a blank or an end-of-string Null, this assumption is incorrect and the count is decremented to zero.

Section 9.2

1. a. ```*text = 'n'
   *(text + 3) = ' '
   *(text + 10) = ' '```

c. ```*text = 'H'
   *(text + 3) = 'p'
   *(text + 10) = 'd'```

b. ```*text = 'r'
   *(text + 3) = 'k'
   *(text + 10) = 'o'```

d. ```*text = 'T'
   *(text + 3) = ' '
   *(text + 10) = 'h'```

3.
```c
#include <stdio.h>
main()
{
   char line[81];

   printf("Enter a string.\n");
   gets(line);
   vowels(line);
}

vowels(strng)
char *strng;      /* strng can be treated as a pointer variable */
{
   int v = 0;    /* v = vowel counter */
   char c;

   while((c = *strng++) != '\0')   /* an address is incremented */
   switch(c)
   {
     case 'a':
     case 'e':
     case 'i':
     case 'o':
     case 'u':
        putchar(c);
        ++v;
   }
   putchar('\n');
   printf("There were %d vowels.", v);
}
```

5.
```
main()
{
   char strng[81];

   printf("Enter a line of text\n");
   gets(strng);
   count_str(strng);
   }


count_str(message)
char *message;        /* message can be used as a pointer variable */
{
   int count;

   for(count = 0; *message++ != '\0'; ++count) ; /* The semicolon at the  */
                                                 /* end of this statement */
                                                 /* is the null statement */
   printf("\nThe number of total characters, including blanks, in");
   printf(" the line just entered is %d.", count);
}
```

7.
```
main()
{
   char forward[81], rever[81];

   printf("Enter a line of text:\n");
   gets(forward);
   reverse(forward,rever);
   printf("\n\nThe text: %s \n",forward);
   printf("spelled backwards is: %s \n",rever);
}


reverse(forw, rev)
char *forw, *rev;    /* these may be used as pointer variables */
{
   int i = 0;

   while(*(forw + i) != '\0')        /* count the elements */
      ++i;                           /* in the string       */
   for(--i; i >= 0; --i)
     *rev++ = *(forw + i);
   *rev = '\0';                  /* close off reverse string */
   return;
}
```

9. The function is included within a complete program.

```
#include <stdio.h>
main()
{
   char ch, line[81];

   printf("Enter a line of text: ");
   gets(line);
   printf("Enter a single character: ");
   ch = getchar();
   append_c(line,ch);
   printf("The new line of text with the appended last character is:\n");
   puts(line);
}

append_c(strng,c)
char c, *strng;
{

   while(*strng++ != '\0')    /* this advances the pointer */
      ;                       /* one character beyond '\0 '*/
   --strng;                   /* point to the '\0') */
   *strng++ = c;              /* replace it with the new char */
   *strng = '\0';             /* close the new string       */
}
```

13.
```
trimrear(strng)
   char *strng;
   {

      while(*strng != '\0') ++strng;  /* move to end of string     */
      --strng;                        /* move to char before '\0' */
      while(*strng == ' ') --strng;   /* skip over blank characters */
      *(++strng) = '\0';              /* close off string */
      return;
   }
```

Section 9.3

1.
```
char *text = "Hooray!";
char test[] = {'H','o','o','r','a','y','\0'};
```

3. message is a pointer constant. Therefore, the statement ++message, which attempts to alter its address, is invalid. A correct statement is

```
putchar(*(message + i));
```

Here the address in message is unaltered and the character pointed to is the character offset i bytes from the address corresponding to message.

Section 9.4

1. a. !four score and ten! /* field width specifier is ignored */
  b. !   Home!!
  c. !Home!   !
  d. !Ho   !
  e. !   Ho!

3. main()
```
{
   char strn[30];
   float num1, num2, num3;

   printf("Enter three numbers on the same line,");
   printf("\n separating the numbers with one or more spaces: ");
   gets(strn);      /* read the numbers in as a string */
   separate(strn, &num1, &num2, &num3);
   printf("The three numbers are %f %f %f",num1, num2, num3);
}

separate(st_addr, n1_addr, n2_addr, n3_addr)
char *st_addr;
float *n1_addr, *n2_addr, *n3_addr;   /* three pointers */
{
   sscanf(st_addr,"%f %f %f",n1_addr, n2_addr, n3_addr);
   return;
}
```

Functions like separate() are useful when reading data from a file. Rather than read individual items sequentially, a complete line of the file is read in as a string and then dissembled internally within the program. This isolates any line that does not have the required number and types of data items.

5. main()
```
{
   char strng1[80], strng2[100];
   int num1, num2;

   printf("Enter a string: ");
   gets(strng1);
   printf("Enter an integer number: ");
   scanf("%d",&num1);
   printf("Enter a second integer number: ");
   scanf("%d",&num2);
   combine(strng1, strng2, num1, num2);
   printf("A string containing all inputs is: ");
   puts(strng2);
}

     /* continued on next page */
```

```
combine(source, dest, n1, n2)
char *source, *dest;
int n1, n2;
{
   sprintf(dest,"%s %d %d",source, n1, n2); /* write the string */
   return;
}
```

Functions like `combine()` are useful in assembling separate data items into a single line for output to a file. The file will then contain identically formatted lines, each line containing the same number and types of data items. Additionally, the file will be in ASCII, which can easily be read by any word processing program, for easy inspection external to the program that created it.

Section 10.1

1. a.
```
struct s_temp
   {
      int id_num;
      int credits;
      float avg;
   };
```
b.
```
struct s_temp
   {
      char name[40];
      int month;
      int day;
      int year;
      int credits;
      float avg;
   };
```
c.
```
struct s_temp
   {
      char name[40];
      char street[80];
      char city[40];
      char state[2];
      int zip;            /* or char zip[5];   */
   };
```
d.
```
struct s_temp
   {
      char name[40];
      float price;
      char date[8];     /* Assumes a date in the form XX/XX/XX */
   };
```

e.
```
struct s_temp
  {
    int part_no;
    char desc[100];
    int quant;
    int reorder;
  };
```

3. a.
```
main()
  {
    struct
    {
      int month;
      int day;
      int year;
    } date;        /* define a structure variable named date */


    printf("Enter the current month: ");
    scanf("%d", &date.month);
    printf("Enter the current day: ");
    scanf("%d", &date.day);
    printf("Enter the current year: ");
    scanf("%d", &date.year);
    printf("\n\nThe date entered is %d/%d/%d.",
            date.month, date.day, date.year);
  }
```

b.
```
main()
  {
    struct clock
    {
      int hours;
      int minutes;
      int seconds;
    } time;              /* define a structure variable named time */

    printf("Enter the current hour: ");
    scanf("%d", &time.hours);
    printf("Enter the current minute: ");
    scanf("%d", &time.minutes);
    printf("Enter the current second: ");
    scanf("%d", &time.seconds);
    printf("\n\nThe time entered is %02d:%02d:%02d", time.hours,
            time.minutes, time.seconds);
  }
```

Note the use of the conversion sequence %02d. The 0 forces the field of 2 to be filled with leading zeros.

```
5. main()
   {
      struct
      {
        int hours;
        int minutes;
      } time;

      printf("Enter the current hour: ");
      scanf("%d", &time.hours);
      printf("Enter the current minute: ");
      scanf("%d", &time.minutes);
      if(time.minutes != 59)
        time.minutes += 1;
      else
      {
        time.minutes = 0;
        if(time.hours != 12)
           time.hours += 1;
        else
           time.hours = 1;
      }
      printf("\nThe time in one minute will be %02d:%02d",
             time.hours, time.minutes);
   }
```

Note the use of the conversion sequence %02d. The 0 forces the field of 2 to be filled with leading zeros.

Section 10.2

1. a.
```
struct s_temp
   {
      int id_num;
      int credits;
      float avg;
   };

   main()
   {
      struct s_temp student[100];
```

b.
```
struct s_temp
  {
    char name[40];
    int month;
    int day;
    int year;
    int credits;
    float avg;
  };

main()
  {
    struct s_temp student[100];
```
c.
```
struct s_temp
  {
    char name[40];
    char street[80];
    char city[40];
    char state[2];
    int zip;              /* or char zip[5];  */
  };

main()
  {
    struct s_temp address[100];
```
d.
```
struct s_temp
  {
    char name[40];
    float price;
    char date[8];     /* Assumes a date in the form XX/XX/XX  */
  };
main()
  {
    struct s_temp stock[100];
```
e.
```
struct s_temp
  {
    int part_no;
    char desc[100];
    int quant;
    int reorder;
  };
main()
  {
    struct s_temp inven[100];
```

3.
```
struct mon_days
{
 char name[10];
 int days;
};

main()
{
    static struct mon_days convert[12] =
                                { "January", 31,"February", 28,
                                  "March", 31, "April", 30,
                                  "May", 31, "June", 30,
                                  "July", 31, "August", 31,
                                  "September", 30, "October", 31,
                                  "November", 30, "December", 31
                                };

    int i;

    printf("\nEnter the number of a month: ");
    scanf("%d", &i);
    printf("\n%s has %d days.", convert[i-1].name, convert[i-1].days);
}
```

Section 10.3

1.
```
struct date
{
   int month;
   int day;
   int year;
};

main()
{
   struct date present;
   long num, days();

   printf("Enter the month: ");
   scanf("%d", &present.month);
   printf("Enter the day: ");
   scanf("%d", &present.day);
   printf("Enter the year: ");
   scanf("%d", &present.year);
   num = days(present);
   printf("\nThe number of days since the turn of the century is %ld", num);
}

long days(temp)
struct date temp;
{
   return(temp.day + 30*(temp.month - 1) + 360*temp.year);
}
```

Note: The pointer version of the function `long days()` is written for Exercise 3.

3.
```c
struct date
{
   int month;
   int day;
   int year;
};

main()
{
   struct date present;
   long num, days();

   printf("Enter the month: ");
   scanf("%d", &present.month);
   printf("Enter the day: ");
   scanf("%d", &present.day);
   printf("Enter the year: ");
   scanf("%d", &present.year);
   num = days(&present);
   printf("\n\nThe number of days since the turn of the century is %ld", num);
}

long days(temp)
struct date *temp;
{
   return(temp->day + 30*(temp->month - 1) + 360*temp->year);
}
```

5.
```c
static struct date
{
   int month;
   int day;
   int year;
};

main()
{
   struct date present;
   long num, days();

   printf("Enter the date as mm/dd/yy: ");
   scanf("%d/%d/%d", &present.month, &present.day, &present.year);
   num = days(present);
   printf("\nThe number of days since the turn of the century is %ld", num);
}

long days(temp)
struct date temp;
{
   long act_days;
   static int daycount[12] = { 0, 31, 59, 90, 120, 151,
                               180, 211, 241, 271, 302, 333};
   act_days = temp.day + daycount[temp.month - 1] + 364*temp.year;
   return(act_days);
}
```

Section 10.4

1.
```
#include <stdio.h>
struct tele_typ
{
    char name[30];
    char phone_no[15];
    struct tele_typ *nextaddr;
};

main()
{
    static struct tele_typ t1 = {"Acme, Sam", "(201) 898-2392"};
    static struct tele_typ t2 = {"Dolan, Edith", "(213) 682-3104"};
    static struct tele_typ t3 = {"Lanfrank, John", "(415) 718-4518"};
    static struct tele_typ *first;
    char strng[30];

    first = &t1;
    t1.nextaddr = &t2;
    t2.nextaddr = &t3;
    t3.nextaddr = NULL;
    printf("Enter a name: ");
    gets(strng);
    search(first, strng);
}

search(contents, strng)
struct tele_typ *contents;
char *strng;
{

    printf("\n%s",strng);
    while(contents != NULL)
    {
        if(strcmp(contents->name,strng) == 0)
        {
            printf("\nFound. The number is %s.", contents->phone_no);
            return;
        }
        else
        {
            contents = contents->nextaddr;
        }
    }
    printf("\nThe name is not in the current phone directory.");
}
```

3. To delete the second record, the pointer in the first record must be changed to point to the third record.

5. a.
```
struct phone_bk
    {
        char name[30];
        char phone_no[15];
        struct phone_bk *previous;
        struct phone_bk *next;
    };
```

Section 10.5

1. The `check()` function is included below in a complete program used to verify that `check()` works correctly.

```
#include <stdio.h>
struct tel_typ
{
    char name[25];
    char phone_no[15];
    struct tel_typ *nextaddr;
};

main()
{
    int i;
    struct tel_typ *list, *current;
    char *malloc();

    list = (struct tel_typ *) malloc(sizeof(struct tel_typ));
    check(list);
    current = list;
    for(i = 0; i < 2; ++i)
    {
        populate(current);
        current->nextaddr = (struct tel_typ *) malloc(sizeof(struct tel_typ));
        check(current->nextaddr);
        current = current->nextaddr;
    }
    populate(current);
    current->nextaddr = NULL;
    printf("\nThe list consists of the following records:\n");
    display(list);
}

check(addr)
struct tel_typ *addr;
{

    if(addr == NULL)
    {
        printf("No available memory remains. Program terminating");
        exit(0); /* Function to stop program and return to operating system */
    }                /* continued on next page */
```

```
  else
    return;
}

populate(record)
struct tel_typ *record;
{
  printf("\nEnter a name: ");
  gets(record->name);
  printf("Enter the phone number: ");
  gets(record->phone_no);
  return;
}

display(contents)
struct tel_typ *contents;
{
  while(contents != NULL)
  {
    printf("\n%-30s %-20s", contents->name, contents->phone_no);
    contents = contents->nextaddr;
  }
  return;
}
```

3. The `insert()` function is included below in a complete program used to verify that `insert()` works correctly. As written, the function will insert a structure after the structure whose address is passed to it. Since the address of the first structure is passed to it, the new structure is inserted between the first and second structures.

Note that if the `populate` function call is removed from the `insert` function then `insert()` becomes a general insertion program that simply creates a structure and correctly adjusts the address members of each structure. Also notice the notation used in `insert()`. The expression

```
addr->nextaddr->nextaddr
```

is equivalent to

```
(addr->nextaddr)->nextaddr
```

This notation was not used in `main()` because the pointer variable current is first used to store the address in `list->nextaddr` using the statement:

```
current = list->nextaddr;
```

The statement:

```
current->nextaddr = NULL;
```

in `main()`, however, could have been written as:

```
list->nextaddr->nextaddr = NULL;
```

An interesting exercise is to rewrite `main()` such that the pointer variable named current is removed entirely from the function.

```
#include <stdio.h>
struct tel_typ
{
  char name[25];
  char phone_no[15];
  struct tel_typ *nextaddr;
};
main()
{
  int i;
  struct tel_typ *list, *current;
  char *malloc();

  list = (struct tel_typ *) malloc(sizeof(struct tel_typ));
  populate(list); /* populate the first structure */
  list->nextaddr = (struct tel_typ *) malloc(sizeof(struct tel_typ));
  current = list->nextaddr;
  populate(current); /* populate the second structure */
  current->nextaddr = NULL;
  printf("\nThe list initially consists of the following records:");
  display(list);
  insert(list);   /* insert between first and second structures */
  printf("\nThe new list now consists of the following records:");
  display(list);
}

insert(addr)
struct tel_typ *addr;
{
  struct tel_typ *temp;
  char *malloc();

  temp = addr->nextaddr;    /* save pointer to next structure */
  /* now change the address to point to the inserted structure */
  addr->nextaddr =  (struct tel_typ *) malloc(sizeof(struct tel_typ));
  populate(addr->nextaddr);  /* populate the new structure */
  /* set the address member of the new structure to the saved addr */
  addr->nextaddr->nextaddr = temp;
  return;
}
populate(record)
struct tel_typ *record;
{
  printf("\nEnter a name: ");
  gets(record->name);
  printf("Enter the phone number: ");
  gets(record->phone_no);
  return;
}
display(contents)
struct tel_typ *contents;
{
  while(contents != NULL)
  {
    printf("\n%-30s %-20s", contents->name, contents->phone_no);
    contents = contents->nextaddr;
  }
  return;
}
```

5. The modify() function is included below in a complete program used to verify that modify() works correctly. The driver function creates a single structure, populates it, and then calls modify(). modify() itself calls the function repop(). An interesting extension is to write repop() such that an ENTER key response retains the original structure member value.

```c
#include <stdio.h>
struct tel_typ
{
  char name[25];
  char phone_no[15];
  struct tel_typ *nextaddr;
};

main()
{
  int i;
  struct tel_typ *list;
  char *malloc();

  list = (struct tel_typ *) malloc(sizeof(struct tel_typ));
  populate(list); /* populate the first structure */
  list->nextaddr = NULL;
  modify(list);   /* modify the structure members */
}

modify(addr)
struct tel_typ *addr;
{

  printf("\nThe current structure members are: ");
  display(addr);
  repop(addr);
  printf("\nThe structure members are now: ");
  display(addr);
  return;
}

populate(record)
struct tel_typ *record;
{
  printf("\nEnter a name: ");
  gets(record->name);
  printf("Enter the phone number: ");
  gets(record->phone_no);
  return;
}
            /* continued on next page */
```

```
repop(record)
struct tel_typ *record;
{
  printf("\n\nEnter a new name: ");
  gets(record->name);
  printf("Enter a new phone number: ");
  gets(record->phone_no);
  return;
}

display(contents)
struct tel_typ *contents;
{
  while(contents != NULL)
  {
    printf("\n%-30s %-20s", contents->name, contents->phone_no);
    contents = contents->nextaddr;
  }
  return;
}
```

Section 10.6

1. printf() function calls, with the correct control sequences, are contained within the following program.

```
union
{
  float rate;
  double taxes;
  int num;
} flag;
main()
{
  flag.rate = 22.5;
  printf("\nThe rate is %f",flag.rate);
  flag.taxes = 44.7;
  printf("\ntaxes are %f",flag.taxes);
  flag.num = 6;
  printf("\nnum is %d",flag.num);
}
```

5. Since a value has not been assigned to alt.btype, the display produced is unpredictable (the code for a 'y' resides in the storage locations overlapped by the variables alt.ch and alt.btype). Thus, either a garbage value will be displayed or the program could even crash.

Section 11.1

1. a. On an IBM or IBM-compatible personal computer (PC, XT, or AT), a file name may have up to eight characters, and optionally a decimal point followed by three more characters. If a string is used to hold the file name, an extra character should be provided for the NULL, for a total of 13 characters.

3.
```
FILE *prices;
FILE *fp;
FILE *coupons;
FILE *distance;
FILE *in_data;
FILE *out_data;
```

Note: If all of these file pointers were used in the same program, the single declaration

```
FILE *prices, *fp, *coupons, *distance, *in_data, *out_data;
```

could be used.

5.
```
FILE *fopen(), *memo;
FILE *fopen(), *letter;
FILE *fopen(), *coups;
FILE *fopen(), *pt_yield;
FILE *fopen(), *pri_file;
FILE *fopen(), *rates;
```

Section 11.2

1. a.
```
#include <stdio.h>
main()
{
    FILE *out, *fopen();
    char strng[81];

    out = fopen("text.dat", "w");
    printf("Enter lines of text to be stored in the file.\n");
    printf("Enter a carriage return only to terminate input.\n\n");
    gets(strng);
    while (*strng != '\0')
    {
        fputs(strng, out);   /* fputs() does not add the '\n' */
        putc('\n', out);     /* write a newline escape sequence */
        gets(strng);
    }
    fclose(out);
    printf("End of data input.");
    printf("\nThe file has been written.");
}
```

Notes:

i. Recall that the `gets()` function does not return the newline escape sequence that terminates each input line, but appends a `'\0'` in its place. Therefore, when a single RETURN is entered a single `'\0'` is generated; it is this single character that is used to terminate the `while` loop.

ii. Since the `gets()` function does not store the newline escape sequence on input, a separate `'\n'` must be appended to each line on output. This is done using the `putc()` function.

iii. Since the `gets()` returns a `NULL` (`'\0'`) value when an end-of-file (EOF) is encountered, the `while` statement could have been written as:

```
while (gets(strng) != NULL)
```

If this form is used, however, an EOF must be generated at the keyboard. For many systems this keyboard EOF is created when the ctrl-Z keys are pushed, followed by a RETURN to actually enter the EOF.

b.
```
#include <stdio.h>
main()
{
   FILE *out, *fopen();
   char strng[81];

   out = fopen("text.dat", "w");
   printf("Enter lines of text to be stored in the file.\n");
   printf("Enter a carriage return only to terminate input.\n\n");
   fgets(strng,81,stdin);
   while(*strng != '\n')
   {
      fputs(strng, out);   /* fputs() does not add the '\n' */
      fgets(strng,81,stdin);
   }
   fclose(out);
   printf("End of data input.");
   printf("\nThe file has been written.");
}
```

Notes:

i. Recall that the `fgets()` function does return the newline escape sequence that terminates each input line. Therefore, when a single RETURN is entered a single `'\n'` is generated; it is this single character that is used to terminate the `while` loop.

ii. Unlike the `gets()` function used in Exercise 1a, the `fgets()` function does transmit the carriage return typed at the end of each line input. Therefore, it is not necessary to add a newline escape sequence on output as was done in Exercise 1a.

iii. Since the `fgets()` returns a `NULL` (`'\0'`) value when an end-of-file (EOF) is encountered, the `while` statement could have been written as:

```
while (fgets(strng,81,stdin) != NULL)
```

If this form is used, however, an EOF must be generated at the keyboard. For many systems this keyboard EOF is created when the ctrl-Z keys are pushed, followed by a RETURN to actually enter the EOF.

c.
```
#include <stdio.h>
main()

{
  FILE *fopen(), *in_file;
  char line[81];

  in_file = fopen("text.dat","r");
  if(in_file == NULL)
  {
    printf("The text.dat file does not exist.\n");
    printf("Please create this file before running this program.");
    exit();
  }
  while( fgets(line, 81, in_file) != NULL)
    puts(line);
  fclose(in_file);
}
```

Notes:

i. The fgets() function returns a NULL ('\0') when it encounters the end-of-file (EOF) marker. Therefore, it is the NULL that is checked for to determine when to stop reading the file.

ii. Since the fgets() function retains the newline escape sequence at the end of each line in the file, and the puts() function adds a newline when it displays a line, the file is displayed on the screen in double spacing. To avoid this either the fputs() function can be used or character-by-character input and output can be used (see the solution to Exercise 1 of Section 14.4).

iii. The exit() function terminates the running program and closes all files.

3. a. The data may be entered in a variety of ways. One possibility is to enter the data, line by line, and write each line to a file as was done in Exercise 1a. A second method is to use a text editor to write the data to a file. A third possibility is to enter the data as individual items for each line, assemble the items into a complete string, formatted as desired, and then write the string out. A fourth possibility is to enter the data as individual items and write the file as individual items. The following program uses the third approach, which illustrates the construction of an in-memory string.

```
#include <stdio.h>
main()
{
  FILE *out, *fopen();
  char name[30], date[30], strng[81];
  int i, id;
  float rate;

  out = fopen("employ.dat", "w");
  for (i = 1; i <= 5; ++i)    /* get and write 5 records */
  {
    printf("\nEnter the name: ");
    gets(name);
    printf("Enter the ID No: ");
    scanf("%d", &id);
    printf("Enter the rate: ");
    scanf("%f",&rate);
    printf("Enter the date (ex. 12/6/65): ");
    scanf("%s",date);
    /* now the line to be written is assembled in memory */
    sprintf(strng, "%-18.15s %5d %6.2f %18.8s",name,id,rate,date);
    fputs(strng,out);        /* write the string out */
    putc('\n',out);          /* append a newline character */
    getchar();               /* clear out the input buffer */
  }
  fclose(out);
  printf("\nEnd of data input.");
  printf("\nThe file has been written.");
}
```

b.
```
#include <stdio.h>
main()
{
  FILE *fopen(), *in_file, *out_file;
  char line[81];

  in_file = fopen("employ.dat","r");
  out_file = fopen("employ.bak","w");
  while( fgets(line, 81,in_file) != NULL)
      fputs(line,out_file);
  printf("\nFile copy completed.");
  fclose(in_file);
  fclose(out_file);
}
```

c. ```
#include <stdio.h>
#include <string.h>
main()
{
    FILE *fopen(), *in_file, *out_file;
    char f_name[15], s_name[15], line[81];

    printf("Enter the name of the file to be copied: ");
    gets(f_name);
    printf("Enter the name of the new file: ");
    gets(s_name);
    if(strcmp(f_name,s_name) == NULL)
    {
        printf("\nYou have specified the same name for both files.");
        printf("\nPlease rerun using different names.");
        exit();
    }
    in_file = fopen(f_name,"r");
    out_file = fopen(s_name,"w");
    while(fgets(line, 81,in_file) != NULL)
        fputs(line,out_file);
    printf("\nFile copy completed.");
    fclose(in_file);
    fclose(out_file);
}
```

*Note:* The strcmp() function checks that the same file name is not attempted to be used for both input and output. Use of this function requires inclusion of the string.h header file. The exit() function terminates program execution.

*d.* A better way would be to enter the source and destination file names on the line used to invoke the executable program. Data entered in this manner are called command line arguments. Command line arguments are the topics of Section 14.4

## Section 11.3

*1.* The fseek() function call moves the character pointer to the last character in the file, which is the EOF character at offset position 12. The ftell() function reports the offset of the character currently pointed to. This is the EOF character. Thus, a 12 is returned by ftell().
```

5. The `f_chars()` function is included within the working program listed below:

```
#include <stdio.h>
main()
{
  FILE *fopen(), *in;
  char f_name[13];

  printf("\nEnter a file name: ");
  scanf("%s", f_name);
  in = fopen(f_name, "r");
  f_chars(in);
  fclose(in);
}

f_chars(fname)      /* this is the required function */
FILE *fname;        /* a pointer to a FILE is passed */
{
  long ftell();

  fseek(fname,0L,2);   /* move to the end of the file */
  printf("There are %ld characters in the file.\n",ftell(fname));
  return;
}
```

Section 11.4

1. The file name referred to in the Exercise is an internal pointer name. The definition of `p_file()` is:

```
p_file(fname)
FILE *fname;
```

3. The `fcheck()` function is included below with a driver function used to test it:

```
#include <stdio.h>
main()    /* driver function to test fcheck() */
{
  int fcheck();
  char name[13];

  printf("Enter a file name: ");
  scanf("%s", name);
  if(fcheck(name) == 1)
   printf("The file exists and can be opened.");
  else
   printf("The file cannot be opened - check that it exists.");
}

          /* continued on next page */
```

```
int fcheck(fname)
char *fname;
{
   FILE *fopen();

   if(fopen(fname, "r") == 0)
      return(0);
   else
      return(1);
}
```

Note: The `fcheck()` function performs essentially the same check as `fopen()`, except `fopen()` returns a `non_zero` pointer instead of an integer value.

Chapter 12

1. a. 11001010   **b.**   11001010   **c.**   11001010
     &10100101 |10100101   ^10100101
     ---------   ---------   ---------
     10000000   11101111   01101111

3. a. 0157 = 001 101 111; 001 101 111 << 1 = 011 011 110 = 0336
   b. 0701 = 111 000 001; 111 000 001 << 2 = 100 000 100 = 0404
   c. 0873 = undefined, there is no octal digit higher than 7.
   d. 087 = undefined.

5. a. The binary number 00001100, which equals octal 014, is the required mask pattern.
   b. Two zeros could be placed in the third and fourth positions to reproduce the flag bits in these positions. However, the inclusive OR operation cannot set the remaining bits to zero.
   c. The binary number 00001100, which equals octal 014, is the required mask pattern.

7. Any character whose ASCII binary code has bit six equal to zero will be unaffected by the conversion of Program 12-2. These include all the characters listed in Appendix B having either a one-digit hexadecimal code or a two-digit hexadecimal code beginning in either a 1, 4, or 5. Conversely, any character whose ASCII binary code has bit six equal to one will be affected. This includes all the characters listed in Appendix B having a two-digit hexadecimal code beginning in either 2, 3, 6, or 7.

9.
```c
#include <stdio.h>
main()
{
  char word[81];       /* enough storage for a complete line */

  printf("Enter a string of both upper and lowercase letters:\n");
  gets(word);
  printf("\nThe string of letters just entered is:\n");
  puts(word);
  lower(word);
  printf("\nThis string, in lowercase letters is:\n");
  puts(word);
}
lower(word)
char *word;
{
  while (*word != '\0')
    if( *word >= 'A' && *word <= 'Z')
     *word++ |= 0X20;
    else
     ++word;
}
```

11.
```c
#include <stdio.h>
main()
{
  char message[81];      /* enough storage for a complete line */
  FILE *fopen(), *outfile;

  printf("Enter a sentence:\n");
  gets(message);
  printf("\nThe sentence just entered is:\n");
  puts(message);
  encrypt(message);
  outfile = fopen("coded.dat","w");
  fputs(message,outfile);
  printf("\nThe encrypted message has been written to coded.dat");
  close(outfile);
}
encrypt(message)
char *message;
{
  while (*message != '\0')
    *message++ ^= 52;
}
```

```
13. #include <stdio.h>
    main()
    {
        char ch;

        printf("\nType in a character: ");
        ch = getchar();
        printf("\nThe character just read is: %c", ch);
        printf("\n\nThe binary code of this character is: ");
        showbits(ch);
    }
    showbits(ch)
    char ch;
    {
        int i, mask = 0X80;
        for(i = 1; i <= 8; ++i)
        {
            /* print a 1 if the next bit is 1, else print a 0 */
            if ( (mask  & ch) > 0 )
                printf("%d ", 1);
            else
                printf("%d ", 0);
            mask >>= 1;        /* shift the mask to inspect the next bit */
        }
    }
```

Section 13.1

1. a. The value of the expression is 6.
  b. The value of the expression is 6.
  c. The value of the expression is 13.
  d. The value of the expression is 3.
  e. The value of the expression is 0.
  f. The value of the expression is 0.
  g. The value of the expression a + b > 20 is a + 0 = 2.
  h. The value of the expression num = a + b > 20 is 2.
  i. The value of the expression a || b is 2 || 3, which is 1 (True).
  j. The value of the expression num = a || b is the same as the value assigned to num, which is 1.

3.
```
c = amount*rate;
b = c;
a = b;
```

5. a.
```
flag = (a >= b) ? 1 : 0
```
  b.
```
flag = (a == b || c == d) ? 1 : 0
```

Section 13.3

1. a. `#define NEGATE (x) -(x)`

  b.
```
#define NEGATE(x) -(x)
main()
{
  float num;

  printf("Enter a number: ");
  scanf("%f", &num);
  printf("\nThe negative of %f is %f.", num, NEGATE(num));
}
```

3. a.
```
#define PI 3.1416
#define CIRCUM(x) 2.0 * PI * (x) b.
```

  b.
```
#define PI 3.1416
#define CIRCUM(x) 2.0 * PI * (x)
main()
{
  float radius;

  printf("Enter a radius: ");
  scanf("%f", &radius);
  printf("\nThe circumference is %f.", CIRCUM(radius));
}
```

5. a. `#define MAX(x,y) ((x) >= (y)) ? (x) : (y)`

  b.
```
#define MAX(x,y) ((x) >= (y)) ? (x) : (y)
main()
{
  float num1, num2;

  printf("Enter two numbers, separated by at least a space: ");
  scanf("%f %f", &num1, &num2);
  printf("\nThe largest number entered is %f", MAX(num1,num2));
}
```

Section 13.4

1. a. The following program opens the file, reads each character, and displays it. For a line-by-line input/output approach to reading and displaying a file, see the solution to Exercise 1c of Section 11.2.

```
#include <stdio.h>
main(argc, argv)
int argc;               /* standard argument declarations */
char *argv[];           /* for command line arguments      */
{
  FILE *fopen(), *in_file;
  char cc;

  in_file = fopen(argv[1],"r");
  while( (cc = getc(in_file)) != EOF)
     putchar(cc);
  fclose(in_file);
}
```

Note: Instead of reading each character until the end-of-file is reached, the `fgets()` function could have been used to read in a line at a time. Since `fgets()` returns a NULL when it encounters the end-of-file sentinel, the appropriate statement would be

```
while (fgets(line, 81, in_file) != NULL);
```

If this statement is used, line would have to be declared as

```
char line[81];
```

To output a line at a time either the `puts()` or `fputs()` functions can be used. The `puts()` function adds its own newline escape sequence at the end of each line; the `fputs()` function does not.

b. The program will open and display the contents of any file. The file can, therefore, be either a data or a program file.

Chapter 14

1. a. `factorial()` expects to receive one integer value and returns an integer value. A suitable function prototype is:

```
int factorial(int);
```

b. `price()` expects to receive one integer value, and two double precision values, in that order. It returns a double precision value. A suitable function prototype is:

```
double price(int, double, double);
```

c. An integer, a double precision value, and an integer in that order, must be passed to `yield()`. (Note that the data type of the third argument is, by default, an integer.) The function returns a double precision value. A suitable function prototype is:

```
double yield(int, double, int);
```

d. A character and two floating point values, in that order must be passed to `interest()`. The function returns a character. A suitable function prototype is:

```
char interest(char, float, float);
```

e. By default, the arguments of total() are two integer values. Also, by default, the return data type of total() is an integer. A suitable function prototype is:

```
int total(int, int);
```

f. Two integers, two characters, and two floating point values, in that order, are expected by roi(). The function returns a floating point value. A suitable function prototype is:

```
float roi(int, int, char, char, float, float);
```

g. Two integer values and a character, in that order, are expected by get_val(). The function returns no value. A suitable function prototype is:

```
void get_val(int, int, char);
```

3.
```
#include <stdio.h>
main()
{
  int count;                         /* start of declarations */
  double fahren, tempvert(double);   /* including a function prototype */
  for(count = 1; count <= 4; ++count)
  {
    printf("Enter a Fahrenheit temperature: ");
    scanf("%lf", &fahren);
    printf("The Celsius equivalent is %6.2f\n\n", tempvert(fahren) );
  }
}

double tempvert(double in_temp)           /* function header */
{
  return( (5.0/9.0) * (in_temp - 32.0) );
}
```

5. *a.* The mult() function is included in the program written for Exercise 5b.

b.
```
#include <stdio.h>
main()
{
  double mult(double, double);  /* function prototype for mult() */
  double first,second;

  printf("Please enter a number: ");
  scanf("%lf",&first);
        printf("Please enter another number: ");
        scanf("%lf", &second);
        printf("The product of these numbers is %f",mult(first,second));
    }

double mult(double num1, double num2)  /* function header */
{
    return (num1*num2);
}
```

7. a. The polynomial function is included within the program written for Exercise 7b.

   b.
```c
#include <stdio.h>
main ()
{
   double a, b, c, x, result;
   double poly_two(double, double, double, double);

   printf("Enter the coefficient for the x squared term: ");
   scanf("%lf", &a);
   printf("\nEnter the coefficient for x : ");
   scanf("%lf", &b);
   printf("\nEnter the constant: ");
   scanf("%lf", &c);
   printf("\nEnter the value for x: ");
   scanf("%lf", &x);
   result = poly_two(a, b, c, x);
   printf("\n\n\nThe result is  %f", result);
}

double poly_two(double a, double b, double c, double x)
{
   return (a*x*x + b*x + c);
}
```

Index

QUICK C REFERENCE

A FIRST BOOK OF C by Gary Bronson and Stephen Menconi

Reserved Words

auto	do	for	return	typedef
break	double	goto	short	union
case	else	if	sizeof	unsigned
char	enum	int	static	void
continue	extern	long	struct	while
default	float	register	switch	

Operators

Type	Symbols	Associativity
		left to right
Primary	( ) [ ] . ->	right to left
Unary	+ + − − & * − ! ~ sizeof	left to right
Arithmetic	* / %	left to right
Arithmetic	+ −	left to right
Shift	<< >>	left to right
Relational	< <= > >=	left to right
Relational	== !=	left to right
Bitwise	& (AND)	left to right
Bitwise	^ (XOR)	left to right
Bitwise	| (OR)	left to right
Logical	&& (AND)	left to right
Logical	|| (OR)	right to left
Conditional	?:	right to left
Assignment	= += −= /= %= etc.	left to right
Comma		

Scalar Data Types

Type		Sample Declaration
char		char key;
int		int num;
short	(or short int)	short count;
long	(or long int)	long int date;
unsigned	(or unsigned int)	unsigned val;
float		float rate;
double	(or long float)	double taxes;

Arrays

An *array* is a list of elements of the same data type. The first element in an array is referred to as the zeroth element.

> *Examples:* int prices[5];
> char name[20];
> float rates [4][15];

Structures

A *structure* (or record) is a data type whose elements need not be of the same data type.

> *Example:* struct tel_rec   /* tel_rec is a tag name */
> {
>   char name[20];
>   int id;
>   double rate;
> } phone;   /* phone is a structure variable */

Comments

Comments are enclosed within a /* and */.

> /* this is a sample of a comment */

Statements

A *Null* statement consists of a semicolon only.

     ;   /* the Null statement */

A *Simple* statement is either a Null, declaration, expression, or function statement.

```
double a;                      /* declaration statement */
taxes = rate * income;         /* an expression statement */
printf("Hello World!");        /* function statement */
```

A *Compound* statement consists of one or more statements enclosed within braces.

```
Example:  {                    /* start of compound statement */
             taxes = rate * income;
             + +count;
          }                    /* end of compound statement */
```

Flow control statements are structured statements consisting of a keyword (if, while, for, do, switch) followed by an expression within parentheses and a simple or compound statement.

Statement	Example
```if (expression)``` ``` statement;```	```if (age == 13)``` ``` printf("Welcome Teenager!");```

```if (expression)```
```   statement1;```
```else```
```   statement2;```
	```if (num == 5)```
	``` printf("Bingo!");```
	```else```
	``` printf("You Lose!");```

```if (expression)```
```   statement1;```
```else if (expression)```
```   statement2;```
```   .```
```   .```
```else```
```   statement3;```
	```if (grade >= 90)```
	``` printf("You got an A");```
	```else if (grade >= 80)```
	``` printf("You got a B");```
	```else if (grade >= 70)```
	``` printf("You got a C");```
	```else```
	``` printf("You got a D");```

```switch (expression)```
```{```
``` case value_1: statement1;```
``` case value_2: statement2;```
```   .```
``` default: statementn;```
```}```
	```switch (marcode)```
	```{```
	``` case 1: printf("Good Morning");```
	``` case 2: printf("Good Afternoon");```
	``` case 3: printf("Good Night");```
	``` default: printf("Good Grief");```
	```}```

```for (init; expression; alter)``` ``` statement;```	```for (i = 0; i < 10; ++i)``` ``` printf("%d %d", i, i*i);```

```while (expression)```
```   statement;```
	```while (num < 10)```
	```{```
	``` printf("number is %d",num);```
	``` + +num;```
	```}```

```do```
```   statement;```
```while (expression);```
	```do```
	```{```
	``` printf("Hello");```
	``` + + count;```
	```}```
	```while (count < 10);```